SCHOLARSHIP AND PARTISANSHIP: *Essays on Max Weber*

SCHOLARSHIP AND PARTISANSHIP:
Essays on Max Weber

by Reinhard Bendix and Guenther Roth

UNIVERSITY OF CALIFORNIA PRESS

BERKELEY, LOS ANGELES, LONDON, 1971

University of California Press / Berkeley and Los Angeles, California
University of California Press, Ltd. / London, England
Copyright © 1971, by The Regents of the University of California
First paperback edition 1971
ISBN: 0-520-01833-8 cloth
      0-520-02032-4 paper
Library of Congress Catalog Card Number: 75-131196
Printed in the United States of America

ACKNOWLEDGMENTS

We gratefully acknowledge permission to reprint the following essays, which appear here in revised form:

Ch. II, G. Roth, "Max Weber's Empirical Sociology in Germany and the United States," *Central European History*, II:3, Sept. 1969, 196–215.

Ch. III, G. Roth, "Political Critiques of Max Weber: Some Implications for Political Sociology," *American Sociological Review*, 30:2, April 1965, 213–223.

Ch. IV., R. Bendix, "Der Einzelne und die Gesellschaft," in Willy Hochkeppel, ed., *Soziologie zwischen Theorie und Empirie* (Munich: Nymphenburger Verlagsbuchhandlung, 1970), 97–113.

Ch. V, R. Bendix, "Sociology and the Distrust of Reason," *American Sociological Review*, 35:5, Oct. 1970, 831–843.

Ch. VII, R. Bendix, "Bureaucracy," *International Encyclopedia of the Social Sciences* (New York: The Macmillan Co. and The Free Press, II, 1968, 206–219.

Ch. VIII, G. Roth, "Personal Rulership, Patrimonialism, and Empire-Building in the New States," *World Politics*, XX:2, Jan. 1968, 194–206.

Ch. IX, R. Bendix, "Reflections on Charismatic Leadership," in Bendix *et al.*, eds., *State and Society* (Boston: Little, Brown, 1968), 616–629.

Ch. X, R. Bendix, "A Case Study in Cultural and Educational Mobility: Japan and the Protestant Ethic," in Neil J. Smelser and Seymour M. Lipset, eds., *Social Structure and Mobility in Economic Development* (Chicago: Aldine Publishing Co., 1966), 262–279.

Ch. XI, R. Bendix, "The Comparative Analysis of Historical Change," in Tom Burns and S. B. Saul, eds., *Social Theory and*

v

Economic Change (London: Tavistock Publications, 1967), 67–86.

Ch. XII, G. Roth, "Das historische Verhältnis der Weberschen Soziologie zum Marxismus," *Kölner Zeitschrift für Soziologie und Sozialpsychologie*, XX:3, 1968, 432–440. Postscript from "Robert Michels and Max Weber on Socialist Party Organization," in *The Social Democrats in Imperial Germany* (Totowa: Bedminster Press, 1963), 249–256.

Ch. XIV, R. Bendix, "Jacob Burckhardt and Max Weber," *American Sociological Review*, 30:2, April 1965, 176–184.

Ch. XVI, R. Bendix, "The Protestant Ethic—Revisited," *Comparative Studies in Society and History*, IX:3, April 1967, 266–273.

We also would like to acknowledge permission by the following publishers:

Bedminster Press, for quotations from Max Weber, *Economy and Society* (New York 1968), G. Roth and C. Wittich, eds.

J. C. B. Mohr, for quotations from Marianne Weber, *Frauenfragen und Frauengedanken* (Tübingen 1919).

CONTENTS

INTRODUCTION

In a famous comparison between Napoleon and Louis Bonaparte, Marx writes that in history similar events first occur as tragedy and then as farce. Had he lived to compare Mussolini with Hitler, he might have reversed that judgment. And had he compared the 1960's with the years before and after World War I, he might have concluded that in some instances historical experiences are repeated.

For the present issues and passions resemble those that commanded attention during the lifetime of Max Weber, whose work is the major scholarly reference in the chapters of this book. The relationship between scholarship and politics is as controversial today as it was then. Against the detached rationalism of an older generation, youth once more demands action and commitment. The *élan vital* and chiliastic hopes have been rekindled. A revived *Jugendstil,* the renewed popularity of Hermann Hesse, and still another erotic emancipation appeal again to the longing for authentic experience. Men over seventy like Martin Heidegger or Herbert Marcuse can view the present time as a renaissance of their youthful days and a vindication of what they have said for half a century, since cultural pessimism is in vogue again.

Accordingly, scholars find themselves today in much the same position as Max Weber and his contemporaries did before and after World War I. As preoccupied with the problematical character of social observation as he was, they too must defend their work against a radical skepticism and various forms of anti-intellectualism. Historical parallels do not teach lessons by themselves. But where parallel issues arise, a later generation may well learn from the intellectual responses of an earlier one.

In his work Weber accentuated critical self-awareness, but fought "every step of the way to salvage as much as possible of the rationalist heritage," as H. S. Hughes has remarked. He was impatient with cyclical as well as evolutionary philosophies of history. He wanted to comprehend what was specific to a given historical constellation and grasp the course of history in terms of its significance for his own time. He preferred historical research to philosophical speculation. He held that in his day there was too much easy speculation and fashionable soul-searching and not enough interest and persistence in empirical inquiry. He immersed himself in the lives of previous generations, but also took his stand on contemporary issues. Like so many of today's young radicals, he too engaged in a furious generational rebellion, yet he came to choose science as a vocation even before his breakdown at the threshold of middle age. But unlike so many others, he did not adjust to the social and political realities after a revolutionary and utopian youth. Instead, he retained a peculiar radicalism and an explosive political temper. Nowadays he appears to many younger rebels as the patron saint of "value-neutral" social science, the symbolic target representing a conformist and opportunist profession. Yet he was, in many respects, a political and academic outsider, who faced the younger generation of his day with a profoundly pedagogic combination of sympathy and skepticism.

American sociologists have dealt mostly with Weber's scholarly work, though in recent years there has been a growing concern with his beliefs and politics, just like in Europe. Our essays go into both, his substantive and methodological contributions as well as the relation of his life to his place in intellectual and political history. Both aspects are legitimate scholarly concerns, but the relation between them should be balanced carefully. The intellectual critique of a scholar's work must be based in the first instance on tests of logical consistency and empirical adequacy. It is also worth-while to investigate an author's intellectual biography once his work has become important for his discipline. There are sociologists who would exclude such biographical and historical interests, leaving them to historians or psychoanalysts. Yet exclusive emphasis on systemic abstractions or strict verification ignores at its peril the wider context in which all scholarly work occurs. For certain theoretical purposes it may be appropriate to disregard the historical setting or the biographical dimension, but their assessment is indispensable for contextual understanding. Today, we are learning once again that the scientist's, and especially the social scientist's, detachment from the society of his time is never more than conditional and precarious.

The task is to investigate the historical and biographical context without falling prey to psychological, ideological, or social-structural reductionism. Recent studies of Weber like those by Wolfgang Mommsen and Arthur Mitzman are not free of this difficulty, in part one suspects because the authors did not sufficiently reflect upon the genesis of their own perspectives. Our purpose is to advance a balanced understanding of Weber's work and thereby to define and refine our intellectual position—with the proviso that we do not raise questions about Weber's work which we would be unable or unwilling to answer about our own. The potential gains seem clear.

A better understanding of generational conflict—both Weber's own and his subsequent encounter with youths—can make us more sensitive to the conflicts of our own time. The many, emotionally charged debates of the Weberian meaning of "value-neutrality" can benefit from a clear grasp not only of its intrinsic logic but also of Weber's strategic considerations and the academic situation of his time. The uses and abuses to which Weber's treatment of bureaucracy and charisma has been put call for better understanding of his whole typological architecture as well as its intellectual context. Similarly, the many polemics surrounding *The Protestant Ethic and the Spirit of Capitalism* have too often ignored Weber's specific purpose, his historical inspiration, and his subsequent comparative studies of the world religions.

Inquiries of this kind have a relevance beyond their manifest content. The critical but sympathetic consideration of earlier contributions is a vital link with the past in contrast to a mindless contemporaneity which sees past contributions only as a history of errors. Such consideration is also a token of continuity with the future, for sociological knowledge does not accumulate as unequivocally or become obsolescent as clearly as knowledge in the natural sciences. Where the progress of knowledge is often imperceptible and slow-moving, it ill becomes us to act as if it were clear-cut and rapid.

Part A of this volume focuses on the tensions between scholarship and partisanship. The first chapter examines Weber's own generational revolt and maturation. We recognize the grave and, in part, debilitating tensions evident in his life, and at the same time the intellectual position from which he developed his work. Emphasis on the first aspect should not lead to a denigration of the second. Otherwise, no one's intellectual creativity would survive an analysis of its motives. The second essay deals with Weber's attempt to establish a purely research-oriented German Sociological Association;

it shows why an autonomous university must in crucial respects be a sanctuary maintained by political armistice. The same problem recurs at another level with regard to politically motivated critiques of a scholarly position. The parallels in the political critique of Weber from the Marxist, Nazi, and natural-law views of the world —the subject of chapter III—were evoked by the renewed campaign against empirical sociology at the centenary exercises of 1964. In particular, Herbert Marcuse's Marxist and existentialist arguments against Weber, along with the critique by the New Left, continue the indictment of Western industrialization that has been reiterated for two centuries. Chapter IV contrasts some of these ideological views with a scholarly approach, while chapter V analyzes the ideological and institutional background of the modern attack upon the university and scholarship. This latter essay—Bendix' Presidential Address before the American Sociological Association in 1970—may be seen as a reflection on Weber's "Science as a Vocation" after an interval of half a century.

When political turmoil threatens to engulf the university, every practicing scholar takes a stand by conscientiously continuing his work. The voice of scholarship may be small, but the values of knowledge are precious. The tradition of the Enlightenment is always our responsibility for work to be done. Therefore, in Part B, we deal with the comparative study of values, authority, and legitimation as a continuation of Weberian themes. We begin with a consideration of Weber's comparative strategy as contrasted with the present-day functionalist and neo-evolutionary approaches to development problems in the new and old states. Chapter VI aims at elucidating the way in which ideal types (historical models) are prerequisites for specific historical explanations (secular theories); Weber's typology of bureaucracy, patrimonialism, and political as well as religious charisma is investigated in relation to his explanations for the course of Western history. The three subsequent chapters take up each of the three types of domination by providing a historical overview of bureaucracy, suggesting the applicability of patrimonialism to contemporary conditions, and making charisma a more precise typological concept. Chapter X links the impact of religious beliefs facilitating modernization to the political context, and explores the problem of a common "capacity for development" in Western Europe and Japan. We conclude Part B with a summary statement on the comparative analysis of historical change.

In Part C we examine some of the historical and analytical relationships that should be considered in assessing intellectual influences and similarities. Marx and Weber have frequently been compared, and there has been a tendency to overemphasize the Marxian impact on Weber's work and to lose sight of the academic currents of the time. Chapter XII examines the historical relationships of Weber's work to Marxism, and chapter XIII addresses itself to Weber's typological approach, which developed from a critique of evolutionism and from a sociological elaboration of Georg Jellinek's "social theory of the state." In general, analytical comparisons should be informed by a knowledge of historical relationships, but some comparisons are appropriate on theoretical grounds alone. In certain respects, Jacob Burckhardt was one of Weber's predecessors. Although Weber wrote only a few, and mostly critical, comments on him, he seems to have admired Burckhardt's genius. Here an analytical comparison (chapter XIV) brings out some of the substantial affinities between the two men's views of society. Conversely, despite Talcott Parsons' perception of convergence in Durkheim and Weber, an analytical comparison (chapter XV) can show differences in theory and method that have come to constitute two divergent sociological traditions. The last chapter reviews some literary antecedents of *The Protestant Ethic and the Spirit of Capitalism* and thus provides an intellectual context for the essay which has been too often ignored.

Most of the chapters have been published previously, in widely scattered places. It appeared desirable to bring them together so that readers could have an overview of Weber's work in his time and in ours. We have benefited from each other's criticism, but think it best to record the authorship of the individual essays, as indicated at the beginning of each chapter. Unless otherwise noted, all translations are by the authors.

Max Weber died on June 14, 1920. Believing in the continuity of scholarship, he was confident that others would carry on where his own studies remained incomplete. This volume is offered as a tribute to Weber's memory, because we feel greatly indebted to his work. It is a small contribution to scholarship in another time of confrontation and adversity.

REINHARD BENDIX
GUENTHER ROTH

Göttingen and Berkeley
May 1970

Part A

IDEOLOGICAL CONFLICT AND SCHOLARLY COMMITMENT

MAX WEBER'S GENERATIONAL REBELLION AND MATURATION

Politics and religion were Max Weber's dominant intellectual interests. They were awakened in his parents' home, where genuine faith and urbane secularism stood in unrelieved tension against one another. For young Weber the irreconcilability of the parents' values was a crucial formative experience. He learned early about the opposition between the pragmatic ethic of responsibility *(Verantwortungsethik)* and the absolutist ethic of sheer commitment *(Gesinnungsethik)*. His eventual solution was to affirm secular pursuits while respecting religious convictions, and to advocate politics as the art of the possible while espousing rigorous standards of personal conduct.

The present period of generational rebellion has drawn attention to the sociology and history of generational conflict. Currently, Weber is a major target as the patron saint of value-neutrality and hence a symbol of political irresponsibility. Therefore, his own generational revolt and maturation warrant closer scrutiny. His struggle for empirical sociology was part of the conflict between two political generations. Both generations agreed that partisanship and scholarship should be linked, but they fought over the appropriate forms of this relationship.

I shall deal first with the ideological conflicts in Weber's "family of orientation"—alas, a family with mutually exclusive values. Then I shall treat Weber as spokesman of a new political generation. After contrasting his thinking with Nietzsche's, I shall turn to Weber's concern with Tolstoy and the two ethics, the central issue in his involved relations with the next political generation. I shall conclude with his attitude toward the youth movement and

---

By Guenther Roth; written for this volume.

his advice to the young in the last years of his life. Since feminism has also become a renewed issue, I shall touch at various points on the feminist attitudes of Max Weber and his wife, Marianne.

In dealing first with the family conflicts, I do not presume that a one-to-one relationship between Weber's personal experiences and his intellectual activities can be established. Such an assumption would denigrate the importance of historical events and of intellectual influences. It would be undue psychological reductionism to derive Weber's political views as a simple projection of his aggressive feelings toward the father. It is true that his filial challenge had a dramatic Oedipal outcome: Max senior died soon after a confrontation over the mother, a catastrophe that almost destroyed the son.[1] But neither before nor after this event did Weber deny the legitimacy of the political order, although his aggressive political stand appeared extraordinary to contemporaries. The parental differences taught him that ideological disagreements existed within each generation. This may have attenuated his political rebellion and made him immune to the utopianism that is a frequent symptom of youthful revolt.

FAMILY CONFLICTS

The conflicts between Weber's parents concerned not only religion, but also involved traditional male authoritarianism and incipient feminism. The father was a Victorian archetype, patriarchal at home and liberal outside. In politics, Max senior was a patient and skillful parliamentarian, but at home he found it hard to be flexible and conciliatory. Devoid of religious feeling, he

---

[1] The English reader can now reconstruct much of Weber's personal history. Much pertinent information is contained in Paul Honigsheim, *On Max Weber,* trans. by Joan Rytina (New York: Free Press, 1968), and in Arthur Mitzman's psychoanalytic interpretation, *The Iron Cage* (New York: Knopf, 1970). For older biographical treatments, see the well-known introduction by Hans Gerth and C. Wright Mills in *From Max Weber* (New York: Oxford, 1946); H. Stuart Hughes, *Consciousness and Society* (New York: Knopf, 1961), ch. 8; Gerhard Masur, *Prophets of Yesterday* (New York: Harper and Row, 1961), 176–203. The major German biographical literature is Marianne Weber, ed., *Max Weber, Jugendbriefe* (Tübingen: Mohr, 1936); *idem, Max Weber: Ein Lebensbild* (Tübingen: Mohr, 1925; cited after reprint, Heidelberg, Schneider, 1950); *idem, Lebenserinnerungen* (Bremen: Storm, 1948); Eduard Baumgarten, ed., *Max Weber: Werk und Person* (Tübingen: Mohr, 1964); Wolfgang J. Mommsen, *Max Weber und die deutsche Politik. 1890–1920* (Tübingen: Mohr, 1959); René König and Johannes Winckelmann, eds., *Max Weber zum Gedächtnis* (Cologne: Westdeutscher Verlag, 1963).

sought instead the good life of intellectual glamor and creature comfort. His wife, Helene, was a moralistic archetype, puritanical in morals although not in doctrine. She embraced the life of the spirit and had a horror of sexuality. It was proper for a Victorian lady to have a spiritual bent, but the wife took her moral concerns too seriously for the husband's ease. She was also much concerned with the "Social Question" and advocated women's rights. In this dualistic environment, a struggle for the children's minds and souls was inevitable. This was most serious for the two oldest sons, Max and Alfred, who were faced with two models of thought and action and two possible targets of rebellion. In his early teens Max Weber eluded his mother's spiritual demands, but in his twenties he moved closer to her as the conflict with the father intensified. Alfred Weber, who also became a famous sociologist, rebelled against both parents, in addition to developing a lifelong rivalry with his older brother.

The Weber household in Berlin was a meeting place for the academic and political elite, since for many years the father, a National Liberal, played a leading role in the subcommittee on educational and academic affairs in the Budget Commission of the Prussian Diet. Max and Alfred had an early opportunity to overhear the conversation of some of the most prestigious members of the older generations, among them the liberal leaders Rudolf von Bennigsen, Heinrich Rickert senior, Johannes von Miquel, and Friedrich Kapp, and scholars such as Theodor Mommsen, Wilhelm Dilthey, Heinrich von Treitschke, Heinrich von Sybel, and Levin Goldschmidt. Inevitably the brothers would ask themselves how they could ever equal the achievements of these men. The sense of self-esteem resulting from such exposure was deflated by the anxiety over belonging to a generation of epigoni.

At first Max Weber's political views were largely a reflection of his father's, but in his late teens his outlook changed significantly when he stepped into the extended family—a tight circle he was not to leave for another decade. In the formation of his political identity, the comparatively equalitarian relationship with his uncle Herman Baumgarten (1825–93) became of paramount importance. Baumgarten had been active in the 1848 revolution and, after political persecution, had resigned himself to the writing of Reformation history. By the time Weber began his studies in Heidelberg in 1882, Baumgarten, author of a famous liberal self-critique in 1866, had withdrawn his temporary support of Bismarck and was just getting embroiled in a spectacular clash with his erstwhile friend Heinrich

von Treitschke—a dispute closely followed by the educated public.[2] Here Weber encountered the first man who radically doubted
the wisdom of his father's National Liberal politics; here was his
first Jeremian prophet of doom.

Baumgarten was married to Ida Fallenstein, the older sister of
Weber's mother, Helene. In view of Weber's later concern with
Calvinism, it is worth noting that the two sisters descended, on the
maternal side, from a wealthy Huguenot family, the Souchays.
Their parents' marriage already suffered from a severe split, ag-
gravated by the circumstance that the deeply religious mother had
brought with her the wealth of the father, Georg Friedrich Fallenstein. Ida Baumgarten was more assertive than Weber's mother,
whose emotional stance against her husband was silent sufferance.
Ida openly disdained the business of politics and the vanities of the
academic market place. Thus there was a psychological balance of
power in the Baumgarten household.

In his Heidelberg student days, Weber became a close friend of
his cousin Otto Baumgarten, then finishing his study of theology.
Ida Baumgarten's power over this son had been strong enough to
make him choose theology against his inclinations. Now she attempted to determine her nephew's course of action as well, after
Weber's mother had not succeeded in this respect. Weber responded intellectually, but not spiritually. He did take a careful
look at Ida's favorite author, William Ellery Channing, the "apostle
of Unitarianism," and found his writings moving. But the young
reserve officer rejected Channing's pacifism and absolutist ethics.
Weber was concerned lest Channing's version of Christianity create
"a cleavage in men's minds between the (alleged) demands of Christianity and the social order of the states and the world." And he
argued that the "uncompromising striving for consistency on the
basis of certain presupposed principles can give the individual an
exalted sense of inner strength, even if misplaced, but then it con-
tradicts certain basic social facts *(Ordnungen)* . . . and involves a
reliance on one's own ego that rejects the label of 'egoism' only
because of self-deception."[3]

---

[2] Cf. Hermann Baumgarten, *Treitschke's Deutsche Geschichte* (Strassburg:
Trübner, 1883), third rev. edition.

[3] Max Weber, *Jugendbriefe*, op. cit., 191f. In an era of violent dissension
over the Vietnam war, it may be worth noting that Weber understood Channing's pacifism as a reaction against the mercenary system under which the
"predatory wars of the democratic American government against Mexico" were
later conducted—Channing died in 1842, before the Mexican War. Against

These remarks against Channing's ethic of ultimate ends were of a piece with Weber's dislike of Ida's inclination to turn every household decision into a moral issue. Yet it was through her that he came to understand his own mother, who had slapped his duel-scarred face when she saw that his students days in Heidelberg had turned him into a hard-drinking, strutting he-man. He began to honor his mother's moral expectations as against the code of his student peers as well as his father's alumni views, convinced that his tempestuous nature needed a counterbalance. Moreover, during these years Weber was attached to Ida's daughter Emmy, a devout but emotionally disturbed young woman. Thus the three women closest to him in his student days were deeply religious and highly critical of the world of politically minded men. It seems reasonable to conclude that Weber's lifelong respect for true believers and his scholarly interest in religion had its affective source in these family experiences.

After Weber passed his law examinations in Göttingen in 1886, his father recalled him to Berlin, ostensibly to curb his student expenditures. Without income of his own, Weber had to spend seven more years in the patriarchal household, from age twenty-two until twenty-nine—a personal dependence then common for professionals-to-be but today unimaginable to most students. The father seems to have ordered the son home to isolate him from the Baumgarten household with its politically and religiously unwelcome influences. Max senior disliked Otto Baumgarten, whom his wife "adopted" as a religious son, since she felt helpless in the face of her own son's intractable secularism. The mother also had close religious ties with a young tutor of her son Karl, whose own rebellion brought him to the brink of juvenile delinquency. When the father fired the tutor in the early nineties, Max junior broke inwardly with him. Many years later he explained about the incident: "Father had a deep antipathy toward both men. Basically, religion was to him identical with cant, theologians with hypocrites. At that time terrible letters resulted from [this situation] and completely alienated me from him."[4] Several years earlier the mother had in-

Channing's view that it was a moral honor for a deserter to be put before the firing squad or behind prison bars, the twenty-one-year-old Weber wrote his mother that he "could simply not understand how public morality would be raised by putting professional military men on a footing with murderers and by upholding them to public contempt—wars would not become more humane on that account" (loc. cit.).

[4] E. Baumgarten, op. cit.; 629.

herited a substantial fortune from her Huguenot family; the father
used a portion for rebuilding his house to make it a more splendid
place of entertainment for academic and political luminaries. Yet
he completely controlled his wife's household purse and tried to
prevent her from "wasting" money on charities. Secretly the mother
gave away part of her allowance and did some of the maid's chores,
thereby saving wages and hiding her good deed.

In her feminist writings, Max's wife, Marianne, later depicted in
ideal typical terms the tensions inherent in such a patriarchal household—a thinly veiled portrayal of the older Webers' home.

It is unavoidable that the patriarchal husband wants to regiment and
control his wife's inner life. The richer and the more autonomous her
personality, the more difficult must be her principled subjection. If she
strongly strives for independent activities and intellectual growth, her
husband, concerned about his authority, must necessarily feel ill at ease.
His anxiety is not calmed as long as he is not continuously certain of
mastery over her inner life. He will feel the urge to supervise her reading, her friendships, and all her outside interests. Even today this half-
conscious tendency, frequently a merely traditionalist influence,
prompts countless husbands to be suspicious toward any serious activity
beyond the household. For outside, women are put under an impersonal
order which removes them from personal domination, just like the
men. . . . There is a tragic irony: the wife who, for her husband's sake,
does not develop her moral faculty and intellectual talents, is in most
cases and in the long run left far behind the more agile man. . . . The
other possibility is that time and life's vicissitudes make the woman
mature in spite of her submission. Then comes the day when her will
and judgment break through the barriers, but it remains very difficult
for her to find the courage of her own convictions toward a husband
accustomed to her subordination, and hence to upset the marital equilibrium. How often have even noble and brave women found no other
way out of the conflict between the command of their own conscience
and their husbands' orders than to comply ostensibly but to circumvent
them secretly. Then the woman's autonomous life, which had remained
latent for so long, confronts him as an alien, hostile element disrupting
marital harmony. The unconditional trust dissolves, an irreparable
break occurs in the marriage, and this only because the woman has
found herself so late and the man has not learned to value her as equally
destined for self-determination.[5]

In Max Weber's eyes, the father's treatment of the mother was an

[5] Marianne Weber, "Authority and Autonomy in Marriage" (1912), in *Frauenfragen und Frauengedanken. Gesammelte Aufsätze* (Tübingen: Mohr, 1919),
76f.

almost intolerable degradation. But he put up with it for the time
being, serving as his mother's confidant. Increasingly frustrated by
his inability to do something decisive about this situation or even
to walk away from it, he drove himself even harder to achieve financial independence. After failing to find employment as legal
counselor for the city of Bremen—a position vacated by Werner
Sombart—he chose, tentatively and hesitantly, the academic career
as the shortest road.

In addition to extended financial dependence, other factors made
for a very prolonged adolescence among the offspring of the well-
to-do, frequently even more prolonged than the extended adolescence resulting from mass education today.[6] In contrast to the
present, adolescence then meant late marriage. Marianne Weber
remarked:

For the upper strata, small in numbers but culturally of paramount
importance by virtue of their example and intellectual influence, moral
behavior is made more difficult by the custom of late marriage. One must
understand that the underlying motives differ morally. There is, first
of all, the necessity of a long preparation for a professional career. This
is hard to change. Next, there are the social and economic aspirations of
these strata, especially the view that one cannot marry without socially
appropriate furnishings, a precondition of social intercourse. Such
purely conventional expectations must be combatted forcefully in favor
of early marriage. [However,] modern cultured man makes higher intellectual and spiritual demands on marriage than medieval man. On
the one hand, the refinement of our sentiments increases the likelihood
that initially happy marriages are ruined and, on the other, makes the
continuation of broken marriages intolerable. Nowadays young intellectuals frequently hesitate to follow an early liking not only because of
philistine ambitions and economic calculation, but also—and justifiably
so—because they do not want to be fettered for life to another person
until they feel ready.[7]

For Weber financial independence and a self-consciously equalitarian marriage came at last in 1893, at the age of twenty-nine. Four
years later, and now in his own house, he finally challenged his

[6] On the present-day prolongation of adolescence, see Bennett M. Berger,
"The New Stage of American Man—Almost Endless Adolescence," *New York
Times Magazine*, Nov. 2, 1969, 32ff.

[7] The two quotations are from Marianne Weber, "Basic Problems of Sexual
Ethics," *Frauenfragen und Frauengedanken, op. cit.*, 46, and "The Divorce
Issue," *ibid.*, 61f.

father's treatment of the mother, condemning him to his face in front of her and his young wife. Max senior left and died abroad a few weeks later without reconciliation with wife and son. Thus Weber not only condemned his father symbolically but was bound to feel that he had actually contributed to his death. After another few weeks, in the fall of 1897 he suffered the breakdown that incapacitated him for several years. He had to renounce his strenuous round of political and academic activities and to abandon his hard-won independence. Like his father, he became a capitalist rentier. Despite his later protestations that the confrontation had been right in substance if wrong in form, his guilt feeling almost destroyed his creativity. But in the long run he made the most of the opportunities hidden in this breakdown. It gave him the leisure necessary for brooding over the course of Western history and for conceiving his sweeping historical inquiries into the major forms of domination and religion.

Spokesman of a New Political Generation

A new generation tends to waver between extravagant hopes for the future and a pessimistic view of the world; it feels entrapped by the previous generation; it draws attention to itself by a sharply dichotomized rhetoric; it takes a heroic stance or indulges in hero worship; in line with its ingrained elitism, it finds fault not only with its elders but also with the majority of its peers; it puts a universal interest—the nation, the race, mankind—above particular social interests, though this often complicates the search for a social power base; finally, after its youthful period, it must face middle age.

Weber became a generational spokesman at the age of twenty-nine. From then on he attracted public attention by virtue of his determined effort to link politics and scholarship, to be a politically engaged scholar. He advanced rapidly after turning from the arcana of ancient and medieval history to contemporary agrarian and industrial matters that aroused great public interest. His writings after 1892 appeared so pertinent to major economic issues that the chair of general economics at the University of Freiburg was offered to him in 1894, although he had prepared himself for the narrower field of legal and commercial history. His expertise remained the intellectual underpinning of his political activity, but the attention of his public was intensified by his dramatic generational posture. The rhetoric of generational difference enabled him to be alternately aggressive and conciliatory, to give the older generation its due and to stake the claims of the younger one.

Weber came to be much less optimistic than most members of his father's generation, but this was a gradual development, not an abrupt change occasioned by the family catastrophe.[8] In his immediate environment there was the personal precedent of Hermann Baumgarten and Theodor Mommsen, disappointed members of the political generation of 1848, who had grown increasingly pessimistic. Moreover, the cultural climate was gradually chilled by *Kulturpessimismus* and the mood of *fin de siècle*. For young Weber the overwhelming nation-building success of the father's generation became as fateful as the unusually severe incompatibility between the parents. The most ambitious of his cohort had no choice but to live in their fathers' mansion, an imposing political edifice with powerful authoritarian controls but also solid guarantees of civil liberties. Youthful energy and idealism could not easily make their own mark. The mere fact of their being late-comers—similar to the fathers' late appearance in the international arena—made it impossible for the sons to accomplish anything as spectacular as national unification and threatened to reduce them to the status of *epigoni,* a self-image the twenty-nine-year-old Weber put before his elders in the Welfare Policies Association:

You will probably have noticed that I am speaking under the weight of a certain resignation and that my demands . . . too are shaped by it. The reason—and I have the honor to address here primarily older and more experienced gentlemen—lies in the different historical situation. . . . I do not know whether my age mates feel as strongly as I do at this

[8] Friedrich Meinecke, the most renowned historian of Weber's generation, balanced the personal and the political score when he wrote: "One could see Orestes in Max Weber upon hearing how he attacked the father recklessly out of love for the mother and, shortly thereafter, was shaken by his sudden death. The inner difference between father and son reflects the historical opposition of two generations. The father was . . . a prestigious National Liberal parliamentarian, affable and full of *joie de vivre,* but a bourgeois without a social conscience. He represented that smooth surface of life which in the new empire seemed to have been achieved in the wake of the old liberal ideas. This surface was shattered under the impact of the grave social problems and the stronger and more passionate sentiments of the younger generation that began to influence the political and intellectual spheres after 1890. Max Weber became the most energetic representative of this new generation. Among the scholars of his generation he was perhaps the only one whom one can call ingenious without reservation." From Meinecke's review of Marianne Weber's *Lebensbild* in the *Historische Zeitschrift,* 135, 1927, 244. Reprinted in König and Winckelmann, eds, *op. cit.,* 144.

moment the grave curse of being epigoni, which burdens the nation from top to bottom. We cannot revive the naïve, enthusiastic drive that animated the preceding generation, since we are faced with tasks different from those our fathers had so solve.

Yet Weber refused to end on a pessimistic note and concluded with a flourish:

Gentlemen, we make greater demands on the future [than just trying our hand and failing]; we believe that the drafts we draw on it will be honored, and we hope that at the end of our days we will be able to enjoy what has been denied in our youth—approaching, with a calm look into the nation's future, the solution of the cultural tasks then before us on the basis of a strengthened social organization of state and people.[9]

While recognizing the achievements of his elders, Weber showed himself more concerned about the unresolved issues, the persistent social and political cleavages, and the pernicious consequences of Bismarck's long rule. For many older men it was difficult to comprehend his sense of urgency and, increasingly, of impending disaster.[10] However, irrespective of his sharpness of tone, he never proclaimed his own generation morally superior or bound to achieve more than its predecessors. Even in the Freiburg inaugural address of 1895, when he shocked his listeners with calculated matter-of-factness, he only asserted the right of youth to make another historical effort idealistically, leaving the outcome open:

Even in the face of the terrible misery of the masses, which weighs heavily on the sensitized conscience of the new generation, we must honestly profess that more burdensome is the awareness of our respon-

[9] Weber, *Gesammelte Aufsätze zur Soziologie und Sozialpolitik* (Tübingen: Mohr, 1924), 467ff. (abbr. *GAzSS*)

[10] Here is a historical parallel to the contemporary scene. In Germany, the older generations have built parliamentary democracy and economic prosperity out of the ruins of war, but the most recent generation considers these achievements "irrelevant" in view of what appear to be unsolved problems or negative consequences. Similarly, in the United States, the New Deal generation, which learned and applied its lessons in the Depression and the Second World War and its aftermath, finds itself challenged and negated by a new one for which its accomplishments count for nought. There is, however, one major difference: whereas today the new American and German generation feels compelled to reject the institutions and the international role of their countries, Weber could identify without guilt feelings with the new nation-state. Conversely, he could not accuse the older generation of criminal conduct in foreign politics, although in domestic politics he pointed insistently to the harsh facts of impersonal economic domination under "peaceful" conditions.

sibility before history. Our generation is not fortunate enough to know whether its struggle will bear fruit [as the nation-builders of 1870 knew] and whether posterity will accept us as its ancestors. We shall not succeed in banning the spell cast on us—to be epigoni of a great political era—unless we succeed in becoming something else—precursors of an even greater one. Will this be our place in history? I don't know, and merely say: It is the right of youth to be true to itself and to its ideals. It is not the passage of years that makes man senile; he remains young as long as he can feel the great passions with which nature endowed us.[11]

Youthful passion involves heroism of a radical or conformist variety. Weber too adhered to the cult of the heroic. But instead of the eschatological imagery of the youthful band of armed rebels so fashionable today, he employed the Social Darwinist rhetoric of the struggle for existence—and this implied the notion of perennial generational conflict. Nothing in the world, he believed, could be accomplished without strenuous effort; in that respect the future would not be different. He rejected, as too shallow a standard of conduct, the utilitarian pleasure-pain calculus and the liberal doctrine of the greatest happiness of the greatest number. He demanded, as a matter of course, a higher standard of living for the working class, but—like today's radicals—did not want the workers to develop a consumers' mentality. He also opposed monarchist and socialist notions of the welfare state being the highest of all possible social achievements. But if he pitted a heroic activism against the hedonism of complacent Victorians, he also condemned, as an insult to human dignity, the authoritarian habits of aristocratic officers and civil servants as well as of bourgeois teachers and employers. Moreover, he had a powerful affect against "philistine" or "petty-bourgeois" attitudes, which he discovered among Social Democratic workers no less than in higher social regions.

Weber also found fault with most of his age mates, typical of the ingrained elitism of those who perceive themselves as a new political generation. Most of his peers did not engage in political revolt, although they were given to youthful emotionalism and hero worship inside and outside the conformist fraternity culture. On Bastille Day 1885, the twenty-one-year-old Weber wrote to Hermann Baumgarten about his fellow students:

It is very fortunate that the huge election rallies involving the whole student body have been abolished now that the student committee has

---

[11] Weber, "Der Nationalstaat und die Volkswirtschaftspolitik," in *Gesammelte politische Schriften* (Tübingen: Mohr, 1958), 24 (abbr. *PS*).

been set up. This has just about cut the ground from under all that agitation. Now the mob finds an outlet only in the frenzied enthusiasm that breaks out whenever Treitschke makes some outrageous anti-Semitic allusions in his lectures. The more or less vicious slogans scribbled on many walls and most tables, etc., are the only other remaining outlet. However, the most incredible part of the matter is the fantastic ignorance of my age mates about the history of this century. Those from the metropolis are a bit more knowledgeable than the others. But for the rest, there is tabula rasa, excepting some notions about the ill deeds of the Liberals and the feats of the students' hero Bismarck. In their heads, domestic politics began less than a decade ago.[12]

Such ignorance and mindless emotionalism could not be remedied by detached instruction alone. Ten years later, in the inaugural speech, Weber demanded that economics be truly "political economy" and that economists engage in a "tremendous effort in political education." This did not contradict his later statements on *Wertfreiheit*. Quite apart from the fact that at an inaugural a new professor was expected to put forth his beliefs, Weber took it for granted that "as an explanatory and analytical science economics was international."[13] His demand, then, was not identical with a call to indoctrinate students from the lectern. But he did ask economists to be politically active and provide insights into the economic and social dynamics of the time. The traditional humanist training of his elders and peers left many of them largely ignorant about the workings of capitalism, the imperatives of industrialization, and the character of the Social Democratic labor movement. Weber wanted scholars to study contemporary society more intensively— which later became one of his reasons for favoring the term "sociology." He also wanted them to feel responsible for the public's political state of mind; they ought to carry their empirically informed understanding into the public arena and make policy proposals— without, of course, claiming that their science could legitimate their choices. Thus did Weber advocate a balance of passion and reason, politics and scholarship.

In addition to his professorial chores, Weber tried his best to promote "political education." He became an active political speaker and writer, appearing before the Welfare Policies Association, the Evangelic-Social Congress, the Pan-German Association, and even workers' education classes. In the Evangelic-Social Congress (founded in 1890) he endeavored to disabuse the well-meaning

[12] *Weber: Jugendbriefe, op. cit.,* 174.
[13] Weber, *Politische Schriften, op. cit.,* 14, 24, 13.

liberal pastors of their social sentimentalism and teach them the realities of the class struggle in an industrial society. In the Pan-German Association (founded in 1891) he presented his ideas on the Polish migrant workers, but he left this conservative body several years later when he found no resonance. He conducted another agrarian survey for the Evangelic-Social Congress and wrote articles for the *Christliche Welt, Evangelisch-soziale Zeitfragen* (published by cousin Otto Baumgarten), *Sozialpolitisches Zentralblatt, Soziale Praxis,* the ultraconservative *Preussische Kreuzzeitung,* and the liberal *Die Hilfe,* Friedrich Naumann's journal. In spite of grave doubts, Weber helped Naumann found the National-Social Association in 1896. This, the most ambitious attempt by the new reformist generation to build a political party and provide a political alternative, did not gain a broad social constituency and soon failed at the ballot box, remaining a party of intellectuals.

In line with the universalist appeals of generational revolt, Weber took the national interest as his political yardstick, subordinating the interests of the social classes and interest groups to the lofty purposes of strengthening Germany's political, economic, and cultural position in the world. He operated with a notion of national interest reminding us today of John F. Kennedy's rhetoric—"Let's get the nation moving again" and "Ask not what your country can do for you—ask what you can do for your country." In contrast to the older generation, which had a primarily national or Continental horizon, Weber tried to face the fact that Germany was now a great power and an industrial state with inevitable involvements in the steadily intensifying world-wide competition of the major powers. His most general proposal was a national policy of social integration, granting the labor movement at least as many rights as it had gained in England, his political model. He admired the ability of that relatively small country to build effective representative institutions and become a world power. However, he was fully aware of the weight of historical legacies. The formative experiences of England, the United States, and France could not simply be repeated. Weber deeply regretted one religious and one political omission in German history: "That our nation never went through the school of hard asceticism, in no form whatever, is the source of all I hate about it and about myself." And: "A people which—as we Germans—has never had the nerve to behead the traditional powers will never gain the proud self-assurance that makes the Anglo-Saxons and the Latins so superior to us in the world, in spite of all our 'victories' (owed to discipline) in war and technology."[14] It is true that these were radical statements of the mature Weber, but both his youthful rebellion and continued nonconformism in later years appear to be motivated, in part, by his sense that as a German he should make a particular effort to fight authoritarian proclivities —submissive as well as oppressive ones—inside and outside himself.

Putting the national cause above social-class interests did not resolve a typical difficulty of generational revolt—locating a social base for its struggle. In his 1895 inaugural address Weber examined in turn the Junkers, the liberal bourgeoisie, and the Social Democratic working class; he determined that none of them was capable of leading the nation into a future fraught with danger. Given the universalist appeals, on the one hand, and the lack of a power base on the other, Weber's policy proposals tended to be vague and impractical. In the early nineties he demanded the closure of the frontiers to Polish seasonal labor in order to raise the standard of living of the German farmworkers and to preserve a higher cultural *niveau* against a lower one. With equal lack of success he advocated a variant of homestead farming in the eastern provinces.[15]

In the second half of the nineties Friedrich Naumann became the mouthpiece of "liberal imperialism." Wolfgang Mommsen and

[14] The first quotation is from a letter to the church historian Adolf von Harnack, dated Feb. 5, 1906; see E. Baumgarten, *op. cit.*, 450. The second quotation is from a letter to the philosopher Count Keyserling, dated June 21, 1911; *ibid.*, 429. Honigsheim remembers a more drastic version: "A people who has never beheaded its monarch is not a *Kulturvolk*"; see König and Winckelmann, eds., *op. cit.*, 172; cf. *On Max Weber*, *op. cit.*, 13. For a very attenuated version, see Marianne Weber, *Lebensbild, op. cit.*, 447, and Wolfgang Mommsen, "Universalgeschichtliches und politisches Denken bei Max Weber," *Historische Zeitschrift*, 201, 1965, 574.

[15] In 1888, when Weber participated in maneuvers in Poznan province, he observed the inconclusive effects of the rather modest Prussian policy of creating small farms for German farmworkers. The capitalist transformation of the large landed estates set free many of the German workers who used to be attached to them. In their stead Polish seasonal laborers came across the Russian border. This made sense from the viewpoint of capitalist productivity, but it violated national interest. In fact, the Junkers, the self-appointed guardians of national interest, were undermining German culture in the East. Weber observed a peculiar kind of Social Darwinist selection: Those with the lower level of cultural aspirations—the Polish peasants—displaced those with higher ones. He believed that many German workers left the countryside not only for material reasons but in search of personal freedom. This was one of the conclusions of the study undertaken for the Verein für Sozialpolitik, which he joined in the same year, 1888.

others have seen its intellectual source in the inaugural address, since Naumann was heavily dependent on Weber's superior intellect. In line with his perception of the English model, Weber, who supported the incipient naval expansion, was indeed a tough-minded "liberal imperialist" at the time. But the stridency of his tone had a largely polemical purpose: his targets were William II's rhetoric of benevolent, welfare-minded patriarchalism and the "ethical culture" movement. In 1911 Weber looked back:

In ethical matters the pacifists are, without doubt, superior to us. As early as in my Freiburg inaugural address, immature as it may have been in many respects, I stressed in the most reckless fashion the sovereignty of national ideas in all areas of practical politics, including welfare matters, when the great majority of my colleagues ran after the swindle of the so-called 'welfare monarchy.' Then too I emphasized very deliberately that politics cannot be a morally buttressed enterprise, nor will it ever be."[16]

Since there is no agreed-upon moral standard in politics and the imperatives of the power struggle compromise the ethical commitments of anybody entering the political arena, Weber demanded a maximum of rational self-discipline. He frequently and sharply disagreed with Naumann's emotionalist stance, opposing especially his anti-intellectualism and animus against scholarship. Naumann feared, like Nietzsche before him, that scholarly detachment and immersion in the past inevitably weakened the will to political activism—today again a popular prejudice among young radicals. Weber maintained that the two should be compatible.

At the age of thirty-four, Weber was politically prominent enough to receive the offer of a *Reichstag* candidacy from the National Liberals. He declined to run, since he had only recently accepted a chair in Heidelberg and felt honor-bound to fulfil his academic obligations. This was shortly before the onset of his illness. He dragged himself through meetings and lectures until he reached the point of complete exhaustion. Thus ended his period of youthful struggle. The man who returned to scholarship several years later was much more aware of his personal limitations. He now accepted "scholarship as a vocation" and research into the past as a particular kind of resignation. But he did not change his politics significantly, nor did he cease to see himself as a spokesman for his generation.

[16] Marianne Weber, *Lebensbild, op. cit.,* 454.

In the last years before the First World War, the generational differences in the Verein für Sozialpolitik became more pronounced, as the generation of 1890—now middle-aged—challenged the rule of the septuagenarian generation of the Schmollers and Wagners. One and one-half decades after his first appearance as generational spokesman in the Association, Weber openly clashed with his elders, who believed that the monarchic bureaucracy was the best instrument for accomplishing social harmony. He and a few others doubted the older generation's assumption that nationalization or increased state control was more beneficent than the existing economic domination by the large-scale private enterprises. Weber argued that

when the Verein für Sozialpolitik was founded [in 1872], the generation of Privy Councillor [Adolf] Wagner called for more than purely technical yardsticks in economic affairs; at the time this group was just as small as we who think differently are today in relation to you. Gentlemen, you then had to fight the salvo of applause for the purely technological accomplishments of industrial mechanization emanating from the laissez-faire doctrine. It appears to me that today you are in danger of providing such cheap applause to mechanical efficiency as an administrative and political criterion. . . . Rational calculation . . . reduces every worker to a cog in this [bureaucratic] machine and, seeing himself in this light, he will merely ask how to transform himself from a little into a somewhat bigger cog, . . . an attitude you find, just as in the Egyptian *papyri,* increasingly among our civil servants and especially their successors, our students. The passion for bureaucratization at this meeting drives us to despair."[17]

Weber had a better sociological grasp of the consequences of bureaucratization than most of the older scholars, but his strong sentiments on this score were rooted in the basic world view. He perceived a massive threat to individual spontaneity and liberty and became much concerned with rescuing some conditions for their preservation in a highly organized industrial civilization. He rejected the view popular among the "literati" that there was too much personal and political freedom in Imperial Germany, and especially in more democratic countries. The older generation was no less individualist than Weber, but he enlarged his liberal inheritance by giving attention to some of the major critics of liberalism, prominently Marx and Nietzsche.

[17] Weber, *GAzSS, op. cit.,* 413f.

NIETZSCHE

It was part of Weber's generational stance to take seriously the very men whom the older generation had rejected or neglected. As in his relation to Marx, Weber was impressed by Nietzsche's Promethean effort and intellectual radicalism. But in spite of lauding the two men and occasionally referring to their work, he retained a critical distance and maintained a basic difference. In the last two weeks of his life he is said to have remarked to a student:

Today a scholar's honesty, and especially that of a philosopher, can be measured by his attitude toward Nietzsche and Marx. Whoever does not admit that he could not have accomplished crucial parts of his own work without the contributions of these two men deceives himself and others. Our intellectual universe has largely been formed by Marx and Nietzsche.[18]

This profession was characteristic of Weber's sense of fairness and intellectual integrity. But the remark had a polemical context. Earlier on the same day Weber had had a showdown with Oswald Spengler, who aroused his ire by disparaging Marx and Nietzsche. In fact, Spengler stood much closer to Nietzsche than he did. Regardless of Weber's acknowledgment, his reception of Nietzsche and Marx cannot simply be gleaned from such a statement. His response was complex and subtle. Neither was his political sociology the fulfilment of Nietzsche's thought—as Eugène Fleischmann has claimed—nor was it primarily a bourgeois reaction to Marxism, as others have asserted.[19] Weber meant what he said: By pointing to the economic and the psychological factors in history Marx and Nietzsche had shaped an intellectual universe within which those after them had to orient themselves in one way or another. Yet this does not answer the question of the specific relationship between his work and theirs.

References to Nietzsche in Weber's work are sparse and mostly critical. The usual philological method needs to be supplemented by biographical evidence, no matter how tenuous, and by analytical comparisons which probe into thematic and psychological affinities. There is no reference to Nietzsche in Weber's published letters

[18] Quoted in E. Baumgarten, *op. cit.*, 554.
[19] Eugène Fleischmann, "De Weber à Nietzsche," *Archives Européen de sociologie*, V, 1964, 190–238. For a critique of Fleischmann's thesis, see W. Mommsen, *op. cit.*, 598.

from his student days, but he became familiar early with the intel-
lectual setting of his writings. Nietzsche began as a follower of
Schopenhauer, who was long disregarded by academic philosophy.
Weber, however, heard in his first semester "a brilliant critique of
Schopenhauer's system" by Kuno Fischer. At the time (1882)
Weber also read, together with cousin Otto Baumgarten, David
Strauss' *The Old Faith and the New* and reported home that the
book "does not contain much that is new and one doesn't more or
less know already. It is intended to be a brief encyclopedia of the
freethinker's *Weltanschauung,* and therefore must appear in many
respects quite superficial."[20] The popular Strauss was a vulgar rationalist and Darwinist, who made easy attacks on clerics and miracles—an attitude too simplistic for Weber's tastes. Now, one of
Nietzsche's earliest writings, published a few years before, was a
savage attack on Strauss, in which he also made short shrift of a
public state of mind for which the victory of Prussian arms was
tantamount to a victory of German over French culture. Albeit we
cannot date Weber's first reading of Nietzsche, we can say that both
the critique of Strauss' shallow rationalism and of the public's smug-
ness in the wake of national unification had an affinity to Weber's
outlook. Similarly, Nietzsche's early *Birth of Tragedy from the
Spirit of Music* (1872) and his later essay on *The Uses and Disadvantages of History* (1876) were likely to appeal to Weber in their
antipathy to the widespread uncritical belief in progress, to utilitarianism, to the antitragic notion of civilization and to the "Alex-
andrian culture of science."

Nietzsche had gone through a more severe youthful identity crisis
than Weber. In fact, one could say that he was an adult before he
became an adolescent. In his childhood he had been so prematurely
self-controlled and pious as to be called "the little pastor." At
twenty-three he already held a chair of classical philology next to
his colleague and friend Jacob Burckhardt. The young Nietzsche
is said to have "lived" in antiquity. But then a tremendous reaction
set in and he lashed out, with a vengeance, against Christianity as
a slave religion and historical research as a threat to life. Young
Weber too did not want to dedicate his life to historical contempla-

---

[20] *Weber: Jugendbriefe, op. cit.,* 53, and Marianne Weber, *Lebensbild, op.
cit.,* 76f. In 1886, Weber wrote to his brother Alfred that at the age of sixteen,
he had read David Strauss' *The Life of Jesus* (1835) and found it very impressive. But he warned his brother, then eighteen, against supposing that Strauss'
notion of the "myth" could elucidate early Christianity. Cf. Weber: *Jugendbriefe, op. cit.,* 205–209.

tion and disregarded Theodor Mommsen's wish to have him take his place in ancient historiography. But in turning to contemporary issues of industrialization and democratization he remained steadfastly committed to canons of scholarship; and therein lies a crucial difference from Nietzsche and, for that matter, many of the present-day rebels, who knowingly or unknowingly repeat Nietzsche's affects and arguments against scholarship.

Nietzsche insisted that illusions, not science, were necessary for invigorating life. In his 1893 address before the Verein für Sozialpolitik, Weber acknowledged that "tremendous illusions were necessary for establishing the German empire." Yet in contrast to Nietzsche's maxim, he did not honestly believe that his own generation could hold such illusions: "They dissolved together with the honeymoon of national unity and cannot be reproduced artificially and by reflection."[21] Therefore, Weber endeavored to put hard-won empirical knowledge in the place of lost illusion, trying to sustain "life" through rational inquiry. In his scholarship and politics Weber definitely rejected the core of Nietzsche's mode of thought—heroic aestheticism. He was morally opposed to Nietzsche's conviction that great men should make history irrespective of the interests of the masses. Weber fought for parliamentary rule and full citizenship of the workers, in diametric contrast to Nietzsche's vast loathing of liberal and democratic forms of government. When his friend Georg Simmel wrote in *Schopenhauer und Nietzsche* that the latter "should at least have clearly delimited his will to power from common acquisitiveness by making it clear that the quality of the sovereign mind, not domination and force as external reality, constitute the will to power," Weber noted in the margin: "That exactly was not Nietzsche's view. Even in that regard he was a German philistine *(Spiesser)*."[22]

On balance, then, Weber's political and scholarly indebtedness to Nietzsche appears rather limited. However, there is another side to the matter. Scholarship and politics were for Weber merely demanding rational "vocations"—necessary for human survival. But they could not answer the most profound spiritual needs of man. Religion, philosophy, and the arts were in crucial ways more satisfying. In this regard Weber felt some affinity to Nietzsche—his concern with "meaning" and "relevance" in modern life. During his years of illness he must also have been aware of the disquieting par-

---

[21] *GAzSS, op. cit.,* 467f.
[22] Cited in E. Baumgarten, *op. cit.,* 615.

allel between Nietzsche's suffering and his own: the forced retreat from academic life and the rootless drifting and traveling in search of recovery. Afterward, however, Weber gave more attention to the Russian mystic and radical movements, and particularly to Tolstoy and Dostoevsky. Again, there are few traces in his scholarly writings, and a projected book on Tolstoy remained unwritten. However, in view of the present eruption of the ethic of ultimate ends, these traces merit our attention.

Tolstoy and the Two Ethics

Whereas Weber maintained his own generational posture against the leaders of the *Verein für Sozialpolitik*, he too, in his forties, became for younger men a member of an older generation. After he had regained his productivity, he still did not feel up to the routines of academic life. But in compensation for his academic marginality, he brought together in his Heidelberg salon some eminent older scholars and writers and a select group of younger men. During these years he acquired a reputation as a passionate critic of the academic establishment. He opposed Schmoller's well-nigh monopolistic appointment powers in economics. He labored, unsuccessfully, to assure Simmel and Sombart of a chair and Robert Michels at least of the right to teach *(venia legendi)*. In 1908, he carried his fight for Michels—then a Social Democrat—before a broad public in the pages of the *Frankfurter Zeitung*, the most important liberal newspaper in Germany. He condemned the universities' policy of refusing appointments to Social Democrats. In 1911, he backed the *Frankfurter Zeitung's* editorial critique of a general's vulgar antipacifist speech before students at the University of Freiburg, after faculty members had replied to the newspaper with a collective declaration. At the same time he wrote several articles against the academic appointment policies of the Prussian ministry of education. Thus his credentials as a foe of vested interests, anti-Semitic and antisocialist biases, and "zoological nationalism" among students and professors were well established. In his campaign against active and passive authoritarianism he went to rhetorical extremes: "If I ever regain my health and can again give a seminar, I shall admit only Russians, Poles and Jews, not Germans."[23] Not surprisingly, some influential members of the aca-

[23] See Honigsheim in König and Winckelmann, *op. cit.*, 172 (English version in *On Max Weber, op. cit.*, 13).

demy, like the neo-Kantian philosopher Wilhelm Windelband—privy councillor and member of the upper house in Baden—reacted acidly. Informed that Weber was sympathetic to a relatively moderate Russian revolutionary, Windelband retorted: "Of course only because the man has been in prison."[24]

Such a reputation explains Weber's attractiveness to East European students, who frequented his house. They were preoccupied with ultimate commitments, ranging from mysticism to secular radicalism. Weber respected their seriousness and courage. Among them was Fedor Stepun, who seems to have introduced him to Soloviev's work. Another visitor, the young *Privatdozent* Nikolai von Bubnoff, worked on mysticism and Dostoevsky. Weber befriended the young Georg von Lukács, who also introduced Ernst Bloch. Lukács and Bloch appeared as "representatives of the antipole" *(Gestalten vom Gegenpol)*, as Marianne Weber dubbed them.[25] Although not yet in their Marxist-Leninist phase, they opposed bourgeois liberalism, relativism, and socialist revisionism in favor of Russian-type collectivism and mysticism. Weber took great interest in Russian events. On the one hand, he was greatly concerned about czarist autocracy and imperialism, and on the other he paid close attention to the religious and revolutionary currents. He considered it faintly possible that Russia might take a course different from Western rationalization.

We have Paul Honigheim's testimony that during those Sunday afternoon meetings "he could not remember one talk during which the name of Dostoevsky did not crop up. But perhaps even more urgent . . . was it for Weber to come to grips with Tolstoy."[26] In dealing with them Weber responded, in some measure, to the intellectual interests of younger men around him. There is no evidence that the two Russians had been a formative influence, although at the age of nineteen Weber knew Ivan Turgenev's works well and the avant-garde of his own generation chose Dostoevsky and Tolstoy as literary models in the 1880's.[27] Yet after his own crisis Weber

[24] *Op. cit.,* 176 (*On Max Weber,* 16).

[25] Marianne Weber, *Lebensbild, op. cit.,* 508.

[26] Honigsheim, *op. cit.,* 241 (*On Max Weber,* 81).

[27] For Weber's 1883 comments on Turgenev, see *Jugendbriefe, op. cit.,* 79 and 87. The *Jugendbriefe* contain no references to Dostoevsky and Tolstoy. The first German translations of *Crime and Punishment, War and Peace,* and *Anna Karenina* appeared in 1885. In the same year Georg Conrad started the major journal of Naturalism, *Die Gesellschaft,* contributing a long essay on Dostoevsky. After 1890, the literature on Dostoevsky and Tolstoy grew steadily. In con-

was likely to have a greater interest than before in the psychological complexities of the two men.

Weber considered Tolstoy's pacifism representative of the ethic of ultimate ends and antithetical to his own political outlook. However, he himself tended to alternate between political pragmatism and a highly personal rigorism. Even close political friends found it often impossible to predict his reaction to a new situation. As a political and academic outsider he did not have to operate within institutional constraints and was free to make a personal decision as he saw fit. Indeed, Weber's critical stance appeared so deeply rooted in an ethic of ultimate ends that Lukács could exclaim: "Max Weber would be the right man to free socialism from the miserable relativism" of the Revisionists.[28] In fact, however, Weber sided with the Revisionists in the Social Democratic labor movement. If Lukács could see Weber in this light, it is not surprising that the Russian students should have asked him to help dedicate their new library in Heidelberg in 1913. In a midnight speech Weber extolled their human strength and praised their good intentions but ended soberly: "If the tensions between the states should reach the breaking point and Russians should feel obliged to back up Serbia, then we will meet again on the field of honor."[29]

The following year Europe was engulfed by the holocaust. Weber was prevented by his age from rushing to the battlefields where so many of the students and his friends—and his brother and brother-in-law—were to die. Instead he took up the pen and wrote "Between Two Ethics." The immediate occasion was a polemic between a Swiss pacifist woman and Gertrud Baeumer, who alongside Marianne Weber was a leader of the feminist movement in Germany. The wartime setting and the polemical context made Weber insist on a razor-sharp distinction between the two ethics. He explained first what he meant by the "admittedly pathetic" notion of "our responsibility before history." Great states, he reasoned, had greater responsibilities than smaller countries, which were, of course, no less "valuable" on that account. In fact, certain values could be realized only in polities that had forsaken political power. For-

---

trast to Dostoevsky, who died early, in 1881, Tolstoy was one of Weber's political contemporaries, since his many ethical tracts appeared mostly between 1880 and 1910. However, the first reference to Tolstoy in Weber's extant letters dates back only to 1908.

[28] Honigsheim, *op. cit.*, 186 (*On Max Weber,* 27).

[29] *Op. cit.*, 169 (*On Max Weber,* 13).

tunately, German culture flourished outside the Empire, as in Switzerland. But Germany happened to be a great state and therefore "must be an armed camp." As he had done twenty years before in his inaugural speech, Weber suggested that national unification had merely been a "costly vain luxury" unless it was meant to enable Germany to do "her damned duty before history, that means, posterity, in opposing the dominance of the whole world by the bureaucratic regulations of Russian officials and the conventions of Anglo-Saxon 'society.'" The specter of a world divided between Russia and the Anglo-Saxon countries was old. Nietzsche had conjured it up, but so had Tocqueville before him. Weber's was a nationalism embraced in good conscience at a time when Germany had not yet committed the crimes that would permanently disqualify her from making any cultural claims to political leadership.

After declaring that the "tragic burden of historic duties" could not be lightened by pacifist goodwill, Weber came to the point. It was inappropriate for anyone to appeal to the gospel unless he was willing to live up to its prescriptions:

There is only Tolstoy's consistency, nothing else. Whoever takes only one penny of interest from others, directly or indirectly, whoever owns or uses a commodity produced with another person's sweat, lives off the machinery of that loveless and pitiless economic struggle for existence which the bourgeois ideologists like to call "peaceful civilization": it is but another form of the struggle of man against man in which not millions, but hundreds of millions are physically and spiritually crippled year after year . . . or at least condemned to lead a life which is infinitely more bereft of recognizable meaning than if all stand up for honor—and that means simply, for the historical duties which fate decreed for one's own people. On this score, the evangels are unambiguous in all decisive respects. They are irreconcilable not just with war—they don't even mention it—but ultimately with all rules of the "world," as long as it wants to be a realm of thisworldly culture—of beauty, dignity, honor, and greatness of man (Kreatur). Whoever does not face the consequences —and Tolstoy did so only under the shadow of death—should be reminded that he is tied to the rules of this world, and that includes for an unforeseeably long time the possibility and inevitability of war.[30]

Weber reaffirmed his adherence to the political ethic of responsibility at the same time that he emerged as one of the most outspoken critics of the "irresponsible" conduct of wartime policies. He tried to promote a negotiated peace, but worried about the rapid spread

[30] Weber, "Zwischen zwei Gesetzen" (1916), in PS, op. cit., 140ff.

of pacifist sentiments, which he believed would undermine the chances of a peace settlement. He respected pacifism only as the outlook of virtuosi, but did not accept it as a realistic solution to social problems. In a letter to his wife, dated April 21, 1908, he remarked that Tolstoy "expected in too utopian a way" that love of one's fellow man could solve life's problems. He insisted that pacifists be totally consistent, thus denying them moral legitimacy as a political mass movement. In the wake of the Freiburg affair of 1911, he wrote to one of the editors of the *Frankfurter Zeitung* that "I judge the all-out-pacifists not differently, or even more severely, than Prof. F. did, unless they take Tolstoy's consequences not just as a literary dessert but carry them through in all directions, including domestic politics. Whoever considers war the worst of all evils in foreign politics must not be enthusiastic about revolutionaries and also must turn the other cheek in his personal life. Only this can impress me; everything else I consider inconsistent and sentimental humbug."[31]

Although a genuinely pacifist mass movement was politically a contradiction in terms, adherence to an ethic of ultimate ends could give rise to a new religious movement. Weber paid a segment of the Russian revolutionary intelligentsia the compliment of considering their movement the last new religion, but he scoffed at the religious pretenses of Western literati, whether in mystical or ascetic cloak. In the only reference to Dostoevsky and Tolstoy in *Economy and Society*—written sometime between 1910 and 1913—he drew an invidious comparison between Russian and western intellectuals.

The last great movement of intellectuals which, though not sustained by a uniform faith, shared enough basic elements to approximate a religion was that of the Russian revolutionary intelligentsia in which patrician, academic, and aristocratic intellectuals stood next to plebeian ones . . . Under the influence of Dostoevsky and Tolstoy, an ascetic and acosmistic patterning of personal life was created among some relatively large groups of these Russian intellectuals. . . . In Western Europe . . . the practical importance of such movements for the sphere of culture was greater in the past than now. Many elements conspire to render unlikely any serious possibility of a new congregational religion borne by intellectuals. . . . The 'need of literary, academic, or café society intellectuals to include "religious" feelings in the inventory of their

[31] The last two quotations from Marianne Weber, *Lebensbild, op. cit.*, 428, 455.

sources of impressions and sensations, and among their topics for discussion, has never yet given rise to a new religion. Nor can a religious renascence be generated by the need of authors to compose books on such interesting topics or by the far more effective need of clever publishers to sell such books. No matter how much the appearance of a widespread religious interest may be simulated, no new religion has ever resulted from such needs of intellectuals or from their chatter.[32]

If Weber was skeptical about the religious potential of Western intellectual fashions, he seems to have held a more positive view of the German youth movement, which flourished in the last decade before the First World War, propagating a new world view and a new way of life. Here was another movement with an ethic of ultimate ends.

THE YOUTH MOVEMENT AND
ADVICE TO THE YOUNG

In the last year of the First World War Marianne Weber delivered a speech on "The Cultural Tasks of Woman." This feminist address also addressed itself to the generational conflict precipitated by the youth movement.[33] Some of her remarks could have been

written today, indicating parallels between the pioneering youth movement of six decades ago and the present situation. Since her writings are not available to the English reader, extensive quotation is in order. Today, she said, there is a

---

[32] Weber, *Economy and Society* (New York: Bedminster, 1968), G. Roth and C. Wittich, eds., 516f.

[33] The young Weber earnestly set out to make his wife an equal not only in their personal relationship but also in the public sphere. This was a response to his father's failure to accept his mother as an intellectual and political equal. But Weber's intellectual influence remained dominant. However, his breakdown made Marianne indeed more of a psychological equal and also a mouthpiece for some of his ideas during his years of public silence. Afterwards she continued to reflect his views; for instance, in 1916 she paralleled her husband's "Between Two Ethics" with a longish essay of her own on "War as an Ethical Problem." During their lifetimes, Marianne Weber never strayed far from the ideas of her husband, Georg Simmel, and Ernst Troeltsch. After Weber's death she not only salvaged the fragments of *Economy and Society* but also wrote a highly personal and reverential biography in a valiant attempt to preserve his memory before a largely indifferent academic public. Because of her unusually close identification it is possible to take much of her written work as a statement of Weber's own views, as will be done here with regard to the youth movement.

far-flung movement which claims for youth the right to codetermine its own education. This movement wants to enlarge the awareness of youth's inherent value and to wrest from the older generation the right to determine their lives "autonomously, on their own responsibility and with truthfulness before themselves." Of course, this formula from the [1913] program of the Free-German *(Freideutsche)* youth is subject to misunderstanding and open to objection, since it sounds as if it intended to exclude the older generation from any educational participation. But it makes sense as a protest against education exclusively through authority and compulsion in home and school. It also is meaningful as a defense against purposes inappropriately imposed on young people, for instance, their training solely for political and vocational roles. The point is that modern youth wants to be young and not to be used up in getting ready for maturity. Modern youth rebels against the ravages of big city life; it seeks to return to the simple pleasures of living in nature, and defends itself, above all, against the one-sided utilization of all energies for vocational purposes, by emphasizing the value of a harmonically developed, uncrippled humanity. . . . The old generation must always be aware that life comes to a standstill if young people, without searching and testing on their own, are pushed into the routines of the old ones. The German educational system, in particular, should give freer rein to adolescence and should set itself the task of making young people independent as early as possible. In Anglo-Saxon countries, above all in America, such ideas have long been accepted as educational principles. A relatively equalitarian, rather than an authoritarian, kind of influence is exerted in school and home out of respect for the "civil rights" of young people. . . . Tensions and battles between growing and grown-up persons, most of all inner resistance of the young against domination by the old, belong to the most inevitable conflicts of life, for every energetic young man must have the confidence that he can arrange the world better than his ancestors, and he prefers to seek his goal through trial and error rather than to be forced into an old mold. . . .

But whatever youth organizations Germany will have after the war, they will be constructive only if the young and their leaders recognize that the idea of self-determination and of educating yourself is only a valuable and necessary supplement, not a substitute and displacement, of education by the mature generation. . . .

Since the number of years alone does not make a human being mature, criticism directed toward the educators, toward the home and the schools, is in order, but only insofar as it is done in proper form and not meant to be basic opposition to the older generation. Especially when the inner voice and the special gifts of young men involve them in conflicts with those closest to them, self-control, a noble tone, and tactfulness in daily relations are particularly necessary, for respect and reverence are indispensable conditions of morality. A young person must acquire these values not primarily for the benefit of others, but for his own good. It has happened that not only school conflicts but also events in the parents' home have been treated literarily and exposed to the broad public in a youth magazine. This means the destruction of irre- placeable values and the degradation of self-education to the level of psychic barbarism and *Unkultur*. The core of the Free-German youth movement has recognized these dangers and unambiguously rejected the mode of expression of those young literati.[34]

Thus Marianne Weber went a long way with the young, advocat- ing their cause, but she firmly drew a line that runs counter to the temper of present-day rebels—what she called "expressive culture" *(Ausdruckskultur)*. Nowadays the term denotes phenomena such as the "politics of kicks," but she meant the opposite—good man- ners.

For Max Weber, too, good manners were a major public good, especially in adversity. He continued to adhere to them when his political universe collapsed at the end of 1918. The work of the fathers and the hopes of the sons were shattered. Weber threw him- self into postwar politics, addressing election meetings and acting as advisor on the republican constitution and the Versailles Treaty. But earnestly as he tried, he ran out of advice in many respects. He accurately foresaw that the parliamentary form of government, which he had advocated for so long, would eventually be over- thrown from the Right, since it was burdened with the responsibil- ity for accepting the Versailles "dictate." He also perceived that the efforts of the extreme Left were inherently doomed to failure. More than ever before, politics appeared as a matter of choosing between evils of almost imperceptible difference. In this situation he stuck to his norms of chivalry toward his political opponents, from General Ludendorff to Otto Neurath, who had joined the short-lived Communist government in Bavaria as nationalization commissioner. When Neurath was released from prison, Weber in- vited him to address his seminar; told afterward by a colleague that he had not learned anything new, Weber replied that his single purpose had been to make it clear that he still considered Neurath a gentleman.[35] Such gestures were honorable but politically ineffec-

---

[34] Marianne Weber, "Die besonderen Kulturaufgaben der Frau" (1918), in *Frauenfragen, op. cit.*, 246ff. On the Free-German youth movement and its program, see Walter Laqueur, *Young Germany* (New York: Basic Books, 1962), 31ff.

[35] Witnessed by Carl Landauer.

tive now that crude force was decisive. Gone were the days of polite disputation with Lukács and Bloch before the war, and the intense talks with Ernst Toller and Erich Mühsam during the war. New right- and left-wing groups maneuvered in a power vacuum, and control of the streets was decisive. Weber's house was picketed and his lectures were disrupted by right-wing students, although he took a stridently nationalist stance; they found unpardonable his affirmation of parliamentary government and his appeal to standards of fairness.

Once more Weber retreated into scholarship, but not before he had addressed a small group of democratic students on politics and science as a vocation. This became his political testament. The speeches were meant for young men and women who might still be willing to listen to a voice of reason. But in the country at large many people—young and old—yearned to be led out of historical catastrophe by leaders promising the millennium of class or race. Weber's stand was truly pedagogic. He refused to deliver utopian promises and affirmed a sociological reality principle: "Age is not decisive; what is decisive is the trained relentlessness in viewing the realities of life, and the ability to face such realities and to measure up to them inwardly."[36]

Weber believed that the empirical study of society was a precondition for understanding the "realities of life." Therefore he demanded a research-oriented ("value-free") sociology. Let us therefore look at his struggle for empirical sociology from the viewpoint of the present political conflicts within the German and American universities.

[36] From "Politics as a Vocation," in Gerth and Mills, *op. cit.*, 126.

II

"VALUE-NEUTRALITY" IN GERMANY
AND THE UNITED STATES

More than any other man of his generation Max Weber remains today influential as well as controversial. Neither intellectually nor politically are scholars done with the man and his work. However, his impact has not been steady over the five decades since his death. At various times Emile Durkheim, Georg Simmel, Ferdinand Tönnies, Robert Michels, Vilfredo Pareto, and Sigmund Freud have attracted more attention and approbation. Among these members of the "generation of 1890"—as H. S. Hughes has called them—Durkheim emerges, in the long run, as Weber's closest rival in sociology. In one respect his reception has outstripped Weber's: he was incorporated with less strain into structural functionalism, the only contemporary "school" in American sociology that may deserve the label. It is indicative of this difference that the Parsonian or Durkheimian approach is often contrasted with the Weberian, usually as a juxtaposition of an integration versus a conflict model of society.[1]

In their home countries, too, Weber and Durkheim differed in

[1] For an illuminating comparison, see Randall Collins, "A Comparative Approach to Political Sociology," in Reinhard Bendix *et al.*, eds., *State and Society: A Reader in Comparative Political Sociology* (Boston: Little, Brown, 1968), 42–67.

Guenther Roth, "Max Weber's Empirical Sociology in Germany and the United States: Tensions Between Partisanship and Scholarship," *Central European History*, II:3, Sept. 1969, 196–215. A first draft of this essay was presented at the meeting of the American Historical Association, New York City, Dec. 29, 1968, in the session on "The Diffusion of Social Scientific Ideas in the Twentieth Century." I wish to acknowledge the comments of Jeffrey Schevitz and Stephen Warner.

their school-making success. Durkheim established an institutional monopoly for his sociology with the backing of the authorities of the French Third Republic.[2] Weber neither held a chair during most of his creative years—from 1903 until 1919—nor had Durkheim's direct influence in the councils of the university and the ministry of education, although he was acknowledged to be an inconvenient critic. In France, Durkheim's pervasive influence declined after a generation, and today he is no longer widely read, sharing the fate of Tocqueville. In Germany, Weber's epistemology and politics continue to receive greater attention than his empirical works and his interpretive sociology.

Weber's long-range impact may appear surprising, at first sight, given the absence of a school or a group of scholars systematically promoting his work. "Influence" or "impact" are, of course, metaphors. Unless a scholar has left behind devoted pupils, his "afterlife" depends on receptiveness, which usually derives from interests extraneous to his work. If by a school we mean a cohesive group carrying on a master's teachings in an existing or newly established institutional setting, we imply that his work has become the core of a tradition. If the group is merely conservative, this tradition tends to become lifeless as competing groups forge ahead; if the group is innovative, it is even more certain that the master's work will soon become dated, no matter how much of an inspiration it remains. In "Science as a Vocation" Weber declared that it is the fate of scholarship to be "antiquated in ten, twenty, fifty years." By this reckoning, parts of his work have fared unusually well in the United States. This survival is due partly to the work's slow and gradual reception, which was handicapped by the discontinuous and incomplete translations. Thus Weber's impact was bound to be fragmentary. In general, his work has been appropriated piecemeal by social scientists with a particular theoretical need or research problem. The result might be called "creative misinterpretation," a familiar aspect of scholarly productivity. Since Weber's world-historical vision was, after all, not readily adaptable to the much narrower, if not outright ahistorical, focus of American social scientists, they wrenched pieces out of context and resolutely used them for all they were worth. This pragmatic approach had considerable payoff. But the price, sometimes self-defeating, was intellectual discontinuity;

[2] See Terry N. Clark, "Emile Durkheim and the Institutionalization of Sociology in the French University System," *European Journal of Sociology*, IX:1, 1968, 37–71.

many "improvements" turned out to be marginal or spurious, many critical revisions without base.

Weber's impact has remained more intellectual than institutional, if by institutionalization is meant (as in T. N. Clark's treatment of Durkheim) the establishment of a new academic discipline or the monopolistic dominance of one theory. I prefer, however, to use the term "institutionalization" more widely to encompass phenomena ranging from the ethos of scholarship to literary indices (standard textbook treatment, ritual footnotes),[3] professional indices (graduate study requirements), and organizational indicators, such as institutes (the Max Weber Institute at the University of Munich), distinguished chairs (the Max Weber Professorship at Washington University, St. Louis), and commemorative meetings of professional societies (the 1964 centenary exercises of the American and German Sociological Association). In the United States, the most striking aspect of Weber's institutionalization in this wider sense has been his status as the patron saint of "value-neutrality," whose champion he certainly was, albeit under different academic and political conditions. His scholarly testament, "Science as a Vocation," has become the vade mecum of many a sociologist, indicating an "elective affinity" (in his sense and Goethe's words). But today the New Radicalism rejects the ill-understood notion of academic neutrality and turns against Weber insofar as he appears to be an ideological buttress of the "establishment" in American social science. Perhaps both sides may better understand some of the underlying issues if Weber's reasons for creating his sociology and for insisting on *Wertfreiheit* are reviewed—he did not expect more than a clearer analytical understanding of any scholarly exchange on divergent value commitments. I shall be primarily concerned with the institutional and nonpartisan, not the epistemological, aspect of value-neutrality, two sides which Weber clearly distinguished.[4]

I shall deal first with the meaning of "sociology" in Weber's time and his reasons for accepting the term in spite of his opposition to

---

[3] Cf. Mark Jay Oromaner, "The Most Cited Sociologists: An Analysis of Introductory Text Citations," *The American Sociologist*, III:2, May 1968, 124ff.

[4] Weber habitually put the term *Wertfreiheit* in quotation marks in order to indicate its technical nature. This emphasis is retained in the present chapter. There is no one English or German term that would make a satisfactory shorthand expression. Weber's attempt to neutralize emotional reactions to his terminology failed; he complained that "endless misunderstanding and a great deal of terminological—and hence sterile—conflict have taken place about the

the older sociology, secondly with his futile efforts to shape the German Sociological Association according to his ideas on "purely scientific" research, and thirdly with his lack of any broad influence on German sociology during the Weimar Republic and his renewed controversiality in the 1960's. In conclusion, I will return to Weber's impact in the United States and the present situation of research-oriented sociology.

The Meanings of Sociology

At the turn of the century, sociology meant for Weber an inflated approach, vainly claiming the status of a master science in pursuit of the empirical and normative laws of social life. At best it meant the three-stage evolutionary scheme of Auguste Comte, the mechanistic similes of Herbert Spencer, or the organicist analogies of Albert Schäffle; at worst it was identified with the eccentric endeavors of marginal professors, such as the pathetic Johannes Scherrer, who represented sociology at the University of Heidelberg.[5] Yet by 1910 Weber accepted the term "sociology" for his interpretive study of social action as well as his comparative approach.[6] What happened to bring about this outward change? For it was not really a change of heart or mind, and up to the end of his life he considered "sociology" just a convenient label. Indeed, he seems to have adopted the term for reasons of expediency. For a time he thought of his empirical interests largely in terms of *Sozialökonomik*. In 1909 he accepted the editorship of a handbook series which he termed *Outline of Social Economics*; the series was meant to supplant the outdated *Handbook of Political Economy*, which Gus-

term 'value judgment.' Obviously neither of these has contributed anything to the solution of the problem." Weber, "The Meaning of 'Ethical Neutrality' in Sociology and Economics," in Edward Shils and Henry Finch, eds. and trans., *The Methodology of the Social Sciences* (Glencoe: Free Press, 1949), 10. In this essay published in 1917–18 Weber set aside the institutional aspect of *Wertfreiheit* after some brief remarks. Moreover, the essay omitted references to the Verein für Sozialpolitik, for which he prepared it in 1913. The early version was not published until 1964; see Eduard Baumgarten, ed., *Max Weber: Werk und Person* (Tübingen: Mohr, 1964) 102–139.

[5] For an anecdotal sketch of Scherrer, see Paul Honigsheim, *On Max Weber*, Joan Rytina, trans. (New York: Free Press; East Lansing: Social Science Research Bureau, 1968), 58f.

[6] In his methodological essays between 1903 and 1906 Weber has in mind economics whenever he writes of "our science." As late as 1919, he spoke of "we economists" in "Science as a Vocation."

tav Schönberg had edited in the 1880's.[7] When Weber wrote the first pages of *Economy and Society* for the series he defined *Sozialökonomik* as a field that "considers actual human activities as they are conditioned by the necessity to take into account the facts of economic life."[8] The term, however, was too limited for the wide-ranging themes of the work, which originally had the more accurate, if more awkward, title, "The Economy and the Arena of Normative and De Facto Powers."

Weber came to use the term "sociology" to denote three orientations either marginal to, or incompatible with, the older meaning: (1) the separation between a normative and an empirical approach—sociology was to be an empirical science; (2) the distinction between causal explanation and its logical antecedent, comparative and configurative analysis—a distinction between history and sociology; and (3) the empirical investigation of contemporary phenomena with quantitative tools and teams of researchers —sociology was to be a fact-finding enterprise providing information especially about industrialization and bureaucratization.

(1) For Weber scientific ethics was impossible; the study of the reciprocal relationship between the ethics of a group and its social matrix could not, in turn, establish a scientifically buttressed ethics.[9] Logically, empirical research could deal only with the empirical validity, not the normative existence, of ideals; that means, with the degree to which people acted according to them. Besides, the normative (*dogmatische*) nature of jurisprudence and the *specific* normative assumptions of laissez-faire and state-socialist economics had too often handicapped the study of empirical relationships among legal, political, and economic phenomena.

(2) Weber's distinction between the tasks of history and sociology is most succinctly stated in his letter to the medievalist Georg

[7] For details, see my introduction to Max Weber, *Economy and Society*, which I edited with Claus Wittich (New York: Bedminster, 1968), sec. 9. The term *Sozialökonomik* was introduced by Heinrich Dietzel, *Theoretische Sozialökonomik* (Leipzig, 1895).

[8] *Economy and Society*, p. 312.

[9] Like his friends Georg Simmel, Werner Sombart, and Georg Jellinek, Weber took issue with the neo-Kantian philosopher Rudolf Stammler, who maintained the identity of social ideal and social law. Cf. Rudolf Stammler, *Wirtschaft und Recht nach der materialistischen Geschichtsauffassung* (Leipzig: Veit, 1906), 2d rev. ed. For a sketch of Weber's arguments against Stammler, see *Economy and Society, op. cit.*, 325ff, 32f., and my introduction, lxi. Weber's two lengthy essays on Stammler have not been translated; see *Gesammelte Aufsätze zur Wissenschaftslehre* (Tübingen: Mohr, 1951), 291–383.

von Below, to whom he wrote in 1914 about the intent of *Economy and Society*:

I am dealing with the structure of the political organizations in a comparative and systematic manner, at the risk of falling under the anathema: "dilettantes compare." We are absolutely in accord that history should establish what is specific to, say, the medieval city; but this is possible only if we first find what is missing in other cities (ancient, Chinese, Islamic). And so it is with everything else. It is the subsequent task of history to find a causal explanation for these specific traits. Sociology as I understand it can perform this very modest preparatory work. In this endeavor it is unfortunately almost inevitable to give offense to the researcher who masters a broad field, since it is, after all, impossible to be a specialist in all areas. But this does not convince me that such work is scientifically futile.[10]

(3) Weber wanted to promote social research in order to enlarge the basis of rational discourse on contemporary developments. Such research, he realized, would require considerable funds to pay teams of fieldworkers and statisticians; he envisioned a research institute supported by private funds. When a privately endowed Academy of Science was founded in Heidelberg, he argued that the natural sciences commanded sufficient resources and that the old-style scholars did not need many, but his plea for an investment in contemporary social research went unheeded. By 1909, he was looking for a different organizational vehicle—one reason for his involvement in the founding of the German Sociological Association. Another reason for his interest in establishing a research association was his clash with the older men in the Verein für Sozialpolitik at the Vienna meeting of 1909.[11]

THE FOUNDING OF THE GERMAN SOCIOLOGICAL ASSOCIATION

The young Weber had risen to sudden prominence through his contributions to the surveys of the Verein für Sozialpolitik in

[10] The letter is reprinted in the second edition of Georg von Below, *Der deutsche Staat des Mittelalters* (Leipzig: Quelle und Meyer, 1925), xxiv. This diplomatic statement addressed to a vociferous opponent of sociology must be taken at face value since Weber made similar remarks in less personal contexts.

[11] For an excellent study of the Verein and the tensions between scholarship and politics, see Dieter Lindenlaub, *Richtungskämpfe im Verein für Sozialpolitik* (Wiesbaden: Steiner, 1967); for a general background, see Fritz Ringer, *The Decline of the German Mandarins. The German Academic Community 1890–1933* (Cambridge: Harvard University Press, 1969), ch. 3.

the early nineties.[12] But he came to feel increasingly that many of
the older scholars overestimated the efficacy and beneficent nature
of extending the monarchic bureaucracies into the realm of economy and society. To fight their "passion for bureaucratization" he
strove for "purely scientific discussion": he wanted his opponents,
many of whom were erudite scholars but ill-equipped for contemporary research, to detach themselves long enough from their habitual perspectives to look at new facts or at old facts with new eyes.
Insofar as he tried to gain a hearing for his own political and social
views, the demand for a strictly scientific or "value-neutral" approach had, of course, a strategic aspect. Yet it would be misleading
to reduce Weber's plea to a mere stratagem. He was fully aware
that intransigent political opponents could not be persuaded by
any fact or any kind of research, no matter how carefully and conscientiously done. Hence he could introduce his great attack on
the governmental system in the midst of World War I with the
remark that he did not invoke "the protective authority of any
science. A choice among ultimate commitments cannot be made
with the tools of science." [13] After Vienna, Weber suggested a *pragmatic* solution to the problem of fact-finding in the midst of political controversy. Since he had observed that scholarly self-restraint
and vigorous partisanship tended to interfere with one another if
linked within the same organization, he proposed to separate research from propaganda—two functions often intertwined in the
Verein für Sozialpolitik. Thus he supported the plan to found a
sociological association. But some of those most interested in the
project considered sociology a normative science. Hence the organization of the German Sociological Association—founded in Berlin
on January 3, 1909—became a struggle between these two sides.
The two protagonists were Weber and Rudolf Goldscheid; Weber
won the first round of the contest, Goldscheid the second, but the
outcome remained open, since the association ceased to function
with the outbreak of the First World War. As Leopold von Wiese
reminisced, sociology was "a kind of religion" to Goldscheid and
others of like mind.[14] Weber, however, insisted successfully on
the principle of *Wertfreiheit* in the first paragraph of the statute:

[12] For a discussion of these studies, see Reinhard Bendix, *Max Weber* (New
York: Doubleday, 1962), ch. II.
[13] Weber, "Parliament and Government in a Reconstructed Germany. A Contribution to the Political Critique of Officialdom and Party Politics," Appendix
II of *Economy and Society, op. cit.,* 1381.
[14] See Leopold von Wiese, "Die deutsche Gesellschaft für Soziologie. Per-

Under the name "German Sociological Association" an association has been founded with its seat in Berlin. Its purpose is the advancement of sociological knowledge through conducting purely scientific investigations and surveys, through publishing and supporting purely scientific works, and through organizing periodic meetings. The society recognizes equally all scientific orientations and methods and rejects the representation of all practical ends (ethical, religious, political, esthetic.)[15]

At the first congress in Frankfurt in October 1910, Weber reaffirmed that the "association rejects, in principle and definitely, all propaganda for action-oriented ideas in its midst"; he was quick to add that this did not imply general political nonpartisanship. He tried to commit the association to studying "what is, why something is the way it is, for what historical and social reasons." [16] Although he was adamant, he did not doubt his adversaries' good intentions. Indeed, he had to resolve an inner conflict, which Paul Honigsheim has described to us:

Goldscheid . . . was a progressive evolutionist and he thought, as did others of that persuasion, that his inspiring belief in progress could be given a scientific foundation. This notion was based on the implicit conviction that it was possible to evaluate unequivocally the diverse cultural phenomena and cultural levels. Weber found this idea untenable. On the other hand, Weber knew, and he told Goldscheid freely, that most of the persons who favored such an association tended to be progressive evolutionists. From a democratic standpoint, Goldscheid's position ought to take precedence. Thus Weber was forced to choose between two obligations: on the one hand, integrity of scientific practice, and on the other, respect for the convictions of people who thought differently, and who constituted the majority. The decision was made even more difficult because of another consideration: he was well aware of the sincerity and selflessness of Rudolph Goldscheid, who, as a private scholar, was above any suspicion of acting for the sake of personal gain. Many years later [in 1931] Marianne [Weber] confirmed this to me in the presence of other witnesses in Cologne, and added that Max had suffered greatly because he felt obliged to hurt such a good man. From my own experience I can confirm the fact that Goldscheid was a most decent sort of person. I had worked with him for years at pacifist enterprises, par-

---

sönliche Eindrücke in den ersten fünfzig Jahren (1909 bis 1959)," *Kölner Zeitschrift für Soziologie*, 11:1, 1959, 11–20.
[15] *Verhandlungen des Ersten Deutschen Soziologentages, Frankfurt, Oct. 19–22, 1910* (Tübingen: Mohr, 1911), v.
[16] *Op. cit.*, 39f.

ticularly at international peace congresses, to our mutual enrichment. Weber decided to give precedence to the principle of value neutrality, a condition that would be the sine qua non of his cooperation.[17]

Since Weber could not persuade the majority of the association to practice "value-neutrality," he withdrew from the executive after the second meeting of the association in Berlin in 1912. He wrote at the time:

Will the gentlemen, none of whom can manage to hold back his subjective "valuations," all infinitely uninteresting to me, please stay with their kind. I am absolutely tired of appearing time and again as the Don Quixote of an allegedly unworkable approach and of provoking embarrassing scenes.[18]

Weber was not the only one to withdraw from the association. Georg Simmel and Alfred Vierkandt also left the executive, if for different reasons, whereas Goldscheid entered it. The association did not gain a recognizable professional profile. Those in attendance at the meetings of 1910 and 1912 were, after all, members of various academic disciplines and the group's heterogeneity was not overcome by the joint interest in "sociology," which meant different things to different minds.

Weber was equally unsuccessful in his promotion of social research through the association. He suggested team projects on the press, voluntary associations, and the relationship of technology and culture. He did manage to gather funds for the press study, but the project collapsed when he resigned from the directorship after a lawsuit against a journalist. Other team projects never materialized, since his colleagues were unwilling to abandon their accustomed individual work style.[19] Moreover, some men whose careers had suffered because their sociological interests were not esteemed by the academic powers-that-be preferred to consider the association primarily as a means of status elevation—hence Weber's injunction, at the first congress, against turning it into a club of notables.

[17] Honigsheim, *op. cit.*, 60; cf. *id.*, "Die Gründung der deutschen Gesellschaft für Soziologie in ihren geistesgeschichtlichen Zusammenhängen," *Kölner Zeitschrift für Soziologie*, 11:1, 1959, 8ff.

[18] Marianne Weber, *Max Weber: Ein Lebensbild* (Heidelberg: Schneider, 1950), 468f.

[19] Weber had in mind a research institute rather than a professional association as we understand it today. On the pioneering efforts of Ferdinand Tönnies and Weber, see Anthony R. Oberschall, *Empirical Social Research in Germany, 1848–1914* (The Hague: Mouton, 1965).

Consonant with his plea to separate the institutional settings of research and political action, Weber tried in 1912 to gather other men from the left wing of the Verein für Sozialpolitik; he intended periodic meetings on the lagging welfare legislation. However, differences of opinion proved too great, and the group never became active.[20]

This cursory enumeration of Weber's failures is meant to show the great obstacles he met, not to understate his intellectual influence. Weber created two institutional settings for his ideas. First, he edited the foremost journal of his generation on social science and welfare politics, the *Archiv für Sozialwissenschaft und Sozialpolitik,* together with Werner Sombart and Edgar Jaffé, later also Robert Michels and Emil Lederer. Second, his was perhaps the last of the German salons of the nineteenth century—a century soon to end with the "guns of August." Into this circle he attracted men of the most diverse political persuasions. At the Sunday afternoon gatherings, renowned scholars met radical foreign students and elitist poets; at times the Sunday meetings resembled more a *"salon des refusés"* (as Weber occasionally quipped) than the vaunted German "aristocracy of the spirit." However, if it was an aristocratic assembly of sorts, it was also democratic. There were no sanctions apart from the possibility that someone might wear out his welcome. This was very different from Durkheim's "school-making" setting at the Sorbonne, where every future secondary school teacher in France had to take his courses.

GERMAN SOCIOLOGY 1918–1968

After his death in 1920 Weber's influence was discernible in various disciplines, but it was not particularly strong in sociology. More scholars dealt with his work outside than inside sociology —an indication of Weber's tenuous link to the nascent sociological profession. His works were not widely read; in a quarter-century less than 2,000 copies of *Economy and Society* (first published in 1921–22) were sold. However, his ideas left their mark on a small number of well-known men. His concern with historical typologies was continued by the economist Alfred Müller-Armack and the historians Otto Hintze and Otto Brunner. His substantive views on capitalism, socialism, and democracy were carried further by Joseph

[20] Cf. Weber's post-mortem circular to the participants dated Nov. 15, 1912, in Bernhard Schäfer, ed., "Ein Rundschreiben Max Webers zur Sozialpolitik," *Soziale Welt,* XVIII, 1967, 261–271.

Schumpeter. Carl Schmitt and Christoph Steding reinterpreted, or outright distorted, Weber from the right, Georg Lukács from the left; the latter even used Weber's influence on him as an apology for his ideological "errors." Theodor Heuss and Carlo Mierendorf claimed him for democracy. Karl Jaspers extolled him as the greatest German philosopher of the twentieth century. Alexander von Schelting, Karl Löwith, and Alfred Schütz rendered constructive philosophical and methodological critiques. In jurisprudence and *Staatswissenschaft,* Hermann Kantorowicz, Hans Kelsen, and Karl Loewenstein gave close attention to his work. Karl Mannheim's Sociology of Knowledge, which largely remained social philosophy and epistemology, was a grand attempt to transcend both Marx and Weber. Among sociologists the young Theodor Geiger and the aging Ferdinand Tönnies adhered to the spirit of Weber's "value-neutral" social research, but they belonged to the minority.[21]

As an academic discipline German sociology did not advance significantly in the Weimar Republic. In contrast to France, Germany remained a country with sociologists but without sociology, as Albert Salomon once put it.[22] When the empire collapsed in 1918 some sociologists expected an academic advancement of their marginal discipline, yet the persistence of many institutional and social structures prevented any major change in the universities. Before his death Weber was immersed in the political turmoil of the early postwar period and, for the rest, occupied with the revision of *Economy and Society.* It is true that, after an intermission of sixteen years, he accepted a permanent teaching position in 1919— Lujo Brentano's prestigious economics chair—but he made no attempt to set up another sociological organization. However, at the time the establishment of sociology chairs was favored by Carl Becker, *Staatssekretär* in the Prussian ministry of education, who hoped that sociology would help democratize German society. Conservatives like Georg von Below objected vociferously. Loyal to the *status quo ante,* they considered his proposal an ideological in-

[21] On the link between Geiger and Weber, see Kurt Lenk, "Das Werturteils-problem bei Max Weber," *Zeitschrift für die gesamten Staatswissenschaften,* 120, 1964, 56f.; for Tönnies on Weber, see his *Soziologische Studien und Kritiken* (Jena: Fischer, 1926), 419f.

[22] Albert Salomon, "German Sociology," in Georges Gurvitch and Wilbert E. Moore, eds., *Twentieth Century Sociology* (New York: Philosophical Library, 1945), 587.

filtration of the university.[23] Others, like Otto Hintze, who before 1918 had upheld the empire's monarchic constitutionalism against Weber's advocacy of parliamentary government, now advocated a measure of "value-neutrality" because it was the only way in which they could honestly come to terms with the new republican order.[24]

In the face of general resistance, only a few sociology chairs were established, although sociology was taught more frequently than before the war, if mostly by instructors (Lehrbeauftragte) . As early as 1919, a Research Institute for Social Science was founded at the University of Cologne. Leopold von Wiese, the head of the sociology section, suggested the reestablishment of the Sociological Association to Tönnies and Sombart, two members of the prewar executive; they agreed with the stipulation that members be recruited by cooptation. But not until September 1922 did the third sociology congress meet, in Jena. Only four more biennial meetings took place before the end of the Weimar period. The main theme of the last meeting, in Berlin in 1930, was "the press and public opinion," Weber's first suggestion to the association. The occasion was ambitious; numerous public officials and newspapermen assembled. But just as twenty years before, the diversity of orientations and interests remained more troublesome than advantageous. Once again it was painfully obvious that the sociologists were a minority at their own meetings.[25] Yet at the end of the Weimar period empirical social research did make progress. Marie Jahoda and Paul Lazarsfeld began their work in Austria, Rudolf Heberle and some others continued Tönnies' pioneering efforts, and the Frankfurt Institute of Social Research was founded. But it was too late: with the Nazi ascendancy the great exodus of social scientists began.

[23] See Ferdinand Tönnies, "Hochschulreform und Soziologie. Kritische Anmerkungen über Becker's Gedanken zur Hochschulreform und Belows Soziologie als Lehrfach," Weltwirtschaftliches Archiv, 16, 1920, 212–245; Georg von Below, Soziologie als Lehrfach (Munich: Duncker, 1920).

[24] On Hintze's adoption of "value-neutrality" see Walter M. Simon, "Power and Responsibility: Otto Hintze's Place in German Historiography," in Leonard Krieger and Fritz Stern, eds., The Responsibility of Power. Historical Essays in Honor of Hajo Holborn (New York: Doubleday, 1967), 215–237. On the constitutional differences of opinion between Hintze and Weber see my Social Democrats in Imperial Germany (Totowa: Bedminster, 1963), 60ff., 285f., 296ff.

[25] For Leopold von Wiese's concerned comments, see "Zwei Soziologenkongresse," Kölner Zeitschrift für Soziologie, 9:3 (old series), 1931, 233–243.

In spite of its obliteration during the Nazi period, sociology developed faster in Germany than in any other western European country after the Second World War. It also became "Americanized"—which in part meant receiving back some of the orientations and methods developed by refugees. Survey methods were eagerly adopted, much literature—often outdated—was translated, functionalism had a vogue, and even Weber's sociology returned because of the attention given to it in the United States.

The 1960's have produced a situation with highly contradictory elements. On the one hand, sociology has expanded rapidly as an academic discipline; the number of chairs has been increased considerably and thousands of students have chosen sociology as their major. On the other hand, the holders of chairs are primarily administrators, not researchers, the assistants are overburdened with teaching and neglect their professional training. Sociology and political science, which faces the same dilemma, have become so fashionable that they suddenly have reached a crisis because of the sheer number of students. Moreover, just as sociology finally seems to have "arrived" as an empirical discipline, it is challenged by a new radical minority as a positivistic tool of the Establishment.

As in the twenties and thirties, Weber is singled out as the prototype of positivistic and "liberalistic" sociology. Again there is controversy about his politics, not his sociology, or else his sociology is treated as mere ideology. The turning point appears to have come in 1964 when the German Sociological Association devoted its Heidelberg meeting ostensibly to commemorating the centenary of Weber's birth. What in fact occurred was a turning away from the sociological substance of his work. Political dispute overshadowed scholarly concerns. Marxists of the old generation, like Herbert Marcuse, made common cause with younger liberals, like Wolfgang Mommsen, who had been influenced by natural-law doctrines in the wake of the American reeducation efforts after 1945. They were applauded by the youthful radicals, whereas staid government representatives claimed Weber as one of the intellectual ancestors of German parliamentary democracy—a sure-fire way to intensify the attacks.[26]

The trend toward nonprofessional sociology meetings continued at the chaotic Frankfurt convention of April 1968—neither were

[26] Cf. Otto Stammer, ed., *Max Weber und die Soziologie heute. Verhandlungen des 15. deutschen Soziologentages* (Tübingen: Mohr, 1965); report in *Kölner Zeitschrift für Soziologie*, 16 (1964), 404–424; Carl Cerny, "Storm over Max Weber," *Encounter*, Aug. 1964, 57–59.

research results presented nor serious research proposals submitted. Instead, under the lenses of television cameras and within view of reporters, a confrontation occurred in which once more political declaration and epistemological confession became primary. The few sociologists willing to speak before a majority of persons without professional commitment to the discipline clashed with the spokesmen of a new anarchism and a Marxism turned voluntaristic. One year later, in April 1969, the executive committee of the German Sociological Association drew some conclusions from these developments: it recognized that for the mass of sociology students there was no room either inside or outside the university; therefore, the diploma for the sociology major should be abolished in its present form and those universities which had been slow to promote sociology should not introduce the degree. A new combination of fields, it was hoped, would offer students greater job opportunities. This was a sober call for retrenchment on the part of a discipline overwhelmed by an undesired kind of success. The dream of catching up with the American sociological profession has been rudely interrupted.

WEBER IN AMERICAN SOCIOLOGY 1945–68

The Second World War and its antecedents, the Depression and the rise of totalitarianism, greatly influenced American sociology between the 1940's and the early 1960's. Sociologists moved beyond the concerns of the once dominant Chicago School with its attention to the underdog: the poor, the derelicts, the hoboes, the prostitutes, in short, the political and social peripheries of American society. The Chicago School, which prospered between the two world wars, desired to ameliorate the strains of industrialization; its outlook was largely that of the reform-minded Midwest with its dislike for the industrial and financial centers, their capitalist exploitation, boss rule, and religious "superstitions." In this respect the school was heir to the muckraking tradition, with the difference that monographs replaced newspaper exposés. Given the orientation of sociologists to "social issues," much of Weber's work appeared too "historical"; and insofar as sociologists still adhered to evolutionist doctrines or holistic theories of society, they found no ally in Weber. The study of the city was instead influenced by Georg Simmel through the works and the teaching of Robert Park and Louis Wirth, two leaders of the Chicago School. Ferdinand Tönnies also received much attention, but more for his evolutionary dichotomy of Gemeinschaft versus Gesellschaft than for his advancement of empirical social research. Karl Mannheim's wartime writings held out the hope that a sociology of knowledge might, after all, provide sound policy recommendations.

In spite of the theoretical importance Parsons attributed to Weber in *The Structure of Social Action* as early as 1937, Weber's reception did not become significant until a decade later when sociologists turned to the organizational complexities of industrial and governmental bureaucracies and the political aspects of social stratification. In these areas Weber was more pertinent than Tönnies, Simmel, or Durkheim. If the Chicago School may be placed in the intellectual neighborhood of Midwestern isolationism, the "coastal sociology" of New England and California may be viewed, at least in part, as a parallel to the international involvements of the United States after the Second World War. Between the mid-fifties and mid-sixties the most important growth of American sociology (and political science) occurred in the areas of political, social, and economic development. For the new states with their old societies Weber's studies had direct relevance, since his comparative interest centered on the historical varieties of ethical beliefs and of political and economic organization. However, the receptivity of the last quarter-century would not have been as broad without the influx of refugees from Nazi Germany, who provided a supply of skills necessary for interpretation and translation.[27]

The severe domestic crisis in the United States since the mid-sixties in general, and fiascoes such as the abortive Project Camelot in particular, have resulted in a refocusing on domestic issues and a retrenchment of foreign-area studies. Even as government support for social research is declining, foundations are redirecting their funds to the racial and urban crisis. At first sight, Weber's studies may appear less pertinent to this renewed interest in domestic social problems. After all, he was not a student of slums and of urban renewal. His approach, however, remains valuable if the Sociology of Domination—the core of *Economy and Society*—is applied to the political struggles within the ghettos and the universities; it revolves around the poles of legitimacy and usurpation, analyzing the perennial triangular struggle among rulers, staffs, and subjects throughout history.

[27] For a summary of Weber's reception up to the end of the fifties see an essay jointly written with Reinhard Bendix, "Max Webers Einfluss auf die amerikanische Soziologie," *Kölner Zeitschrift für Soziologie*, 11:1, 1959, 38–53.

The question of the quality of a man's scholarly work differs from that of evaluating his political convictions: this is the established view in American social science. One feature, in particular, of Weber's political outlook has been unsympathetic to the liberal temper of many American social scientists: his strong identification with the fate of the German nation-state and his acceptance of a major role for Germany in world affairs, although it was combined with a critical attitude toward the fashions of *Realpolitik* and Social Darwinism. Some of his other political views have made him more sympathetic: his commitment to political democratization and his plea for parliamentary government; the one-man, one-vote principle; recognition of unions and of collective bargaining. More radical spirits found it appealing that he decried the monopolistic interests of the academic guild—a form of domination by notables —just as he disdained the degree-hunting of the masses of security-minded students. But to the New Radicalism a key part of Weber's outlook is unacceptable: his conviction that in the large-scale organizations of industrialized countries the imperatives of authority cannot be wished away. This politically significant view is rejected together with academic neutrality at the same time that the possibility and desirability of distinguishing between politics and scholarship is increasingly denied. If the Chicago-trained sociologists blended their liberal creed almost unconsciously with their reform-oriented research, many of the young radicals advocate a purposive fusion of creed, research, and political action; the present organizational and role separations appear to them mere sham, and adherents of academic neutrality either naive or corrupt. However, the polemical interpretations of "ethical neutrality" are frequently so shallow and misinformed that, in conclusion, it may be worthwhile to compare Weber's reasons for insisting on an *institutionally* circumscribed "value-neutrality" with the present situation.

The postulate of *Wertfreiheit* has a moral base and an institutional setting. Weber pointed to the moral aspect behind the epistemological issue when he stated "a very trivial demand: The researcher and teacher must keep apart the ascertainment of empirical facts and his practical evaluation in terms of likes and dislikes, because fact-finding and evaluation happen to be two different things." [28] As a student of institutions, Weber realized better than

---

[28] Weber, "Der Sinn der 'Wertfreiheit' der soziologischen und ökonomischen Wissenschaften," *Gesammelte Aufsätze zur Wissenschaftslehre*, ed. by Johannes Winckelmann (Tübingen: Mohr, 1951), 485; cf. *The Methodology, op. cit.*, 11.

many of his peers that adherence to such a distinction required not just good will, but an explicit consensus about a set of rules. The university could augment substantive rationality only if administrators accepted some form of political pluralism and professors and students adhered to standards of intellectual self-discipline.

Weber was one of the few academic men in Imperial Germany who consistently objected to the use of political criteria on the part of the ministries of education, especially to discrimination against qualified scholars on the grounds that they were Jewish, pacifist, or socialist. He also went beyond those tolerant enough to accept everybody but an anarchist: "An anarchist can surely be a good legal scholar. And if he is, then indeed the Archimedean point of his convictions, which is outside the conventions and the presuppositions which are so self-evident to us, can equip him to perceive problems in the fundamental postulates of legal theory which escape those who take them for granted. Fundamental doubt is the father of knowledge." Weber objected especially to Gustav Schmoller, the long-time, powerful head of the Verein für Sozialpolitik; both men esteemed one another as scholars but disagreed strongly in politics. Schmoller, who himself was at times considered too liberal, and slighted, by the government, affirmed that teachers should propound values, but did not consider Marxists and Manchesterites qualified to hold academic chairs, since it was the university's task to train loyal servants for the monarchic welfare state. To Weber this meant turning the university back into a "theological seminary—but without the latter's religious dignity." He also carried on the fight of the preceding liberal generation for a "science without presuppositions"—Theodor Mommsen's war cry against the use of religious criteria in academic appointments.

Weber, then, was a champion of the liberal university, which endeavors to be open to all political and philosophical orientations, with the proviso, of course, that professors be competent and productive scholars, not just propagandists of their cause. This required a more active toleration by the ministries of education than just their willingness to permit the establishment of new universities, as in the Netherlands, if dissenters had the necessary funds and qualifications: "This gives the advantage to those with large sums of money and to groups which are already in power." However, the

---

The other Weber quotations in the rest of the essay are from the first nine pages of *The Methodology, op. cit.*

German state governments did not grant the university—with the partial exception of Heidelberg—enough leeway to become a forum of national debate. "Today the most decisive and important questions of practical and political values are excluded from German universities by the very nature of the present political situation." Weber hoped that a more pluralist university would provide an intellectual corrective to the rigidities of political life in the empire. He assumed, of course, that the constitutional system would not disintegrate or be overthrown and that only incremental change would occur in the foreseeable future. Not until 1918 did he consider it possible that an extreme right- or left-wing movement could destroy the existing university and preclude the one desired by him. The extent to which the coming dictatorships would totally politicize the universities was barely imaginable when he died.

Compared to the days of Imperial Germany or even the American thirties, the contemporary American university enjoys a remarkably high level of freedom from direct political controls, unless some recent developments indicate the reversal of a trend toward greater autonomy for what is, in effect, an intramural liberal establishment. Concurrently, social science has achieved a degree of scholarly objectivity which is probably unparalleled in the history of the Western university. Theses and books are judged primary by their empirical adequacy, not by their political orientation or conformity to a school; professors are less likely to be appointed for ideological reasons and partisan zeal, and students less frequently must prove political conformity to earn their degrees. This state of affairs is a cause of chagrin to extreme right-wingers who deplore the university's abdication of the "spirit-building function" of education. On the left, the precarious achievements of the American university, especially in social science, are played down, if not discounted, with the argument that they intrinsically amount to a sell-out to the "military-industrial complex" or the "power elite." It is charged that the improvement—if there is any at all—of the quality and matter-of-factness of research has been paralleled by a diminution of the university's "critical function," without which it cannot help but support the vested interests. The reformist version of this argument, still within the realm of political pluralism, points to social groups that have not received the same attention and support, material and intellectual, from the university as those better organized. The radical version, incompatible with the liberal university as a free market place of ideas, insists that social science as such must be revolutionary and that it is not enough for the individual social scientist to be politically active as a citizen.[29]

Weber considered the question of professing values before students subordinate to the logical problem of *Wertfreiheit* and the political problem of intellectual freedom. The teacher's behavior in the classroom was largely a pedagogical question. Weber was far from asking that the teacher minimize his value judgments and not show his emotions. However, he made a distinction between lecturing and speech-making. He combated the use of the lecture hall as a propaganda forum for the instructor's political views: "The least tolerable of all prophecies is surely the professor's with its highly personal tinge." [30] Students then had no way to talk back individually, although they freely drummed their approval on the desk or shuffled their feet in disapproval—traditions alive until the sixties, before more radical collective responses emerged. Weber stood firm against emotional overheating of the classroom; he regretted especially Treitschke's excesses, but given the choice between a highly dramatic style and a completely bland presentation he preferred the former because it would enable the students to perceive more clearly the connection between affect and reasoning.[31] He opposed pseudo-objectivity, which disguised a vested interest, no less than the personality cult. Frequently the requirements of rational discourse were also undermined by the students' desire to hear a "profession": "Every teacher has observed that the

[29] For a recent answer from a liberal perspective, which distinguishes between the social role of the sociologist and the logical possibilities of sociology, see Ralf Dahrendorf, *Die Soziologie und der Soziologe—Zur Frage von Theorie und Praxis* (Konstanz: Universitätsverlag, 1967).

[30] For reminiscences of classroom propaganda shortly before and after the downfall of Imperial Germany, see Franz Neumann, "The Social Sciences," in Neumann *et al., The Cultural Migration. The European Scholar in America* (New York: Barnes, 1961), 15f. Neumann, a prominent member of the Old Left, comments: "I do not consider it the task of universities to preach democracy. In this, I fully stand with the ideas of Max Weber. . . . But it is most certainly not the function of the universities to ridicule democracy, to arouse nationalist passions, to sing the praise of past systems—and to cover this up by asserting that one is 'nonpolitical.' "

[31] On Treitschke, see a letter from Weber's student days addressed to Hermann Baumgarten, July 14, 1885, in Marianne Weber, ed., Max Weber, *Jugendbriefe* (Tübingen: Mohr, 1936), 174; the reference in *The Methodology, op. cit.*, 2, is written from a distance of three decades.

faces of his students light up and they become more attentive at his lectures when he begins to set forth his personal evaluations, and that the attendance at his lectures is greatly increased by the expectation that he will do so. . . . I fear that a lecturer who overemphasizes his personal style will, in the long run, weaken the students' taste for sober empirical analysis."

In the United States, classroom instruction has long been more informal and much less authoritarian than in Germany, and in this sense Weber's pedagogical problem is far less acute today. However, recently the very fact of the instructor's authority in drawing up an outline and in giving grades has been challenged as "repressive," and the content of professional courses has come under attack for its "irrelevance"—to the passionate yearnings and high-minded ideals of the young radicals. This brings up the last institutional issue with which Weber was concerned: the ineradicable conflict between the liberal scholar and the radical student.

Weber fought what he called the "zoological nationalism" of large numbers of students, who demanded ringing chauvinist and anti-Semitic declarations from their teachers. At the moment, students in the United States (and in Western Europe) are much less patriotic than they used to be in previous decades. For the time being, this proclivity is dormant. However, at the end of his life Weber moved toward a showdown with a minority of students who fell under the spell of an "apolitical ethos of brotherhood," as he called the turn toward romantic anarchism and syndicalism. This ethos now has again erupted with great force. Its believers stress the "ethic of ultimate ends" (Gesinnungsethik) to the exclusion of the "ethic of responsibility." He wanted the students —and the teachers—of whatever political persuasion to face up to the consequences of their beliefs, not to be content with "good intentions." He greatly respected the idealism of these young radicals and did not deny his sympathy and personal help. But he also recognized the irreconcilability of the conflict that transcended the boundaries of the universities.

It is the Weberian position that intellectually disciplined instruction and research require a basic political consensus or "armistice" within the academic arena. Weber made it clear that fighting for institutional nonpartisanship has nothing to do with the "popular middle-of-the-road line"; rather, it aims at safeguarding the right to examine the facts and at maximizing the opportunities for empirical research. Today the American university is under attack as a relatively neutral arena. Persistent pressures toward politicalization from inside and outside can possibly ruin it, for the insistence that researchers and teachers orient their work exclusively to one set of political and moral imperatives is likely to turn the university into an armed camp occupied by one or the other side.

III

POLITICAL CRITIQUES

Max Weber has been a major target for a series of critiques aimed at political sociology in general, if not at most of social science. These critiques either use a sociological approach for political purposes or deny altogether the present rationale of political sociology and to some extent even the viability of Western pluralist society. Because Weber had a highly articulate view of politics and took his stand on political issues that have remained controversial to this day, it is not always easy to distinguish specific critiques of Weber's politics and scholarship from the general implications for political sociology. There is considerable room for different historical interpretations; it is, of course, also possible to put different accents on the definition of politics. At any rate, my intent is not a historical defense of Weber but a review of critiques so far as they seem to bear on the *raison d'être* of political sociology. In my judgment, this rationale is imperiled if Weber's insights into the nature of politics are denied.

Since sociological anlysis properly endeavors to look at the world dispassionately or, more correctly, from a "theoretical" perspective, in the strict contemplative sense of the word, it must appear relativist and Machiavellian to all those who, for ideological reasons, cannot recognize any dividing line between political sociology and political ideology. Weber emphatically insisted on such a distinction. He always made it clear that he did not claim scientific support for his political views. Of course, in his political writings he drew on his sociological learning; he also put concrete political issues into the universal historical context with which his studies were concerned. But since his political critics refuse to distinguish between

Guenther Roth, "Political Critiques of Max Weber," *American Sociological Review*, 30:2, April 1965, 213–223; first read at the annual meeting of the American Sociological Association, Montreal, 1964.

his scholarship and his politics, they can quote sociological statements—his or anyone else's—as articulations of political views.

A Sociological Ethic

The vehemence of various critiques must be attributed not
only to Weber's insistence on a scholarly study of power and authority, but also to his own political decision that politics is the art of
the possible—a rational craft. Here, indeed, is a connection between
Weber's sociological work and his political commitment, which
may be said to imply a sociological ethic: it was sociological because
he considered it empirically indisputable that recurrent ideological
conflict was as basic a fact of social life as the impossibility of recon-
ciling any Is with any Ought, so far as large-scale social structures
were concerned; it was an ethic because he advocated moral stamina
in the face of these "iron" facts.[1] His recognition of the realities of
power was not identical with the glorification of the state and of
Realpolitik by many of his contemporaries. Rather, his views were
the secular counterpart of the age-old Christian dualism revived as
a major literary topic by Dostoevsky and Tolstoy, about whom
Weber planned to write a book.[2] Those who would remain pure and
innocent must stay out of politics altogether, yet even this is not entirely safe, since values may be compromised by a refusal to act; witness the pacifists who refuse to fight the enemies of humanitarianism. Whoever enters politics encounters the need to exercise power,
and this implies ethical as well as political compromise.

These sociological insights did not shake Weber's resolve that
man should act decently toward his fellow man, even if there was
no absolute supernatural or scientific justification for it. For him
this was a simple rational affirmation of the humanitarian element
in Western civilization. He had no illusions about the dark side of
progress, and this was one reason for his aversion to abstract moral-
izing. He was convinced that responsible political leadership can-

---

[1] This seems to me related to what Benjamin Nelson has called the "social
reality principle," in derivation from Freudian terminology (see n. 3). The
term "sociological ethic" is gleaned from Carlo Antoni, *From History to Sociology* (1939), Hayden V. White, trans. (Detroit: Wayne State University Press,
1959), 141. Since Antoni is a follower of Benedetto Croce's idealist intuitionism,
the object of his study must appear to him as "the decline of German thought
from historicism to typological sociologism" (see his preface).

[2] See Weber, "Politics as a Vocation," *From Max Weber,* H. Gerth and C. W.
Mills, eds. and trans. (New York: Oxford, 1946), 126; Marianne Weber, *Max
Weber: Ein Lebensbild* (Heidelberg: Schneider, 1950), 509.

not afford to adhere to moralistic, legalistic or any other kind of ideological absolutism, since these are inherently self-defeating. His sociological ethic was thus a latter-day version of Stoic philosophy in that virtuous conduct was more important than any notion of ultimate salvation in a this-worldly or other-worldly millennium— and only in this ethical sense was Weber a Machiavellian.

This anti-ideological insistence on measure has provoked the true believers in political panaceas, Left, Right, and Center. Accordingly, the ideological critiques of Weber have come mainly from three quarters: Marxism, Nazism, and Natural Law with its liberal and conservative wings. In the United States, advocates of moralistic liberalism, which is rooted in a strong natural-rights tradition, have been especially provoked by Weber. Many of the other attacks, however, seem at first sight to refer to another land and another time. Most of the participants in the extended debate were born in Germany; many left involuntarily, some on their own initiative; some returned; and some merely studied there. (As I proceed, it should become clear that more is involved than a mere quarrel between Germans, ex-Germans, Germanophiles, and Germanophobes.)

The three ideologies are substantively opposed to one another, but they are all instances of an "ethic of good intentions" or "ultimate ends" (Gesinnungsethik) and, methodologically, they all resort to historical reductionism. To be sure, Marxism does not recognize the existence of absolute values in the sense of natural rights (a self-interested bourgeois postulate), but it adheres dogmatically to a correspondence theory of concept and object, maintaining that only critical, dialectical concepts can express the "truth." Nazism, in turn, was an "ethic of good intentions" only in the most formal sense.

THE MARXIST CRITIQUE

Not surprisingly, the only Marxist critiques that warrant attention have come from writers who opposed Communist totalitarianism from the outside[3] or who eventually clashed with party

---

[3] Prominent among Western spokesmen for a sophisticated "critical theory of society" are T. W. Adorno and Max Horkheimer. In an address as president of the German Sociological Association at the 1964 annual convention in Heidelberg, Adorno called for a critique of Weber's political philosophy, and Herbert Marcuse delivered the main attack at the same occasion. See Otto Stammer, ed., *Max Weber und die Soziologie heute. Verhandlungen des 15. deutschen Sozi-*

orthodoxy from the inside. Among the latter, Georg Lukács was the only writer on sociology in the Moscow of the Stalinist purges who approached serious scholarship. At the time he kept himself busy—and out of the way—with an attempt to construe German intellectual history as a road to irrationalism leading from Schelling to Hitler via Weber and all other major German sociologists.[4]

Despite important political and philosophical differences among these Marxist writers, their views on Weber appear very similar:

(1) Weber refused to accept the dialectical idea of potentiality; he studied the facts of social life and tried to extrapolate future trends instead of measuring reality against the great possibilities postulated by Marx's theory of human nature.

(2) Epistemologically, this was due to the fact that Weber was a Neo-Kantian, adhering to the belief that the phenomenal world can be conceptualized in many different ways.

(3) Therefore, Weber postulated a universe of conflicting values among which no scientific choices are possible; this opens the way to irrationalism, leading directly to imperialism and ultimately to fascism. For if Weber denies the truth of Marxism and is too much of a secular relativist to subscribe to outmoded religious metaphysics, he must perforce take the nationalist and militarist nationstate as his major political and even moral reference.

(4) Weber's mode of thinking was typically bourgeois, insensitive to the truth that capitalism has been the most extreme exploitation of man. In class defense, men like Weber and Georg Simmel—

---

ologentages (Tübingen: Mohr, 1965). For the English version of Marcuse's speech see his Negations. Essays in Critical Theory (Boston: Beacon, 1968), 201–226. For critical rejoinders by R. Bendix and B. Nelson, see Stammer, op. cit., 184–201. For Horkheimer's critique of Weber, see his Eclipse of Reason (New York: Oxford, 1947), 6.

[4] See Georg Lukács, Die Zerstörung der Vernunft (Berlin: Aufbau-Verlag, 1955), on Weber especially 474–488. Lukács followed the Stalinist line before 1953 but joined the intraparty opposition before the Hungarian revolution of 1956. After a period of banishment he emerged again with an appeal for a selfcritical Marxism that can even accept Franz Kafka's bureaucratic nightmare. Cf. Melvin Lasky's perceptive review of two Lukács translations in the New York Times Book Review, May 10, 1964, 4, especially his remarks on the "simple-minded thirties." Less known in this country is Hans Mayer, who abandoned his professorship of modern literature at the University of Leipzig in 1963 and sought asylum in West Germany. For Mayer's views on Weber, see "Die Krise der deutschen Staatslehre von Bismarck bis Weimar" (partly written before 1933), in his Karl Marx und das Elend des Geistes (Meissenheim: Westkulturverlag, 1948), 48–75.

both capitalist rentiers and parasites, "objectively" speaking[5]—
view social reality in formalized terms, conceiving of capitalism as
a system of rational calculation based on the abstract medium of
money. Significantly, Weber is also concerned with the "spirit"
(Geist) of capitalism and its affinity to the Calvinist ethic. But in
his most detached scholarly work, Economy and Society, an "orgy
of formalism" in its casuistic definitions of types of action and of
domination, Weber reveals the depravity, the Ungeist, of capitalist
society.[6]

(5) Weber's interest in a comparative study of social structure
and ideology "reflects" the imperialist interests of the capitalist
countries; it is "expansionist" sociology.

Most of these charges clearly apply to contemporary American
social science as well. In spite of their basic optimism, most American social scientists are skeptical of the idea of potentiality, have
been vaguely Neo-Kantian, and have focused on the methodological
and conceptual elaboration of their disciplines—hence have been
guilty of "positivistic formalism." Moreover, American social science tends to appear as a defensive Cold War instrument, in view
of its increasing interest in newly developing countries.

THE NAZI CRITIQUE

In general, the Nazi critique has been even less sophisticated
than the Marxist critique, but there are also some striking parallels.
Exceptions to the rule of ignorance and incompetence were Carl
Schmitt, the renowned and notorious political scientist and constitutional expert, and the forgotten Christoph Steding, the unful-
filled hope of Nazi philosophy. Both men share two features with
the Marxists mentioned above: they held substantially the same
opinion of positivistic sociology—except for the race issue—and
they were prominent but politically marginal ideologists. I shall
limit myself to Steding, who was more direct and typical than the
elusive and more capable Carl Schmitt.[7]

Steding made a limited effort to conform to some of the canons
of scholarship in his Ph.D. dissertation of 1932 on Max Weber's

[5] Lukács, op. cit., 361.
[6] Cf. Marcuse, op. cit., 203.
[7] Carl Schmitt started from an authoritarian Catholic position. His major
scholarly work is his Verfassungslehre (Munich: Duncker und Humblot, 1928),
3d unchanged ed., 1957; on Weber, see pp. 286f., 307, 314, 335f., 341, and 347.

politics and science, in which he asserted their identity and found Weber's notion of charismatic leadership very congenial.[8] Steding's major concoction, begun on a Rockefeller Foundation grant in the early thirties, grew into a violent attack on the "disease of European culture." [9] Mixing historical fact and paranoid fantasy, he argued that this disease originated with the Westphalian Peace of 1648 when the Western European nation states established a balance of power that made an effective *Reich* impossible and hence vitiated a universalist political and cultural order that would have restored philosophic realism. The age of neutralism arrived and championed the liberal theory of the laissez-faire state, philosophical nominalism and value-free sociology.[10]

In vivid organic imagery, Steding showed that the "disease carriers" that threatened the Reich were located in the Rhein valley; Weber had suggested that terms like "nation," *"Nationalgefühl,"* or *"Volk"* were not really applicable to "neutralized" areas like Switzerland, Alsace-Lorraine, Luxemburg and Liechtenstein, for which opposition to "militarist" Germany provided a strong basis of their sense of political community.[11] The old Calvinist territories of Switzerland and the Netherlands became the cornerstones of the hostile wall of Rhenish cities which had been Free Imperial cities or anti-Prussian court residences. Basle was the preferred domicile of Jacob Burckhardt and Friedrich Nietzsche, the two most formidable intellectual enemies of the Reich in the last third of the nineteenth century; the old universities of Freiburg, Heidelberg, and

---

Scholarly in substance too is his essay *Der Begriff des Politischen* (1927). See the text of 1932 with a new defensive preface (Berlin: Duncker und Humblot, 1963). This essay contains his famous friend-foe distinction as the basic criterion of the political process. The Nazified edition of 1933 (Hamburg: Hanseatische Verlagsanstalt) differs only—but decisively—in tone, terminology, and omission. Weber, for whom Schmitt had high regard, is no longer mentioned, but Franz Oppenheimer is suddenly identified as a "Berlin-Frankfurt sociologist"—evoking the image of the two cities as citadels of liberalism-capitalism-bolshevism-Judaism-sociologism. Schmitt suffered quick decline after 1933, but he was one of the most effective opponents of the Weimar Republic and of sociology during the late twenties.

[8] Steding, *Politik und Wissenschaft bei Max Weber* (Breslau: Korn, 1932).

[9] *Das Reich und die Krankheit der europäischen Kultur* (Hamburg: Hanseatische Verlagsanstalt, 1938).

[10] Carl Schmitt also construed a theory of political decline from the sixteenth century to the liberal-bourgeois age of "neutral" and "unpolitical" attitudes and social spheres. See "Das Zeitalter der Neutralisierungen und Entpolitisierungen" (1929), reprinted in *Der Begriff des Politischen, op. cit.*, 1963, 79–95.

[11] See Weber, *Economy and Society* (New York: Bedminster, 1968), 395ff.

Marburg excelled in "quasi-Calvinist" and "quasi-Jewish" Neo-Kantianism; the old court residence Darmstadt was the home of several figures of the charismatic George circle, which was suspect because of its esthetically refined vision of a Third Reich; [12] the trade and university centers of Frankfurt and Cologne, which pioneered institutes for economic and sociological research, provided the link to Amsterdam.

In this context Max Weber and Thomas Mann appear as the last two outstanding and personally admirable representatives of bourgeois civilization in its terminal stage of decadence and fatal disease —exactly as they do for the Marxists.[13] Their work is the last achievement of the bourgeois spirit: it is capitalist, urban, abstract, nominalist, neutralist, Neo-Kantian and, for Steding, of course, "Jewish" by association.

As in the Marxist perspective, there is no basic difference between Imperial Germany and the Weimar Republic: both are capitalist societies. The personnel and the personalities are largely the same: William II and Weber, his stormiest critic, appear akin in their haste, nervousness and imperialist posturing, lacking a real power-drive. But Weber and Thomas Mann are also acknowledged to have been more perceptive than most other members of their class. Their support of parliamentary government made them ideological spokesmen or symbols of the Weimar Republic, the spirit of which, alas, was that of Locarno—another "neutralist" locality.[14]

Christoph Steding and his Marxist counterparts read their sociologists with malicious care so as to use sociological insights as political weapons and turn the tables on Weber, Simmel and other members of the Generation of 1890. Both Steding and the Marxists adhere to a vulgar sociology of knowledge, an all too easy and superficial notion of correspondence between ideas and social structure. The facts are sometimes correct, but the political conclusions arbi-

[12] For Weber's own dead-pan references to George's charismatic exaltation, see *ibid.*, 245, 1114.

[13] See, for example, Hans Mayer, *Thomas Mann: Werk und Entwicklung* (Berlin: Volk und Welt, 1950), and "Thomas Manns 'Doktor Faustus': Roman einer Endzeit und Endzeit eines Romans," in *Von Lessing bis Thomas Mann* (Pfullingen: Neske, 1959), 383–404; Georg Lukács, *Thomas Mann* (Berlin: Aufbau-Verlag, 1949); see also Hans Mayer's "revisionist" review essay, "Georg Lukács' Grösse und Grenze," *Die Zeit,* July 24, 1964, 12.

[14] In Locarno, Switzerland, in 1925, Germany, Belgium, France, and Great Britain concluded a treaty that guaranteed the western frontiers and seemed to create the basis for lasting peace among the European nations. This was the era of the "spirit of Locarno."

trary. Thus, Steding points out that Weber became interested in Confucianism only after Germany took over Kiaochow in 1898. Weber wrote *Ancient Judaism* and some of his most passionate political essays in the midst of the turmoil of the First World War, when he felt like a lonely prophet.[15] Steding, the proud peasant son, also charged Weber with the inability of the decadent to finish their work and to defend their political interests successfully. Yet, ironically, he died at the age of 35 in 1938, before finishing his long and rambling work, and the two most notorious Nazi henchmen, Himmler and Heydrich, who considered using his book as a major indoctrination text,[16] perished within a few years, eliminating for the time being this kind of threat to the social sciences.

THE NATURAL-RIGHT CRITIQUE

In reaction to the rise of totalitarian Nazism and Communism some prominent writers have urged a return to natural right, which posits a natural or rational hierarchy of values. Adherents believe that this hierarchy can be discovered by philosophic reflection or intuition, or that it has been revealed to man. But because this latter-day revival of natural right is so obviously a reactive phenomenon, it has a strong instrumental or functionalist admixture. Those of Weber's critics who more or less fall back on natural rights have either stressed philosophical implications or they have been concerned primarily with political consequences, especially with the course of German history.

Politico-philosophical critiques. The attacks on this level have been carried in particular by Leo Strauss and Eric Voegelin.[17] For them, Weber is the greatest and most typical representative of modern social science. "No one since Weber," says Strauss, "has devoted a comparable amount of intelligence, assiduity, and almost fanatical relativism." According to Strauss and Voegelin, science should be understood no longer positivistically, but again ontologically as the search for *prima principia*. Whoever does not believe in the

[15] Cf. Steding, *Politik und Wissenschaft, op. cit.,* 108 and 31.

[16] See Heinrich Himmler's letter to Reinhard Heydrich, Feb. 1, 1939, in Leon Poliakov and Josef Ulf, eds., *Das Dritte Reich und seine Denker* (Berlin: Arani, 1959), 282.

[17] See Leo Strauss, *Natural Right and History* (Chicago: University of Chicago Press, 1953), ch. 2; Eric Voegelin, *The New Science of Politics* (University of Chicago Press, 1952), 13–26.

devotion to the basic problem of the social sciences. Whatever may have been his errors, he is the greatest social scientist of our century." [18] But Weber helped lead social science into the "morass of oneness of truth cannot help but succumb to a chaos of random values. Without the acceptance of natural rights, relativism and its dialectical counterpart, totalitarian absolutism, appear inevitable.

Like the Marxists and Steding, Voegelin develops a formula identifying the forces of evil in history. Instead of focusing on the capitalist spirit of inhuman rationality and neutrality, he attacks the whole "gnostic search for a civil theology," for a perfect order on earth.[19] For Voegelin, the Nazis' belief in the Third Reich, and the Marxists' hopes for a classless society after the Revolution, are gnostic fantasies about the millennium. Their very attempt to create total goodness by their own definition is bound to turn government into a force of total evil. Furthermore, gnosticism is not just a matter of totalitarianism but is typical of Westernization in general, a global process that is continuing in the United States and Western Europe.

Positivistic gnosticism has destroyed political science proper: methods have subordinated relevance, useless facts are accumulated, objectivity is equated with the exclusion of value judgments. In this scheme Weber occupies a transitional position. He was a "positivist with regrets," who tabooed classic and Christian metaphysics. Voegelin finds it revealing that Weber neglected these two traditions in his vast comparative studies of the affinity between status groups and ethical ideas. If he had not shied away from them he would have discovered there "the belief in a rational science of human and social order and especially of natural law. Moreover, this science was not simply a belief, but was actually elaborated as a work of reason." [20] Weber's positivism made him see history as a process of rationalization, whereas modern history was actually a downfall from the grace of reason—in the light of the *scientia prima*. Because Weber did not recognize natural right, he had to demonize politics. Only his ethics of responsibility was a rational counterforce. Voegelin concedes that Weber made a stronger effort than all other positivists to turn social science in a meaningful direction, but since Voegelin adopts a Christian dualism, he feels compelled to reject Weber in the end.[21]

[18] Strauss, *op. cit.*, 36.
[19] Voegelin, *op. cit.*, 163.
[20] *Op. cit.*, 20.
[21] As a young man, Voegelin was under Weber's spell and wrote an excellent

For Strauss, too, the troubles of recent history have been due basically to the denial of natural right. Its rejection is tantamount to nihilism, and in Weber's case it led to "noble nihilism." Since American social science largely agrees with Weber's relativism, it has become something of a German aberration (says the German philosopher):

It would not be the first time that a nation, defeated on the battlefield and, as it were, annihilated as a political being, has deprived its conquerors of the most sublime fruit of victory by imposing on them the yoke of its own thought. Whatever might be true of the thought of the American people, certainly American social science has adopted the very attitude toward natural right which, a generation ago, could still be described, with some plausibility, as characteristic of German thought.[22]

This is an extreme statement, which may have been advanced for its shock value. But Strauss is fair enough to denounce the *reductio ad Hitlerum*,[23] the assertion that Weber's thinking led to fascism. This kind of reductionism has been typical of the historical critique associated with moralistic liberalism.

The critique of moralistic liberalism. American liberals have traditionally shown exasperation with the reverses of democracy abroad. Moreover, their pragmatist background has made them especially skeptical toward German idealism and to a lesser extent toward historical materialism, another German product.[24] Times have changed, however, since 1935 when Ellsworth Faris rejected Pareto from implied moral premises, without conceding any utility what-

---

analysis of his rationalism, in particular of the difference between the necessary resignation of the responsible political activist (Weber's theory) and that of the esthetic creator (Simmel's theory); see Voegelin, "Über Max Weber," *Deutsche Vierteljahrsschrift für Literatur*, III, 1925, 177–193.

[22] Strauss, *op. cit.*, 2. By contrast, in the wake of the First World War some English scholars felt that one of its benefits had been liberation from the yoke of "German" value-free science; see Voegelin, *op. cit.*, 189.

[23] See Strauss, *op. cit.*, 42.

[24] Paradoxically, however, some liberals have been more sympathetic with the extreme German left than with the convinced supporters of parliamentary government in the Social Democratic labor movement—after both 1918 and 1945—because the former seemed to promise a utopian reconstruction. See my *Social Democrats in Imperial Germany* (Totowa: Bedminster, 1963), 323ff. For a recent textbook illustration of this moralistic bias, see John E. Rodes, *Germany:* 278–287.

ever to Pareto's political sociology.[25] But many liberals still tend to distrust the detached sociological study of power and of nondemocratic systems of government, except Communism and Nazism—the most extreme negations of liberalism they fit into a moralistic black-white scheme. Until very recently, at least, there were few studies of the growing number of authoritarian governments not just as variants of Fascism or Communism but as different types of domination, age-old or brand-new. This traditional distrust may also explain some of the uneasiness toward Weber's insistence on the facts of power and toward his nationalism which at best is regarded as a characteristic he shared with most scholars of his generation, especially Durkheim. Moreover, the experience of Nazism provides a powerful moral perspective on German history and makes it hard to be fair to past generations.

The interest among American social scientists, first in fascism and then in totalitarianism in general, was shared and stimulated by German political exiles. In reflecting upon the rise of Nazism, some writers began to view Weber, not so much as a direct Nazi forerunner, but as a symptom of things to come.[26] This concern has now been taken up by a new generation of German scholars. Intent on understanding the causes of the German catastrophe, some of them have been so preoccupied with the political interpretation of Weber that they tend to lose sight not only of his scholarly intentions and achievements but also of the rationale of sociology. Weber, a major argument goes, emphasized too strongly the instrumental instead of the inherent value of democracy—that is, democracy as decreed by natural law. He advocated charismatic leadership in the face of bureaucratization, and therefore favored the direct election of the president of the Weimar Republic, a constitutional provision that proved fatal in 1933. Hence the conclusion: Neither from the viewpoint of natural rights nor from that of pragmatic compromise does Weber's position provide reliable support for a pluralist system in which mundane group interests

[25] See Ellsworth Faris, "An Estimate of Pareto," *American Journal of Sociology*, 41, 1935, 657–668.

[26] J. P. Mayer, who feels more at home with Tocqueville's older conservative liberalism, wrote his reflections on Weber and German politics in the early thirties, contemporaneous with the work of Lukács, Hans Mayer, and Steding, and published them in wartime England. J. P. Mayer, *Max Weber and German Politics* (London, Faber, 1943). Hans Kohn, lifelong student of nationalism, has echoed Mayer and placed Weber squarely in the ranks of narrow-minded nationalists; see his *The Mind of Germany* (New York: Scribner, 1960), 269, *A History* (New York: Holt, 1964), preface,

must continually be readjusted, a task that can be accomplished best with a minimum of charismatic excitement.[27]

Related to these arguments is another kind of historical reductionism, which assumes a downfall from the Age of Reason. A number of younger German writers, holding a natural-rights position at least for polemical purposes, have construed an ideological line leading to Nazism which runs, for example, from Kant's formalistic Categorical Imperative, through Ranke's view of states and peoples as historical individualities, through the legal positivism since the 1860's, to Weber's sociological definition of politics and the state, and from there to Carl Schmitt's theory of politics as friend-foe relations—only one last step removed from Hitler's views and crimes.[28] In the same fashion, other writers have tried to trace the rise of totalitarian democracy from Rousseau's general will, through Saint-Simon's technocratic elite and Marx's theory of the

[27] The most impressive study on this score, superseding J. P. Mayer, is Wolfgang Mommsen's *Max Weber und die deutsche Politik, 1890–1920* (Tübingen: Mohr, 1959); for Mommsen's implicit natural-rights view, see 407. As a German historian, Mommsen is, of course, far removed from the interest of American sociologists in Weber, but his treatment becomes questionable to them the moment he interprets Weber's sociological analyses as political ideology. Accordingly, he was criticized on both historical and methodological grounds in a symposium by three American (formerly German) social scientists: Reinhard Bendix, Karl Loewenstein, and the late Paul Honigsheim in *Kölner Zeitschrift für Soziologie*, 13, 1961, 258ff. Mommsen replied at length against what he called the Weber orthodoxy in *ibid.*, 15, 1963, 295–321.

The facts on the presidential issue have now been uncovered in the excellent study by Gerhard Schulz, *Zwischen Demokratie und Diktatur: Verfassungspolitik und Reichsreform in der Weimarer Republik* (Berlin: Gruyter, 1963), I, 114–142. Schulz points out that far from taking a blunt position in favor of a "Caesarist" leader, Weber gradually shifted his opinions in response to the changing political situation and the diversity of opinion in committee meetings. Eventually he came to favor a popularly elected president as a mediator between the Reichstag and the States, between the unitary and the federative principles. Cf. Weber, *Gesammelte politische Schriften*, Johannes Winckelmann, ed. (Tübingen: Mohr, 1958), 394–471, 486–489. Schulz also delivered the commemorative address on "Weber as a Political Critic" before the Friedrich-Naumann-Stiftung, Heidelberg, 1964.

[28] See Wilhelm Hennis, "Zum Problem der deutschen Staatsanschauung," *Vierteljahrshefte für Zeitgeschichte*, 7, 1959, 1–23. For a similar construction making Schmitt a terminal point of a long development passing through Weber, see Heinz Laufer, *Das Kriterium politischen Handelns: Eine Studie zur Freund-Feind-Doktrin von Carl Schmitt* (Munich: Institut für politische Wissenschaften der Universität München, 1961). For Mommsen's interpretation of Schmitt's "logical" elaboration of Weber, see Mommsen, *op. cit.*, 379–386. For a judicious assessment, in the wake of the 1964 Heidelberg convention, of the link and the

class struggle, to Lenin's democratic centralism—only one last step removed from Stalin.[29]

The tracing of such ideological lineages is a challenging and fascinating task, but it is also very difficult, since the scholar must do justice to the individual's subjective intentions and to the complexities of historical reality; he must avoid a facile theory of antecedents, stepping stones, and parallels, since it is in the nature of politics that differences of degree in belief and action are critical (the rule of the lesser evil). With regard to Max Weber before fascism, Ernst Nolte has brilliantly balanced the account.[30]

SUBJECT INTENT AND OBJECTIVE CONSEQUENCES

There is no effective protection against the misuse of ideas, against their deterioration into ideological coins and political weapons. The doctrine of natural rights, too, has been susceptible to political misuse, not least in this century.[31] Ideas always have unintended consequences, and sociology largely lives off this fact. Weber himself showed the possible relations between the Protestant ethic and the spirit of capitalism. But he was never concerned with declaring Calvin or Baxter responsible for the materialism of the capitalist era, or Karl Marx, for the intransigence of the labor movement. His grasp of historical reality protected him from subscribing to any Devil theory of history.

Since my main interest is not an historical defense of Weber, I shall merely summarize some of the factors to be taken into consideration in this context:

difference between Weber and Schmitt, see Karl Loewith, "Max Weber und Carl Schmitt," a full-page essay in the *Frankfurt Allgemeine Zeitung*, June 27, 1964. Loewith also delivered the main address on "Science as a Vocation" at the Weber commemoration of the University of Heidelberg, April 1964.

[29] In addition to Eric Voegelin, see Jacob L. Talmon, *The Origins of Totalitarian Democracy* (New York: Praeger, 1960) and *Political Messianism: The Romantic Phase* (London: Secker and Warburg, 1960); Georg Iggers, *The Cult of Authority: The Political Philosophy of the Saint-Simonians* (The Hague: M. Nijhoff, 1958) and *idem*, ed., *The Doctrine of Saint-Simon: An Exposition* (Boston: Beacon, 1958), ix-xlvii. For a critique of this approach, see Alfred Cobban, *In Search of Humanity: The Role of the Enlightenment in Modern History* (New York: Braziller, 1960).

[30] "Max Weber vor dem Faschismus," *Der Staat*, 2, 1963, 295–321; see also his major comparative study of French, Italian, and German fascism, *Der Faschismus in seiner Epoche* (Munich: Piper, 1963).

[31] See Ernst Topitsch, "Max Weber und die Soziologie heute," address before the 1964 Heidelberg convention, in Stammer, *op. cit.*, 19–38.

(1) Weber insisted on realism in politics because the politically dominant Right adhered to idealist and romanticist notions to provide motive and cover for irresponsible power politics.

(2) Weber insisted on realistic politics also because for decades the sterile left-wing liberal opposition of Imperial Germany stuck to "principles" regardless of political feasibility.

(3) He insisted that he was patriotic as anybody else because (before 1918) he could not hope to exert any influence at all on the German Establishment unless he turned its own values against it by repeatedly pointing out that Imperial Germany and its ruling groups violated national ideals and national interests.

(4) He insisted on value-neutrality in the classroom because the nationalist historian Treitschke and similar "professors" of ideological creeds indoctrinated students from the rostrum.

(5) He insisted it was the university's business to make the students face the logical consequences of their beliefs because most of his listeners were middle- and upper-class students predisposed to nationalist sentiments.

(6) He insisted, finally, on an ethic of responsibility and of the politically possible (while conceding the abstract honorableness of an ethic of good intentions) because in 1919 the ideologists of the Right and the Left were interested in anything but the creation of parliamentary government in Germany.

It is true that national welfare was Weber's ultimate political yardstick, since he considered himself a political man, not a theologian or philosopher—two very different types, who are not forced to operate within a given political unit. Constitutional problems were secondary to national welfare only in this abstract regard, not in the realm of practical politics or of sociological analysis. Weber gave much more thought to the instrumentalities of parliamentary government than almost anybody else, including the Left, during the last decade of the Empire. His only hope for public effectiveness lay in the persuasiveness of the technical arguments for parliamentary government; the Empire's history had proven that ideological appeals for parliamentarism were in vain.

Political critiques of Weber can to some extent be considered merely the price a scholar must be prepared to pay for entering the political arena and exposing himself to the crude vehemence of political controversy. Most social scientists since Weber's time have refrained from playing the dual role of scholar and political man, but the critiques reviewed here illustrate that this does not guarantee protection. On the one hand, adherents of Marxism, Nazism, and Natural Law have not only refused to recognize any dividing line between ideology and sociology, but they have also shown a common tendency toward a historical reductionism which is a challenge to serious scholarship. On the other, political sociologists are liable to provoke political opposition by dealing with the facts of national power and domestic group interests. This makes them controversial in their professional roles and ultimately makes it impossible for them to avoid taking an explicit political stand. Weber's scholarly canons and his sociological ethic were a major attempt to cope with this perennial tension.

IV

IDEOLOGICAL AND
SCHOLARLY APPROACHES TO
INDUSTRIALIZATION

In 1901, Theodor Mommsen, the well-known German historian, issued a proclamation in defense of academic freedom. In it he spoke of "research without presuppositions" as the vital nerve of academic life. The conscientious scholar arrives at conclusions which appear to him right in view of logical and factual considerations. Truthfulness is his watchword. It is the basis of his self-esteem, his honor, and his influence on youth. This simple canon is in jeopardy where the religious affiliation of candidates affects their selection for university appointments, as it had at the University of Strasbourg. This simple canon is violated where the scholar comes to conclusions because they satisfy practical goals or pragmatic considerations outside the realm of scholarship, or simply because they satisfy what the mind dwells on with peculiar satisfaction.

In 1904, Max Weber assumed the editorship of the *Archiv für Sozialwissenschaft und Sozialpolitik*. On the occasion he published an essay in which he advanced the idea that responsible work in the social sciences must be free of value judgments. Weber's meaning was the same as Mommsen's. He spoke for an ethics of truthfulness in scholarship which demands a kind of mental hygiene. Every scholar is obliged to separate what he can assert in his scholarly capacity from the wishes or feelings he shares with everyone else.

Mommsen and Weber were unfortunate in their choice of

Reinhard Bendix, "Der Einzelne und die Gesellschaft," in Willy Hochkeppel, ed., *Soziologie zwischen Theorie und Empirie* (Munich: Nymphenburger Verlagsbuchhandlung, 1970), 97–113.

words. They did not contend that inquiry can be without presuppositions or that it is possible to eliminate value judgments from research, especially in the social sciences. In fact, Weber made it clear that "no science is absolutely free from presuppositions, and no science can prove its fundamental value to the man who rejects these presuppositions." [1] The canon of truthfulness demands only that scholars reflect on the presuppositions and values of their work and that they make them public. These are minimal demands against self-deception and the deception of others. Such demands will not solve methodological difficulties. But Mommsen and Weber thought them appropriate where the climate of opinion militates against candor and intellectual self-discipline.

Today, as so often before, scholarship is in jeopardy where problems of sociological inquiry border on the broader issues of social philosophy. The position of the individual in society is such a concern. The question is whether in this borderline area it is possible to distinguish between scholarly judgments and expressions of ideological commitment.

Intellectual Ambivalence

It is difficult to deal with the changing position of the individual in society and focus on the experience of ordinary men, rather than express the emotions one feels in reflecting upon that experience. When Bacon wrote that we must be on guard against ideas on which the mind dwells with peculiar satisfaction he did not realize how difficult it is to follow this admirable injunction in the study of culture. Only intellectuals comment on the individual's role in society, and this is unavoidable. One should take into account that the characteristics of the intellectual have some bearing on his social philosophical speculations in this field. It may be difficult to avoid special preoccupations completely, but their causes can be examined and their unwitting influence on our thought reduced. The intellectual is not exempt from critical scrutiny. The object of that scrutiny is enlightenment; it should not be confused with anti-intellectualism.

The position of the intellectual in modern society is equivocal. Ordinarily, the concept is applied only to persons who make their living by mental exertions and as free professionals rather than as

[1] Weber, "Science as a Vocation," in H. Gerth and C. W. Mills, eds. and trans., *From Max Weber* (New York: Oxford, 1946), 153.

salaried employees. Intellectuals as an especially designated group have been a by-product of modern societies since the eighteenth century. In Western Europe artists and scholars became emancipated from their earlier dependence on the Church or rich secular patrons when industrialization created a market and a mass demand for cultural products of all kinds.

Typically intellectuals responded to this mass demand in an ambivalent manner. On the one hand they glorified the public. In the second half of the eighteenth century the English novelist Oliver Goldsmith spoke of his many readers as good and generous masters in pointed contrast to the patrons in whose service he had stood previously. Ever since, the people have been glorified as a source of genuine cultural values. Marxism and nationalism are two variants of this theme. On the other hand, many intellectuals reacted to the same development with considerable apprehension, seeing mass society as a threat to cultural values, an evaluation which has recurred from the eighteenth century to the present.

As a result of these disparate reactions, intellectuals have frequently wavered between populism and elitism. And two centuries of ambivalence between glorification of the people and the consciousness of a cultural elite have been accompanied by lack of comprehension of economic affairs and sweeping criticism of commercialization. These opinions and sentiments have colored analyses of the individual's role in society to such an extent that a modern assessment of this theme must concern itself with the prevalent interpretations of the past.

CRITIQUES OF INDUSTRIAL SOCIETY

Man and society has been a favorite theme of social criticism since the middle of the eighteenth century. From a scholarly standpoint speculative images of man are questionable and must be considered with a certain reserve. For these images express our wishes and fears and hence manifest a religious attitude even in people who are superficially irreligious. But in the literature of social philosophy the question is not raised how such talk about man in general can be kept free of wishes and fears. Nor is it asked how we can form a judgment about man in the large when we deal with complex societies and millions of people. Instead such judgments are considered necessary for understanding social change, and justified by certain fundamental conditions of different social structures. Each structure, say of medieval or industrial society, is characterized by a particular organization of production, and by typical relations of men to nature and to each other. The results of such speculations vary widely, since each author is free to select one or another aspect for emphasis. It is all the more striking, therefore, that in a period of two centuries critiques of culture have come to broadly similar conclusions, though arising from and approaching the subject from widely divergent angles. Some forty years ago Karl Mannheim pointed this out when he emphasized the convergence of conservative and radical critiques of industrial society.

Although the nuances of divergent political positions are necessarily neglected, this convergence can be summarized as follows. All critiques of industrial society have seen in its development since the late eighteenth century a profound cultural crisis. One aspect of this crisis is said to be the changed relation between the worker and the product of his labor. It is tacitly assumed that in preindustrial societies man had a natural relationship to the process of work but that this relationship has deteriorated with industrialization. Another aspect of the cultural crisis is said to be that human relationships have changed and that social norms have declined. Both aspects are related in the attribution to preindustrial societies of a stable morality and orderly human relations based on that morality. Basic to this concept is the idea of a social order in which every individual knows and accepts his rights and duties; this gives him a firm purpose in life and provides him with unmistakable guidelines in his relations with others. On the whole, radical critics emphasize changes in the work process whereas conservative critics emphasize the decline of social norms. It should be noted, however, that even radical critics refer to declining social norms while putting their major emphasis on the fate of the laborer. Similarly, conservative critics note the lack of human satisfaction in the industrial work process, although they put their major emphasis on the decline of morality.

A good way to summarize the major themes of these radical and conservative critiques of culture in an industrial civilization is to emphasize in each case the human consequences of social change. On the first theme: Industrialization depends on the division of labor. As specialization advances, man ceases to be the master of the machine he uses and becomes its victim. Work becomes more monotonous and deprives the worker increasingly of the possibility of developing and applying his human faculties. More generally: the specialized development of one faculty in the interest of productivity and economic success leads necessarily to the atrophy of many or all other capacities. Industrial man appears at all levels of the social structure as a contrast conception to Renaissance man.

On the second theme: Industrialization and democratization destroy human relationships. The individual obtains his freedom from patriarchal domination and from a hierarchical rank order, but only at the price of fraternal relationships within the community. In an industrial society, human relations lose their emotional quality and the feeling of moral obligation, because gradually they come to depend upon economic interests alone. Cooperation on an equal basis is replaced by a struggle for survival. The traditional rights and duties that once existed between master and servant lose all their personal reciprocity, and employers and employees come to agreement only on the basis of material advantage.

In evaluating these widespread opinions one will admit readily that modern industrialization has brought profound changes. The critical question is only how these changes are to be described and assessed. The opinions I have characterized are not so much false as distorted by contrasts in black and white. In part this distortion arises from the tendency of intellectuals to generalize their own mentality as an attribute of people at large. This generalization cannot be ignored. Intellectuals are a cultural elite and their critical assessment of industrial civilization is of historical importance, whether true or false. Yet social scientists must ask whether it is probable that people in general will respond to the division of labor and the changing norms of an industrial society as intellectuals have.

THE DIVISION OF LABOR

Karl Marx's characterization of the division of labor and its development is a classic instance of the cultural critique advanced by intellectuals:

The knowledge, the judgment, and the will, which, though in ever so small a degree, are practised by the independent peasant or handicraftsman, in the same way as the savage makes the whole art of war consist in the exercise of his personal cunning—these faculties are now required only for the workshop as a whole. . . . It is a result of the division of labour in manufactures, that the labourer is brought face to face with the intellectual potencies of the material process of production, as the property of another, and as a ruling power.[2]

In another equally well-known passage Marx characterizes the significance of industrial labor for the individual worker. Note that in these passages the peasant, craftsman, or worker is made into a general symbol of man as a working creature and hence a symbol of the several social structures as well. Marx writes:

Within the capitalist system all methods for raising the social productiveness of labour are brought about at the cost of the individual labourer; all means for the development of production transform themselves into means of domination over, and exploitation of, the producers; they mutilate the labourer into a fragment of a man, degrade him to the level of an appendage of a machine, destroy every remnant of charm in his work and turn it into a hated toil; they estrange from him the intellectual potentialities of the labour-process in the same proportion as science is incorporated in it as an independent power; they distort the conditions under which he works, subject him during the labour-process to a despotism the more hateful for its meanness; they transform his life-time into working-time, and drag his wife and child beneath the wheels of the Juggernaut of capital.[3]

There is no doubt that mechanical work represents a difficult psychological burden, especially if it takes the form of repetitive manual operations such as those Charlie Chaplin depicted sardonically in his film *Modern Times*. But the question is how a manual worker comes to terms with this burden, an issue that was not even raised in the socialist literature of the nineteenth century. It was assumed instead that this burden was oppressive and that the division of labor itself had to be overcome to undo the inhumanity of the capitalist system. Accordingly, *The German Ideology* by Marx and Engels opposes the division of labor with its famous idealization of man in a future social order:

In Communist society, where nobody has one exclusive sphere of activity, but each can become accomplished in any branch he wishes, society regulates the general production and thus makes it possible for me to do one thing today and another tomorrow, to hunt in the morning, fish in the afternoon, rear cattle in the evening, criticize after dinner, just as

[2] Karl Marx, *Capital* (New York: Modern Library, 1936), 396f.
[3] *Op. cit.*, 708.

I have a mind, without ever becoming hunter, fisherman, shepherd or critic.[4]

I consider it improbable that workers on the average would react in this fashion to the special burdens of the division of labor and of mechanization. There exists some indication, however, that this was indeed Marx's opinion.

Apparently Marx presupposed that the average worker is endowed with a creative potential in many fields of activity. Therefore, he imputes to the worker a desire for creative effort, not only for increased consumption, leisure, and diversion. In a footnote to which little attention has been paid, he quotes the autobiographical report of a French worker who had emigrated to California and whose many-sided experience roughly corresponds to the ideal image Marx projected. This footnote reads as follows:

I never could have believed, that I was capable of working at the various occupations I was employed on in California. I was firmly convinced that I was fit for nothing but letter-press printing. . . . Once in the midst of this world of adventurers, who change their occupation as often as they do their shirt, egad, I did as the others. As mining did not turn out remunerative enough, I left it for the town, where in succession I became typographer, slater, plumber, etc. In consequence of thus finding out that I am fit for any sort of work, I feel less of a mollusk and more of a man.[5]

One should note that this was written by a printer, a member of the labor aristocracy, to use Marxian categories. Anyone familiar with California labor conditions of that time will recognize in this description conditions of employment characterized by rapid labor turnover and employment conditions of an improvising, transitory kind. But in using this quotation Marx probably had in mind the ideal of a worker with abundant creative capacities, all the while generalizing the special abilities of this man and ignoring the special working conditions of California in its pioneering period.

The point is that cultural critiques of the industrial division of labor frequently operate with an ideal contrast conception that does not correspond to the experience either of primitive men or of medieval craftsmen, or yet to the possibilities of a socialist so-

    [4] Karl Marx and Friedrich Engels, *The German Ideology* (New York: International Publishers, 1947), 22.
    [5] Marx, *Capital, op. cit.,* 534.

ciety of the future. This contrast conception is based on a generalized ideal of genius, for example of a Leonardo da Vinci. An almost
inexhaustible range of talents is attributed to man generally, a
conception derived from the wishful thinking of intellectuals im-
bued with the personality ideal of the Romantic period. This idea
has little basis in what is known of human possibilities and limitations. In most cases gifted men achieve the development of their
talents by concentration, though rare examples exist of men who
continuously extend their creative activities. But a generalization
of these exceptions deserves the label of promethean fallacy. It may
be an expression of intellectual narcissism that this fallacy continues to be reiterated.

How else is one to explain that Herbert Marcuse continues to
dream of multi-dimensional or Renaissance man as he attacks
one-dimensional man for his travesty on human aspirations? Men
with intellectual aspirations engage in wishful self-deceit when
they conceive a social order in which the division of labor will be
overcome so that everyone may give free reign to the unused capacities within him. To say it more positively: Every future reorgani-
zation of society will face the problem of endowing the necessary
specialization of labor with a meaningful human content and to
develop satisfying uses of leisure time. This problem exists in every
society of the future since all will depend upon specialization to
combat the poverty of the world. Yet certain utopian thinkers give
their attention to an idealized Renaissance man, writ large, forgetting the poverty and hunger of people in whose behalf they
claim to speak. Even Lenin appreciated the positive contribution
of modern technology, and since his day automation has achieved
extraordinary results in the simplification of labor. However, many
cultural critics look upon these innovations only in terms of their
negative consequences. Unlike their predecessors of the nineteenth
century they seem to have no hope that such developments might
be pointed in a positive direction.

Social Norms

Now to the second critique of industrial society: the decline of social norms. Here also there are many works in which
the common theme of the deterioration of human relationships is
examined in ever new variations. I select one quotation from the
work of Alexis de Tocqueville in which he describes the traditional
relations between masters and servants. (In passing it should be

noted that Tocqueville had a balanced and relatively non-ideological conception of human relationships in their transformation from the medieval to the modern world.)

[The] aristocratic constitution does not exert a less powerful influence on the notions and manners of servants than on those of masters; and although the effects are different, the same cause may easily be traced. Both classes constitute small communities in the heart of the nation, and certain permanent notions of right and wrong are ultimately established among them. The different acts of human life are viewed by one peculiar and unchanging light. In the society of servants, as in that of masters, men exercise a great influence over one another: they acknowledge settled rules, and in the absence of law they are guided by a sort of public opinion; their habits are settled, and their conduct is placed under a certain control. . . . Although in aristocratic society the master and servant have no natural resemblance, although, on the contrary, they are placed at an immense distance on the scale of human beings by their fortune, education, and opinions, yet time ultimately binds them together. They are connected by a long series of common reminiscences, and however different they may be, they grow alike. . . . the master gets to look upon his servants as an inferior and secondary part of himself, and he often takes an interest in their lot by a last stretch of selfishness. Servants, on their part, are not averse to regarding themselves in the same light; and they sometimes identify themselves with the person of the master, so that they become an appendage to him in their own eyes as well as in his.[6]

Thus it is said of an earlier social order that the individual had definite rights and duties and accordingly enjoyed a clear integration within the community. And this characterization is delineated more sharply, the more it is contrasted with an industrial society with its individualism based on formal legal rights and its lack of social and moral integration.

An example can illuminate this idea and its problematic character. Otto Brunner has shown that in the preindustrial societies of Europe problems of economic life were discussed in treatises on estate and household management.[7] Here instruction on agriculture, animal breeding, and budget keeping were presented along with advice on the education of children, marital relations, and the

[6] Alexis de Tocqueville, *Democracy in America* (New York: Vintage, 1945), II, 188f.

[7] Cf. Otto Brunner, *Adeliges Landleben und europäischer Geist* (Salzburg: Otto Müller, 1949).

proper treatment of servants. Technical and economic questions were, therefore, part of a moral regulation of human relationships. This "mixture" belongs to a world in which the household and the estate encompassed a community in which production and consumption were part of an integrated way of life. The separation of moral from economic concerns therefore belongs to a society in which the work place is typically separated from the family household.

Now, no one will contend that the development of modern industrial societies has been without effect on human relationships and has not led to a decline of formerly valid social norms. But in assessing this change we should keep in mind that the intellectual minority which is preoccupied with these questions is all too easily inclined to present its own concerns as the general destiny of man. The problem of norms makes a direct appeal to the fears of those of conservative inclination. Their concern with social norms is different from the promethean fallacy. It represents the intellectual diagnosis of what all other men require in order to maintain the social order. One may call this the fallacy of a biological conception of society or, more briefly, the organic fallacy.

This organic interpretation of changing social norms is just as questionable as the promethean interpretation of specialization. One should avoid the romantic fallacy that a traditional society with its relatively high integration under a patriarchal authority and universally accepted religious norms is also characterized to a high degree by social harmony and human happiness. A strong integration of the family household or of the small community means at the same time an isolation of families and communities from one another. Integration within small groups and isolation between them go together. Moreover, integration within family or community means also that everyday life is characterized by a proud and cruel publicity, as Huizinga has said. Men are personally dependent upon one another, since their life occurs largely within the household and estate or within the small community. This may mean not only a firm integration of the individual in the group, but also the intensification of all emotional ties, which include hatred, distrust, and mutual supervision, because the fate of each is affected directly by the actions of those next to him. This kind of life is not idyllic. We may indeed speak of change from such a social pattern as a separation of familial from economic concerns, as well as a decline of group solidarity and firm social norms. But we should always add that this earlier society was at the same time lacking in privacy and those forms of intimacy dependent on privacy; it was characterized by the compulsions of living in close proximity to others. A change of this society meant a decline of isolation of different households and increasing interdependence of each household with the market. Change also meant increasing personal freedom, with the chances and problems implied thereby.

We must never cease to pay close attention to the burdens and advantages of each social structure. Yet critiques of industrial society have frequently contrasted the burdens and problems of the present with the advantages of the past. That way we obtain a view of the past that results from our wishes and dreams and a view of the present that expresses our fears and discontents.

A SCHOLARLY PERSPECTIVE

The contrast between traditional and modern society can avoid the systematic distortions which I have pointed out. To do this, the advantages and special burdens of both types of social structure must be made explicit. One may distinguish such structures in terms of the social solidarity they achieve and the typical psychological problems that achievement engenders. This is one way of arriving at scholarly propositions about man and society as distinguished from ideological expressions of wishes and fears.

In traditional societies, one finds small groups with personal relations of great intensity in love and hate. Inside these groups, affection and dislike are on public display in a manner which modern men would probably find personally intolerable. It may be true that traditional societies are characterized by generally recognized cultural norms but this goes hand in hand with the subservience of educated men and the predominance of illiteracy in the population. Such a framework of norms goes together with a low level of production and communication and with a society composed of small economic, legal, and political units. In such a fragmentary society legal disputes among a large number of solidary groups predominate. Their cohesion depends not only on common norms but on the necessity of self-help and of a common defense.

Each of these groups and the community as a whole is characterized, moreover, by a sharp division between rulers and ruled. Men of noble family background have a predominant share of wealth and ready access to positions of formal authority, and they enjoy the sociability, the leisure, and the culture of their class. By contrast the mass of the population lives in poverty and follows a daily round of heavy physical labor, without access to education, culture, or influential position, and without any visible means by which its members may alleviate their impoverished existence. Under these conditions it is difficult to apply the concept "society." The people at large live in fragmented subordination, and only the leading strata have enough cohesion to constitute a society. To speak here of a life secured by a firm moral order or of the warmth of human relationships in family and community would make sense only if all the hatred, illiteracy, poverty, and physical insecurity are disregarded.

What then are the related considerations pertaining to modern industrial society? It may be true that such societies possess relatively few cultural norms that are universally accepted and strictly mandatory. This absence of a universal moral framework is probably related to the relative emancipation of intellectuals and to the high level of education in the population at large. Moreover, structural differentiation in technology and communication has produced a high level of production as well as a high degree of impersonal inter-dependence. Associated with this interdependence are the characteristics of the nation-state. Legal enactments and adjudication of disputes, taxation, control of the currency, military organization, a postal system, public services, and other activities have become functions of a national government. The political struggle now relates to this national level and no longer consists in feuds between relatively autonomous authorities. Another related characteristic of modern society is the fundamental democratization of which Karl Mannheim spoke when he referred to those classes becoming active which until then had played only a passive role in political life. Rulers and ruled are no longer divided as sharply as they once were, since the ruled have the vote and the rulers are subject to formal controls in many respects. Status distinctions are no longer synonymous with inherited privileges.

In this general context it is appropriate to use the concept "society" with reference to the population of an entire country, in view of the mutual interdependence among the people and their equality as citizens. Now, human relations are characterized by affection or aversion on two levels which hardly exist in traditional societies. On the one hand, there is the nuclear family with all the advantages and disadvantages of its intense, affective ties. On the other hand, there are national loyalties which fluctuate between two extremes. In normal times such loyalties are accepted as a matter of course; they involve little intensity of feeling or may be replaced entirely by political skepticism. However, in times of national crisis or in other direct confrontaitons with foreign cultures, national loyalties can quickly rise to fever pitch. Love and hate in the nuclear family or at the national level are characteristics of modern society.

THE INDIVIDUAL AND THE ORGANIZATION

In this discussion of the individual and society, I have dwelled on the contrast between ideological and scholarly interpretations, because black-and-white contrasts between traditional and modern societies have obstructed our understanding of these matters. By examining the ideological tradition critically I wanted to obtain a vantage point for a more balanced analysis. A consideration of modern problems appears to me possible only when that vantage point is secured. But in conclusion it is perhaps useful to single out one modern issue to indicate in which direction further work on these questions might be attempted.

One of the most important questions of our time is the relation between the individual and large bureaucratic organizations. In this connection American sociology has emphasized the willingness of individuals to adapt or adjust in response to the expectations of others, and the dangers to personal values which arise from this other-directed orientation. David Riesman's *The Lonely Crowd* and William Whyte's *The Organization Man* are well-known writings on this theme. One should be aware, of course, that the tendency toward an other-directed orientation goes back in American society to the tradition of the Puritan sects and is thus not simply an aspect of the modern experience. But there is no question that this tendency to live up to the expectations of others is a special burden for the individual whose personal integrity is already placed in jeopardy by the demands which large organizations make upon him. There is no simple solution to this problem. But in assessing it one should keep in mind that the relevant standards of judgment are themselves questionable.

Neither personalities who pursue their own way to the bitter end without any regard for the opinions of others, nor personalities who lack all inner strength and merely do what others expect of them correspond to the life experience of most people. These are caricatures, unmasking critiques that exaggerate existing tendencies. In the nineteenth century we had an exaggerated ideal of personality. These twentieth-century critiques present a contrary exaggeration that attributes a complete lack of personality to all men who are other-directed, in Riesman's terms. This is a good example of the ideological component I have criticized here. Social tendencies are personified and generalized. The personality ideal in one of its versions corresponds to economic man in a free market just as the other-directed personality belongs to economic man in the large organizations of a modern economy.

What remains true is that each economic structure confronts men with specific psychological tasks which everyone must solve as best he can. To characterize this situation, it is appropriate to cite Arnold Gehlen:

The catchword that mass culture threatens the personality is only half true. . . . Never before has there been this much differentiated and expressive subjectivity as today. . . . Every time has its own name and honor for that action and impact which are extraordinary and indeed improbable. If today the term personality is used in the sense of a particularly admirable productivity, we are perhaps less likely to find it in the separate realm of high culture, literature or art; we are more likely to find it where someone makes the exacting demands of the human spirit prevail within the organizational apparatus, rather than keep his distance from it. That man has personality in this specific sense who has the strength and inventiveness to give effect in everyday life to the finer and more precarious values; who has the spiritual strength to give meaning to everyday situations and to respond to them in all their respects.[8]

[8] Arnold Gehlen, *Die Seele im technischen Zeitalter* (Hamburg: Rowohlt, 1957), 114, 118.

V

SOCIOLOGY AND THE DISTRUST
OF REASON

Historical Perspectives and Sociological Inquiry as the theme of an American sociological convention would have been incongruous twenty years ago. It is not so today. We meet amidst upheaval directly affecting the academic community. The social sciences and sociology in particular are at the center of the storm. The freedom to do scholarly work has been questioned when it is not directed to problems considered "relevant" by the critics. In this setting we must demonstrate to those willing to listen that great issues of the day can be examined with that combination of passionate concern and scholarly detachment which is the hallmark of reasoned inquiry in our field.

But there are those unwilling to listen. Detachment and analysis as hitherto practiced, and almost regardless of content, appear to them fatally impaired because they feel that even in the midst of great wealth they must live by an ethic of social despair. Here is one expression of this sentiment, taken from the privately circulated manuscript of a sociologist who is a respected member of a university faculty.

Time is short; we cannot wait years for research to give us impregnable theses. America's academia fiddles while the fires are burning. Where are the studies of the new corporate power, of the Defense Department, of the military-industrial complex, of the new bureaucracies, of Vietnam? American academics are prisoners of liberal democratic ideology. Even as the chains rust, they do not move. A new current of reason and

Reinhard Bendix, from *American Sociological Review*, 35:5, Oct. 1970, 00–00; prepared as Presidential Address, 65th Annual Meetings of the American Sociological Association, Washington, D. C., Sept. 1970.

passion is arising in America—outside of its conventional institutions. The current of reason must flow faster to create an image of reality and hope for the future, for a ruling class in despair will soon reach for some other kind of ideology, and all that is left for the American establishment is "patriotism," that is fascism.

In this view the evils of the world loom so large that only those energies are employed legitimately which attack these evils head on. By that standard much or most scholarship fails.

You will say they are a minority. This is true. But the social despair that motivates this minority also moves larger numbers, perhaps at a distance but still significantly. Why do the few who feel moved by social despair evoke such resonance among the many?

In posing this question I am mindful of several contributions. The sharp rise in student unrest during recent years has been analyzed in terms of generational conflict. Lewis Feuer has amassed evidence on this theme from far and wide and on this basis delineated the symptoms of student protest. Bruno Bettelheim has provided us with "a psychograph of adolescent rebellion." His emphasis, like that of Kenneth Keniston and Bennett Berger, is on an age-cohort of anxiety. In modern society there is a prolonged period of dependence between childhood and adult responsibility. In effect youths are permitted very early sexual experience. But when on that or other bases they claim or expect the independence of adults, education prolongs their dependence and an automated technology makes them feel obsolete. Edward Shils has analyzed the resulting protest in terms of a utopian fantasy of plenitude, a belief in the sacredness of immediate experience, and the consequent attack on all boundaries of discipline, institutions and authority.[1]

I have learned much from these and related analyses. But I also note that they end rather regularly with an appeal to the people over thirty. We are called upon to "stand firmly by the traditions of teaching, training, and research as the proper task of universities"; we should "not allow ourselves to be swept away by the desire to be 'with it', to relive our lost youth or to prolong our fading

[1] See Lewis Feuer, *The Conflict of Generations* (New York: Basic Books, 1969), esp. chs. I and X; Bruno Bettelheim, "Obsolete Youth," *Encounter,* XXXIII, Sept. 1969, 29–42; Kenneth Keniston, *Young Radicals,* (New York: Harcourt, 1968), 257ff. and *passim;* Bennett Berger, "The New Stage of American Man—Almost Endless Adolescence," *New York Times Magazine* (Nov. 2, 1969); and Edward Shils, "Plenitude and Scarcity," *Encounter,* XXXII, May 1969, 37–57.

youth." [2] I agree, but I ask myself whether this is enough. The literature on student protest often gives the impression of having been written by kindly uncles whose air of concern or sympathy and whose analytical stance give one no intimation of mortality. But we are mortal. When the value of scholarship is in question, an analysis confined to the protest of youth will appear patronizing. It will miss the fact that the protest expresses not only the disquiet of the children but also the growing uncertainty of their parents. In the midst of a crisis of legitimacy we must try once again to interpret the values we cherish and understand why our adherence to them has become ambivalent.

In addressing myself to this task I shall first characterize the belief in science that has become the central legitimation of universities. Second, I shall examine the attack on the value of academic scholarship which the great critics of modern civilization launched during the nineteenth century. Third, I want to show that, in the twentieth century, Western culture has been marked by a changed sensibility in the arts, which has increased the distrust of reason. Fourth, I will make reference to political aspects of this distrust of reason, especially by examining the rhetorical use of the term "fascism." Fifth, I shall note the greater institutional vulnerability of universities owing to the changed role of science since the Second World War. Finally, I shall offer an assessment of the problems facing sociology in a period when the belief in progress through knowledge has been impaired and the legitimacy of scholarship is in question.

The Belief in Science

The belief in science has remained remarkably consistent from the time of its first articulation in the seventeenth century to our own day. Francis Bacon wanted to inspire men with confidence that knowledge enhances human power. "Nature to be commanded must be obeyed; where the cause is not known the effect cannot be produced." He attacked the zealots who opposed science because they feared for religious faith and state authority.

. . . surely there is a great distinction between matters of state and the arts (science) . . . In matters of state a change even for the better is distrusted, because it unsettles what is established, these things resting on authority, consent, fame and opinion, not on demonstration. But arts

[2] Shils, *op. cit.,* 56.

and sciences should be like mines, where the noise of new works and further advances is heard on every side. . . ."[3]

By the mid-nineteenth century, the "noise of new works" was on all sides and scientists could speak with the confidence of great success.

For a representative statement we may turn to the physiologist Helmholtz who considered the purposes of the university in terms of the relation between the natural sciences and all other disciplines. In 1862, he noted the specialization and frequent incomprehension among the several disciplines and asked whether it made sense to have them continue in the same institution of learning. Helmholtz compared the disciplines in terms of the way in which they achieved their results and noted—as so many have since—the greater precision in the natural sciences and the greater richness and human interest in the *Geisteswissenschaften*. The latter have a higher and more difficult task and contribute to order and moral discipline. But in respect of method they can learn much from the sciences proper.

Indeed I believe that our time has already learned a good many things from the natural sciences. The absolute, unconditional respect for facts and the fidelity with which they are collected, a certain distrust of appearances, the effort to detect in all cases relations of cause and effect, and the tendency to assume their existence—[all this] distinguishes our time from earlier ones and seems to indicate such an [exemplary] influence [of the natural sciences].[4]

The progress achieved through the advancement of science appeared to justify this position of the natural sciences as the model. Scientific knowledge is power and increases "the benefit and use of life." Helmholtz made two reservations only, as an aside. The scientist must become increasingly narrow in his specialization and "each student must be content to find his reward in rejoicing over new discoveries." Implicitly, all other qualities of the human mind were diminished.[5]

[3] Francis Bacon, "Novum Organum," in E. A. Burtt, ed., *The English Philosophers from Bacon to Mill* (New York: Modern Library, 1939), 64.

[4] Hermann Helmholtz, "Über das Verhältniss der Naturwissenschaften zur Gesamtheit der Wissenschaft," *Populäre Wissenschaftliche Vorträge* (Brunswick: Friedrich Vieweg, 1865), I, 23. The lecture was delivered in 1862.

[5] The second point is noted in *ibid.*, 27; the first point is found in "Über das Ziel und die Fortschritte der Naturwissenschaft," *Populäre Wissenschaftliche*

For a contemporary statement it is perhaps best to recall the thesis of C. P. Snow that "the intellectual life of the whole of Western society is increasingly being split into two polar groups." [6] World War II and the postwar years had been a period of unprecedented scientific advance and unprecedented public support of science. As a former research scientist Snow shared the resulting buoyancy of the scientific community. But as a writer sensitive to the critiques of science he put the case of science more sensitively than most. Everyone, he says, is aware of human tragedy at the individual level. Scientists certainly are. "But there is plenty in our condition which is not fate, and against which we are less than human unless we do struggle . . . As a group, the scientists . . . are inclined to be impatient to see if something can be done: and inclined to think that it can be done, until it's proved otherwise. That is their real optimism, and it's an optimism that the rest of us badly need." [7] Snow contrasts this scientific creed with the cultural pessimism of literary intellectuals, whom he calls "natural Luddites." Ever since the industrial revolution men of letters have stood uncomprehending at the tremendous advances of science and technology, unable or unwilling to see that the age-old scourges of hunger and poverty could be relieved only in this way.

The history of the belief in science still needs to be written, but the three examples I have cited are prominent enough. The commitment to scientific work makes sense if there is hope that in the long run the constructive uses of knowledge will prevail. Science presupposes a belief in the perfectibility of man; it does not flourish amidst preoccupation with its own potential evil. These are among the reasons why the scholar is freed of purposes extraneous to his inquiry, and why the institutional immunities of the university were considered legitimate.

THE ROMANTIC CRITIQUE

We accept these beliefs and institutional arrangements as long as we cherish the pursuit of knowledge. But during the last

Vorträge (Brunswick: Friedrich Vieweg, 1876), II, 186. This lecture was delivered in 1869.

[6] C. P. Snow, *The Two Cultures and a Second Look* (New York: Mentor Books, New American Library, 1964), 11. Originally formulated in 1956, these lectures were given and published in 1959; the addendum dates from 1963.

[7] *Ibid.*, 13–14.

two centuries the legitimacy of this pursuit has been challenged repeatedly by appeals to the imagination and to authentic experience. Generational revolts have reflected this conflict of values between reason and the "poetry of life." Such revolts have erupted in movements of liberation during the nineteenth century and in radical movements at the end of World War I, during the Depression, and in the 1960's. Conflicts over the belief in reason are a major characteristic of Western civilization.

Schopenhauer, Kierkegaard, Nietzsche, Marx, and Freud are among the great iconoclasts of the last century. All of them questioned the autonomy of knowledge and asserted that knowledge is inseparable from its preconditions, whether these are called will, commitment, will to power, class situation, or libidinal sublimation. On this basis all five deny the possibility of scholarly detachment, and some deny that scientific knowledge is desirable at all.

Two distinct premises are involved. To Schopenhauer, Kierkegaard, and Nietzsche the search for knowledge appears as an arid suppression of life; they seek a true way to knowledge through Indian mysticism, or religious experiences, or a cultural regeneration by men larger than life. For these writers the sickness of our time is a deadened feeling and a mediocrity of spirit of which the universities are an especially glaring manifestation. Their attack on scholarship is part of a more general critique of culture.

By contrast, Marx and Freud believe in the pursuit of knowledge and its promise of emancipation, at the same time that they reject academic scholarship. According to Marx, universities are involved in the contentions of society and their claim to be above the battle is false. For him, true awareness of history requires a critique of the ideological foundation of scientific work. And this awareness is achieved through a unity of theory and practice only to be found in revolutionary movement, not in universities. By a similar reductionism Freud considers every intellectual position in terms of its function in the "psychic economy" of the individual. The quest for knowledge cannot escape this psychological process, just as for Marx it cannot escape the historical process. Hence the path to knowledge in psychology lies in a heightened awareness of self, induced by the analysis and control-analysis of psychoanalytic training. This extramural recruitment and training of psychoanalysis is as incompatible with academic psychology as Marx's unity of theory and practice is incompatible with academic sociology.

Whereas Marx and Freud believed in the pursuit of knowledge

and its promise of emancipation, Schopenhauer or Kierkegaard, who revolted against the Enlightenment, believed in neither. Shelley's *Defence of Poetry* (1821) puts the case with great lucidity. Science and reason are distinguished from poetry and the imagination. The poets, says Shelley, "have been challenged to resign the civic crown to reasoners and mechanics" and he acknowledges that these have their utility. The banishment of want, the security of life, the dispersal of superstition, and the conciliation of interests are utilities promoted by the calculating faculty. This is of value as long as it remains confined to "the inferior powers of our nature." But poetry and imagination represent another, higher utility. "The great secret of morals is love; or a going out of our own nature, and an identification of ourselves with the beautiful which exists in thought, action, or person, not our own. A man, to be greatly good, must imagine intensely and comprehensively; he must put himself in the place of another and of many others; the pains and pleasures of his species must become his own." [8] The great difficulty is that in scientific and economic systems of thought "the poetry . . . is concealed by the accumulation of facts and calculating processes." Certainly, the sciences have enlarged our "empire over the external world." But in proportion as the poetical faculty is wanting, the sciences have also circumscribed the empire of the internal world.[9] Here is Shelley's own summation:

We want the creative faculty to imagine that which we know; we want the generous impulse to act that which we imagine; we want the poetry of life: our calculations have outrun conception; we have eaten more than we can digest. . . . The cultivation of poetry is never more to be desired that at periods when, from an excess of the selfish and calculating principle, the accumulation of the materials of external life exceed the quantity of the power of assimilating them to the internal laws of human nature.[10]

It could not have been said more soberly.

But the romantic protest was not frequently sober. The praise of art was linked with a promethean image of the poet as godlike, rising above mere humanity and achieving ends which nature is incapable of achieving by herself. These views from Shaftesbury

[8] P. B. Shelley, "A Defence of Poetry," in R. J. White, ed., *Political Tracts of Wordsworth, Coleridge and Shelley* (Cambridge: Cambridge University Press, 1953), 202.

[9] *Ibid.*, 205.

[10] *Ibid.*, 205–206.

and Goethe to Carlyle and Nietzsche meant, as Novalis put it, that "poets know nature better than scientists." [11] Such sentiments have a close kinship to attacks on the abstractions characteristic of all academic work. For Nietzsche all scientists were plebeian specialists and the worst enemies of art and artists. Kierkegaard made the central theme of his work the primacy of living over reflecting. Philosophy deals with man in general only and thus is a treason to life. What matters is man's personal situation and his vital relation to God.[12] In calling for more life and less thought, for more poetic imagination and less abstract reason, the romantics also attacked considerations of utility and the idea of material progress. Since the eighteenth century, scores of writers have elaborated the notion that the division of labor turns men into fragments, strangling their capacities and stultifying their emotions. This sentiment has implied an irrationalist, antiscientific stance so frequently since the industrial revolution that C. P. Snow is quite correct when he refers to literary intellectuals as "natural Luddites."

Yet the romantic protest of the nineteenth century was still bound up with the conventions of feeling and language that are the bases of discourse in ordinary life as well as in scholarship. By contrast, since before World War I a new sensibility in the arts has increasingly rejected that universe of discourse. The form and content of artistic expression have questioned the values of Western industrial civilization to such an extent that today the "Luddism" of literary intellectuals jeopardizes the legitimacy of academic pursuits and of much else besides. I can do little more here than sketch some tendencies that provide a ready arsenal for attacks upon universities and scholarship.

SUBJECTIVISM AND THE LOSS OF LANGUAGE

It is convenient to start with the generation of scholars and writers born in the 1850's and 1860's who were on the average a bit over forty around 1900. The classic writers of modern sociology belong to this generation. Beyond all the differences dividing them, men like Freud, Durkheim, Weber, Pareto, Park, Thomas, Cooley,

[11] See Judith Shklar, *After Utopia* (Princeton: Princeton University Press, 1969), 44–45, 54–57 and *passim,* for documentation of this point.

[12] See the cultural critique based on these convictions in Sören Kierkegaard, *The Present Age* (New York: Harper Torchbooks, Harper and Row, 1962), *passim.* On this basis Kierkegaard directed a virulent polemic against scholars and universities.

and Mead are discernible as a group by their common concern with
the subjective presuppositions of thought. This increased self-
consciousness could easily become self-defeating. With Dilthey, for
example, self-consciousness led to a skeptical relativism, while in
the work of Sorel it produced a radical commitment in thought and
action to overcome that relativism. Yet men like Freud, Durkheim,
and Weber, while making room for this new awareness, fought
"every step of the way to salvage as much as possible of the rationalist heritage." [13]

Max Weber's essay "Science as A Vocation," written just half a
century ago, is a document of this generation. It represents a careful blend of rationalist convictions and romantic sensibility. Like
the great rationalists before him, but with none of their optimism,
Weber commits himself to the scientist's calling. For him science is
the affair of an intellectual aristocracy. It demands concentration,
hard work, inspiration, and the passionate devotion to a task that
can only be accomplished if all extraneous considerations are excluded. Increasing knowledge can enhance the "technical mastery
of life." It helps us to perfect methods of thought and to achieve
intellectual clarity about the relation of means and ends. Weber
stated these goals with deliberate restraint. Like the great romantic
iconoclasts before him, he viewed the ideal of progress through
knowledge with profound skepticism. The very achievements of
science have "chained [us] to the idea of progress." For every scientific achievement poses new questions and calls for investigations
that will lead to the quick obsolescence of the scholar's contribution.
Weber states: "It is not self-evident that something subordinate
to such a law [of progress] is sensible and meaningful in itself. Why
does one engage in doing something that in reality never comes,
and never can come, to an end?" [14] Tolstoy attacked science because
for men on this endless frontier death has no meaning; the logical
goal of progress would be man's immortality. But in fact the scientific world view leaves the meaning of life and death undefined.
Thus stating his case Weber deliberately rejected the idea that
youth could find leadership and authentic experience in the universities.

Those academicians who want to assume the role of leader should
engage in it where they can be challenged politically. Nor can the

[13] H. Stuart Hughes, *Consciousness and Society* (New York: Knopf, 1958), 17.
[14] Max Weber, *Essays in Sociology,* tr. and ed. by H. H. Gerth and C. W. Mills
(New York: Oxford, 1946), 138.

university teacher provide experience in the sense in which the churches offer it to the believer. Let those who search for authenticity learn that the individual who simply fulfills the exacting demands of the day, if he has found himself, expresses the creative spark that is within him. Weber addressed these remarks to a generation which rejected his own skeptical commitment to the Enlightenment tradition. The young men of the 1920's, like their age-mates in the years before World War I, demanded experience and action rather than words. Their drive had culminated in the enthusiasm with which they greeted the outbreak of war in 1914, and with which they were joining extremist movements of the Right or Left in 1918 to 1920.

But meanwhile imaginative writers had begun to explore the possibilities of relativism in a world without values, further helping to undermine the legacy of the Enlightenment still viable in men like Freud or Weber. The arts may have little direct bearing on science or scholarship, except where they destroy the notion of competence. However, their development in the twentieth century jeopardized the standards of discourse on which all academic work is based. The nature of this jeopardy is conveyed by two interrelated tendencies of modern art: the retreat from intelligibility and the emergence of a radical subjectivism. As Saul Bellow put it in *Mr. Sammler's Planet*: "When people are so desperately impotent, they play that instrument, the personality, louder and wilder."

Some nineteenth-century writers anticipated these developments. The German poet Novalis (1772–1801) wrote of poetry as a defense against ordinary life, a magical union of fantasy and thought, a productive language which like mathematics is a playful world of its own, intelligible only to a few.[15] Novalis was read in France. Many of these elements are elaborated by Baudelaire, whose poems are deliberately impersonal so that they can express every possible human emotion, preferably the most extreme. Baudelaire uses the term "modernity" to refer to the ugliness of large cities, their artificiality and sinfulness, their loneliness in large crowds, their technology and progress. He despised advertising, newspapers, the tide of a leveling democracy. But modernity also meant to him that these and other features of modern civilization result in a profusion of evil, decay, poverty, and artifice which fascinates the poetic imagination. Baudelaire and the many who

---

[15] These paraphrases are taken from the profound book by Hugo Friedrich, *Die Struktur der Modern-Lyrik* (Hamburg: Rowohlt, 1967), 28–29.

followed him have had a desperate urge to escape this reality. Most of them were unbelievers with a religious longing. For them poetry became a magical incantation, designed to cast a spell rather than reveal a meaning. To this end fantasy decomposes the whole created world and by reordering the component parts out of the wellsprings of human experience fashions a new world of its own.[16]

A retreat from meaning and coherence is evident in this orientation. When the poet does not want to recognize the existing world, ordinary themes and objects lose their relevance. Instead, style and sound are the prevalent means of expression at the expense of meaning. The poet has no object, says one writer. Pure poetry must be devoid of content so that the creative movement of language can have free rein, says another. A third speaks of formal tricks maintaining the verve of style; nothing is interrelated either thematically or psychologically, everything is nailed up rather than developed. Writers like Rimbaud, Apollinaire, Saint-John Perse, Yeats, Benn, search for a "new language" which is tantamount to the destruction of grammatical rules and rhetorical order.[17] The spirit of this endeavor is beautifully expressed in T. S. Eliot's "East Coker." The poet is

> Trying to learn to use words, and every attempt
> Is a wholly new start, and a different kind of failure . . .
> And so each venture
> Is a new beginning, a raid on the inarticulate . . .

And in "Burnt Norton" Eliot writes that "words strain, crack and sometimes break, under the burden, under the tension."

Where language thus loses its communicative power, a radical subjectivism comes into its own, much as in painting and sculpture a free experimentation with colors and forms followed the classical ideal of representation. In his study of poetry, Friedrich refers to this tendency as "dictatorial fantasy." Rimbaud had said that memory and the senses are only food for the creative impulse; the world which the poet leaves will no longer resemble its former appearance, because artistic fantasy has cruelly disfigured it.[18] Baudelaire, Mallarmé, Garcia Lorca, Proust, and Benn expressed similar ideas. In *The Counterfeiters* by André Gide, Edouard intends to write a

---

[16] See *ibid.*, 35–58, for an analysis of Baudelaire on which this statement is based.

[17] *Ibid.*, 149–152.

[18] *Ibid.*, 81–83, 136–138, 202–203.

novel which will be a sum of destructions, or a "rivalry between the
real world and the representation of it which we make to ourselves.
The manner in which the world of appearances imposes itself upon
us, and the manner in which we try to impose on the outside world
our own interpretation—this is the drama of our lives." [19]

In the main this drama has been "resolved" by a radical subjectivism of the artist. Not only language has been destroyed, but
persons and objects as means and ends of creative activity. In the
futurist manifesto of 1909 the rejection of language and of the human subject are linked directly. The author, Marinetti, argues for
the destruction of syntax, the elimination of adverbs and adjectives,
and the serial listing of nouns, in order among other things to destroy the ego in literature. "People are completely stupefied by
libraries and museums, and they are subjected to a terrible logic
and science. Man is no longer interesting. Therefore, one has to
eliminate people from literature." [20] A parallel destruction of the
object is evident in a comment of Picasso's. "I noticed that painting
has a value of its own, independent of the factual depiction of
things. I asked myself, whether one should not paint things the way
one knows them rather than the way one sees them . . . In my pictures I use the things I like. I do not care, how things fare in this
regard—they will have to get used to it. Formerly, pictures approached their completion in stages . . . A picture used to be a
sum of completions. With me a picture is a sum of destructions." [21]

Here then is the paradox of the development I have sketched.
Since the later Nineteenth century modern art has been characterized increasingly by a retreat from meaning and coherence. That
is to say, an ethics of social despair has led by circuitous routes to
self-created, hermetic worlds of pure subjectivity in which neither
the old romantic ideal of the human personality nor the objects
and themes of ordinary experience have a recognized place or meaning. Thus, in the dominant culture of the West a type of sensibility
has developed which reacts to the world as a provocation, and which
is hostile to intellectual positions that retain a belief in the constructive possibilities of knowledge for all their questioning of

[19] Quoted in Wylie Sypher, *From Rococo to Cubism* (New York: Random
House, 1960), 300–301.

[20] Quoted from Walter Höllerer, ed., *Theorie der modernen Lyrik* (Hamburg: Rowohlt, 1965), 138.

[21] Quoted from Walter Hess, ed., *Dokumente zum Verständnis der Modernen
Malerei* (Hamburg: Rowohlt, 1956), 53.

fundamentals. In this way, the ground was prepared for protests which are based on

the view that every human being simply by virtue of his humanity is an essence of unquestionable, undiscriminatable value with the fullest right to the realization of what is essential in him. What is essential is his sensibility, his experienced sensation, the contents of his imagination, and the gratification of his desires. Not only has man become the measure of all things; his sentiments have become the measure of man.[22]

Here is a statement which exemplifies this interpretation:

We are fed reason in order to give an inferiority complex to the rest of our emotions and senses. . . .
    We are trapped in a philosophical system of cause and effect. Rationality binds the mind and restricts the soul. It might even destroy the brain cells. We need to be liberated. We should be constrained no longer by possible rational consequences. We should begin to allow other emotions to dictate our actions.[23]

There is an "elective affinity" between a changed sensibility in the arts and the sectarian modes of protest which are inspired by a mystique of plenitude and subjectivism.

    There is as well a political dimension to which brief reference must be made.

THE RHETORIC OF FASCISM

I emphasize the transformation of artistic sensibility for two reasons. The retreat from intelligibility and its radical subjectivism have long since prepared the ground for a distrust of reason among the educated middle class, including members of faculties as long as their own field is not in question. Also I emphasize the affinity between this changed sensibility and current student protests because

----

[22] Shils, *op. cit.*, 44. See the related comments by George Steiner, "The Language Animal," and by David Martin, "Visit to Inner Space," *Encounter*, XXXIII, Aug. 1969, 23, 71–73. Robert Nisbet's argument in "Who Killed the Student Revolution?" *Encounter*, XXXIV, Feb. 1970, 10–18 that the protest aimed at the society rather than the university, misses the amorphous quality of these sentiments. The "web of iniquity" critique does not allow for institutional distinctions.
[23] Richard Hyland in *The Harvard Crimson* (Oct. 22, 1969) quoted in *Encounter*, XXXIV, April 1970, 30.

I see little evidence that these protests have arisen from communist or fascist doctrines. To be sure, Bolshevism after the Russian Revolution of 1917 and the Nazi movement before and after 1933 launched a concerted attack upon the universities as bastions of false claims to scholarly objectivity. For example, A. A. Bogdanov declared in 1918 that with the exception of the social sciences transformed by Marxism "all the present sciences are bourgeois [though] not in the sense that they defend the interests of the bourgeoisie directly. [They are bourgeois] in that they have been worked out and presented from the bourgeois standpoint, in that they are suffused by the bourgeois Weltanschauung and as such have a bourgeoisifying influence. . . ." Bogdanov also added that all teaching and research must be transformed from the proletarian standpoint and based thenceforth on the "living, brotherly cooperation between teachers and students, rather than on authority and intellectual subjugation." [24] Overtones reminiscent of current protest themes will be noted, yet I believe that these are distinct.

The rhetorical use of the word "fascism" helps to characterize the situation in which we find ourselves. Students proclaim that the Establishment is fascist, and critics over thirty reciprocate by calling the protesters fascists or, as Jürgen Habermas had it, "left fascists." There is no clearer indication of mutual incomprehension. What does this mean? Let me take each side in turn, though, of course, there is much diversity I must ignore.

Broadly speaking, "fascism" is for some students, some faculty members, and not a few writers an expressive term of utter derogation. It has a proven shock value for the older generation when applied to democratic institutions or indeed any aspect of industrial society. The term is also a potent weapon for a policy of escalation. Agitation may lead to police action, which proves that the regime is repressive like fascism. But if agitation does not lead to this result, then the question is raised: What did we do wrong? Since the regime is "objectively fascist" and the police was not called, the strategy of protest must have been at fault. There is no entry into this circle of a self-fulfilling prophecy.

Note the ethic of social despair that lies behind the provocation.

[24] Quoted in Richard Lorenz, ed., *Proletarische Kulturrevolution in Sowjetrussland (1917–1921)* (Munich: Deutscher Taschenbuchverlag, 1969), 218f. Analogous declarations, but with the accent on blood and soil, race purity, and the rest can be cited from the Nazi period. See the documentation in Hans Peter Bleuel and Ernst Klinnert, *Deutsche Studenten auf dem Weg ins Dritte Reich* (Gütersloh: Sigbert Mohn, 1967), 237f. and *passim*.

Time has run out. No landing on the moon can assuage the prospect of a nuclear holocaust. The liberation movements around the
world and the race problem at home have exposed the hypocrisy of
the Western claim to liberty, justice, and equality. The invasion of
Czechoslovakia and the manifest inequalities and repressions of
Soviet society have exposed the hypocrisy of the Communist claim
to represent the people and end the exploitation of man by man.
Faced with ultimate horrors and proximate evils, protest draws
once more on the arsenal of cultural pessimism with its total rejection of competition, efficiency, the division of labor, considerations
of utility, and the whole world of technology. Last but not least is
the visible tarnishing of the old promise of the Enlightenment, that
knowledge is power for the benefit and use of life.

In the face of these massive evils, the first and sometimes the only
response is to see everything as connected with everything else, and
to call this web of iniquity fascism. Thus, universities, a central
institution in a technological society, are a prime target. Their
values of dispassionate inquiry and free discussion, of tolerance
for ambiguity and diversity, presuppose an ethic of social hope,
that means, a freedom to choose and to wait, to discuss and deliberate. To the protester this appears utterly incommensurate with the
dire threats confronting us. An academia "which fiddles while the
fires are burning" appears as actually engaged in an insidious
"fascist repression," for discussion delays decision, and words are
seen as a smoke screen for inaction. All the values of scholarship
turn to dross: tolerance is repressive, objectivity or neutrality serve
the "system," lectures become an abuse of authority, and indeed
scholarship which uses abstract terms, as it must, "crumbles in the
mouth like mouldy fungi," [25] which phrase helped to initiate the
change of sensibility I have traced. At one level or another a good
many people respond positively to these sentiments, faced as they
are with a world of local wars and international stalemates in which
the threat of nuclear destruction hangs over every move.

On the other hand there are the liberals, young or old, who are
outraged by these attacks upon the values of civilization. To be
sure, conservatives rather than liberals call for law and order. But
as the legal system is dragged into the vortex of political polarization, "fascism" comes to be used by liberals as a term of alarm at

---

[25] The phrase is taken from Hugo von Hofmannsthal, "The Letter of Lord
Chandos," in *Selected Prose* (New York: Bollingen Series XXXII, Pantheon
Books, 1952), 134; originally published in 1902.

the deliberate abandon with which standards of academic and democratic civility are flouted. It is a term of abuse against those who reject tolerance, discussion, and the rule of law—or in an academic setting against those who reject free inquiry, the quest for objectivity, and the civilities of academic deliberation. It refers as well to the all-or-nothing perspective which fails to distinguish between authority and oppression, normal national interest and violent aggression, political compromise and political corruption.

Liberals believe that the indiscriminate and immoderate attack upon all social and political conventions and upon traditional values is profoundly unpolitical. The liberals see protesters frequently attacking not only political abuses and empty pretensions, but the very institutions that protect their right to protest. To liberal critics it is clear that protesters are blind to the ways in which their activities consolidate opinion on the far right. But this characterization is answered by the protesters by saying that nothing else can be done, since ordinary politics have brought us to this impasse. Theirs is a sectarian mode of protest outside of time, of political calculation, and of technical efficiency.

Indeed, it is outside of ordinary communication when one considers how declamation has crowded out discussion. With or without drugs "the mystic finds himself exploring every negative experience in order to make possible his return to the world of a 'total' human being." [26] Meanwhile, his more activist brother develops a cult of distant savior-leaders like Mao or Che, identifies with populist causes everywhere, and unites with others in a desperate, if superficially euphoric, rejection of his own civilization.[27] In their indiscriminate attack upon social and political conventions the protesters begin to resemble intellectuals of the Weimar Republic, who were equally sweeping in their condemnations. Walter Laqueur has dubbed this the "Tucholsky Complaint" after the German satirist of the 1920:

Tucholsky and his friends thought that the German Judge of their day was the most evil person imaginable and that the German prisons were the most inhumane; later they got Freisler and Auschwitz. They imagined that Stresemann and the Social Democrats were the most reactionary politicians in the world; soon after they had to face Hitler, Goebbels,

---

[26] David Martin, *op. cit.*, 73.

[27] The two modes are well described by Shils, *op. cit.*, 43–46, and Richard Lowenthal, "Unreason and Revolution," *Encounter*, XXXIII, Nov. 1969, 28–32.

and Goering. They sincerely believed that fascism was already ruling Germany, until the horrors of the Third Reich overtook them.[28]

In a book entitled *Deutschland, Deutschland über Alles,* Tucholsky said "no" to everything except the landscape of Germany. But at least he despaired of a society without democratic traditions. Some recent critics like Herbert Marcuse simply despair of civilization altogether—without telling us how they would live without it.

Today, discussion within the academic community is gravely impaired by the distrust of reason of the present generation of dissenters. This rise of irrationalism in the cultural sphere is due in part to a failure of the national political community. In their relations with the young generation the universities cannot tackle issues like the Vietnam war, race relations, or the uses of technology which the political leadership has so far failed to resolve. The universities should not be asked to make the attempt. Nevertheless, protesters and politicians have misused the universities as a convenient battleground without immediate and obvious disadvantage to themselves. They have done so in part, because we are faced with a crisis of legitimacy within the walls of academe.

THE CHANGED ROLE OF SCIENCE

Agonizing questions are raised concerning the purposes to be served by a quest for knowledge wherever it may lead. When scientists help to create powers of destruction which threaten civilization, the authority of scholarship is placed in jeopardy, because the belief in progress through knowledge is impaired.

Strictly speaking, the uses of knowledge and the conditions that facilitate its pursuit are extraneous concerns. As Don Price has stated: "Science has achieved its great power by insisting on defining for itself the problems it proposes to solve, and by refusing to take on problems merely because some outside authority considers them important. But that power, and the precision of thought on which it depends, is purchased by a refusal to deal with many aspects of such problems." [29] The power referred to is the capacity to advance knowledge. But the capacity to define problems auton-

___

[28] Walter Laqueur, "The Tucholsky Complaint," *Encounter,* XXXIII, Oct. 1969, 78.
[29] Don K. Price, *The Scientific Estate* (Cambridge: Harvard University Press, 1967), 105.

omously depends upon authority. And this autonomous authority has become more difficult to maintain in recent decades.

The role of science has changed. Scientific research in World War II and its culmination in the military and peaceful employment of atomic energy produced a marked rise in the authority of the scientific community. In his report to the president in 1945, Vannevar Bush spoke for that community when he argued strongly that basic scientific research is indispensable for the nation's welfare in war and peace.[30] Remember: only a year later Bernard Baruch declared that we tremble with fear as we think of the power science has put at our disposal, but science does *not* show us how we can control the dangers inherent in that power.[31] Nevertheless, for a time, the positive claims of science were accepted very generally. Between 1953 and 1966, gross national product in the United States doubled, but total funds for basic research increased more than six times. During the same period the federal government increased its support of basic research from one half to two thirds of the national total.[32] In the five-year period from 1959–60 to 1963–64, federal support of research in universities more than doubled.[33]

In the last twenty-five years science has become very prominent; even the social sciences have advanced, albeit at a great distance. Clark Kerr, in his Godkin lectures, has analyzed the resulting changes in academic decision-making. By offering projects, federal agencies exert a subtle but potent influence upon the directions which research at universities will take. They affect the allocation of funds and space and hence the establishment of priorities. As extramural research funds become a major portion of a university's research budget, many scholars are prompted to shift their identifi-

[30] Vannevar Bush, *Endless Horizons* (Washington: Public Affairs Press, 1946), 39–81. Progress in the social sciences and humanities is "likewise important," Bush said then, but that appears to be the only reference of this kind in the report.

[31] See Bernard Baruch, The United States Proposals for the International Control of Atomic Energy, presented to the U. N. Atomic Energy Commission (June 14, 1946) in U. S. State Department, *The International Control of Atomic Energy, Growth of a Policy* (Washington, D. C.: U. S. Government Printing Office, 1946), 138.

[32] U. S. Department of Health, Education, and Welfare, *Digest of Education Statistics, 1968 Edition* (Washington, D. C.: U. S. Government Printing Office, 1968), 128 (Table 160).

[33] *Ibid.*, 95 (Table 115). It should perhaps be added that the total of $3.2 billion spent for basic research in 1966 compared with $18.9 billion spent for applied research and development.

cation and loyalty from their university to the grant-giving agency. Increased emphasis on research through extramural funds entails a shift of resources to graduate, at the expense of undergraduate, education, and to the employment of research personnel without faculty status. Projects, costly facilities, and program planning introduce a new managerial dimension. Scientists who launch a series of projects can become caught up in the apparatus they have helped to create, and may be deflected permanently from what they would prefer to do if they still had a free hand.[34] Thus the earlier autonomy of science and of universities is in doubt just at the time when the destructiveness of weapons and the dangerous side effects of modern technology have become urgent concerns.

In addition, the demands on the educational system have increased greatly. In 1939/40 50 percent of those aged 17 were high-school graduates. By 1967/68 that percentage had risen to 74. During the same period college enrolments and the total number of college degrees increased by a factor of four and the number of higher degrees by a factor of seven. Nor is it a question of numbers alone. Increasingly, politicians, administrators, the general public, and not a few scientists, who should know better, have called upon the university to help solve the race problem, the urban crisis, generational conflict, pollution, the arms race. Scientists are called upon to be responsible for the application of their increasing knowledge at the same time that questions are raised whether the consequences of science are still beneficial. These and other demands subject the universities to a barrage of expectations which they cannot possibly fulfill. From being a method of inquiry to answer carefully delimited questions, science has been turned into a fetish with which to interpret the world, advise politicians, examine the future, provide an education, and entertain the public.

A crisis of legitimacy results whenever in critical periods the very claims of authority are used to question its justification. The claim is that "basic research performed without thought of practical ends" is indispensable for the nation's welfare.[35] But this claim has led to public support for science, which undermines the freedom of scientists from practical ends. The claim has also led to uses of

[34] Clark Kerr, *The Uses of the University* (New York: Harper Torchbooks, Harper and Row, 1966), 57–69. This summary selects the aspects most directly related to the autonomy of decision-making by scholars and universities. It should be noted that Kerr concentrates on the "federal grant university," but that analogous considerations apply to research funds from private foundations.
[35] Bush, *op. cit.*, 52.

knowledge which have a destructive potential that appears incompatible with welfare. In their eagerness to advance knowledge scientists have made claims for the unequivocal beneficence of their results. Inadvertently, they have contributed to the distrust of reason which is upon us.

THE PLACE OF SOCIOLOGY

Ordinarily we do not think of science and scholarship as bases of authority. But knowledge has an authority of its own, and I have tried to show why the legitimacy of that authority is now in question. Protest aimed at the foundations of academic institutions has found considerable resonance among people ostensibly committed to the life of the mind. What then of sociology?

Like all academic disciplines sociology depends on the existence of a scholarly community. A modern university comprises a congeries of such communities. Teachers and students in the different disciplines may communicate little or not at all. But while they live with their different interests and obligations, all of them can share an interest in the advance of knowledge—an advance facilitated by independent inquiry, free discussion, and academic self-government. When this shared interest is in doubt, more is at stake than spurious talk about an academic community. For when the legitimacy of the pursuit of knowledge is questioned, discourse itself is threatened by a withdrawal of affect. Let me spell this out in relation to sociology.

As in other disciplines, scholarship in sociology depends on communication concerning the findings and methods of study. In this context every statement made invites consent and helps to define the circle of those who agree, while to some extent marking off those who do not. We are all familiar with the feeling of dismay and anxiety, or with the displays of aggression, when such agreement is not achieved. We are also familiar with the school- or clique-building tendencies that arise from this desire for consensual validation. Accordingly, the twin principles of toleration and free discussion are more difficult to achieve within disciplines than in the university at large. Indeed, there is more to discuss within disciplines than between them, and withdrawal of affect within disciplines threatens discourse quite directly.

Many sociologists aspire to bring their field of study to the status of a science of society. To an extent this is salutary. The aspiration to engage in empirical inquiry is an indispensable bulwark against speculations which are complacent towards idiosyncrasies and take a lofty view of the merely factual. Yet today sociologists as scientists face a crisis of legitimacy. The destructive possibilities of knowledge and the diminished autonomy of science have prompted a questioning of premises which is bound to affect a discipline whose scientific aspirations are well ahead of its achievements. Moreover, sociologists of this persuasion should have noted the antihumanistic impulse of their model all along. It appears that the qualities of the scientific mind have been extolled at the expense of philosophical breadth and historical perspective, of literary distinction and aesthetic sensibility, of moral imagination and the cultivation of judgment. To be sure, much has been gained in the process. But a sociology that takes the natural sciences as its model also falls heir to a tradition in which these other qualities are at a discount.

At the same time we are all aware that in our discipline there have always been those who thought science not enough, who believed that the cultivation of judgment and moral sensibility was indispensable for sociology as a scholarly discipline. Such cultivation provides a bulwark against the dangers of scientism, against the preoccupation with techniques for their own sake, and against the unthinking denigration of contextual understanding. At the same time, sociologists of this persuasion are committed to empirical inquiry, broadly conceived. But today they, also, face a crisis of legitimacy. For the destructive possibilities of the distrust of reason, with its craving for authenticity and relevance, are evident once again. Hence the plea for more cultivation of judgment and sensibility in sociology should be made with care. A humanistic sociology which takes the distrust of reason as its model thereby undermines its own existence.

To me the tensions and debates between the scientific and the humanistic impulses appear as the foundation of modern sociology. Twenty years ago I wrote an essay on social science and the distrust of reason. My purpose then was to contrast an unreflective faith in science with the tradition of critical self-scrutiny reaching from Francis Bacon to Sigmund Freud. I wanted to warn that methodological preoccupations not be permitted to encroach on substantive concerns, lest we do harm to our discipline.[36] In the meantime there have been notable attempts to redirect our efforts, to which I have tried to contribute. Hence today I would emphasize that the distrust

[36] Reinhard Bendix, *Social Science and the Distrust of Reason* (Berkeley: University of California Press, 1951), *passim*.

of reason is not furthered by scientism alone. It consists also in a consciousness of crisis, an ethic of despair, and a call for action which do away with learning and deliberation altogether. I think sociology is as endangered by this retreat from meaning and coherence as it was by spurious analogies from the natural sciences.

Still, we are also enriched by the creative interplay of the traditions that have formed us. Their constructive use depends upon faith in the possibilities of human reason. Those who would destroy that use and that faith would not long survive in a world in which the ideals of reasoned inquiry have been abandoned. As long as we do not go back to the caves in anticipation of holocausts to come, learning has a creative role to play in the human community. It can do so only in universities which exist in the society and for it, and which provide institutional protection for learning in order to perform their mission.

Part B

COMPARATIVE STUDIES OF AUTHORITY
AND LEGITIMATION

VI

SOCIOLOGICAL TYPOLOGY AND
HISTORICAL EXPLANATION

In the aftermath of the Second World War, a large number of African and Asian countries became formally independent, joining some of the older Latin American countries as the Third World. This course of events has been accompanied by the proliferation of development studies, which took as their starting point the question of how an "underdeveloped" country could become a "developed" one. After more than two decades the formidable practical difficulties and the theoretical complexities have been widely recognized, and much of the initial political and academic optimism has been greatly attenuated. There is increasing understanding that in most instances the patterns of Western, Soviet, or Japanese industrialization will not be repeated. Instead, in many cases a different road or prolonged stagnation appear likely.

The rise of the Third World has been a result of Western penetration followed by political retreat. The impact has been great enough to bring about a radically new historical situation: for better or worse, Western technology and institutions are being adapted piecemeal all over the world. Many of the "follower countries" now face an amalgam of borrowed and indigenous elements. Their old social fabric has been rent apart at the same time that modernization remains partial, and heterogeneous traditionalist groups are strengthened by borrowed institutions such as mass parties and universal suffrage. Political instability has become endemic.

In response to the strains of modernization, much of the literature has been preoccupied with two major development issues: the

By Guenther Roth.

preservation or creation of (1) an innovative spirit and (2) effective political authority. One set of studies has searched for "functional equivalents" to the Protestant ethic and the spirit of capitalism, ranging from traditionalist religious incentives to sectarian Communist party discipline. Another set has dealt with legitimation and authority, particularly with regard to bureaucratic and charismatic organization. In addition, the neo-evolutionist literature has attempted to place contemporary developed and underdeveloped countries within a world-historical scheme of developmental stages.

In all three lines of inquiry the importance of Weber's work has been acknowledged by many scholars with purposes divergent from his.[1] Changing historical situations and shifting theoretical interests require the modification, in varying degrees, of older approaches. In many instances it may be neither necessary nor feasible to follow Weber's path but, whatever strategy a scholar may want to adopt, it should be informed by a clear understanding of what Weber and others have tried to accomplish in the past. Such understanding may be useful for the clarification of his own purposes. Therefore, this chapter will contrast Weber's intent and strategy with those in the recent literature. I shall first comment on the difference between his studies in the sociology of religion and the current search for functional equivalents. Section 2 will contrast the developmental approach of Almond and Powell to comparative politics with Weber's typological approach.[2] Section 3 will sketch the model character of Weber's types in relation to his long-range historical explanations. (The adaptation of his political typologies to developed and underdeveloped countries will be the theme of chapter VIII.)

---

[1] No survey of the literature is attempted here. Representative of the first line of inquiry is Robert N. Bellah's work; for an overview see his "Reflections on the Protestant Ethic Analogy in Asia," *Journal of Social Issues*, XIX: 1, Jan. 1963, 52–60, reprinted in S. N. Eisenstadt, ed., *The Protestant Ethic and Modernization* (New York: Basic Books, 1968), 243–251. Representative of the inquiries into legitimation and authority is David Apter's work, especially *Ghana in Transition* (New York: Atheneum, 1966); for his own reassessment, see "Nkrumah, Charisma, and the Coup," *Daedalus*, 97: 3, Summer 1968, 757–792. The neo-evolutionary approach has been most prominently espoused in Talcott Parsons, *Societies. Evolutionary and Comparative Perspectives* (Englewood Cliffs: Prentice-Hall, 1966).

[2] Gabriel Almond and Bingham Powell, Jr., *Comparative Politics: A Developmental Approach* (Boston: Little, Brown, 1966).

WEBER IN THE DEVELOPMENT LITERATURE

Weber's studies on the world religions endeavored to explain the rise of Western rationalism. But what was a specific historical question for him has since become a general issue of "development" and "modernization." The analytical focus has shifted from a unique course of events to the conditions under which cultural borrowing, combined with indigenous mobilization, can lead to similar results. This shift has often involved a reinterpretation, sometimes subtle and sometimes blatant, of Weber's purposes.

A subtle example is Neil Smelser's remark that "one of Weber's enduring preoccupations was with the conditions under which industrial capitalism of the modern Western type would arise and flourish. . . . The 'Weber thesis' has stimulated much analysis of the economic implications of religious systems other than those Weber himself studied. Other analysts have argued that secular beliefs, especially nationalism, exert an even more direct force on economic development." [3] Strictly speaking, however, Weber attempted to explain the *absence* of these conditions outside of Western Europe and the United States. His purpose was not the positive identification of optimal conditions for industrialization. And in his work on India he referred to the modern nationalist intelligentsia only to indicate that it did not belong in the historical context of his research.[4] Weber did not address himself to the issue of industrializing and modernizing underdeveloped countries. In his time Japan had already demonstrated that an Asian country could copy Western institutions and technology. He did not doubt that other countries would follow suit, although he recognized the much greater obstacles in India. But his study of Hinduism and Buddhism dealt with the purely historical question of the absence of the "spirit of capitalism." Only in passing did he touch on the modern development problem:

Obviously it was unthinkable that a community dominated by such

[3] Neil J. Smelser, *The Sociology of Economic Life* (Englewood Cliffs: Prentice-Hall, 1963), 15, 41.

[4] Weber, *Hinduismus und Buddhismus,* vol. II of *Gesammelte Aufsätze zur Religionssoziologie* (Tübingen: Mohr, 1920), 362f.; cf. Hans H. Gerth and Don Martindale, eds. and trans., *The Religion of India* (New York: Free Press, 1958), 328.

spiritual forces could have created on its own what we call here the "spirit of capitalism." Even the reception, in the Japanese manner, of the economically and technically ready-made artifact has here met, understandably enough, with very serious, and apparently greater, difficulties, in spite of the English domination. Today the penetration of Indian society by capitalist interests is so thorough that it can probably not be eradicated, but only a few decades ago very knowledgeable Englishmen could remain convinced that . . . the old feudal robber romanticism of the Indian Middle Ages would erupt again with undiminished force if the thin stratum of European masters and the **Pax Britannica** enforced by it should disappear.[5]

There is, then, a considerable hiatus between Weber's studies in the sociology of religion and the bulk of the development literature. The fact is that they deal with bygone days, not with present and future development. Still, the historical content of these writings is far from irrelevant to the new concerns, since each country labors under persistent age-old legacies. It appears to me that the hiatus is less significant in the case of *Economy and Society*. True, it too deals with the events of many centuries, but its historically saturated typologies may be more readily adaptable to the study of present-day development than the "mental experiments" in the sociology of religion. These experiments were the last, if very precarious, step in a long series of comparisons in which similarities were identified for the sake of narrowing down crucial differences.

Without claiming any misplaced "scientific" precision, Weber tried to hold political, social, and economic factors relatively constant on a world-historical scale in order to suggest explanations for the differential impact of the ethical prescriptions of the world religions. His familiar conclusion was that, within a long chain of historical causation involving many nonreligious phenomena, only Puritanism had the effect of furthering economic capitalism (in contrast to political capitalism) . Yet the sweep of these mental experiments was so vast that the "results" (as Weber called them) were not meant to be more than rough hypotheses. In fact, Weber advanced a very modest claim for the essays in the sociology of religion: "They are perhaps useful, in some way, for supplementing the formulation of questions in the sociology of religion and here and there probably also in economic sociology." [6] That may have

---

[5] Weber, *op. cit.*, 359; for a different wording see *The Religion of India, op. cit.*, 325.

[6] Introduction, *Gesammelte Aufsätze zur Religionssoziologie, op. cit.*, I, 237. Weber took up the first of these studies—on Confucianism and Taoism—in

been a deliberate understatement. As a self-confident scholar, he believed that he had divined tenable answers and taken some steps toward their empirical support. But the "results" were indeed not sufficient in guiding new research in various fields. Feasible answers —as will be shown in section 3—remained dependent on the typologies employed prior to the historical theses.

Since the "results" of the essays concerned religious beliefs, much of the subsequent functionalist literature could easily integrate them into its own theoretical framework, in which values appear crucial. The essays on China and India, however, also drew on the typologies of organization and domination in *Economy and Society,* in which the social structural level predominates.[7] When Weber prepared the first volume of his collected essays on the sociology of religion in 1919–20—the only one readied before his death—he reminded the reader that "only a systematic presentation could demonstrate how far the [typological] distinctions and terminology chosen here are expedient." [8] Since the systematic exposi-

---

1913, without having finished *Economy and Society,* especially the chapters on religion and charisma. When he first published the studies in 1915, he called them merely "Sketches in the Sociology of Religion," later—in 1920—"Essays *(Versuche)* in the Comparative Sociology of Religion."

[7] In fact, Weber dealt with the level both of values and of organization as early as his two works on the Protestant ethic (1904) and the Protestant sects (1906). Stephen Berger has recently pointed out that "if people understood the relationship between the Protestant sect essay and the Protestant Ethic thesis, they would be more sensitive to questions like: What kinds of groups become autonomous and separate in a given society and what makes this possible? They would also be somewhat more suspicious about the possibilities of using premodern values and social structures to generate modern ones. But they have not been so suspicious in the past, and their attempts to find analogies to the Protestant Ethic have been largely searches for similarities in values, not in social structures. Hence my plea to become more sophisticated users of Max Weber's ideas." See Stephen D. Berger, "The Sects and the Breakthrough into the Modern World," paper presented at the April 1970 meetings of the Midwest Sociological Society (mimeographed), 8.

[8] H. Gerth and C. W. Mills, eds. and trans., *From Max Weber* (New York: Oxford, 1946), 299. In an untranslated explanatory note on the essays in the sociology of religion Weber pointed to their close connection with *Economy and Society:* "The essays were intended . . . to be published together with the treatise on *Economy and Society* . . . and to interpret and supplement the section on the sociology of religion (but also to be interpreted by it in many ways). Even in their present state they can probably serve this purpose, albeit in a more incomplete manner. Whatever the present essays lack because of their sketchiness and unevenness, the work of other men will certainly accomplish much better than I could do it here. Even if the essays had been finished, they

tion is contained in *Economy and Society*—then unpublished—the typologies and generalizations will be explored on the basis of the earlier opus (1909–13).

THE DEVELOPMENTAL VERSUS THE TYPOLOGICAL APPROACH

Weber's typologies constitute the basic instruments of his comparative approach, which gradually emerged from his critique of organicist and evolutionary theories.[9] By contrast, the current development literature is largely functionalist and/or neo-evolutionary. From Parsons and Eisenstadt to Almond and Powell, systems analysis and evolutionary schemes, usually as three-stage patterns, have become prominent again.[10] Their approach differs in some respects from Weber's targets. Cybernetic analogies have replaced organicist ones, and the new evolutionism no longer postulates a unilinear development or inevitable stages for each society. However, from Weber's perspective significant similarities are left. It is true that Weber too was interested in "developmental forms" (*Entwicklungsformen*), but he meant not general patterns of development but the more complex historical forms of political, economic, and religious organization. Since he was concerned with the unique course of Western rationalization, he did not view it as a generic phenomenon, and in line with his critique of organicist and functionalist conceptions he did not equate the "developmental forms" with "whole" or "total" societies. Of course, he perceived a "general development of culture" (*allgemeine Kulturentwicklung*) from lower to more complex forms of rationalization, but he considered such "progress" subject neither to scientific laws nor to objective evaluation.[11]

The difference between the present-day evolutionary approach and Weber's typological one can be illustrated with reference to the work of Almond and Powell, which is singled out here because

---

could never have claimed 'definiteness,' since the author had to rely on translated sources." *Gesammelte Aufsätze, op. cit.,* I, 237.

[9] See ch. XIII below.

[10] A three-stage scheme is found in Parsons, *op. cit.,* Almond and Powell, *op. cit.,* and S. N. Eisenstadt, *The Political Systems of Empires* (New York: Free Press, 1963).

[11] My treatment here and in ch. XIII contrasts with Talcott Parsons' attempt to recognize in Weber a "basically evolutionary" approach. See his introduction to Weber, *The Sociology of Religion,* Ephraim Fischoff, trans. (Boston: Beacon, 1963), xxvii.

of its very attempt to utilize Weber's typologies. Before bringing out the differences, I shall sketch some similarities, showing the limited parallels between the functionalist terminology and Weber's.

Terminological Equivalents. One of the standard misconceptions about Weber's work is that it provides the basic categories of social action but nothing comparable to larger systems analysis. In view of the methodological situation of his time, Weber insisted that *interpretive* sociology must start with the individual, not the group ("system"). Perhaps because of this emphasis, the fundamental categories of social action in the famed first chapter of *Economy and Society* (written as late as 1918–20) have been remembered more clearly than those of the social group (*Gemeinschaft*). Thus, the kinds of action orientation, but also the concepts of conflict, power and domination are more familiar than aspects of organization ("system properties"), such as openness and closure, monopolist and expansionist tendencies, representation and joint responsibility, consensual and imposed order, or administrative and regulative order. In fact, the first chapter is just as much a contribution to "group functioning" as to the analysis of individual action—except that Weber insisted on the individual as the ultimate referent. Weber's conception of the social group, then, is as free of time and space as is the functionalist "system." Both must be universally applicable.

Weber supplemented his categories of social action and organization with the "adaptation" dimension of economic action and organization—the modes of want satisfaction. Subsequently he appended a broad historical distinction between production for the direct satisfaction of one's own needs and production for the market. Contrary to the evolutionary schemes of economic historians, he considered this distinction applicable in varying degrees throughout history.

Almond and Powell "agree with Max Weber that legitimate force is the thread that runs through the action of the political system, giving it its special quality and importance, and its coherence as a system."[12] They acknowledge the existence of systems theory in the older literature—for instance, the *Federalist Papers*—but claim that their "concept of 'system' is more explicit." They believe that the older terminology of political science directed too much atten-

---

[12] Almond and Powell, *op. cit.,* 17f.

tion to the formal governmental institutions, and therefore propose a historically "neutral" terminology. Weber, however, avoided the term "system" because in his days it still reflected its older philosophical meaning as well as the organicist analogy. His terminological equivalent for "political system" is "political organization" (*Verband*), but his concept of "political community" is already a historical notion. Moreover, he retained well-established political, economic, theological, and legal terms because of his concrete historical interests; he wanted to understand the corresponding institutions. Yet he added a sociological dimension. Thus, he meant by "constitution," following Ferdinand Lassalle, the actual operating condition of a political system, which according to Almond and Powell, "includes not only governmental institutions" but also parties, interest groups, and media of communication. However, he did not go so far as to include "all structures in their political aspects,"[13] although he spoke of the political *functions* of relatively universal groups, such as kinship units, at a time in early history when the political community was not yet a group of *sui generis*.

Conceptual Differences. The systems approach is in itself insufficient for historical analysis because of its level of abstraction. Here lies the well-known difficulty of filling "empty boxes": the matrix fits every case irrespective of its historical context, whereas the historical dynamics remain elusive. The functionalist approach has often been accused of being "static" and incapable of explaining basic changes. However, on the basis of what Weber called "rules of experience," functionalist analysis does assume systemic strains preventing long-range stability and equilibrium. Yet the basic issue is the explanation of major historical changes. In order to cope with history, functionalist systems analysis has increasingly turned to an evolutionary perspective. Historically more complex forms appear as necessary products of responses to systemic strains; structures become more differentiated and values and standards more generalized. Thus, historical development "makes sense" in general, although the specific reasons for major historical changes remain elusive. Weber, however, did not see much sense in explanations based on the principle of differentiation, for instance; instead he was concerned with the "actual" reasons for specific historical changes.

In turning to historical development, Almond and Powell present a three-stage evolutionary scheme: I. Primitive systems with

---

[13] The last three quotations are from *ibid.*, 12 and 18.

intermittent political structures; II. Traditional systems with differentiated governmental-political structures; III. Modern systems with differentiated political infrastructures. Structural differentiation (especially "subsystem autonomy") and secularization appear as the two major continuous variables. The three kinds of systems differ in their capabilities, an aspect to which Almond and Powell give particular attention because "the analysis of capabilities . . . enables us to classify and compare political systems more effectively."[14] But it appears to me that the comparison of capabilities suffers from the evolutionary scheme. The authors point out that "although historical appearance was not itself a basis of classification, it is no accident that most systems in Classes I and II are historical systems, and that Class III is largely composed of modern and modernizing systems." Here an optical problem arises that can easily create a tautology, depending on whether systems are dead or alive. In a secular perspective it may be feasible to say that "the capability of intermittent systems to deal with complex problems, including expansion of neighbors, is very limited."[15] But if it is true that with increasing internal and environmental complexity a political system's tasks also grow by leaps and bounds, the generalization appears doubtful that "in capability terms, [political systems] with high subsystem autonomy have relatively versatile and continuous capacity (i.e., they have the capability both of adapting to their environments and of shaping them), while those characterized by limited subsystem autonomy tend to have a fluctuating pattern of capability."[16] Thus, the difference between "differentiated governmental-political structures" (Class II) and "differentiated political infrastructures" (Class III) becomes precarious, and with it the dichotomy of "traditional" and "modern" (the other two labels for II and III). Finally, the charge of ideological bias is invited if the comparison of totalitarian and democratic systems comes to the conclusion that "the profile of capability of the most developed democracies is more versatile and adaptive." [17] Certainly this depends on the intensity of internal pressures and external challenges, and here it may be preferable to suggest with Weber that the capacity of most organizations to deal with their gravest problems is notoriously poor. For instance, Weber considered the bu-

[14] *Ibid.*, 192.
[15] *Ibid.*, 217f.
[16] *Ibid.*, 310.
[17] *Ibid.*, 313.

reaucracy of Imperial Germany technically superior to all others, but he did not at all trust its ability to cope with the most urgent national and international issues.

After conceptualizing the properties of the political system and following it up with a historical typology, Almond and Powell take a third step, like Weber, and elaborate a substantive theory of modern democratization, on the one hand, and of persistent authoritarianism on the other. Here the issue of prediction is most acute. Almond and Powell are correct in stating that the very act of comparison and classification facilitates structural predictions, but a chasm remains between predicting, on the one hand, structural features and trends, and, on the other, specific historical events. The authors predict "that higher capabilities depend upon the emergence of 'rational' bureaucratic organizations" and here refer to "Weber's hypothesis about the increasing 'rationalization' or 'bureaucratization' of modern society." [18] Weber, however, was concerned not with structural predictions of development toward higher forms, but with certain facts of Western history. Bureaucratization was a fact. Predictions could only identify alternative historical possibilities. His hypothesis was that unless certain trends toward state intervention were reversed, a new era of "Egyptianization" was likely. This was already an explicit value position, on which he took his political stand.

In conclusion, I shall summarize some of the analytical consequences of the two approaches. The evolutionary approach focuses on long-range changes and basic transformations by depicting the evolution from primitive and traditional systems to contemporary ones. Almond and Powell's basic purpose is to provide a framework for studying contemporary developed and underdeveloped countries. However, their evolutionary perspective is not well suited for studies that cover only the span of one to three generations and concern the short-run capabilities of a political community—and this includes most of the research. Paradoxically, Almond and Powell's developmental scheme is too sweepingly historical. Contemporary development theory needs a typology demarcating the range of alternatives potentially open to new and old states. What is needed is a detailed, descriptively rich typology, which has historical depth as well as contemporary applicability. This need may be satisfied, in part, by the Weberian typology, which encompasses

[18] *Ibid.,* 323f.

three thousand years in a relatively "static" fashion—if compared to the evolutionary scheme.[19] The typology elaborates the varieties of rulership in a nonevolutionary fashion, emphasizing instead logical adequacy and historical utility. It facilitates the analysis of the historical combinations and mixtures, since each historical case can be treated in terms of its own dynamics and potentialities. De-emphasizing the evolutionary dimension and relativizing the progression from the traditional to the modern can make it easier for the researcher to work with all categories on a given case.

HISTORICAL MODELS AND SECULAR THEORIES

In contrast to the analysis of systems and of long-range differentiation in functionalist and evolutionary terms, Weber addressed himself to some of the big historical issues and to the construction of historical types, which are a logical prerequisite for their elucidation. His strategy was to elaborate historical summaries of similar cases, which will here be called "historical models," in order to suggest specific historical explanations, here called "secular theories." I want to speak of Weber's ideal types as "historical models" to make the point that they involve historical dynamics and are not just static descriptions of structural properties. In his first exposition of the ideal type in 1904, Weber did not deal explicitly with its model character; rather, he took it for granted, as is demonstrated by the fact that the "laws" and developmental constructs of academic and Marxian economic theory appeared to him as outstanding examples of the ideal type.[20] At that time Weber was polemically concerned with the difference between scientific laws proper and ideal types,

[19] Fairly recently substantive theories of development patterned closely after Western precedents have been abandoned as inadequate for the study of the new states with their various forms of authoritarian rulership. Increasingly there is disagreement about what constitutes more or less "development," excepting some measures of economic advance. Almond and Powell make the somber point that instead of proffering contemporary models of pluralism and the welfare state to the leaders and students in the new states "they would have been better prepared for the tasks which confront them had they been exposed to a political theory and history which stressed the long and costly struggle in Europe over the development of the state and of the nation" (op. cit., 327). Weber's comparative study of political organizations throughout the ages can still serve this cautionary purpose.

[20] Cf. Weber, "Objectivity in Social Science and Social Policy," in Edward Shils and Henry Finch, eds. and trans., The Methodology of the Social Sciences (New York: Free Press, 1949), 90f., 103.

arguing that only the latter could reveal the cultural significance of a phenomenon.

Historical models specify how empirically similar, typologically identical cases function under certain conditions, such as absence or presence of a money economy, newly conquered territory, or outside military pressure. They spell out a range of variation, incorporating the tendencies toward greater stability as well as toward decline or transformation. Yet the models remain primarily tools for ex post facto analysis; in view of the limited number of cases they do not permit prediction or quantification and, in this sense, they are not "scientific." There are, after all, only five world religions, or six if Judaism is added—as Weber did because of its great significance for Western rationalism. There are only about half a dozen major examples in European history of the alliance of political and hierocratic powers. For certain features of a model there are sometimes only one or two illustrations, if not just some logical possibilities. Moreover, the transition to secular theories is fluid. Generally, a statement is part of a model if it refers to more than one historical case. The models are meant to facilitate the construction of secular theories, but they must in turn be built from historical explanations proper. Thus, the level of religious rationalization, a historical ("secular") theory, becomes part of the model of hierocracy and caesaropapism, as we shall see below.

The static and dynamic aspects of the models are fused in the major body of *Economy and Society* (Part Two), but this has been obscured by Weber's very attempt at simplification. When he found out that the discursive treatment of a large number of concepts within a massive body of historical data made reception and retention difficult for the reader, he resorted to an enumerative exposition (Part One) in catalogue form. The crystallizing effect of the categorization was so strong that it tempted the reader to overlook Weber's cautionary remarks and his cross references to the subsequent presentation of the workings of a given type of domination; he spoke of the "detailed description" *(Einzeldarstellung)* in contrast to the summary enumeration of the type cases *(Kasuistik)*.[21]

I shall briefly review bureaucracy, patrimonialism, and hierocracy

---

[21] This was a particular handicap for English readers, since Part One of *Economy and Society* appeared under a somewhat misleading title in 1947, whereas Part Two was not published in its entirety until two decades later. See Talcott Parsons, ed. and trans. (with A. M. Henderson), *The Theory of Social and Economic Organization* (New York: Oxford, 1947).

and caesaropapism to illustrate the nature of the models.[22] I am concerned with their formal side, but some descriptiveness is inevitable in view of the concrete historical content.

Modern Bureaucracy. Weber constructed a model by beginning with closely similar phenomena before moving along a declining line of comparability to other historical and contemporary cases. "Modern bureaucracy" was built largely from the French and German cases—historically and geographically proximate—and to a lesser extent from the older bureaucracy of the absolutist state. Since continuous bureaucratic administration presupposed a steady income from taxation or state-owned enterprises, the prevalence of a natural economy made the other "historical bureaucracies" inherently unstable and largely patrimonial—Egypt since the New Kingdom; the Roman principate, especially from the Diocletian monarchy to the Byzantine polity; China from Emperor Shih (third century B.C.); the Roman Catholic Church since the end of the thirteenth century.

Although modern bureaucracy has greater stability on purely technical grounds, its predominance is by no means inevitable. It is true—and has often been quoted—that Weber wrote: "Once *fully established,* bureaucracy is among those social structures which are hardest to destroy. . . . Where administration has been *completely bureaucratized,* the resulting form of domination is practically indestructible." [23] But this was a conditional proposition. In the same context Weber pointed out that the advance of bureaucracy may be slowed down or deflected if older administrative forms remain technically adequate to the tasks at hand, as was the case in England.

Moreover, the dynamics of bureaucracy are related to those of mass democracy: "Bureaucracy inevitably accompanies modern mass democracy." [24] There is typically a tension between the two forces, as there is between both and charismatic rulership. All of them may reinforce as well as conflict with one another. The democratic value of equality before the law is also a bureaucratic norm; the same is true of the preference for examinations as against selec-

[22] The following is a very condensed treatment. For a general exposition of Weber's Sociology of Domination, see my introduction to his *Economy and Society* (New York: Bedminster, 1968), lxxxii–xciv.

[23] *Ibid.,* 987. Emphasis throughout the quotations from Weber is mine.

[24] *Ibid.,* 983.

tion on the basis of ascriptive status. Bureaucrats and democrats alike fight the notables or the nobility, but bureaucrats will resist the development of direct democracy. Both uphold the right to office and tenure as a protection against arbitrary intervention from above. However, the right to office tends to weaken not only the ruler's arbitrariness but also to create a new status group inimical to democratic tendencies. In turn, if the democratic demand for equality changes into a demand for substantive or material justice (equity), it becomes as detrimental to rational (bureaucratic) justice as the star chamber of an absolutist ruler; both forms of justice make an arbitrary will—the people's or the ruler's—the ultimate yardstick. Because of the play of these diverse forces, Weber concluded that "it must remain an open question whether the power of bureaucracy is increasing in the modern states in which it is spreading. . . . Hence, one must *in every historical case* analyze in which particular direction bureaucratization has developed." [25] Thus, Weber first constructed a model of bureaucracy and of the potential directions of bureaucratization. The explanation of the course of bureaucratization in a given country and during a given period was the subsequent task of secular theory.

The American organization literature has not taken sufficient note of the fact that Weber's enumeration of the formal characteristics of modern bureaucracy is part of a historical model of bureaucracy and mass democracy. Instead, a truncated type has frequently been employed as a blueprint to be compared with the "natural system" or the "informal structure" of private and public organizations. Ironically, the famed, if not fabled, "classic Weberian type," comprising mainly the first few pages of the chapter on bureaucracy, is the least original of Weber's contributions, because the formal characteristics were part and parcel of the academic teaching of public administration in his time. Weber did not deal systematically with the distinction between formal and informal structure, because he was not interested in a general theory of organization. Instead, he was concerned, on the one hand, with the formal aspects of modern bureaucracy in relation to other historical forms of organization, and on the other with the politics of bureaucrats and other officeholders. His systematic focus, then, was on the power struggle between ruler, staff, and subjects. Bureaucracies develop their own vested interests. Whereas modern bureaucracy is technically superior to older forms of administration, a given bureau-

[25] *Ibid.,* 991.

cracy can obstruct, in its own self-interest, the intentions of the ruler as well as the subjects.

Patrimonialism. Weber built the dynamics of patrimonialism, a traditionalist form of domination, right into his definitions. Patrimonialism was *"domestic* authority *decentralized* through assignment of land and sometimes equipment." [26] Because the traditionalist obedience of the patriarchal household remained the pattern of patrimonial legitimacy, decentralization of such personalized relationships was likely to weaken the ruler's grip unless it could be buttressed by other means. The conflict potential was even stronger under *political* patrimonialism, Weber's primary concern. In the patrimonial state "the prince organizes his political power over extrapatrimonial areas and political subjects just like the exercise of his patriarchal power"—if he is strong enough.[27] The range of conflict is circumscribed in these terms:

(1) The benefice is a universal phenomenon under patrimonialism;
(2) There is an inherent tendency on the part of the benefice holders and their heirs to appropriate the benefices;
(3) If the ruler can maximize his power, he will usurp contempt powers and turn political subjects into patrimonial dependents;
(4) There is a continuous struggle between the ruler and the local notables.

The outcome of this struggle obviously turns on the distribution of power, which again depends partly on the technical nature of the administration, partly on economic development. Therefore, Weber goes to great length to identify the military and civilian modes of administration, on the one hand, and the relationship of trading and capitalist operations to the political struggle, on the other. In each case he endeavors to draw up a ledger sheet of the advantages and disadvantages from the viewpoint of ruler and staff, an implicitly functionalist procedure. Although the individual ruler could rise and fall rapidly, patrimonialism tended toward a political stalemate, which might last for generations. Here ends the historical model. Weber moves on to the secular level when he

[26] *Ibid.,* 1011.
[27] *Ibid.,* 1013.

shows how the patrimonial stalemate was broken in two ways: In the Orient military conquerors periodically upset the pattern of appropriation and typification in their favor; in the Occident the expanding money economy at first facilitated the appropriation and commercialization of benefices, but in the end permitted the absolutist ruler to reorganize his administration along bureaucratic lines. This resulted in such a different kind of organization that another model had to be applied: modern bureaucracy.

Hierocracy and Caesaropapism. Just as Weber linked the dynamics of bureaucracy and mass democracy, so did he encompass hierocracy and caesaropapism in one historical model. Hierocracy, which in its bureaucratic form is called a church, means the political dominance of priests; in turn, caesaropapism denotes the secular ruler's control over the priesthood. These contrasting types were important both with regard to legitimation and administration. Weber showed the range within which religious and political forces would clash or cooperate with one another. The primeval antagonism between political and magical charisma was reinforced in time by organizational and power interests. Since it was very rare for either side to gain a full victory, the patterns of antagonistic cooperation were more important than the extreme ("pure") forms. Each side had something to offer to the other. For political rulers, hierocracy served two "functions": it provided legitimation for rulers who had some personal or institutionalized charisma but needed further legitimation, a frequent historical case; and it was the "incomparable means of domesticating the subjects in things great and little" and was thus particularly suitable to conquerors.[28] For hierocracy, the political ruler was useful because he could suppress opponents and annihilate heretics, and he could extract taxation in its favor.

The power balance depended on several conditions. (1) The constellation of status groups. This involved an indirect economic codeterminant. The petty bourgeoisie was the typical ally of hierocracy; the secular nobility was its typical opponent. (2) The state of religious rationalization. The political ruler tended to gain the upper hand as long as priestly charisma was of a personal magical nature. Quite similarly to his phrasing of the invincibility of bureaucracy, Weber stated that "a *fully developed* ecclesiastic hierarchy, with an established body of dogmas and particularly well-organized educational system, cannot be uprooted at all."[29] (This

---

[28] *Ibid.*, 1176.
[29] *Ibid.*, 1175.

has proved true of the Catholic Church until now.) (3) The specific character of the religion. Only the Catholic Church and Calvinism had a notion of a divinely ordained ecclesia, in contrast to Lutheranism, the Eastern Church, and Buddhism. (4) The importance of military force. If the religion was established by force, the secular ruler tended to retain control over the priests; witness the caliphs.

After listing the conditions, Weber turned to the consequences. Caesaropapist regimes encouraged stereotyped forms of religion and ritualist manipulations of supernatural powers. Hierocracy had more consequences: regulation of conduct by way of unlimited ethical claims; institutionalization of magic; control over secular education; promotion of transcendental speculation; defense of the "weak"; opposition to innovation, including new social groups. These consequences obtained in spite of the diverse origins of the religions. Among the economic consequences of hierocracy were land accumulation, usually resisted by the secular nobility, competition with bourgeois trading and craft interests, and opposition to inherently nonethical capitalism. However, the policies of a hierocracy had a greater impact than its own economic operations.

After spelling out the consequences of hierocracy in general, Weber turned to the secular theory of Western hierocracy. He considered it impossible to reduce the parallel development of urban trades and religious rationalization to an "unambiguous relation of cause and effect: Religious rationalization has its own dynamics, which economic conditions merely channel; above all, it is linked to the emergence of priestly education." [30] The main channel was the urban setting, but rationalization was also very much affected by hierocracy's gravest problem: the irrepressible conflict between institutional and personal charisma, the clergy and the monks. Therefore, Weber turned his attention to the monastic movements, which required a typology of their own.

Monasticism was charismatic, anti-rational, and anti-economic, but this very fact made for great rational achievements. The double nature of monasticism meant that it could be either an adversary or an ally of hierocracy and caesaropapism. For the latter it reinforced the uses of hierocracy, legitimation, and domestication; in addition, it provided the cheapest kind of clerical and teaching personnel. Most importantly, it could be used as an instrument of patrimonial or bureaucratic rationalization against the nobility. But this cheap methodical work force had a high price; in matters religious, monks were more intransigent than regular clergy, and

[30] *Ibid.*, 1179.

once monasticism gained strength it was bound to clash sooner or later with caesaropapist claims. For hierocracy the uses of monasticism were "far more problematical" in view of the ineradicable tension between institutional and personal charisma.[31] However, there were several advantages; monks served as the troops of the monocratic head of the church, they helped control the urban masses through missionary activities, and in a natural economy they provided, through their communal living, the only defense against feudalization.

Weber envisaged three overlapping uses for his models: comparisons of models with one another, leading to "clear concepts"; comparisons of one model or submodel with cases within its range; comparisons of batteries of models with a given case. The latter two uses led to the construction of secular theories.

Weber made the first kind of comparison hundreds of times, until he had almost exhausted the similarities and differences. For instance, bureaucracy and patrimonialism contrasted sharply with regard to legitimacy and rational division of labor, but both were relatively normative, stable, and routine forms of administration; their armies were centrally supplied and functioned best under a money economy, thus contrasting with popular levies and militias. Weber dealt with similarities between two models in order to call attention to structural correspondence, to bring out the contrast to still another model, or to point to gradual long-range transitions. Example: "In the course of financial rationalization, patrimonialism moves *imperceptibly* toward a rational bureaucratic administration, which resorts to systematic taxation." [32] In this instance, the model shades off into secular theory.

The second application is the blueprint method. A model is compared with a case ("natural system"), occasionally a hypothetical one. The model serves as a set of benchmarks: "By the terminology suggested here, we do not wish to force schematically the infinite and multifarious historical life, but simply to create, for specific purposes, *useful concepts of orientation*." [33] With the help of refinements (subtypes) Weber fixed the typological location of a case as well as its historical drift. Thus, in England domination by the justices of the peace was "a combination of patrimonialism of the estate type with a pure type of autonomous administration by not-

---

[31] *Ibid.*, 1171.
[32] *Ibid.*, 1014.
[33] *From Max Weber, op. cit.*, 300; translation slightly changed.

ables, and it tended much more to the latter than toward the former." [34] Such specifications prepared the secular theory of English history, which explicated its leading role in industrialization and democratization. Weber's great interest in the rise of industrial capitalism accounts for the ubiquity of the English case in the various models. China was a negative test case. Here Weber applied the model of bureaucracy in order to establish both formal fit and functional difference. "From a formal viewpoint [the qualifying examinations and official certificates of conduct] constitute the most radical application of bureaucratic objectivity possible and therefore an equally radical break with typical patrimonial officeholding." This statement on the model level is then followed by historical explanation proper: "Nevertheless, Chinese officialdom did not develop into modern bureaucracy, for the functional differentiation of spheres of jurisdiction was carried through only to a very limited extent in view of the country's huge size. . . . The specifically modern concept of the functional association and of specialized officialdom, a concept which was so important in the course of the gradual modernization of the English administration, would have run counter to everything characteristically Chinese and to all the status trends of Chinese officialdom." [35]

The third, the battery approach, is an extension of the simple blueprint method and facilitates case studies proper. After working out the three models of domination as well as the mixed forms of hierocracy, caesaropapism, and urban polity, Weber applied them to his study of Confucianism and Taoism. This explains why this first study on the "economic ethics of the world religions" reads at the outset like a continuation of the Sociology of Domination in *Economy and Society,* for it begins not with religion but the Chinese city, patrimonial administration, the emperor's charisma, and the country's economic features. The application of models to a given case makes it necessary to devise compound constructs: "We shall be compelled again and again to form expressions like 'patrimonial bureaucracy' in order to make the point that the characteristic traits of the respective phenomenon belong in part to the rational form of domination, whereas other traits belong to a traditionalist form of domination, in this case to that of status groups." [36]

In principle, most models are applicable to tribes no less than

[34] *Economy and Society, op. cit.,* 1063.
[35] *Ibid.,* 1048f.
[36] *From Max Weber, loc. cit.*

modern states. Caesaropapism and hierocracy, for instance, apply backward and forward from their type cases, the Byzantine and Carolingian empires. The Holy Roman Empire was the "exemplary case" [37] for the rivalry between political and religious power. Weber began the construction of these models with familiar medieval examples and ultimately came back to the uniqueness of Europe in the secular theories, which take up the larger part of his analysis. Sometimes he speedily shifted back and forth between model and secular theory. Since his time, some of his contemporary cases have become merely illustrations of a model. But regardless of whether the Second Vatican Council, for instance, has attenuated the doctrine *extra ecclesiam nulla salus,* Weber would hold that the phrase remains valid as "the motto of all churches." [38]

Weber was extremely insistent on the limits of his generalizations. On issues such as the economic codeterminants of religious phenomena "no meaningful generalization can be made." Time and again he pointed to historical imponderables: "Fateful events play a tremendous role." [39] Either Pope or Emperor could have triumphed over the other, with incalculable consequences for European culture, if certain historical "accidents" had not happened. Likewise, if the Irish monks had prevailed, the Church could have become monastic rather than bureaucratic. Instead the monks' integration into the bureaucratic Church became a major step toward modern rationalism. Weber concluded that the uniqueness of Occidental culture resulted, among other reasons, from the tension and balance between office charisma and monasticism, on the one hand, and between the contractual feudal state and the autonomous bureaucratic hierocracy, on the other.[40] Thus although historical accidents and the plurality of historical factors make it impossible to predict the actual course of events, the construction of types (or models) is necessary, for the historical conclusions are couched in typological language. This is the ultimate methodological rationale of their indispensability.

[37] *Economy and Society, op. cit.,* 1159.
[38] *Ibid.,* 1167.
[39] *Ibid.,* 1174, 1176.
[40] Cf. *ibid.,* 1192.

VII

BUREAUCRACY

The term "bureaucracy" is of recent origin. Initially referring to a cloth covering the desks of French government officials in the eighteenth century, the term "bureau" came to be linked with a suffix signifying rule of government (as in "aristocracy" or "democracy"), probably during the struggles against absolutism preceding the French Revolution. During the nineteenth century, the pejorative use of the term spread to many European countries, where liberal critics of absolutist regimes typically employed it to decry the tortuous procedures, narrow outlook, and highhanded manner of autocratic government officials.[1] Since then this pejorative meaning has become general in the sense that any critic of complicated organizations that fail to allocate responsibility clearly, or any critic of rigid rules and routines that are applied with little consideration of the specific case, of blundering officials, of slow operation and buck-passing, of conflicting directives and duplication of effort, of empire-building, and of concentration of control in the hands of a few will use this term regardless of party or political persuasion.[2] During the years following the Second World War this common stereotype was given a new twist by the witty, mock-scientific formulations of Parkinson's Law, which derided empire-building, waste of resources, and inertia by implying that official staffs expand in inverse proportion to the work to be done.[3]

This popular, pejorative usage must be distinguished from "bu-

[1] Karl Heinzen, *Die preussische Büreaukratie* (Darmstadt: Leske, 1845).
[2] Goodwin Watson, "Bureaucracy as Citizens See It," *Journal of Social Issues* 1, 1945, 4–13.
[3] C. Northcote Parkinson, *Parkinson's Law, and Other Studies in Administration* (Boston: Houghton, Mifflin, 1957).

Reinhard Bendix, from *International Encyclopedia of the Social Sciences* (New York: Macmillan and Free Press, 1968), II, 206–219.

reaucracy" used in a technical sense. Although the distinction is beset with difficulties, social scientists have employed the term because it points to the special, modern variant of age-old problems of administration, just as terms like "ideology" and "class" point to modern aspects of intellectual life and social stratification. The analytic task is to conceptualize this modern variant. At the macroscopic level, Max Weber's definition of bureaucracy under the rule of law provides the best available solution to this problem; none of the critics of Weber's analysis has as yet dispensed with his definition. According to Weber, a bureaucracy establishes a relation between legally instated authorities and their subordinate officials which is characterized by defined rights and duties, prescribed in written regulations; authority relations between positions, which are ordered systematically; appointment and promotion based on contractual agreements and regulated accordingly; technical training or experience as a formal condition of employment; fixed monetary salaries; a strict separation of office and incumbent in the sense that the official does not own the "means of administration" and cannot appropriate the position; and administrative work as a full-time occupation.[4]

A government administration so defined must be understood, according to Weber, as part of a legal order that is sustained by a common belief in its legitimacy. That order is reflected in written regulations, such as enacted laws, administrative rules, court precedents, etc., which govern the employment of officials and guide their administrative behavior. Such authoritative ordering of the bureacracy is never more than a proximate achievement; written regulations are often "out of step" with the conditions to which they refer, while codifications and legal and administrative reforms, although designed to cope with that problem, are subject to interpretation. The legal order remains intact as long as such difficulties are resolved through further elaboration of existing regulations and, in relation to the bureaucracy, as long as administrative behavior is oriented toward a system of regulations. In sum, these ideal types of administration and the rule of law are the more fully realized "the more completely [they] succeed in eliminating from official business love, hatred, and all purely personal, irrational, and emotional elements." [5]

[4] Max Weber, *Economy and Society*, G. Roth and C. Wittich, eds. and trans. (New York: Bedminster, 1968), 956ff.; Reinhard Bendix, *Max Weber: An Intellectual Portrait* (Garden City: Doubleday, 1960) 423ff.

[5] Weber, *op. cit.*, 975.

A word is needed concerning the difficulties of these formulations. Weber himself always emphasized that an ideal type simplifies and exaggerates the empirical evidence in the interest of conceptual clarity. No actual government administration is bureaucratic in the strict sense of his definition; this follows from the simplifications needed to arrive at an ideal type. Concrete instances will, therefore, lack one or several of the constituent elements or possess them in varying degrees. Thus Weber speaks of mixed types like "patrimonial bureaucracy" when referring to specific examples. This approach involves methodological problems still under discussion.[6] However, for present purposes it is sufficient to distinguish among and to discuss three possible uses of Weber's definition: as a historical bench mark (modern bureaucracy); as a syndrome of social change (bureaucratization); and as a specification of the problems of bureaucracy in the modern nation-state.

The modern type of bureaucracy. Structures approximating Weber's definition of bureaucracy have existed from time to time in different parts of the world. The historical bureaucratic empires such as ancient Egypt and Rome, and ancient and medieval China, exemplify this point. China, for example, witnessed a close approximation to bureaucracy in the sense that appointment to office depended upon qualifications tested by examination, and authority relations were ordered systematically. On the other hand, Chinese officials qualified through humanistic learning rather than technical proficiency; in the absence of a legal order based on abstract, written norms, administrative performance was based ideally on considerations of equity; and administrative work was not a full-time occupation strictly separated from the official's personal and familial concerns—to mention at least three respects in which administration under the Chinese dynasties was nonbureaucratic or protobureaucratic.[7] In partial contrast with these approximations, Weber recognized a distinctive modern type of bureaucracy, and it is useful to follow him in this respect.

[6] Cf. Paul F. Lazarsfeld and Anthony R. Oberschall, "Max Weber and Empirical Social Research," *American Sociological Review,* 30, 1965, 185–199; Arthur Schweitzer, "Vom Idealtypus zum Prototyp." *Zeitschrift für die gesamte Staatswissenschaft,* 120, 1964, 13–55; Fritz Machlup, "Idealtypus, Wirklichkeit und Konstruktion," *Ordo,* 12, 1960–1961, 21–57; Don Martindale, "Sociological Theory and the Ideal Type," in Llewellyn Gross, ed., *Symposium on Sociological Theory* (Evanston: Row, Peterson, 1959), 57–91.

[7] Cf. Max Weber, *The Religion of China: Confucianism and Taoism* (Glencoe: Free Press, 1951), chs. 2–4.

The several attributes specified in his ideal type have been approximated most closely under the conditions of the modern state. A product of absolutist regimes in Europe since the Renaissance and distinct from the bureaucratic empires mentioned above, the modern state is characterized by a government over a contiguous territory, which is stabilized on the basis of written regulations and the centralized appropriation of all means of administration. Such stability and centrally controlled administration are possible only on the basis of financial resources and revenue administration that are the exclusive prerogative of the central government. Similarly, an army and a police force are at the exclusive disposal of the government. This central appropriation of resources and means of coercion is paralleled by the establishment of a country-wide jurisdiction, with regard both to the creation and application of legal rules and to the provision of public services considered to be in the general interest. It is in this sense that Weber defines the state as based on a monopoly of a physical coercion, which is made legitimate by a system of legal norms binding on rulers and ruled alike and which entails the ultimate subordination of all less inclusive associations under this central jurisdiction.[8] In the setting of the modern state, bureaucracy, as defined above, is the most characteristic form of government administration.

Both ideal types (of the state and of bureaucracy) may be considered historical bench marks designating over-all distinguishing attributes of an entire historical period. The meaning of these ideal types is most clear-cut when they are contrasted with their opposites. Political structures in preabsolutist Europe, for example, lacked a central government with such attributes of states as exclusive financial resources, administrative apparatus, military force, and territorial jurisdiction. Similarly, administration lacked dependence on written regulations, separation of office and incumbent, and several other attributes of bureaucracy.[9] Such distinctions are the results of comparative study and are useful at their general level, but they are also starting points for further analysis. For the attributes defining these ideal types are themselves the several by-products of

[8] Johannes Winckelmann, "Max Webers historische und soziologische Verwaltungsforschung," Fondazione Italiana per la Storia Amministrativa, *Annals*, 1, 1964, 27–67.

[9] Reinhard Bendix, *Nation-Building and Citizenship* (New York: Wiley, 1964).

changes which have culminated in the historical constellations that we call state or bureaucracy.[10]

BUREAUCRATIZATION OF GOVERNMENT

One area of comparative sociological analysis consists in examining the substitution of bureaucratic conditions of governmental administration for nonbureaucratic ones. The term "bureaucratization" serves to designate this pattern of social change, which can be traced to the royal households of medieval Europe, to the eventual employment of university-trained jurists as administrators, to the civilian transformation of military controllers on the Continent, and to the civil-service reforms in England and the United States in the nineteenth century. These several changes were related to other social trends, especially the development of the universities, a money economy, the legal system, and representative institutions; but the present discussion is confined to governmental administration.

Development of European bureaucracies. Bureaucratization may be traced to the royal or princely households of the early Middle Ages, which were composed in part of retainers who made up the military following of the ruler and also performed administrative functions in his service (the German word *Amt,* meaning "office," goes back to a Celtic term meaning "servant"). Rulers would appoint these retainer-officials to the several offices of the royal household, including those charged with organizing and superintending supplies, finances, clothing, horses, weapons, written communications and records, etc. For a time the royal household traveled from place to place, administering the affairs of the realm, dispensing justice, and collecting (and in part consuming) the revenue owed to the ruler.[11] However, eventually a separation occurred, in terms of personnel and location, between the offices of the royal household and the corresponding offices of government. In his classic work T. F. Tout has shown for England, and in a briefer essay Otto Hintze has shown for several western European countries, how the several functions of the royal household provided the starting points of a

[10] William Delany, "The Development and Decline of Patrimonial and Bureaucratic Administration," *Administrative Science Quarterly,* 7, 1963, 458–501.

[11] Hans K. Peyer, "Das Reisekönigtum des Mittelalters," *Vierteljahrshefte für Sozial- und Wirtschaftsgeschichte,* 51, 1964, 1–21.

development eventuating in the establishment of the several ministries of a modern government.[12] This change from personal to public service by officials involved a century-long development.

From an organizational standpoint, this development was partly a by-product of the size and complexity of government affairs. As the territory to be governed grew in size and the complexity of affairs increased, the households of kings and princes grew larger, since they provided lodging, food, and clothing for the officials of the ruler as well as for members of his family and his personal retainers and servants. Sooner or later the corps of officials became too large to be maintained in this manner, and officials came to live in households of their own and to be paid for their services in money rather than in kind. Several factors, both tangible and intangible, facilitated this change. Among the more tangible factors were improved means of transportation, the increased use of money, and the growth of the economy and, hence, of revenue; for the control of officials at a distance depends on the incentives available to the ruler and on the ease with which the officials can be reached. A more intangible factor was the sense of obligation or awe with which subordinate officials regarded those above them. That this partly patriarchal feature remained a part of government employment long after government through the ruler's household had disappeared is suggested by the fact that until the nineteenth century public officials in Prussia were still obliged to obtain permission to marry from their official superior, who would pass judgment on the social standing of the prospective bride.[13]

The development of modern public service has been less uniform in its political than in its organizational features. Service to a ruler in a capacity that combined household functions and official responsibilities soon resulted in honor and social standing for the incumbent, whether or not he originally possessed an aristocratic title. All royal officials came to constitute a lower nobility in contrast to a higher nobility, which was entitled to an autonomous exercise of authority on a hereditary basis. Yet the dividing line was neither clear nor stable, as high royal officials used their positions to gain more independence from the ruler in the conduct of govern-

[12] Thomas F. Tout, *Chapters in the Administrative History of Medieval England* (London: Longmans, 1920–33) 6 vols.; Otto Hintze, "Die Entstehung der modernen Staatsministerien," in his *Staat und Verfassung* (Göttingen: Vandenhoeck und Ruprecht, 1962), 275–320.

[13] Hintze, "Der Beamtenstand," in his *Soziologie und Geschichte* (Göttingen: Vandenhoeck und Ruprecht, 1964), 66–125.

ment affairs as well as for their own advancement. This drive of high-ranking officials for greater independence was supported, moreover, by public demands for greater stability and for an administrative performance that was readily available. One can visualize the development as one alternating between a growing independence of one or another group of officials and a renewed endeavor by the ruler and his "party" to buttress his authority by increasing the dependence of his officials or obtaining the services of more dependent and dependable men. The vicissitudes of these struggles have much to do with the divergent development of representative institutions in the several European countries.

These vicissitudes could lead to nonbureaucratic as well as to bureaucratic conditions of government employment, which suggests that bureaucratization is neither an inevitable nor an irreversible development. The point may be illustrated by reference to developments in France. Under the Carolingian rulers, officeholding and its attendant powers had been annexed to the fiefs granted by the king to his vassals, and these fiefs became hereditary. In this way dependent retainers and officials, exercising only a delegated authority, developed into a landholding aristocracy that exercised the powers of government autonomously, a process facilitated by the undeveloped condition of economy and transport.[14] Later on, French rulers came to delegate authority by making grants of official functions directly rather than making grants of land, with its attendant powers. In so doing they followed the practice of the Catholic Church, which had developed not only a well-organized, clerical officialdom but also a body of secular managers who exercised local authority over the extensive holdings of the church. From the twelfth to the fourteenth century, for example, French district officials (baillis) already possessed several characteristics of the modern bureaucrat: they were outside the fealty relationship, were frequently transferred or recalled, were subject to detailed controls by royal authority, were forbidden to acquire land where they performed their official duties or to have their children marry property owners in that locality, and were dependent upon a money income, albeit one partly derived from fees and tolls accruing to the office. These conditions of employment combined the personalized controls characteristic of the royal household with the personnel management (frequent transfers, detailed controls, monetary compensation) characteristic of bureaucracy.

[14] Peyer, loc. cit.

In the sixteenth and seventeenth centuries, France witnessed a further commercialization of government offices. In response to the need for revenue and the demands of a well-to-do middle class, most positions became a form of property that could be purchased and could also be made hereditary for an annual fee. Soon, offices were created as a means of raising revenue rather than in terms of the functions to be performed. Also, wealthy families came to consider the purchase of an office a form of investment. Salary and office fees yielded a rent income; officeholding itself was exempted from direct tax payments *(taille)*; and hereditary occupancy of a higher office conferred an aristocratic title on the incumbent.[15] Parts of this *noblesse de robe* became an estate of great dignity which was represented in the provincial *parlements* and which, by the mid-eighteenth century, constituted a resurgence of aristocratic privilege.[16] This commercialization of office went furthest in France but, in the early modern period, office-holding as a form of property and as an opportunity for family investment was prevalent in many countries.[17]

So far we have considered the subdivision of administrative tasks and their separation from the royal household as aspects of bureaucratization. The feudalization and the commercialization of public office facilitated that subdivision and separation, because they represented steps away from personal service to a ruler. However, neither process contributed for long or unequivocally to bureaucratization, because each represented a type of private appropriation of public office. Accordingly, European rulers resorted early to the employment of clerics (hence the English word "clerk") in order to obtain the services of dependable men who possessed skills useful in administrative work. Because of their celibate status, members of the clergy had no direct interest in using their position to enlarge a family inheritance, and from this viewpoint they were more reliable than landed aristocrats or men of wealth. On the other hand, in all conflicts between secular rulers and the church, the clergy's subordination to the authority of the church jeopardized their de-

[15] Martin Göhring, *Die Ämterkäuflichkeit im Ancien Regime,* Historische Studien, vol. 346 (Berlin: Ebering, 1938).
[16] Franklin L. Ford, *Robe and Sword: The Regrouping of the French Aristocracy After Louis XIV* (Cambridge: Harvard University Press, 1953).
[17] Cf. Koenraad W. Swart, *Sales of Offices in the Seventeenth Century* (The Hague: Nijhoff, 1949).

pendability as royal servants. Accordingly, toward the end of the fifteenth century clerics were increasingly replaced by laymen trained in the universities as jurists and humanists, a development associated on the Continent with the reception of Roman law.[18]

The employment of trained laymen introduced or greatly furthered the practice of public employment as a contractual relation entered into on the basis of stipulated conditions of service in exchange for a salary and subject to cancellation by either party. This was clearly a major step in the process of bureaucratization. Until the fifteenth century, public service had been a temporary matter, since the knight or cleric still remained a landlord or priest and retained a fief or benefice at the termination of his service. With the employment of university-trained councilors and secretaries, a new status group developed and was greatly strengthened during the sixteenth century when temporary public service was transformed into lifelong employment on a contractual basis.

In the provinces of Prussia persons of bourgeois origin predominated among those acquiring a university education and hence among officials of the new type, a situation often exploited by secular rulers to combat the influence of the aristocracy. However, as sons of aristocratic families came to attend the universities and enter public employment, the prestige of these trained officials, their interest in regular conditions of employment, and their covert resistance to the arbitrary commands of the ruler also increased.[19] Hence the old tendency toward independence among officials recurred, albeit on the new contractual basis; this development paralleled the growth of independence of the *noblesse de robe* in France.

Following Otto Hintze,[20] one may consider the absolutist measures taken against these tendencies a third foundation of modern bureaucracy. The Prussian kings appointed special officials *(kommissarische Beamte)* who were recruited among natives of other provinces and among foreigners and had nothing in common with the indigenous aristocratic cliques. In France the new office of the

[18] Paul Koschaker, *Europa und das römische Recht* (Munich: Beck, 1958) chs. 12 and 13.

[19] Fritz Hartung, "Studien zur Geschichte der preussischen Verwaltung," in his *Staatsbildende Kräfte der Neuzeit: Gesammelte Aufsätze* (Berlin: Duncker und Humblot, 1961), 178–344.

[20] Hintze, "Der Commissarius und seine Bedeutung in der allgemeinen Verwaltungsgeschichte," in *Staat und Verfassung, op. cit.,* 242–274.

provincial *intendants* was made completely dependent upon royal authority, subject to cancellation at will, and entirely free from the commercialization of office mentioned earlier. Both the Prussian commissars and the French *intendants* originated in the procurement officers who accompanied the armies in the field and were then charged with maintaining peace and order in the conquered provinces on the basis of dictatorial powers. The institutionalization of these quartermasters for purposes of civilian administration retained the patriarchal features of government employment but also introduced a new measure of centralized control, which has remained an important feature of Continental bureaucracy.

Three antecedents of modern bureaucracy have been mentioned so far: subdivision of tasks in the service to a ruler and the eventual separation of officials from the ruler's household; employment of university-trained jurists; and the transformation of military controllers into civilian officials. During the nineteenth century, these antecedents eventuated in a regularization of public employment approximating the ideal type as defined by Max Weber. On the Continent, government officials themselves played a dominant role in this development in an endeavor to increase the security, remuneration, and social standing of their position. The independence and impartiality of administrators was also a political objective of groups seeking to curb royal prerogative and to combat privileged access to government employment. These developments on the Continent were paralleled by the civil-service reform movements in England and the United States which exemplify recent antecedents of modern bureaucracy.

Administrative reform in England. Beginning as part of the royal household, English government administration was gradually removed from the court and divided into the different branches of the executive, much as it had been in France and Germany. But in this process the cohesion of the country, the ease of communication, and the absence of a standing army and other factors combined to achieve a balance between royal authority and the local authority of the landed gentry. True, an administration approximating the Continental absolutist system was attempted, beginning with the Tudor monarchy in the late fifteenth century. Yet this absolutist interlude ended with the legislative supremacy of Parliament rather than with the administrative absolutism of the king, while administration at local levels consisted of offices as a species of collective prerogative in the hands of the gentry and urban notables.[21] In France bureaucratization had already been advanced by royal absolutism, and when the revolution swept aside both the *pouvoirs intermédiaires* and the monarchy, the national system of administration that was instituted extended the bureaucratic measures of the *ancien régime*.[22] In England, on the other hand, earlier bureaucratic developments had been arrested by the overthrow of royal absolutism, which was followed by a period in which the private appropriation of public office prevailed. Some reforms curbing a direct financial exploitation of public office and requiring the personal discharge of public duties by officeholders were instituted in the late eighteenth century, and some unsuccessful experimenting with examinations for the public service occurred during the 1830s.[23] But administrative reform became effective only insofar as it was part of the movements for political reform and hence an attack upon the identification of office with family and property. Beginning in practice with the Poor Law Amendment Act of 1834 and the administrative centralization pioneered by Edwin Chadwick,[24] administrative reforms were extended to the personnel field on a programmatic basis following the Northcote-Trevelyan Report of 1853. Selection by competitive examinations and promotion by merit were instituted subsequently by Gladstone's Order in Council of 1870. English bureaucratization was, therefore, in part a manifestation of increasing equalitarianism and in part evidence of the desire to detach the public service from its previous ties with familial and political privilege at a time when governmental services and controls were being expanded rapidly to cope with the problems of a maturing industrial society.

The United States. Bureaucratization in the United States was also the result of a movement for administrative reform, but the setting

[21] Lewis B. Namier, *England in the Age of the American Revolution* (1930; 2d ed., New York: St. Martins, 1962). Reference is to pages 3–41 of a 1961 paperback edition.

[22] Alexis de Tocqueville, *The Old Regime and the French Revolution* (Garden City: Doubleday, 1955); Alfred Cobban, *A History of Modern France* (New York: Braziller, 1965), 2, 18–38.

[23] Emmeline W. Cohen, *The Growth of the British Civil Service: 1780–1939* (London: Allen and Unwin, 1941).

[24] Samuel E. Finer, *The Life and Times of Edwin Chadwick* (London: Methuen, 1952).

and course of this movement differed from the experience of England. In the first decades after independence, political life was largely in the hands of notables, and presidential appointments to the public service reflected not only the privileged access of the dominant upper-class groups but also their competence. Partisan activity as a basis of appointment increased in importance under Adams and Jefferson; in this respect Jackson's administration merely continued previous practices, although because of the altered character of political life, family origin and connections as factors favoring appointment to office declined markedly in importance during this era.[25] Jackson first articulated the ideology of the spoils system, but his reputation as its initiator is undeserved because the abuses incident to that system mounted rapidly only with the growth of machine politics.[26]

The movement for civil-service reform gained momentum in the years following the Civil War and had as its objective the elimination of machine politics from the public service. Accordingly, the reform measures, which were largely borrowed from abroad, were aimed at curbing the abuses of machine politicians rather than, as in England, at destroying privilege. Leadership of the movement for civil-service reform came from socially and politically prominent Eastern liberals. They saw in the destruction of the spoils system a needed emancipation from moral corruption; the movement was second only to the earlier abolitionist movement, in which many had been active as well.[27]

The Western experience. The common denominator of bureaucratization is that the earlier involvement of public employment with family prerogative and the identification of office with property have been superseded, in the course of long and diverse developments, by the emergence of the nation-state in which public officials administer "a service-rendering organization for the protection of rights and the enforcement of duties" of a national citizenry.[28] That is, government is in charge of the currency, the postal system, the construction of public facilities, the provision of social services, the

[25] Sidney H. Aronson, *Status and Kinship in the Higher Civil Service* (Cambridge: Harvard University Press, 1964).

[26] Leonard D. White, *The Jacksonians* (New York: Macmillan, 1954), 347–362.

[27] Paul P. Van Riper, *History of the United States Civil Service* (Evanston: Row, Peterson, 1958), 78–86.

[28] Ernest Barker, *The Development of Public Services in Western Europe: 1660–1930* (Oxford University Press, 1944), 6.

adjudication of legal disputes, the national educational system, the defense establishment, and the collection of revenue to pay for these and other public services. Although the policies that should govern such public functions are often in dispute, the relative neutralization of the civil service and hence the conception of administrators as employees in charge of a public trust may be due ultimately to the growth of consensus concerning the idea of government as a service-rendering institution that should not be preempted by any one of the individuals and groups contending in the political arena. This consensus is both cause and consequence of the growth of government and public employment. Official statistics provide conclusive evidence of that growth, but are not standardized enough to be suitable for comparative study.[29]

Developing areas. The preceding discussion of bureaucratization, which has been confined to the "Western experience," has suggested the importance of at least two characteristics: the long-run continuity of this experience, and the central role played by the clergy and by law and legal experts in effecting the emancipation of government service from ties with personal service, kinship relations, and property interests. These and related preconditions have been absent from other types of bureaucratization, to which at least some reference ought to be made at this point. One type refers to problems of public employment in the so-called developing areas.

However diverse, these areas have at least three features in common. They are latecomers as far as industrial development is concerned. They show little of that diminution of "primordial" ties which preceded or accompanied the development of Western nation-states and their bureaucratization. At the same time, they greatly emphasize the importance of government and rapidly expand public employment.[30] Under conditions of economic scarcity, government posts are much sought after, and the ideology of government initiative in economic development provides no basis for

[29] Cf. Carl H. Ule, ed., *Die Entwicklung des öffentlichen Dienstes* (Cologne: Heymanns, 1961), and the sources cited there.

[30] Edward Shils, *Political Development in the New States* (The Hague: Mouton, 1962); Lloyd A. Fallers, *Bantu Bureaucracy: A Study of Integration and Conflict in the Political Institutions of an East African People* (Cambridge: Heffer, 1956); idem, ed., *The King's Men: Leadership and Status in Buganda on the Eve of Independence* (Oxford University Press, 1964); University of Chicago, Committee For the Comparative Study of the New Nations, *Old Societies and New States: The Quest for Modernity in Asia and Africa,* Clifford Geertz, ed. (New York: Free Press, 1963), 105 ff.

restricting public employment. As a result, such countries are characterized by top-heavy officialdom relative to economic growth; this severely strains the merit system of recruitment, which is a legacy of colonial regimes in many of these areas.[31]

Perhaps it is useful to consider public administration in these cases as an arena of fluctuating contests, in which the primordial ties between officials and the public, the exigencies of governmental planning under conditions of great poverty and in the context of the Cold War, and the ideals of efficient public service by trained administrators all play a part. This novel setting calls for an analysis of bureaucratization in terms appropriate to it (Riggs 1964),[32] especially because bureaucratization in Western societies eventually coincided with the weakening of primordial ties, while in the developing areas it may well strengthen them.

Communist countries. In the modern world the comparative study of bureaucratization must also deal with what may be called the "postbureaucratic" or "quasi-bureaucratic" type of governmental administration in communist societies. It is appropriate, but also easily misleading, to apply Weber's definition of bureaucracy to these societies. Such criteria as experience or training as a condition of public employment, the separation of office and incumbent, the strict exclusion of familial ties, and administrative work as a full-time occupation are clearly applicable in the communist countries. Indeed, these countries appear to be "superbureaucratic," in the sense that centralized planning swells the ranks of governmental employees. At any rate, in the Soviet Union organizations have been set up to deal in coordinated fashion with problems of personnel administration throughout the government hierarchy.[33]

Nevertheless, it would be misleading to treat communist coun-

[31] Morroe Berger, *Bureaucracy and Society in Modern Egypt: A Study of the Higher Civil Service,* Princeton Oriental Studies: Social Science, No. 1 (Princeton; Princeton University Press, 1957), ch. 2.; Ralph Braibanti, "Bureaucracy and Judiciary in Pakistan," in Joseph G. LaPalombara, ed., *Bureaucracy and Political Development,* Studies in Political Development, No. 2 (Princeton: Princeton University Press, 1963), 360–440; John D. Kingsley, "Bureaucracy and Political Development, With Particular Reference to Nigeria," in *Bureaucracy and Political Development, op. cit.,* 301ff.

[32] Fred W. Riggs, *Administration in Developing Countries* (Boston: Houghton, Mifflin, 1964).

[33] Merle Fainsod, *How Russia Is Ruled,* Russian Research Center Studies, No. 11 (Cambridge: Harvard University Press, 1963), 414–417.

tries as if their governments simply represented other instances of bureaucratization in the sense discussed above. This is evident in the policies governing the placement of executive personnel, which depends not only on the standards developed by the Soviet Ministry of Finance and on the separate procedures adopted by the various ministries and agencies concerned but also on decisions of the Central Committee of the Communist Party. Agencies of the Party work out lists of jobs that may not be filled without prior Party clearance, and they also prepare rosters of trusted personnel available for placement.[84] The principle that decisions of any importance require political clearance in addition to their appropriate administrative surveillance applies throughout Soviet society; indeed, it is the distinguishing characteristic of this postbureaucratic society.

In order to mount the desired degree of political mobilization and control over the decision-making centers of an entire society, the Communist Party is itself obliged to undergo a process of bureaucratization. In 1962, between 150,000 and 200,000 persons, or some 4 per cent of the membership, were paid party workers; the actual number was probably higher, since many held temporary assignments in various institutions. Through higher Party schools, first established in 1946, this cadre of activists has become increasingly professionalized; by 1956 there were 29 Party schools officially rated as institutions of higher education, offering a four-year curriculum and affording selected students a stipend from five to eight times higher than stipends at ordinary schools.[85] Thus the most characteristic feature of the postbureaucratic structure of communist societies is the bureaucratization not only of the public service but also of political life, so that the ruling party has the trained activists it needs to politicize the executive and the judicial branches of government and much of civilian life as well.

This degree of centralized, political manipulation indicates that these societies lack a concept of law in the sense of a system of relatively stable, impersonal, and nonpolitical norms and procedures. They are also distinguished from the societies whose further bureaucratization is considered below by their determination to centralize decision-making under the auspices of a single party, by their

[84] Nicholas DeWitt, *Education and Professional Employment in the U.S.S.R.* (Washington, D. C.: National Science Foundation, 1961), 463–466.

[85] Zbigniew Brzezinski and Samuel P. Huntington, *Political Power: USA/ USSR* (New York: Viking, 1964), 140–173; DeWitt, *op. cit.,* 300; John A. Armstrong, *The Soviet Bureaucratic Elite* (New York: Praeger, 1959).

injection of political controls at all levels of the administrative hierarchies, and by their effort to prevent the uncontrolled emergence of organized interests.

PROBLEMS OF MODERN BUREAUCRACY

We have seen that Weber's concept of bureacracy is serviceable as a macro-historical bench mark and that "bureaucratization" is a useful term to characterize an important pattern of social change. But it is also true that, in the course of that change, several elements of Weber's definition have been transformed from political issues into administrative techniques. As long as government administration was in the hands of a social elite or a group of political partisans which had privileged access to office and conducted the "public" business as a species of private prerogative, administrative reforms were aimed at equalizing access, diminishing arbitrariness, and reducing private profiteering. The separation of office and incumbent, appointment by merit, the contractual regulation of appointment and promotion, fixed monetary salaries, and other related measures can be understood as *preventing* the intrusion of kinship relations, property interests, and political partisanship upon the conduct of the public business. This negative effect was bound to decline in importance to the extent that government administration by a social elite or by party politicians became a thing of the past. The exclusion of "every purely personal feeling" remains an important desideratum as well as a proximate characteristic of official conduct. So does the effective separation of office and incumbent. But in most modern governments in the countries of Western civilization these and related aspects of public employment are handled routinely, if only proximately, by departments specializing in the several branches of personnel administration, which are themselves an example of bureaucratization as well as a means of promoting it.

In practice, appointment to public office on the basis of competitive examinations has succeeded in its primary objective of separating office-holding from partisan politics and the vested interests of a social elite. But recruitment to public office on this basis is not a "neutral" instrument, if we mean by this that it would result in a corps of public officials whose social composition corresponds to that of the general population. Rather, under the merit system, recruitment reflects the unequal distribution of opportunity characteristic of society at large. This implication has been the subject of several studies. Generally speaking, higher civil servants come from families in which the father is in an administrative, professional, managerial, or related middle-class occupation at a high or intermediate level, and they do so far in excess of the proportions of these occupational groups in the working population. By contrast, sons of families in which the father is a manual laborer are "underrepresented" among higher civil servants. Since the merit system makes educational qualifications a condition of entry into the public service, it tends to favor recruitment from social groups with a high level of education.[36] Marked regional differences in economic development, as in Italy, may superimpose their own effects on these patterns; Italian higher civil servants come in disproportionate numbers from the disadvantaged south, and their social origin appears to be considerably below that of officials recruited from the north.[37]

There have been efforts to make public employment at all levels more "representative" of the general population by adopting quota systems of selection favorable to those who come from disadvantaged families. In the Soviet Union and in other communist countries this policy was adopted for a time in order to dispense as quickly as possible with the dependence of the revolutionary regime upon old-time public officials. Subsequently, such quotas have been adopted from time to time when political considerations have suggested the advisability of populist appeals and measures against new "pockets of privilege." However, experience has shown that an administrative apparatus dependent upon a skilled staff is limited in the degree to which it can manipulate quotas favoring the disadvantaged without jeopardizing its level of performance. As a result, educational policies favoring the disadvantaged tend to be preferred to quota systems in public employment.[38] In India a

[36] Roger K. Kelsall, *Higher Civil Servants in Britain, From 1870 to the Present Day* (London: Routledge, 1955); Thomas B. Bottomore, "La mobilité sociale dans la haute administration française," *Cahiers Internationaux de Sociologie*, 13, 1952, 167–178; W. Lloyd Warner et al., *The American Federal Executive* (New Haven: Yale University Press, 1963); Reinhard Bendix, *Higher Civil Servants in American Society* (Boulder: University of Colorado Press, 1949).

[37] Luciano Cappelletti, "The Italian Bureaucracy: A Study of the Carriera Direttiva of the Italian Administration," Ph.D. dissertation (University of California, 1966).

[38] Fainsod, *op. cit.*; Alex Inkeles, "Social Stratification and Mobility in the Soviet Union: 1940–1950," *American Sociological Review*, 15, 1950, 465–479; Robert Feldmesser, "Equality and Inequality Under Khrushchev," in *Russia Under Khrushchev: An Anthology* (London: Methuen, 1962), 223–239.

public-employment policy *and* an educational policy are incorporated in the constitution. Quotas for positions in government employment and at the universities are reserved for members from "backward classes," leading to the paradoxical result that various castes, tribes, and other groups seek to be classified as "backward" in order to provide their members with additional opportunities for employment and education.[39]

These instances are cited to suggest that the merit system reflects existing social differences in various ways and that within narrow limits it can be used deliberately to alter such differences. In either case, studies of the social composition of higher civil servants have more to teach us about the social and political structure of a society than about the exercise of governmental authority. The organizational problems encountered in that exercise are by-passed here in order to consider the critical question of political control.

POLITICAL CONTROL OF PUBLIC OFFICIALS

The basic issue of control was formulated by Hegel in his *Philosophy of Right* in 1821, in which he pointed out that the bureacracy will be prevented "from acquiring the isolated position of an aristocracy and [from] using its education and skill as a means to an arbitrary tyranny" by the sovereign working on it from the top and corporation rights working on it from the bottom.[40] Despite its dated and parochial references, the statement identifies three dimensions that should be considered in an analysis of control over the exercise of governmental authority: the tendency of high public officials to develop and display a consciousness of special rank and the dangers of an abuse of authority implicit in the secrecy that is a by-product of expertise; the problems thereby posed for the "sovereign" who seeks to control officials from on high; and, conversely, the problem of the influence on administrative procedure and decision-making exercised by the individuals and organized groups who are subject to governmental authority.

Consciousness of rank among public officials is part of a historically derived "bureaucratic culture pattern." It may reflect the degree to which public office has been associated with the established

---

[39] Backward Classes Commission of India, *Report,* 2 vols. (New Delhi: Manager of Publications, 1955–56).

[40] G. W. F. Hegel, *Philosophy of Right,* trans. with notes by T. M. Knox (Oxford: Clarendon, 1942), 296–297.

privileges of a ruling class,[41] although an element of this consciousness may remain as an attribute of high public office even in the
absence of such traditions.[42] Consciousness of rank is probably related to the prestige accorded to public employment and the confidence or trust with which the public at large regards the work of
governmental officials.[43]

But there is no systematic evidence to indicate how public opinion concerning government is related to the discretionary exercise
of authority. It is as plausible to assume that public officials will
make responsible use of their public trust because they have high
prestige and sense the confidence placed in them as it is to assume
that they will do so in the absence of prestige and trust because they
fear the consequences of abusing their power. One is probably on
safe ground only with the empty assertion that both too much and
too little prestige and privilege tend to be correlated with abuse,
either because the incumbent official assumes that anything *he* does
must be right or because he is so needy as to use his office "for all it
is worth." Generally, civil-service systems have provided public officials with a high degree of economic security and special legal protection in order to enhance their sense of responsibility in the
exercise of discretionary powers. Yet such measures bear an uncertain relation to the conduct of the public business and specifically
the exercise of discretion; with bureaucratization the importance
of professional skills and administrative expertise increases, as does
the difficulty of implementing the principles of accountability.

In his discussion of bureaucracy Max Weber noted one major
obstacle standing in the way of accountability: the tendency of officials to increase their intrinsic superiority as experts by keeping
their knowledge and intentions secret.[44] More recent analyses have
examined the tensions typically arising in the relations between
experts and top administrative officials in public bureaucracies
and, more generally, the inherent difficulty of distinguishing be-

[41] John D. Kingsley, *Representative Bureaucracy: An Interpretation of the
British Civil Service* (Yellow Springs: Antioch College Press, 1944), ch. 7.
[42] Edward Shils, "Charisma, Order and Status," *American Sociological Review*, 30, 1965, 199–213.
[43] Gabriel A. Almond and Sidney Verba, *The Civic Culture: Political Attitudes and Democracy in Five Nations* (Princeton: Princeton University Press,
1963); Franklin P. Kilpatrick, Milton C. Cummings, and M. Kent Jennings,
The Image of the Federal Service (Washington, D. C.: Brookings Institution,
1964).
[44] Weber, *Economy and Society, op. cit.*, 992.

tween policy decisions and administrative implementation where
executives must rely on professionals.[45] The intrinsic dilemma appears to be that ultimately all professional services involve an element of trust in the skill and wisdom with which the professional
makes his judgments, whereas accountability of all administrative
actions implies that on principle these actions are subject to scrutiny and criticism by higher authority. It is only somewhat exaggerated to say that the trust implicit in the employment of professionals is at odds with the distrust implicit in the accountability of
administrators. This incompatibility is enhanced as governments
make increasing use not only of technical and scientific expertise
but also of professional administrative skills. To be "modern" a
government must rely on such skills, but to be responsible it must
nevertheless check on the discretionary judgments that are indispensable for both professional work and good government.

Genuine as this dilemma is, it should not be exaggerated. The
unchecked exercise of discretion by administrators with professional training is *not* simply synonymous with an abuse of authority. A substantial part of such discretion is usually called for by the
general legislative mandate under which officials do their work.
Much of what is kept secret by government officials concerns types
of information involving legitimate personal and social concerns
of individuals, which under the rule of law should not be divulged
despite periodic demands to this effect by partisans of all kinds. It
may be the fundamental tendency of all bureaucratic thought, as
Karl Mannheim has stated, to turn all problems of politics into
problems of administration.[46] Similarly, professionals tend to turn
every problem of decision-making into a question of expertise.
However, such tendencies occur not only (or even primarily) because officials with professional training wish to exceed their authority but also because the perennial difficulties of decision-making at
higher political levels leave a vacuum of action. Then, indeed, officials will proceed in keeping with *their* interpretation of the public

[45] Robert K. Merton, *Social Theory and Social Structure* (Glencoe: Free Press,
1957), 219–224; Alexander Leighton, *Human Relations in a Changing World*
(New York: Dutton, 1949), 129–173; Talcott Parsons, *Structure and Process in
Modern Societies* (Glencoe: Free Press, 1960), 66–69; Carl J. Friedrich, *Man and
His Government: An Empirical Theory of Politics* (New York: McGraw-Hill,
1963), 309–314.

[46] Karl Mannheim, *Ideology and Utopia: An Introduction to the Sociology
of Knowledge* (New York: Harcourt; London: Routledge, 1954).

interest. In so doing they may be influenced by their professional preoccupations, but they are still acting in the context of public authority. Under a system of laws, that context is circumscribed by the controls to which public officials are subject and by their own belief in legitimacy. Such controls and beliefs exert a constraining pressure upon them even in the absence of any direct checks on their performance.

Among the controls to which public officials are subject are the rules pertaining to their civic position. Should these officials be permitted to retain all the rights enjoyed by private citizens, or should certain special restrictions be imposed on them in view of their powers and responsibilities as public employees? The question pertains to those political systems that give legal recognition to the rights of citizens against the government. Under these conditions one viewpoint would concede to public officials the full exercise of their rights as private citizens and hence reject any restriction on the political or trade-union activities of public employees. The other position demands of public officials that they accept special restrictions upon their expression of political views and their participation in partisan political activities in order to safeguard the impartiality of governmental administration as well as public confidence in that impartiality.

According to this second view, governmental employment involves a public trust that can be jeopardized if public officials make injudicious use of their rights as citizens; hence, efforts are made to draw a legally binding distinction between permissible and impermissible political activities.[47] Related to this second position are the various efforts to regulate the relations between public officials and elected representatives, including the question whether and under what conditions officials should be permitted to stand for elective offices.[48] Efforts to control the political activities of public officials have the same objective as the merit system, namely, to ensure the quality and impartiality of the public service. Hence the importance of these efforts will diminish in proportion to the success of the merit system of personnel recruitment.

Direct checks on the performance of administrators are, of course,

[47] Otto Kirchheimer, "The Historical and Comparative Background of the Hatch Law," *Public Policy*, 2, 1941, 341–373; Milton J. Esman, "The Hatch Act: A Reappraisal," *Yale Law Journal*, 60, 1951, 986–1005.

[48] Werner Weber, "Parlamentarische Unvereinbarkeiten," *Archiv des öffentlichen Rechts*, 19 (New Series), 1930, 161–254.

a more important means of ensuring the responsible execution of policies than are general rules concerning the civic status of officials. In his incisive critique of Prussian bureaucracy, Max Weber emphasized parliamentary inquiries as a means by which politicians could check upon the administrative implementation of the legislative intent. He saw such inquiries as a proving ground for politicians in parliament. They would match wits with expert administrators in order to vindicate the supremacy of political decisions over the official's use of his education and skill to preserve the technical integrity of an administrative program.[49] The problems that Weber noted have become, if anything, more complex. Under the conditions of the modern welfare state, legislatures increasingly delegate authority to administrative agencies. With the consequent proliferation of governmental functions and reliance on expertise, the difficulties not only of parliamentary but also of executive control over the administrative process mount. Elected representatives are too few in number in comparison with the officials under their authority, less expert than the latter, and necessarily restricted to spot checks on performance. Moreover, in a context of expanding government functions, political decisions already involve the active participation of top administrators and are then embodied in service-rendering institutions. To an extent, parliamentary control of officials is circumscribed, because past political decisions tend to engender a popular demand for the continuation of government services once these are initiated, even aside from the self-perpetuating momentum of the administration.

It is true that legislative controls have proliferated, as in the annual authorization of agencies or in statutory provisions requiring agencies to obtain legislative clearance for particular programs. But the result has not only been further legislative control of the administrative process. Legislative committees are also transformed into champions of particular administrative agencies, in part because politicians and administrators compete for the allegiance of the same constituency, albeit for different ends. In this way legislative committees combine control and advocacy in their relations with administrative agencies. At the same time the executive branch (in particular, the office of the president) has had to develop its own methods of supervision through the Bureau of the Budget and other

[49] Weber, *Economy and Society, op. cit.,* 1381–1469.

instrumentalities, in order to keep pace with the expansion and decentralization of the administrative process.[50]

We have noted several concurrent and interrelated developments of bureaucracy in the industrialized societies of Western civilization: the relative success of the merit system and the consequent decline of direct political intereference with administration; the professionalization of public administration and the consequent difficulties of parliamentary and executive supervision; and the expansion of governmental functions and the consequent delegation of authority.

The mounting difficulties of supervision are associated, in turn, with the process of democratization. As long as a politics of notables prevailed, it was more or less accurate to think of decision-making as a legislative and ministerial prerogative and of administration as an implementation of policies. Even in this setting, voluntary associations like the Anti-Corn Law League in England and the Bund der Landwirte in Germany were used to influence public policy. However, representatives of such associations had close social ties with political decision-makers and thus appeared as little more than a specially organized section of the ruling elite. With democratization the number of those engaged in political activities has increased; organized interests have proliferated in interaction with the proliferation of governmental functions,[51] and so have the opportunities of individuals and groups to contact and influence administrators as well as legislators. Delegation of authority to administrators has developed along with the mobilization of interest in the government process on the part of the public.[52]

Close and frequent contacts between bureaucracy and organized interests are encouraged where policies are general, where effective administration requires information that is often at the disposal of these interests, and where governmental responsiveness to the public, together with freedom of association, are considered major desiderata of a pluralistic polity. The result is policy formation at

[50] Richard E. Neustadt, "Politicians and Bureaucrats," in David Truman, ed., *The Congress and America's Future* (Englewood Cliffs: Prentice-Hall, 1965), 102–120.

[51] Joseph H. Kaiser, *Die Repräsentation organisierter Interessen* (Berlin: Duncker und Humblot, 1956).

[52] Philip Selznick, *TVA and the Grass Roots: A Study in the Sociology of Formal Organization*, University of California Publications in Culture and Society, 3 (Berkeley: University of California Press, 1949).

many levels of government and outside the government proper, as in licensing boards, advisory committees, and other such institutions. Under these conditions contacts between administrators and the interested public on matters of policy as well as on matters of procedure become frequent, especially if the legislature and the political executive fail to make needed decisions. With only very general policies to guide them, officials may function as resolvers of conflicting claims not previously resolved at higher political levels. In these and other cases there is reason to question how deeply the available controls can still penetrate into the network of interaction between organized interests and the bureaucracy, and it cannot be taken for granted that by gaining ascendancy over the controls exercised by politicians the administrator is also increasing his own autonomy.

Where interest groups do not exist, officials may help to create them in order to have organs of consultation and cooperation, and under certain conditions frequent contacts may lead to a mutual support between interest group and clientele administration.[53] Even in this case, it may be said that groups which obtain a hearing in the executive agency directly concerned with their affairs probably also endorse the political system which grants them that hearing, so that here again it is appropriate to emphasize the important, if imponderable, belief in legitimacy. A spirit of moderation may be created by the consensus of the public as well as by the prudential neutrality of the administrators, but this certainly need not happen. And even where it does, there is still the question of how much decision-making can be decentralized without jeopardizing the capacity for concerted action on the part of the national political community.

The developments sketched here have recurred in the several countries usually considered together under the term "welfare state," and they have evoked certain predictable responses. In the United States, as direct political interference with the administrative process has become less and the influence of interest groups has become more important, conflict-of-interest legislation has been elaborated. By distinguishing between acceptable and unacceptable types of contact between officials and the spokesmen for interest

[53] Henry Ehrmann, "Les groupes d'intérêt et la bureaucratie dans les démocraties occidentales," *Revue française de science politique*, 11, 1961, 541–568; Peter Woll, *Administrative Law: The Informal Process* (Berkeley: University of California Press, 1963); *idem, American Bureaucracy* (New York: Norton, 1963).

groups, such laws seek to safeguard the impersonal character of public employment and day-to-day administration.[54] Where such controls are successful, they probably do more than provide general discouragement and occasional penalties for the worst abuses engendered by close relations between administrators and the interested public. For they also provide the administrator with a ready buttress to his neutrality, which he can use in his handling of the conflicting claims pressed upon him. The same consideration applies to the established legislative and executive controls over the administrative process, which vary in the degree to which they penetrate the contacts between administrators and private interests.

That this penetration is felt to be insufficient is perhaps best exemplified by the Scandinavian institution of the *ombudsman*, a parliamentary commissioner who is charged with the task of screening complaints against the administrative arm of the government and of vigorously prosecuting transgressors, whether they have violated the law or merely neglected the performance of their official duties. The need for an opportunity to redress individual grievances is widely recognized, but the institution of the ombudsman is not easily transferred from one constitutional framework to another, in part because similar functions may be performed in other ways.[55] It remains to be seen whether such new devices, as well as old ones like administrative courts, will be sufficient to counteract the unwitting and undesired effects of interest-group activity upon the impartiality and effectiveness of a corps of professional administrators.

THE STUDY OF BUREAUCRACY

The preceding discussion of recruitment patterns and political controls has certain general implications for the comparative study of bureaucracy. The old argument over the amateur generalist versus the expert technician is a case in point. At one time, the former tended to be the man of privilege, while the latter was the man of technical reasoning. But with the disappearance of privilege, the generalist may be open to considerations of broad policy, while the technician, with his commitment to expertise and perhaps a disinclination to entertain political considera-

[54] Roswell B. Perkins, "The New Federal Conflict-of-Interest Law," *Harvard Law Review*, 76, 1963, 1113–1169; Bayless Manning, *Federal Conflict of Interest Law* (Cambridge: Harvard University Press, 1964).

[55] Donald C. Rowat, ed., *The Ombudsman* (London: Allen and Unwin, 1965).

tions, may be open to influence by special interests clothed in
technical arguments. In an increasingly specialized administration, considerations of technical efficiency can hide a political judgment.[56] Hence, the view that bureaucracy is the most efficient type
of administrative organization remains valid only on the very narrow ground that it is more efficient than an administration governed by kinship ties and property interests. Such considerations
suggest that today we are less concerned with bureaucratization as
such than with the exercise of administrative authority.

With this shift in orientation the study of bureaucracy comes
close to the analysis of organizations, although this is no warrant
for neglecting the separate significance of governmental authority.
The analysis of organizations has called into question the utility of
assuming the unequivocal unity of organizational goals, the uni-
lateral determination of administrative conduct by the commands
of superiors, the hierarchical ordering of superior-subordinate relationships, and hence the significance of hierarchical organizations
as a means to the attainment of well-defined ends.[57] Oriented as it
is to the macroscopic contrast with patrimonialism, Weber's model
of bureaucracy does not provide guidelines in these respects, but
three elements of his analysis may be noted.[58]

The emphasis on the belief in legitimacy as the foundation of
administrative conduct already precludes an interpretation of organizational behavior in terms of specific ends. Thus, democratic
beliefs in legitimacy implicitly endorse the many diverse ends that
are pursued in the interaction between bureaucracy and interest
groups. A second basic characteristic of bureaucracy is the emphasis
on an orientation toward abstract norms as an integral part of the
rule of law. Organizational analysis can be related to the study of
bureaucracy if it takes cognizance not only of informal relations in
hierarchical organizations but also of the continuing efforts to off-
set their effects on the organization or to subject these relations to
norms developed for this purpose. Third, the defining characteris-

---

[56] Philip Selznick, *Leadership in Administration: A Sociological Interpretation* (Evanston: Row, Peterson, 1957).
[57] Norton E. Long, *The Polity* (Chicago: Rand McNally, 1962); Michel
Crozier, *The Bureaucratic Phenomenon* (Chicago: University of Chicago Press,
1964).
[58] Reinhard Bendix, *Work and Authority in Industry: Ideologies of Management in the Course of Industrialization* (New York: Wiley, 1956); *idem, Nation-
Building and Citizenship, op. cit.;* Niklas Luhmann, "Zweck-Herrschaft-System,
Grundbegriffe und Prämissen Max Webers," *Der Staat,* 3, 1964, 129–158.

tics of bureaucracy have one common denominator, namely, the effort to insulate officials from all effects of society that militate against the probability of a faithful and efficient implementation of policies. This is necessarily a proximate achievement that requires continuous reinforcement. We have seen that its original objective—the insulation of officials from the effects of kinship ties and property interests—has become less important with time, while the new problems posed by the contact between officials and interest representatives may not be amenable to over-all solutions. In this respect the managements of large industrial organizations have been more successful, to the extent that they have insulated their top officials by providing their families with a luxurious but manipulated style of life. These perspectives suggest the possibility of linking the study of bureaucracy, with its historical and comparative approach, and the study of organizational behavior, to the benefit of both.

VIII

PERSONAL RULERSHIP, PATRIMONIALISM, AND EMPIRE-BUILDING

The concrete lessons of recent history have helped us to appreciate the paramount importance of the political preconditions of social and economic development in the new states. The basic problem of political stability must be solved before all others—or everything else may be in vain. For this reason, some of the scholarly attention that used to be focused on social and economic development has shifted to political organization and has given prominence to terms such as "nation-building," "political culture," and "democratization." At the same time efforts have been made to modify the usual evolutionary and dichotomous conceptions of social and political development. The two-faced nature of tradition and modernity has come under scrutiny again.

Two basic theoretical choices have been made in the face of the complexity of the subject matter: one choice has been to resort to a relatively novel terminology that is intended to transcend Western historical connotations—witness the attempt by Gabriel Almond and his collaborators to adapt the Parsonian scheme; the other has been to reexamine older terms for their contemporary usefulness and to work with historically more specific concepts.[1]

I shall follow the latter path because I should like to reconsider

[1] Cf. ch. VI: 2 for Gabriel Almond, and ch. XI for Bendix' alternative approach.

Guenther Roth, "Personal Rulership, Patrimonialism, and Empire-Building in the New States," *World Politics*, XX: 2, Jan. 1968, 194–206. First presented at the Sixth World Congress of Sociology, International Sociological Association, Evian, France, Sept. 6, 1966, Session I, "Approaches to Comparative Politics." I greatly appreciate the helpful comments of Juan Linz.

a neglected part of Max Weber's typology of *Herrschaft*, the notion of patrimonial rule, for it seems to me that many of the features of legal-rational modernity may not appear in the new states and that certain basic modes of administration persist, even though traditionalist legitimacy has disintegrated in most cases. From the beginning, it should be clearly understood that Weber's sociology of *Herrschaft* deals not only with beliefs in legitimacy but also with the actual operating modes and administrative arrangements by which rulers "govern," not just "rule" (to paraphrase Adolphe Thiers's constitutional theory). This is made abundantly clear in his historical analyses of patrimonialism, sultanism, feudalism, the routinization of charismatic rule, hierocracy, and the city-state. If you wish, Weber tried to find out "how systems really work." It is true that he organized his great opus *Economy and Society* around a typology of social action and of legitimacy, but both in the terminological exposition (in Part I) and in the more descriptive analyses (in the older Part II) he always dealt with *Herrschaft* in terms of both legitimacy and the typical staff arrangements of the various kinds of rulers. Here lies the great difficulty of translating *Herrschaft*, which in English is usually rendered either as "authority" (Parsons) or "domination" (Bendix, Rheinstein, Shils). Patrimonial rulers, for example, endeavor to maximize their personal control. Like all rulers, they are continually engaged in a struggle with their staff over ultimate control. In this regard, traditionalist legitimacy may be a burden as well as a help for them (as both Weber and Eisenstadt have shown).[2] Such legitimation may fetter them and prevent them from mobilizing the resources needed for empire-building, a handicap that Eisenstadt has considered the fatal flaw of the "historical bureaucratic societies." Rulers, then, avail themselves of various political and administrative devices that transcend the bases of their legitimacy. Patrimonial rulers resort to "extra-patrimonial" recruitment, which may retain the fiction of patriarchal subordination but may in fact be based on a feudal-contractual, bureaucratic-contractual, or merely personal relationship.

TRADITIONALIST PATRIMONIALISM AND PERSONAL RULERSHIP

Lately, some attempts, primarily in the field of African studies, have been made to remember the meaning of patrimonialism, yet by and large Weber's broad typology of *Herrschaft* has

[2] See S. N. Eisenstadt, *The Political Systems of Empires: The Rise and Fall of the Historical Bureaucratic Societies* (New York: Free Press, 1963).

been underutilized and, in fact, reduced to the dichotomy of bureaucracy and charisma. Not only patrimonialism but also collegial
government and rule by notables have been disregarded.

I wish to distinguish two kinds of patrimonialism. One is the historical survival of traditionalist patrimonial regimes; the foremost
example is Ethiopia, where the researcher, if he gains access at all,
can almost perform the feat of traveling into the past.[3] The second
type of patrimonialism is personal rulership on the basis of loyalties
that do not require any belief in the ruler's unique personal qualification, but are inextricably linked to material incentives and rewards. This second variant has been submerged in much of the
literature through the indiscriminate use of the term "charismatic."
As long as patrimonialism is considered to rest exclusively on traditionalist legitimation and hereditary succession, the category obviously loses applicability to the extent that these phenomena decline. Personal rulership, however, is an ineradicable component
of the public and private bureaucracies of highly industralized
countries; some of the newer states lack the institutional matrix,
whether pluralist or totalitarian, of these countries to such an extent that personal rulership becomes the dominant form of government. In terms of traditional political theory, some of these new
states may not be states at all but merely private governments of
those powerful enough to rule; however, this only enhances the
applicability of the notion of personal rulership (in the sense of
detraditionalized, personalized patrimonialism). Such personal governance easily evokes notions of opportunism and corruption from
the perspective of charismatic or legal-rational legitimation.[4] Traditionalist as well as personal patrimonial regimes differ from

---

[3] See Donald N. Levine, "Ethiopia: Identity, Authority, and Realism," in
Lucian W. Pye and Sidney Verba, eds., *Political Culture and Political Development* (Princeton: Princeton University Press, 1965), 245–281; also the same
author's *Wax and Gold: Tradition and Innovation in Ethiopian Culture* (Chicago University Press, 1965). Levine's fascinating accounts disregard the literature on patrimonialism. For a detailed description of personal rulership and
palace intrigues, see Richard Greenfield, *Ethiopia* (London: Pall Mall, 1965).
On the much more precarious Iranian case, see Leonard Binder, *Iran: Political
Development in a Changing Society* (Berkeley: University of California Press,
1962), and Norman Jacobs, *The Sociology of Development: Iran as an Asian
Case Study* (New York: Praeger, 1966).

[4] For one of the latest examples, see Conor Cruise O'Brien, former member of
the Irish delegation to the United Nations and vice-chancellor of the University
of Ghana from 1962 to 1965, "The Counter-revolutionary Reflex," *Columbia
Forum,* IX, Spring 1966, 21f.

charismatic rulership in that the patrimonial ruler need have neither personal charismatic appeal nor a sense of mission; they differ from legal-rational bureaucracies in that neither constitutionally regulated legislation nor advancement on the basis of training and efficiency need be predominant in public administration.

Also, personal rulership should not be mistaken for authoritarianism, which has little to do with authority as such. After the First World War, the doctrine of authoritarianism was developed by right-wing nationalists, who championed the autonomy of the state apparatus as against parliament with its parties and interest groups and even as against the dynastic families and their loyalist supporters. Nowadays, however, the term is usually applied to the many political regimes that lie between democratic and totalitarian ones. These regimes base themselves on a limited structural pluralism, which admits of some interest-group articulation; strategies of *divide et impera* are usually more important than legitimation or ideological integration, and for that reason authoritarian regimes may be less stable and have less "authority" than democratic and totalitarian states.

Many authoritarian regimes have features of traditional and personal patrimonialism, which may be more important than charismatic appeals, the belief in legal rationality, and bureaucratic practices. Typologically, however, it would be inadvisable to equate "patrimonial" with "authoritarian." The latter term has been useful in establishing a continuum ranging from pluralist democracy to totalitarianism; the former category properly belongs to a typology of beliefs *and* organizational practices that can be found at any point of such a continuum.[5]

---

[5] For an excellent discussion of authoritarianism, see Juan J. Linz, "An Authoritarian Regime: Spain," in E. Allardt and Y. Littunen, eds., *Cleavages, Ideologies and Party Systems* (Helsinki: Westermarck Society, 1964), 291–341. Linz argues that "Max Weber's categories can and should be used independently of the distinction between democracy, authoritarianism, and totalitarianism. Within each of these systems the legitimacy of the ruler, for the population or his staff, can be based on one or another of these types of belief. . . . While we want to stress the conceptual difference between authoritarian regimes and traditional rule, we also want to suggest that they sometimes have elements in common and that the students of such regimes could gain as many insights from Weber's analysis of patrimonial rule and bureaucracy as those of totalitarianism have gained from his thinking about charisma" (319, 321). My approach differs from Linz's suggestion in that it treats patrimonialism not only as a type of traditional belief but also as a strategy of rulership. For another treatment of

PERSONAL RULERSHIP IN INDUSTRIALIZED COUNTRIES

In order to emphasize that personal rulership transcends the dichotomy of tradition and modernity, I shall first illustrate its continued functioning in industralized countries, before turning to some African and Asian regimes. In the older political-science literature, the phenomenon has been subsumed under terms such as "machine" and "apparatus," or even "clique" and "faction"; organization analysts have rediscovered some aspects under the names "primary groups" and "informal relations," and they customarily contrast these with the formal structure of bureaucracy, which is usually and misleadingly called the Weberian model (as if Weber had not scrutinized patrimonial bureaucracies and modern higher civil servants as status groups and vested interests).

The old urban machines are a familiar example. They had, of course, some kind of traditionalist legitimation because of the immigrants' Old World ties, but they functioned primarily on the basis of personal loyalty—plebeian, not feudal—and material reward; offices were distributed by a noncharismatic and nonbureaucratic ruler, and occupying them amounted to holding a benefice. The boss might have great power, but his legitimacy was precarious; thus he had little authority and had to envelop his "clients" in an intricate web of reciprocities.[6]

The old machines have largely disappeared, but personal rulership has not. Instead of the Irish bosses of yesteryear there is the Kennedy "clan" with its charismatic appeals to the electorate. However, the organizational power of the Kennedys has been based on an apparatus that some time ago brought its patrimonial character

---

authoritarianism, which does not emphasize the issue of personal rulership, see Lewis A. Coser, "Prospects for the New Nations: Totalitarianism, Authoritarianism, or Democracy?" in Coser, ed., *Political Sociology* (New York: Harper and Row, 1966), 247–271.

[6] In his discussion of patriarchalism and patrimonialism, Weber pointed out that traditionalist authority is not sufficient to ensure conformity with the directives of a patriarchal head; the ruler must be particularly responsive to his group as long as he does not have an efficient staff; once he has it, he must be responsive to his staff, lest he risk his power or even his position. In the language of the pattern variables, patrimonial organizations are particularist, but I shall show below that this is not necessarily so; on the other hand, Parsons himself long ago stressed the inherent instability of universalist orientation within legal-rational bureaucracy. Cf. *The Social System* (New York: Free Press, 1951), 268.

to public attention during the Judge Morrissey affair in Boston.[7] For that matter, every American president, in order to be effective, cannot merely rely on his constitutional (legal-rational) powers, the institutionalized charismatic aura of his office, or any personal charismatic appeals to the public, but must build his own personal apparatus out of the so-called in-and-outers, who efficiently take the place of a permanent civil service of the British kind (as Richard E. Neustadt showed in his comparison of cabinet and presidential government, much of which reads like a description of personal governance).[8] Even the authority of the presidential office does not suffice to hold this apparatus together, and "authoritarian" imposition easily misfires.

The phenomenon of personal rulership is no less important in a totalitarian state than in a pluralist one. Nikita Khrushchev's fabled personal apparatus, which he took from Moscow to the Ukraine and back, served him well until defection eroded it. In the spring of 1966, his successor, Leonid I. Brezhnev, managed to enlarge to thirteen full members and seven candidates the number of Central Committee members who hailed from, or had connections with, the Ukrainian Dnepropetrovsk region, where he was born and began his career. Some of these are said to have been old friends from before the Second World War. At the same time, Kremlinologists identified another ascending group made up of Byelorussians and headed by Politburo member Kirill T. Mazurov, which is alleged to have made unusual gains on the Central Committee and to have taken over important positions.[9]

Far from being a vanishing phenomenon, personal rulership in public bureaucracies is apparently enlarged by the extension of government functions in industrialized countries. Both in Western Europe and in the United States, there are an increasing number of semipublic agencies and corporations in which such patrimonial relationships emerge and officials tend to become "beneficeholders." In the literature on industrial bureaucracies, this development is referred to by the wholly imprecise term of "industrial feudalism," which indicates the appropriation of managerial func-

[7] Almost forgotten are the charges of liberal Democrats in 1960 that J. F. Kennedy "bought" the nomination of his party, meaning that he had such great financial resources that he could build an overpowering nationwide machine.

[8] "White House and Whitehall," *The Public Interest*, I, Winter 1966, 55–69.

[9] See Harry Schwartz, "Brezhnev Favors Old Colleagues," *New York Times*, July 15, 1966.

tions and prerogatives. Such prerogatives include the use of expense accounts, representation funds, official residences, limousines, and first-class tickets. The contractual character of the civil-service relationship may be changed because some officials cannot be dismissed *de jure* or *de facto*. Such officials may also be able to co-opt candidates and thus displace universalist criteria of formalized recruitment. However, along another universalist dimension, the hiring of highly qualified friends (from law school or graduate school days) can be very efficient. Finally, such patrimonial organizations may even be able to levy indirect taxes.

REVOLUTIONARY LEGITIMACY AND PATRIMONIAL PRACTICE

It is my contention that in some of the new states patrimonial features in the detraditionalized, personalized sense are more important than bureaucratic and charismatic ones, and hence that it is too simplified a typology to contrast, for example, "the charisma of party" with "the bureaucracy of the military." [10] Neglect of the patrimonial dimension of government has also led to a tendency to interpret all political leadership as charismatic. Both analytical trends usually ignore Weber's point that bureaucracy and charisma are not necessarily exclusive of each other and that, in fact, bureaucracies can be superior instruments for charismatic leaders.[11] Moreover, the treatment of almost all political leaders in the new states as charismatic has been misleading on at least two counts: it has obscured the difference between charismatic authority and charismatic leadership,[12] and it has taken at face value the international propaganda claims of some of the new leaders. Most heads of government in the new states do not have the magic of personal charisma for many groups in the society, nor do they have the kind of impersonal, institutional charisma that Edward Shils has stressed as a basic requirement for organizational stability.[13] The political situation in many African and Asian countries is so fluid exactly because leadership is merely personal and lacking in both

[10] See Irving Louis Horowitz, *Three Worlds of Development* (New York: Oxford, 1966), 263.

[11] Weber's example was Gladstone and Chamberlain's Liberal Party machine, to which he gave much attention. See Weber, "Politics as a Vocation," in H. H. Gerth and C. W. Mills, eds., *From Max Weber* (New York: Oxford, 1958), 106.

[12] Cf. below, ch. IX, n. 7.

[13] "Charisma, Order, and Status," *American Sociological Review,* 30: 2, April 1965, 199–213.

charismatic qualities, that is, personal as well as office charisma.

For an outside observer it is very hard to gauge to what extent the international charismatic imagery of men like Nkrumah, Sukarno, Ben Bella, and Nasser has had substance for the various strata in their countries. At any rate, the sudden downfall of such men or slow attrition of their leadership shows that they lose power in the same way in which patrimonial rulers have often lost it: by a palace coup, especially by intervention of the army.[14] For reasons of legitimation some of them may be retained as figureheads; this is perhaps a good measure of charismatic efficacy, although in the case of Sukarno in 1966 the military's calculated "neutralization" of the head of state may have been as important a motive for his retention as his charismatic halo in the eyes of millions of Indonesians. At any rate, the successors of these charismatic leaders tend to have a more pragmatic bent—another patrimonial feature.

Much has been written about armies in underdeveloped countries as a major, and sometimes the only, modern bureaucracy and force for modernization. They certainly are hierarchical organizations, and some of them indeed approach the bureaucratic realities of a Western army; but most of them have personal patrimonial traits that facilitate the takeover of government, that is, the troops are more loyal to their immediate commanders than to the governmental leaders. Significantly, some of the more stable countries (Morocco, Iran, Ethiopia, Thailand) still have armies in which the belief in traditionalist legitimacy is alive. However, such legitimation has never been sufficient insurance against the overthrow of the ruler, partly because of the administrative strategies of patrimonial regimes. One such strategy has been the creation of a military force that differed in social, ethnic, or tribal composition from the population, so that the social distance between apparatus and subjects would be maximized. However, this strategy could easily put the ruler at the mercy of his troops. (Weber took his major historical examples for this double-edged role from the Near Eastern armies, particularly the Mamelukes and Janissaries.) [15]

There seems to be a parallel here to the dilemma of present-day nationalist leaders, who want to have a "national" army free from regional and tribal ties. The course of events has proved that they

[14] For the first major study of Nkrumah's downfall, see Henry L. Bretton, *The Rise and Fall of Kwame Nkrumah: A Study of Personal Rule in Africa* (New York: Praeger, 1966).

[15] *Economy and Society* (New York: Bedminster, 1968), Part Two, ch. 12: 5.

can quickly lose control over their own instrument, either because regional or tribal elements in the army resist or because a "nationalized" army becomes the only nationally effective force in an otherwise fragmented state. In the Near East as well as in Africa the pattern of military takeover that was typical of traditional regimes is repeating itself. Some sub-Sahara kingdoms, for example, used to be unstable because army units tended to be more loyal to their immediate commanders (princes or other members of the ruling families) than to the king. In some of these areas political instability is part of the precolonial tradition, not just a phenomenon of transition and modernization.

It should be clearly understood that such patrimonial loyalties are compatible with universalist components. Among the Bantu, where interregnum wars and princely usurpations were frequent, patrons selected their clients among commoners according to administrative and military ability. Conversely, under British control the modern Bantu bureaucracy, which had been modeled after the British civil service, at times had to be "corrupt" (that is, particularist) in order to reconcile conflicting values.[16]

Once in power, army leaders tend to become personal rulers; we can think of the extremely precarious position of the South Vietnamese corps commanders ("Baby Turks"), with their practices of appointment by loyalty and taxation by discretion, or of their much more entrenched neighbors in Thailand.[17] Several years ago Edgar L. Shor considered Thailand an unusual case, but actually the overall pattern he pictured has frequently been repeated. Shor perceived a transitional corruption of the civil-service model, which had been borrowed from England in the 1880's, a corruption that would eventually be overcome. Like many others, his standard was the "classic Weberian model"; however, his description of the "aberrations" in the administrative realities of Thailand amounted to what I mean here by "personal governance":

Deprived of the traditional deference accorded the morally legitimized monarchy, governments have relied upon the disposition of offices and shared material rewards to obtain the support of key leaders. . . . In

[16] See Lloyd Fallers, *Bantu Bureaucracy* (Chicago University Press, 1956), 241f., 248f. In spite of his recognition of universalist elements in traditional relationships, Fallers continues to think in terms of the dichotomy of bureaucracy and charisma (250).

[17] See Denis Warner's account of the practices of the South Vietnamese commanders in *The Reporter*, May 5, 1966, 11f.

the Thai bureaucracy, patterns of authority relationship are habitually hierarchical, predominantly personal, and inherently unstable. . . . The personal clique, based on a feudal-like system of personal obligation, provides the principal focus of bureaucratic loyalty and identification. Bonds of reciprocal obligation, reminiscent of earlier patron-client structures in the traditional social system, informally align a number of dependent subordinates with individual political and administrative leaders in more or less cohesive informal structures. In contrast to primary group ties in some other Asian countries, the clique groupings in Thailand are substantially independent of family or kinship relations. . . . Since the clique generally consists of a ranking superior and his subordinates within the organization, it usually coincides with the legal structures. . . . The dependence of careers on political and personal favor apparently dictates an entrepreneurial career strategy for the ambitious.[18]

The importance of personal loyalties and of material rewards does not exclude a peculiar mixture of reform-mindedness and "corruption" in such regimes. In his vivid description of the Young Turks' patrimonialism—which he never called by this name— Dankwart Rustow pointed to the "uninterrupted chain that links the Kemalists to the Young Turks, to the men of the Tanzimat, and to the classical Ottoman Empire—the sponsors of modernity in the twentieth century with the founders of tradition in the thirteenth." If the Ottoman Empire was "in essence a military camp and an educational institution," it is still true that "the sentiments persist among younger military officers that only an authoritarian regime under military aegis can accomplish the necessary tasks of social, cultural, and economic reform." [19] Rustow's portrayal of Turkish bureaucracy reveals a patrimonial administration that has not changed much since the Ottoman Empire adopted a formal French pattern; then as now there exists what is imprecisely known as "corruption": "connections" count, favoritism prevails, and for the few there is abundant profit in real-estate dealings. Corruption in the conventional sense varies with the strength of puritanical sentiment among reformist or revolutionary functionaries—officeholders or aspirants. However, reforms do not seem to change the largely personal character of loyalty patterns.

[18] E. L. Shor, "The Thai Bureaucracy," *Administrative Science Quarterly*, v, June 1960, 70, 77, 80. See also Fred W. Riggs, *Thailand: The Modernization of a Bureaucratic Polity* (Honolulu: East-West Center Press, 1966).

[19] "Turkey: The Modernity of Tradition," in Pye and Verba, *op. cit.;* 172f., 187.

In sum, nowadays, the nationalist leaders of the new states claim revolutionary legitimacy. Most of them embrace some variation of national socialism, which in the 1930's often came close to Nazism and Japanese fascism and later moved toward communism. Frequently, the same men have made the switch without drastically changing their outlook, whether they were Indonesian or Arab nationalists. Behind the ideological veneer lie goals and means that are closer to native traditions of government than tends to be apparent to the leaders themselves and to many an outside observer. Europeanization, Americanization, Westernization, and simply modernization—there is no similarly accepted term for the influence of Russian or Chinese communism—provide so many influential ideological and institutional models, but are not necessarily dominant in administrative practice.

PERSONAL RULERSHIP AND EMPIRE-BUILDING

One of the major reasons for the predominance of personal rulership over legal-rational legislation and administration in the new states seems to lie in a social, cultural, and political heterogeneity of such magnitude that a more or less viable complementary and countervailing pluralism of the Western type, with its strong but not exclusive components of universality, does not appear feasible. Even the total victory of a totalitarian minority merely leads to a highly centralized variant of personal governance under which the ruler has maximum discretion (what Weber called "sultanism"). The foremost task of these states is the political integration of greatly disparate elements—ethnic, tribal, religious, linguistic, or even economic. Structurally, much of what is today called nation-building should perhaps be called, more precisely, empire-building, if the political connotations of the term do not make it too difficult to use it in a strictly sociological, value-neutral sense. The problem of empire is the problem of establishing political order in the face of social and cultural heterogeneity. By contrast, nation-building finds its historical matrix in the European nation-state, which aimed at the integration of a population with a common culture, especially a common language and common historical legacies shared by various strata. It is no accident that pluralist democracy has been successful, on a larger scale, only in fairly homogeneous countries.[20]

[20] The term "state-building" can perhaps substitute for "empire-building," but it does not imply equally well the integration of disparate elements. In

An empire in the sense meant here was the Austro-Hungarian Double Monarchy, which introduced parliamentary government only for each of its halves and not for the whole realm. Even Imperial Germany faced a substantial problem of integrating diverse cultural and political elements, but because of compensating homogeneous forces this task was ideologically perceived as that of building a nation.[21]

The problem of empire is not one of bigness as such, and the absolute number of people is not decisive. China is commonly called an empire by virtue of a combination of sheer size, historical longevity, military power, and expansionist ideology; but smaller African countries, for instance, face "empire problems" similar to those of India and Indonesia because they have more tribal fragmentation on a smaller geographical scale and perhaps because they have a smaller "critical mass" of elites. In fact, Weber used his model of patrimonialism for African petty kingdoms as well as for the great empires of history.[22]

Despite technological progress—in particular, vastly increased communication facilities—many of the problems that troubled the patrimonial states of the past persist or recur. The agonies of Indonesia provide a stark example. Sukarno adhered to a rhetoric of the nation-state and of racial unity that simply denied the facts of an exceedingly complex pluralism and particularism. In a well-focused community study of social change and economic modernization in

---

Weber's terminology, which is applied here, the state is defined as a group that asserts an effective monopoly of legitimate force over a given territory; this definition does not specify the cultural and social aspects of the problem of political integration. The United States and the Soviet Union, which face tasks of international integration, can be called great or global empires *(Weltreiche)*; expansionist states may be called "imperialist" in the conventional sense.

[21] It should not be forgotten that Imperial Germany remained a federation of states under the hegemony of Prussian monarchic constitutionalism, which combined dominant features of traditionalist patrimonialism with subordinate legal-rational (constitutional and bureaucratic) arrangements.

[22] Weber and Eisenstadt have been alone among sociologists in giving systematic attention to the phenomenon of empire. Weber dealt with it throughout his career: in his book *Roman Agrarian History and Its Importance for Public and Civil Law* (1891), in his essay "The Social Causes of the Decline of Ancient Civilization" (1896), in his book *The Agrarian Conditions of Antiquity* (1909), in the major body of *Economy and Society* (1911–13), and in the collected *Essays in the Sociology of Religion*. Eisenstadt applied structural functionalism to the great "patrimonial-bureaucratic" empires, as Weber called them. Both writers have been particularly concerned with the reasons for the empires' ultimate failure, the causes of stagnation and disintegration.

Indonesia, Clifford Geertz recognized several years ago what I call the problem of empire and stated it succinctly:

The ideologies of modern nationalism, arising as they do out of intense concern with massive social reconstruction, show a strong tendency toward a neglect, even an outright denial, of important variations in domestic cultural patterns and of internal social discontinuities. . . . With regard to national economic planning this leads to a failure to cast proposals in a form which attempts to take maximum advantage of the peculiarities of various local traditions, to an unwillingness even to consider differentiated plans for different cultural and social groups. . . . In the over-concern with national integration, conceived in a wholly monistic sense, the very construction of such integration . . . may be undermined.[23]

Personal rulerships can be more responsive to cultural and social diversity than intensely ideological leaders are willing to be. But this does not imply that such regimes are much more likely to solve the problem of empire in the direction of faster economic growth and modernization. A country's diversity may amount to an inflexible pluralism that is not amenable to integration through the compromise strategies of personal rulers. Moreover, radical intellectuals deny legitimacy to ideologically uninspiring forms of personal rulership and in the long run can undermine them in both domestic and international politics. Since such intellectuals have taken over from traditional ones the role of legitimizers, personal rulerships are likely to have precarious legitimacy; and this is one reason for the pattern of frequent coups and countercoups. If self-proclaimed charismatic leadership with its ideological preoccupations fails to achieve the necessary amount of economic growth, personal rulership may fail to sustain political stability despite its pragmatic tendencies, and hence may also retard economic growth. This vicious circle may make it impossible for many of the new states to solve urgent problems of modernization, not to speak of catching up with the highly industrialized countries in the foreseeable future.

This skeptical conclusion is intentionally set in opposition to the predictions of those who, like Clark Kerr, envisage "the age of

[23] Clifford Geertz, *Peddlers and Princes* (University of Chicago Press, 1963), 155f. For an informative analysis of neotraditionalism in Indonesia, see Ann Ruth Willner, *The Neotraditional Accommodation to Political Independence: The Case of Indonesia* (Princeton: Center of International Studies, Princeton University, Research Monograph No. 26, 1966).

total industrialization" and anticipate that "by the middle of the twenty-first century, industrialization will have swept away most pre-industrial forms of society, except possibly a few odd backwaters." [24] It is equally possible to foresee a century in which the past will repeat itself and issues of personal rulership and empire-building will persist.

[24] Clark Kerr et al., *Industrialism and Industrial Man* (New York: Oxford, 1964), 3, 221.

IX

CHARISMATIC LEADERSHIP

"The term 'charismatic leader' has recently attained widespread and almost debased currency. In the past, it was occasionally applied to Gandhi, Lenin, Hitler, and Roosevelt. Now nearly every leader with marked popular appeal, especially those of new states, is indiscriminately tagged as charismatic." [1] Difficulties in the use of this term arise not only from indiscriminate labeling but also from conflicting theories of societies. Two recent discussions are especially instructive in this respect.

In an assessment of Max Weber's political writings Karl Loewenstein has raised the question of whether or not the term "charisma" can properly be applied in contemporary politics. Charismatic leadership depends upon a widespread belief in the existence of extraordinary or supernatural capacities, but such beliefs are at a discount in secular contexts. Though democratization has increased the plebiscitarian component of modern politics, the qualities of

---

[1] Ann Ruth and Dorothy Willner, "The Rise and Role of Charismatic Leaders," *Annals of the American Academy of Political and Social Studies,* 358, March 1965, 78.

Reinhard Bendix, "Reflections on Charismatic Leadership," from Bendix *et al.,* eds., *State and Society* (Boston: Little, Brown, 1968), 616–629. This essay originated in a symposium organized by the Association of Asian Studies, which met in New York, 1966, under the chairmanship of Professor Rupert Emerson. Subsequently the editors of *Asian Survey* arranged for publication of papers on four Asian leaders, with this essay serving as an introduction (*Asian Survey,* II, June 1967, 341–353). In the republication of the essay, I have made several revisions as well as included factual materials which originally appeared in separate essays by Professor Robert M. Smith, Dr. Margaret Fisher, Professor Chongsik Lee, and Dr. Stuart R. Schram. I wish to thank the authors and the editors of *Asian Survey* for their permission to use materials from the articles in this revised form.

personality which attract voters indicate the popularity, but not necessarily the charisma, of a successful political leader. Accordingly, Loewenstein feels that today charisma in the proper sense is likely to be found in those areas of the world in which a popular belief in supernatural powers is still widespread, as in some parts of Africa or Asia.[2]

Quite the opposite position has been taken by E. A. Shils, who sees a charismatic element in all societies. Shils notes Weber's distinction between the disruptive or innovative effects of charisma and the continuous and routine character of tradition or the legal order; this parallels Loewenstein's distinction between the magico-religious contexts that encourage, and the secular contexts that discourage, charisma. As Shils points out, Weber himself did not confine his use of the term to magical or religious beliefs, and he analyzed the institutionalization of charisma through kinship, heredity, and office. But he also believed that the opportunities for genuine charisma had diminished in the course of an increasing rationalization and bureaucratization of Western society. Shils takes issue with this last point. He maintains that men in all societies confront exigencies of life which demand a comprehensive solution. Man's position in the cosmos, birth, death, marriage, basic ideas of equity, are among these central concerns. The need for establishing some order with reference to these concerns may vary among men, but the point is that charisma attaches itself to those individuals or institutions which satisfy that need or promise to do so. Such ordering may involve philosophical or artistic representations, religious doctrines, interpretations of the law, or the authority of government. Charisma has necessarily a protean character, since it may become a focus of belief whenever ultimate concerns are given an authoritative ordering.[3]

This is not the place to discuss these larger questions substantively, but it is appropriate to refer briefly to one rather topical application of the term "charisma." The new nations provide a setting of rapid change in which charismatic leaders may achieve new forms of political integration. In his analysis, *Ghana in Transition*, David Apter has suggested that charismatic leadership helps to undermine tribal authority and thus helps to make way for the creation of secular, legal institutions in a nation-state. He notes, however, that

[2] Karl Loewenstein, *Max Weber's Political Ideas in the Perspective of Our Time* (Amherst: University of Massachusetts Press, 1966), 74–87.
[3] E. A. Shils, "Charisma, Order and Status," *American Sociological Review*, Vol. 30, April 1965, 199–213.

charismatic leadership is not easily reconciled with secular systems of authority. Perhaps a charismatic leader like Nkrumah can transfer some of the loyalty, traditionally accorded to tribal chiefs, to the agents and symbols of a secular government—as long as he is the leader. But then the problem is: How can the loyalties of a personal following be transferred to the institutions of government ("routinized" in Weber's terminology)? Without such transfer governmental stability is not assured.[4]

In a critique of writings on Ghanaian and African politics Claude Ake has raised the basic question whether or not charismatic leaders can fulfill any such constructive functions in the new nations. They often command a large percentage of the vote, but this may involve a fleeting acclamation and an engineered consent rather than widespread public support. Since in the new nations political instability is rife and integration difficult to achieve, any leader may at times obtain considerable political power if he can command a certain degree of loyalty. Modern means of publicity can give such leadership all the appearance of charisma: the singular gifts of the leader and the unquestioning devotion of his followers. But such appearances can be misleading. The popular celebrations at Nkrumah's overthrow in 1966 suggest either that his charisma had disappeared by then, or that it had been on the wane for some time past, or indeed that there had been little of it in the first place. Such uncertainties only point up the evanescent qualities of charisma, which may come to the fore in times of rapid change but which are neither a substitute for regular leadership nor easily reconciled with enduring political institutions.[5]

These contemporary uncertainties in the use of the term suggest that there are special hazards in drawing analogies between new nations, then and now. S. M. Lipset has noted that George Washington was a source of unity in the early years of the United States and that his commanding military success inspired widespread veneration of his person. But Lipset also notes that Washington was

[4] See David Apter, *Ghana in Transition* (New York: Atheneum, 1966; first published in 1955), 303–306; see also 168, 173f., 296f., 323. For Apter's own reassessment, see "Nkrumah, Charisma, and the Coup," *Daedalus*, 97: 3, Summer 1968, 757–792.

[5] See Claude Ake, "Charismatic Legitimation and Political Integration," *Comparative Studies in Society and History*, Vol. IX, Oct. 1966, 1–13. Mr. Ake raises many appropriate questions but does not seem aware that it is inappropriate to expect a legitimation of regular political institutions from charismatic leadership—these institutions exist already.

oriented to the rule of law, permitted the growth of an embryonic party system, and established a precedent for succession to office by voluntarily stepping down in favor of President-elect Adams. Genuine as Washington's charisma probably was, it was acted out in a framework of received political and legal institutions—and it is just the absence of such a framework which jeopardizes analogies between early American and contemporary experience in new nations.[6]

I have cited the large interpretative questions raised by Loewenstein and Shils and the uncertainties of the contemporary application of the term because I believe that the proper definition and use of the concept "charisma" must be clarified before these larger issues can be addressed. My purpose here is, therefore, to restate Weber's original formulation of the concept and emphasize its dynamic implications. I shall also comment briefly on some analytic problems that arise when the term "charismatic leadership" is applied to four Asian leaders whose careers illustrate different facets of the problem.

In referring now to Weber's specification of the term "charisma" I confine myself to the concept of "charismatic leadership," leaving out the "routinization of charisma" (through its association with kinship, heredity, and office) as well as the positive or negative relations between charisma and social structure. An analysis of individual political leaders need not be concerned with routinization, except insofar as it bears on the problem of succession. Also, the leaders under consideration are politically active in societies undergoing rapid change, that is, in contexts presumably favorable to charismatic appeals.[7]

[6] S. M. Lipset, *The First New Nation* (New York: Basic Books, 1963), 16–45. Cf. the contrasting interpretation by S. P. Huntington, "Political Modernization: America vs. Europe," *World Politics*, XVIII, April 1966, esp. 408–414.

[7] Weber's discussion tends to obscure the distinction between leadership and authority, since he always analyzes the latter in terms of the chances of a command being obeyed, and this criterion can be applied to leadership as well. In Weber's terminology charismatic authority in the sense of routinized charisma can be distinguished from charismatic authority in the sense of personal leadership, but that appears to leave no room for personal leadership that is not charismatic. I return to this question briefly at the end of this chapter. At any rate, the present discussion is confined to charismatic authority in the sense of personal leadership, or what I call charismatic leadership. For an illuminating discussion of this point, see Robert Bierstedt, "The Problem of Authority," in Morroe Berger, Theodore Abel, and Charles Page, eds., *Freedom and Control in Modern Society* (New York: Van Nostrand, 1954), 71f.

Weber defines "charisma" as

a certain quality of an individual personality by virtue of which he is considered extraordinary and treated as endowed with supernatural, superhuman, or at least specifically exceptional powers or qualities. These are such as are not accessible to the ordinary person, but are regarded as of divine origin or as exemplary, and on the basis of them the individual concerned is treated as a leader.[8]

Five specifications are added to this basic definition. Weber notes first that "charisma" is probably the greatest revolutionary power in periods of established tradition, and second that it typically neglects considerations of economic efficiency and rationality.[9] Third, he emphasizes that the charismatic leader and his followers constitute a congregation *(Gemeinde)*; he has no officials assisting him but rather disciples or confidants, who have no career or qualifications in the bureaucratic sense and no privileges. They are personally called by their leader on his peremptory judgment of their own charismatic gifts; they may be as summarily dismissed when he judges that they have failed his trust in them.

Weber's fourth and fifth specifications are of special interest to us here. It is best to quote him verbatim:

It is recognition on the part of those subject to authority which is decisive for the validity of charisma. This recognition is freely given and guaranteed by what is held to be a proof, originally always a miracle, and consists in devotion to the corresponding revelation, hero worship, or absolute trust in the leader. But where charisma is genuine, it is not this which is the basis of the claim to legitimacy. This basis lies rather in the conception that it is the duty of those subject to charismatic authority to recognize its genuineness and to act accordingly. Psychologically this recognition is a matter of complete personal devotion to the possessor of the quality, arising out of enthusiasm, or of despair and hope.

No prophet has ever regarded his quality as dependent on the attitudes of the masses toward him. No elective king or military leader has

---

[8] Weber, *Economy and Society* (New York: Bedminster, 1968), 241.

[9] The first of these points relates to the discussion by Loewenstein and Shils; Weber's statement is obviously conditional. Not the presence of charisma but its power to revolutionize the social order is judged to be greatest where traditions are well established. Weber also makes clear that "pure charisma" is incompatible with economic routine, not with material gain or possessions as such. *Ibid.,* 246f.

ever treated those who have resisted him or tried to ignore him otherwise than as delinquent in duty. . . .

If proof and success elude the leader for long, if he appears deserted by his god or his magical or heroic powers, above all, if his leadership fails to benefit his followers, it is likely that his charismatic authority will disappear. This is the genuine meaning of the divine right of kings (*Gottesgnadentum*).[10]

A first reading of this passage might suggest that a leader is charismatic when his followers recognize him as such, because they see "powerful results achieved in the absence of power." [11] But closer examination suggests that both the recognition by followers and the leader's own claims and actions are fundamentally ambivalent.

For the charisma of a leader to be present, it must be recognized by his followers, and in the ideal typical case this recognition is a matter of duty. But a personal devotion arising from enthusiasm, despair, or hope is easily contaminated by the desire for a "sign" which will confirm the existence of charisma. In turn, the leader demands unconditional devotion from his followers, and he will construe any demand for a sign or proof of his gift of grace as a lack of faith and a dereliction of duty. Yet his "charismatic authority will disappear, . . . if proof and success elude the leader for long." It appears then that charismatic leadership is not a label that can be applied but refers rather to a problematic relation between a leader and his followers which must be investigated. For it is in each case a question of fact: To what extent and in what ways has the followers' desire for a sign—born out of their enthusiasm, despair, or hope—interefered with, modified, or even jeopardized their unconditional devotion to duty? And similarly it is a question of fact: To what extent and in what ways has the leader's unconditional claim to exceptional powers or qualities been interefered with, modified, or even jeopardized by the actions which he construes as proof of his charismatic qualifications?

The following sketches of four political leaders in Asia may be considered with these questions in mind.

PRINCE NORODOM SIHANOUK, CAMBODIA (1922–   )

Prince Sihanouk exemplifies in his own person the transition from prince to plebiscitarian leader. He was called to the

---

[10] *Ibid.*, 242.

[11] The phrase in quotation marks has been suggested by Dankwart Rustow, *The World of Nations* (Washington, D. C.: Brookings Institution, 1967), 165.

throne in 1941, at the age of eighteen, presumably because the French colonial rulers considered him submissive. Yet at an early time, Sihanouk faced up to the problem of procuring Cambodia's independence from French rule, while dealing with the leading political party, which was not only nationalist and anti-French but also opposed to the monarchy. The Prince recognized the difficulties which would surround the emerging state and did not want to foreclose the possibility of appealing to France for assistance. Therefore he chose to negotiate the achievement of independence rather than win it through open revolt. But by winning independence as a monarch in 1953, Sihanouk also succeeded in countering anti-monarchical sentiments. Because the throne was customarily above national politics, Sihanouk recognized that in an independent Cambodia he had to choose between his monarchical position and an active political role. Accordingly, he abdicated in favor of his father in 1955 and founded a party, the Sangkum, in order to arouse greater public interest in political affairs. Originally, the party was not intended to be "political"; however, the people responded enthusiastically, and eventually all other parties were dissolved, and their leaders and followers joined the Sangkum. In 1960, upon the death of his father, Sihanouk was requested to ascend the throne once again, but he refused. Instead, his mother became Queen, while the Prince suggested that the National Assembly amend the constitution and create the position of chief of state. The amendment was passed, and Prince Sihanouk was elected to the newly created position.

In this way the charisma of the royal family was transferred in good part to the position of a plebiscitarian political leader. The concept of the Sangkum party as a loyal following of the entire people may be considered similarly: a transmutation of subjects into citizens with the ideology of the people's loyalty to the king virtually intact. The subsequent dissolution of all competing parties may have the same significance; while pressure was no doubt exerted, it may have involved to a great extent an appeal to loyalty which even the opponents of the Prince could not ignore. The same populist approach is evidenced in the National Congress. Originally designed to provide a forum for the people to voice their opinions and complaints, the agenda of the Congress are arranged in practice by the Sangkum. Prince Sihanouk presides over the meetings of the Congress, while the people in attendance are a largely passive audience. The Prince is generally able to influence the course of the meeting which becomes in effect a royal audience in plebiscitarian disguise.

In his new role of plebiscitarian leadership the Prince has reenacted the attributes of a benevolent ruler with a strong emphasis on good works and modernity. The populist stance, the jokes to get people relaxed, human warmth and personal solicitude, the appeal to the people at large and to the grandeur of the country's traditions, even the Prince's exemplary actions such as the design of textiles or well-publicized acts of manual labor—all these are instances of symbolic identification with the people in a context of popular affection and deference. Reactions are not unequivocal, however. There are signs of discontent among competing groups within the Sangkum, which are critical of the Prince's foreign and domestic policies; there is also unrest among the educated youths who cannot find the opportunities for which they feel themselves qualified. Nevertheless, the Prince apparently uses his protean talents to show his solidarity with the people rather than to manifest his exceptional powers as a leader. And accounts of popular reactions present the people as, on the whole, content and deferential rather than devoted or eager for signs and miracles. In sum, this is a case of institutionalized charisma, with the aura and potential terror of royalty mellowed by populist appeals and an adaptation of plebiscitarian methods of government.

This classification is suggested also by Prince Sihanouk's personnel policy. The men he has employed are not disciples but rather men distinguished by their experience and independent judgment. His present advisors include men who formerly opposed him but whom he appointed apparently because he valued their talents. However, two of the chief advisors are relatives of the Prince. It is speculated that the future leaders of Cambodia will be recruited from this group of advisors, perhaps under the direction of Prince Monireth, Sihanouk's uncle. But the question is whether or not any successor can achieve anything like Prince Sihanouk's very personal combination of royalist tradition and plebiscitarian methods. As long as Sihanouk is still "King" to the people at large, no one is likely to question his right to name his successor; indeed, some years ago the Prince designated one of his sons as the future head of the Sangkum party. But how long will this belief in the institutionalized charisma of royalty remain intact? The Prince's son, for example, would succeed not to the throne but to the position of party leader. And unless he is quite as successful as his father in holding the warring party factions at bay by an appeal to the people and by successful actions in their behalf, his image will get tarnished more quickly than it would in the presence of comparable intrigues at a royal court with its base in the sacred blood ties of the royal family.

The strength of institutionalized charisma (as in royalty) is that succession is solved through inheritance; its weakness is that personal qualification for office is a matter of chance. In the case of charismatic leadership proper, the assets and liabilities are reversed: there is no rule for succession, while personal qualifications can be decisive. The relation between Gandhi and Nehru is a case in point.

JAWAHARLAL NEHRU, INDIA (1889–1964)

Among the four leaders considered here, Nehru is the only one clearly a disciple and a publicly designated successor. Since in the eyes of his followers at least, Nehru's charisma was derived from Gandhi, we are obliged to examine the transfer of charisma from teacher to disciple, in order to assess the latter's charismatic appeal. Weber discusses the transfer of charisma as an aspect of "routinization." Since by definition charisma is out of the ordinary and dependent upon manifestations of strictly personal qualities, it exists in pure form only in the person in whom it originates. Yet the disciples of the leader and his followers at large share a strong desire to perpetuate that "gift of grace" and its real or presumed benefits, and efforts at such perpetuation come to the fore when the problem of succession must be solved. In this respect Weber distinguishes six typical alternatives; the one of interest here is that the original charismatic leader designates his own successor, who is then accorded recognition by the community.

Nehru's long schooling in England had prepared him to become a junior member in his father's legal firm, but he found this prospect dull. In 1919, at the age of thirty, he became actively involved in the Indian independence movement. The designation of Nehru as a successor to Gandhi took place over a number of years. During this early period, Nehru emerged as a young, conspicuously Western, relatively wealthy, and intensely theoretical member of the inner circle of disciples. All the disciples were held together by their faith in Gandhi's political and moral leadership. Yet there were divisions among them, for the specific goals of Hindu-Moslem harmony, the elimination of untouchability, and the improvement of village life were broad enough to allow considerable variation with regard to means and ends. In the context of the movement for independence the most noteworthy division concerned nonviolence, which was a creed to some and a tactic to others. This tells us something about Gandhi's tolerance for diversity among his immediate followers, suggesting the permissive preaching of the "exemplary prophet" which "says nothing about a divine mission or an ethical duty of obedience, but rather directs itself to the self-interest of those who crave salvation, recommending to them the same path as he himself traversed." [12]

Nehru's tie to Gandhi was based on deep respect and acceptance of Gandhi's tactical skill, but these sentiments did not affect Nehru's own wide-ranging ideological and political explorations and commitments. Such world-political preoccupations separated Nehru from things Indian even in the midst of intense political activities. Gandhi commented in 1924 that Nehru was one of "the loneliest young men of my acquaintance in India." [13] This personal and cultural isolation was directly related to the articulation of Nehru's political position. His views on international affairs sharpened his conflict with the older Congress leaders, including his father, but these views also enabled Nehru to appeal effectively to labor groups and radical youth, among whom some had lost faith in Gandhi. In this setting Gandhi, choosing to withdraw from the Congress presidency in favor of Nehru (1930), used Nehru to keep the young rebels in line. Gandhi also induced his chosen disciple to accept policies that bewildered him, so that Nehru was forced for the sake of party unity to represent as his own a position in which he did not believe. This pattern recurred during the long years of discipleship, from Gandhi's reconciliation between Nehru and his father in 1919 to his formal designation of Nehru as his political heir in 1942. For Nehru these were also years during which he was pulled in several directions, dedicated to the man in whose charisma he believed but at odds with him in his style and judgments. Yet Nehru served him and the cause of independence with complete devotion despite the false positions and humiliating experiences into which Gandhi's tactics forced him from time to time.

A lesser man might have succumbed to the strain of that relationship, compounded as it was by Gandhi's cooperative and antagonistic relations with Nehru's father. But Nehru was an intense and

[12] Weber, op. cit., 447f.

[13] In a letter to Motilal Nehru, September 2, 1924. Quoted from B. R. Nanda, The Nehrus: Motilal and Jawaharlal (New York: John Day, 1963), 247, in Margaret Fisher, "India's Jawaharlal Nehru," Asian Survey, VII, June 1967, 367.

ebullient man, who apparently overcame the ambiguities of his position and his own ambivalence. He was aided not only by his courage and idealism for India but also by Gandhi's patient trust in his qualities of mind and character despite outbursts of temper, doctrinaire views, and repeated clashes with other Congress leaders. Nehru's relationship with Gandhi reflected his ambivalence to India as a whole. Admiring Gandhi's tactical "magic" and his uniquely Indian means of achieving independence, Nehru still saw nonviolence only as a tactic to achieve a political purpose; thus at the same time he identified with, and dissociated himself from, this symbol of India. While Gandhi gave him his trust during the long years of discipleship, he still mixed expressions of confidence with fatherly admonitions, giving him his blessing but withholding his mandate. There is some suggestion in this context that Nehru's successful campaigns among the Indian masses were an escape from an enervating tutelage as well as a discovery of India. Contacts with the Indian people were a means of attaining confidence in his mission, for he witnessed the unconditional devotion with which they viewed him as the embodiment of Gandhi's charisma and the charisma of his own sacrifices for independence. There is an almost tragic irony in the paradox that what his personality represented to the people was largely independent of what he said to them. Nehru's effect on the masses inspired his confidence in India while increasing the skepticism of his colleagues. Yet this mass enthusiasm and Nehru's continued isolation among the disciples provided Gandhi again and again with the opportunity to weld the factions of the Congress together. And then, at the age of fifty-three, once more in jail, Nehru learned from the book of an Englishman what it was that distinguished him from Gandhi. The book distinguished between the prophet, who pursues the truth relentlessly, and the leader, who strikes a compromise between truth and the views of the average man. Nehru thought his own role to be that of the leader but believed Gandhi had confused the two roles. Apparently Nehru did not recognize Gandhi's unique fusion of prophecy and teaching, which was a part of that specific charisma of India's holy men that was beyond his own grasp. By separating the teacher's role from the educative function of exemplary conduct, Nehru revealed his own Western acculturation as well as the discrepancy between his self-image and the Indian people's recognition of his charismatic gift. He wanted to be their teacher, while they sought in him the exemplary prophet.

In this all too brief consideration I have emphasized the problem of succession, highlighted by the great charisma of Nehru's mentor. It may be noted that the charismatic appeal of Gandhi and of Nehru is entirely the by-product of their personal gifts in the context of the Indian independence movement.

In turning now to a discussion of two leaders in communist countries, we must attempt to disentangle the relationship between the leader and his people from the manipulated representation of that relationship by the mass media.

KIM IL-SŎNG, NORTH KOREA (1919–   )

It is difficult to separate fact from fiction in the life history of Kim Il-sŏng. Kim has concentrated in his hands all power of decision-making in the party, the government, and the army. To account for this fact, and to celebrate it, North Korean historians have written hagiological accounts which twist the story of Kim's childhood, his role as a guerrilla leader, and the first phase of his party leadership into so many anticipations of his present preeminence. For that reason it becomes difficult to assess the rather meager descriptions of Kim's leadership. The Korean party appears to model its mobilization of the people after a shock-troop pattern, giving its civilian appeals and organizational efforts the appearance of simulated combat under conditions of guerrilla warfare. For example, Kim approaches production problems in the manner of a self-confident guerrilla leader who himself masters whatever he asks of his soldiers and by his example encourages them to greater effort. He reportedly learns the technicalities of the factories or collectives he will visit, thus living up to the reputation of the omniscient leader. In this way he emphasizes by his example the party's mission as the teacher of the people. Organized propaganda shows this leadership in action and seeks to enhance its exemplary effects by the testimony of "awed witnesses." But this inevitably raises questions as does Kim's power to divert resources to those farms and enterprises which have been selected for exemplary success in their production efforts. Propagandistic manipulation of this kind can give a hollow ring to the claim of exceptional powers on behalf of the leader, and a mere joke or derisive comment aimed at such manipulation can turn a follower's devotion into a skeptic's "withdrawal of efficiency" (Veblen).[14]

---

[14] According to Chong-sik Lee, biographical data detrimental to Kim's official image have been suppressed, such as his flight to Siberia to escape the Japanese

Here we come to a lacuna in Weber's approach to charisma, due to the time at which his analysis was written (1913–14). He did not foresee that it would be possible to simulate publicly all aspects of charismatic leadership—the manifestations of the leader's extraordinary gift, the unconditional devotion of his disciples, and the awed veneration of his large following—saturating all channels of communication so that no one could escape the message. Modern dictatorships have used such centrally organized, public hagiology extensively; given the possibilities of the "great lie" and the "will to believe," a widespread belief in charisma can be created under favorable conditions. Yet the built-in limitations of "charisma by publicity" should not be overlooked. All hagiological writings contain paeans to the virtues of the saints; in the eyes of the believers the credibility of these writings is enhanced, rather than diminished, by stories showing "powerful results achieved in the absence of power," and such stories are also a regular feature of dictatorial propaganda. But the authors of conventional hagiology were themselves true believers, expressing their own sense of the miraculous for the edification of their readers, in the absence of any claim to be believed other than the authenticity of their own religious experience. In this respect, a manipulated hagiology differs. Where all media are saturated with news of the leader's great deeds and the devotion of his followers, ordinary people may begin to resist the message by various strategies which help them escape the din and the drive to mobilize them. For the saturation of the media means manipulation and can suggest even to the unlettered that "powerful results are 'achieved' in the presence of power" and hence in the absence of miracles.

Nevertheless, it would be a mistake to infer that charismatic leadership cannot occur under these conditions. First of all, central manipulation of news is still compatible with credibility. All totalitarian regimes have an interest, for example, in obtaining testimonials to the leader by prominent individuals with a reputation for probity and independent judgment. Whether or not pressure is used to obtain such testimonials, they can be turned to good ac-

---

invasion, which makes his subsequent political prominence largely the result of Russian or Chinese influence. There is some question, of course, whether the manipulation of such biographical details enters into people's awareness; but even in the absence of knowledge, suspicions and rumors spread quickly if they project popular feelings.

count by the mass media—at least for quite a time. Again, the leader himself may use the media to project his supreme confidence in his mission, and pomp and circumstance can enhance the effect of that message. Thus it is quite wrong to suppose that charismatic leadership implies the absence of deliberate manipulation on the part of the leader. On the contrary, a sense of personal mission will justify the manipulative enhancement of the charismatic appeal, so long as this does not conflict with the appeal itself.[15] Secondly, the leader's career may exemplify his charisma in the eyes of the people, and the mere fact of media manipulation will not necessarily undermine their belief in him. Indeed, a people's recognition of that charisma—born of the will to believe and manifest in their devotion to duty—may endure long after they have begun to discount the credibility of the leader's entourage and of the whole apparatus of media manipulation. This consideration may have some bearing on the case of Mao Tse-tung.

MAO TSE-TUNG, CHINA (1893–   )

The evidence of Mao Tse-tung's leadership is overwhelming, and there is little doubt that this leadership deserves the attribute "charismatic." Stuart Schram points out that Mao gives the appearance of an "average Chinese peasant." [16] The peasant is traditionally a symbol of weakness; Mao's success has made him a symbol of strength. For a great power to develop out of universal weakness is indeed a miracle in the literal sense. Since in this case identification with the peasant also symbolizes the nation, Mao personifies the whole transformation of his country. His grand and remote appearance only intensifies the impression of mystery associated with miracles—whether or not this appearance is a personal trait, a manner acquired during a dramatic life spent in revolutionary politics, an impression created by party propaganda, a sign of old age, or some combination of these.

Three main aspects of Mao's thought are directly related to his rise to power. His nationalism is exemplified in the mobilization of

[15] It is probably more difficult to make testimonials to the leader appear genuine when these are given by his direct collaborators, because the secular context militates against the image of the disciple who is moved by unselfish devotion to duty and who partakes of the leader's charisma.

[16] See Stuart R. Schram, "Mao Tse-tung as a Charismatic Leader," *Asian Survey*, VII, June 1967, 383–384.

the Chinese against Japanese aggression. His concern with military action is related to his long experience in guerrilla warfare with its combination of militancy and populism. And his emphasis on voluntarism and conscious action (though related to Leninist ideas) reflects the special importance he has attributed throughout his career to moral and psychological preparedness as the principal basis of revolution. These themes were articulated in Mao's early writings, and his continued adherence to these basic ideas conveys an impression of extraordinary consistency. In his own mind and those of his devoted followers these ideas are directly related to the success of the Chinese revolution. Accordingly, Mao's outlook is seen as the cause of "powerful results achieved in the absence of power." It is not surprising that an aging leader relies on this inspiration of his successful achievements of the past when his revolutionary regime begins to encounter the resistance of men and the complications of circumstances, as all revolutionary regimes do, once established.

A number of factors have been cited to explain the excesses of the Mao cult in recent years: a struggle for power within the highest ranks of the party, senile vanity, echoes of traditional emperor worship. Mao's penchant for a personalist approach to problems of leadership despite his awareness of the importance of organization, and last but not least his conscious manipulation of his own personality cult as a political weapon. To this plethora of causes an outsider hesitates to add further possibilities. But if the evidence for Mao's charisma is as strong as has been suggested, then it is probable that mounting complexities bring out both the supreme leader's fear of losing his extraordinary powers and that mixture of hope and fear of despair with which the young generation reacts to a charisma placed in jeopardy. As the difficulties of the regime mount, the populist desire for a "sign" or proof of charisma is increasing, just at the time when the leader who embodies that charisma is visibly aging. After all, the paradox is that a personality cult centering on a seventy-four-year-old man comes to a crescendo at a time when he must solve the most difficult problem of charismatic leadership— the problem of succession. The more the cult centers on him personally, the more insoluble that problem becomes, and Mao appears to be quite aware of this fact. Referring to organizational changes involving the delegation of his power to Liu Shao-ch'i and Teng Hsiao-p'ing in 1956, Mao stated in October 1966: "When I retreated into the second line by not conducting the daily work and by letting others execute it, my purpose was to cultivate their prestige so that when I have to see God, the country can avoid great chaos."[17]

In now reversing that earlier decision according to his own interpretation, Mao is apparently attempting to transform the people's recognition of his personal charisma into a cult of sacred objects. It remains to be seen whether such a transformation can capture the imagination of the people and also preserve their devotion to duty—in the absence of visible miracles and eventually in the absence of the charismatic leader himself.

All this is without precedent in the history of communist movements only in the sense that a career of leadership that spans the entire period from the beginning of the revolutionary movement until eighteen years after the seizure of power is also without precedent. This factor must be recognized in making comparisons between Mao and either Lenin or Stalin. Lenin's early death removed him from the contentions arising later, so that the deification of his person and the canonization of his writings became weapons for his immediate followers in their struggle over the succession and in subsequent policy disputes. Mao's position is quite different. Still being alive, he has become the leading participant in struggles in which he uses his own deification and canonization to resolve the problem of succession and the policy disputes associated with that problem. Again, Stalin was the disciple who won out in the struggles for the succession following Lenin's death and in the absence of any clear settlement of that succession by Lenin himself. The purges instigated by Stalin in the 1930's were well removed from that question; they could be compared to Mao's present situation only if, instead, Lenin had lived and had instigated the purges in order to designate his successor and make certain basic policy decisions binding upon him and the Party leadership.

There is reason to anticipate some deification of Mao after his death, as old and young followers alike seek to preserve the power of his charisma for themselves and the community at large.[18] At present Mao appears to anticipate just such a development. By laying the groundwork not only for the choice of his successor but for

[17] Quoted in Gene T. Hsiao, "The Background and Development of 'The Proletarian Cultural Revolution,'" *Asian Survey*, VII, June 1967, 392. Mr. Hsiao has suggested to me that the reference to "God" is meant ironically, and the statement itself is clearly polemical. But these considerations do not, I think, affect the interpretations suggested here.

[18] Cf. Weber's discussion of the impulse behind the routinization of charisma, *op. cit.*, 246ff.

the terms in which that successor will be obliged to implement the legacy of Maoist revolutionary achievements, he may be attempting to foreclose the gross misuse of his charisma by followers whose interest in institutionalization is greater than his own. It is an arresting though that Mao's effort to replace the party elite with new men and to employ the Red Guards as an instrument of "permanent revolution" is in part an old man's struggle over the use that is to be made of his work and his person by those who will live after he is gone.

In conclusion, it is appropriate to consider the distinction between charismatic leadership and leadership *sans phrase,* to which I alluded earlier. The term "charisma" is used indiscriminately, because this distinction is difficult to make in practice, though not in theory. All types of leadership are alike in that they involve an ambivalent interaction between leaders and led. A leader demands unconditional obedience, because he does not want his performance to be tested against criteria over which he has no control. Such tests jeopardize his authoritative right to command. On the other hand, the led withhold an ultimate surrender of their will (if only in the form of mental reservations), because they do not want to forgo their last chance for a quid pro quo, that is to say, for a gain through effective leadership in exchange for the obedience shown. Yet to withhold unconditional obedience in this way always runs the risk that leadership will fail us, because we have not shown our ultimate devotion to duty. The interactions between leaders and led probably trace an erratic path between this Scylla and Charybdis. The hazards of cumulative causation (as actions and reactions reinforce each other) and the reluctance of most men to face the ultimate consequences of their acts frequently lead to a tempering of demands and expectations on both sides. By not claiming ultimate authority and demanding unconditional obedience leaders can avoid being challenged and yet hope to accomplish a modicum of success. And the led are ready to obey when no ultimate commitment is demanded of them, because a mixture of acquiescence and performance leaves them free to hope for benefits with only a moderate inconvenience to themselves. In theory it is easy to see that charisma makes its appearance when leaders and led are convinced that these easy accommodations are no longer enough, when consummate belief, on one side, and the promptings of enthusiasm, despair, or hope, on the other, imperatively call for unconditional authority and obedience. In theory it is even easy to see that charisma appears to be present and yet is in jeopardy when such convictions animate the leader *or* the led, but not both simultaneously. There are many historical examples of a leader who feels the call but cannot find a following, or of people at large searching in vain for a leader who will satisfy their longing for a miracle. Thus charisma appears to occur frequently because the search for it continues. But genuine charisma is a rare event, born as it is of a belief in the mysterious gift of one man which that man shares with those who follow him.

X

JAPAN AND THE PROTESTANT ETHIC

"Cultural-educational mobility and development" suggests that education and mobility are positively related to economic development. This positive relationship exists only, I believe, where the value of economic development is already accepted as a sine qua non of individual and national advance. It is true that this ideology is widespread in the many countries which since the Second World War have been transformed by a turn of phrase (and often by little else), from "underdeveloped" into "developing" nations. But in what general sense is it meaningful to link culture with mobility and economic development? To speak of development is to imply that at one time a given society was not developing or was under- developed. With regard to that contrast, culture typically maintains the established social structure; education helps to transmit and uphold the received tradition. Accordingly, the extensive literature on development contrasts—at least implicitly—tradition and mod- ernity, and much of it is focused on the problem of how a nonindus- trial society can give rise to an industrial society. Each type has cul- tural and educational attributes of its own. It is, therefore, necessary to distinguish between the cultural *preconditions* of development and the cultural and educational *changes* that occur once develop- ment is under way, difficult as it may be to pinpoint this distinction. In this chapter the question will be how cultural patterns suporting tradition can give rise to cultural patterns supporting modernity.

Japan, in contrast with England and France, experienced rapid

Reinhard Bendix, "A Case Study in Cultural and Educational Mobility: Japan and the Protestant Ethic," in Neil J. Smelser and Seymour M. Lipset, eds., *Social Structure and Mobility in Economic Development* (Chicago: Aldine, 1966), 262–279.

economic growth, especially in the industrial sector, only after 1868. She borrowed heavily from abroad in a conscious effort to benefit from the advanced technology and the political institutions of other countries. Today, she is among the most industrialized nations of the world. My principal emphasis will not be on economic development itself, but on its "cultural-educational" preconditions. Since the classic study in this field is still Max Weber's famous essay on *The Protestant Ethic and the Spirit of Capitalism,* I shall begin with a brief, critical discussion of that essay. A comparative consideration of that essay and the Japanese development yields a perspective that illuminates "cultural-educational mobility" as a condition of development in both cases.

DOCTRINE AND CONDUCT

Max Weber's study of this problem in *The Protestant Ethic and the Spirit of Capitalism* begins with the observation that societies develop differentially and that "capitalism" originated in certain areas of Western Europe. Within these areas the traditional Catholic approach to economic pursuits tended in practice to condone what it could not prevent. Continuing a moral and religious posture that condemned usury, monopolistic practices, and generally the dance around the golden calf, the Church allowed erring men to obtain, through indulgences and the confessional, sanctioned release from whatever pangs of conscience or religious tribulations their worldly activities induced in them. In their explicit teachings the great reformers opposed the moneychangers and all their works as clearly as had Catholic doctrine. Here no change is discernible, unless it be the greater ethical rigor that reformist zeal imparted to pastoral practice. But the religious doctrines of the reformers—above all the Calvinist doctrine of predestination—introduced a basic anxiety into the believer's relation to his God, and this anxiety, so Weber's argument runs, introduced a decisive change.[1] In lieu of the permissive pastoral practice by which Catholicism softened the psychological impact of its doctrine, the Protestant believer had to face the divinely ordained uncertainty of his salvation without aid or comfort from anyone. Only his actions

---

[1] No one who has examined some of the personal documents of the period will want to minimize that anxiety. Especially impressive in this respect is the fear induced in children, documented in Sanford Fleming, *Children and Puritanism* (New Haven: Yale University Press, 1933).

could allay that uncertainty, whether through inward contrition and an abiding faith, as in Lutheranism, or through self-discipline and an active life in the service of God, as in Calvinism.

Weber points out that for analytical purposes he presents the ideas of the reformers "in their most consistent and logical forms." In this way he hopes to bring out the drift of these ideas, the direction in which a sincere believer would move. The gist of the argument is to posit an intensified motivation. All men of that time were concerned with their salvation, but the pastoral practice of Catholicism had diminished the concern. It had been greatly heightened, on the other hand, by the religious zeal of the great reformers and by the unintended implications of their theological doctrines as these were revealed in the sermons of Puritan divines. The economic actions consistent with the "Spirit of Capitalism" were, in significant measure, efforts to relieve religious anxiety—at any rate during the sixteenth and seventeenth centuries.

It is difficult, however, to infer the intensification of a motive (the quest for salvation) from the logical implications of a theological doctrine (the believer's uncertainty concerning his salvation, as a corollary of the doctrine of predestination). For all its subtlety and learning, Weber's text contains evidence that he himself remained uncertain concerning the relation between doctrine and conduct.[2] In this case, analysis of the text can help us understand the difference between cultural and behavioral analysis.

Weber writes:

We are naturally not concerned with the question of what was theoretically and officially taught in the ethical compendia of the time, however much practical significance this may have had through the influence of the Church discipline, pastoral work, and preaching. We are interested rather in something entirely different: the influence of those *psychological sanctions* which, originating in religious belief and the practice of religion, gave a direction to practical conduct and held the individual to it.[3]

Since this passage states the specific focus of attention, it is all the more significant that the key word "sanction" is ambiguous. If disci-

---

[2] Cf. the related points made by Paul Lazarsfeld and Anthony R. Oberschall, "Max Weber and Empirical Social Research," *American Sociological Review*, 30: 2, 1965, 191–193. Cf. also the discussion in Reinhard Bendix, *Max Weber. An Intellectual Portrait* (Garden City: Anchor, 1962), ch. 7.

[3] Max Weber, *The Protestant Ethic and the Spirit of Capitalism* (New York: Scribner, 1958), 97. My italics.

pline, pastoral work, and preaching are *not* relevant for understanding the impact of doctrine on conduct, then what of the "psychological sanctions" that are? Weber uses the German word *Antrieb*, impulse; he thus posits psychological impulses originating in the religious beliefs evoked by a theological doctrine. His use of the term "impulse" suggests that a propensity to act in accord with the implications of the doctrine of predestination has already been internalized. But this begs the question, since he is investigating and not presupposing the impact of doctrine on belief and conduct. (The translation unfortunately obscures the passage further, since the word "sanction," which corresponds to German words like *Bestätigung, Genehmigung,* or *Zwangsmassnahme,* refers to external control. "Psychological sanction" is a contradiction in terms—in addition to being a wrong translation of *Antrieb.*) To be clear on this point, Weber would have had to use the word *Anreiz,* incentive. Thus he would have stated what indeed he shows in brilliant fashion, that the religious beliefs of the Puritans contained incentives encouraging a personal conduct of "innerworldly asceticism" *to the extent that these beliefs were internalized*—clearly a conditional assertion. Yet his whole analysis rests on the thesis that Puritan believers differed from Catholics in their greater internalization of religious precepts, their anxious concern with the uncertainty of salvation unrelieved by indulgences or the confessional, each man facing the stern and inscrutable majesty of God alone and unaided. In his responses to critics Weber declared that this intensified motivation had been a causal factor of great, but uncertain, magnitude, because men of that day were more deeply affected by abstract religious dogmas than a more secular age can readily understand.

This reply, it seems to me, does not resolve the issue I have raised, nor does it do justice to the profundity of Weber's analysis. That profundity consists in Weber's paradoxical assertion that the reformers continued to adhere to the traditional, Christian devaluation of mundane pursuits, that Christian believers of this period continued to be concerned with their fate in the hereafter (though in a more intense fashion than hitherto)—but that Western civilization shifted from a predominantly otherworldly to a predominantly innerworldly orientation nonetheless. In other words, the "Spirit of Capitalism" represents a direct outgrowth of the earlier, anti-materialistic tradition of Christianity and, as Weber shows, was all the more powerful for that reason. Was this due in part to the intensified motivation that Weber analyzes?

Questions of this kind have given rise to a large, controversial literature which seems to have resolved very little. One reason for this failure is probably that both critics and defenders have discussed Weber's thesis entirely in the context in which he first formulated it. It may be worthwhile, therefore, to pursue this unresolved problem in Weber's analysis in the different context of the cultural-educational preconditions of Japanese development.[4]

IMPLICATIONS OF TOKUGAWA EDUCATION

To do this, I must note some factors in the background of Tokugawa Japan. That background, I shall suggest, militated against the self-disciplined vigor in action that the samurai displayed in the decades following the Restoration of 1868. There is evidence that under the Tokugawa the education of samurai and of commoners continued to inculcate the traditional ethic of the samurai, but there is evidence also that such education was at best partially successful. If one distinguishes clearly between cultural incentive and internalized psychological impulse (as I believe one should), then the evidence of the Tokugawa regime appears to point to a partial decline (rather than the increased vigor) of the samurai ethic.[5] The post-Restoration experience suggests, on the other hand, that the Western challenge arrested that decline by providing an opportunity for the leading groups of samurai and of commoners to live up to their ideals in modified form, and thus to overcome the discrepancies between ideal and conduct in the pre-Restoration period.

Following a long succession of internecine wars lasting until the end of the sixteenth century, Japan underwent a massive political and administrative consolidation, at the local as well as the national level. By 1560 Japanese fiefs had been amalgamated into large territorial units, and seignorial rights were usurped by the locally

[4] This was made possible for me by Ronald Dore's volume, *Education in Tokugawa Japan* (Berkeley: University of California Press, 1965). I am indebted to Professore Dore for having made the manuscript of the book available to me before publication.

[5] The reiteration of the phrase "cultural incentive" in this altered context calls for an additional comment. In his analysis of Calvinist and other Reformed doctrines Weber was not concerned with their explicit moral injunctions but with their implicit effects. The following discussion of Japanese materials is similar in the sense that explicitly the official code called for militancy while official practice discouraged certain forms of it, and this discrepancy provided the "cultural incentives" of the Tokugawa period.

dominant daimyo families. In this process smaller lords (samurai) were deprived of their seignorial rights and forced to reside, as retainers and officials of the daimyos, in castle-towns, whose construction in the period from 1580 to 1610—together with the destruction of all other fortified places—outwardly symbolized the new dispensation. This transformation of the samurai from rural landholders into urban retainers under the authority of the daimyos occurred when the Tokugawa Shogunate was consolidating its own position at the national level by a determined policy of isolation, the expulsion or extermination of Christians, and the imposition of the alternate-residence system (sankin-kotai) which made all daimyo families personally and politically dependent on the Shogunate in Edo. Within this general context the samurai were transformed from an estate of independent, landed, and self-equipped warriors into one of urbanized, aristocratic retainers, whose privileged social and economic position was universally acknowledged. They remained attached to their tradition of ceremonious conduct, intense pride of rank, and the cultivation of physical prowess. The problem to be explained is how this demilitarized aristocracy could retain, for some two centuries, its individualized military stance and its cult of disciplined action in a thoroughly pacified society in which differences of hereditary rank were strongly emphasized but all forms of military aggression suppressed. For, at the time of the Meiji Restoration, it was against this improbable background that the samurai not only provided the active political and intellectual leadership of the nation, but pioneered in modern entrepreneurial activities as well.[6]

Why is this background improbable? The demilitarization of the samurai, the employment of some of their number as daimyo officials, the opportunities, at least among the better-off samurai families, for corruption in an urbanized, retainer existence, the emphasis on rank and the discouragement of competition, and among many lower samurai families the sheer necessity to supplement rice stipends by some employment, often menial: these were so many reasons why the samurai could be expected to lose their militancy and self-discipline. No doubt some of them did, especially among the highest-ranking samurai and daimyo, for whom the Shogunal court at Edo provided additional opportunities for corruption. But

---

[6] See the data reported by Ronald Dore, "Mobility, Equality, and Individuation in Modern Japan," in Ronald Dore, ed., *Aspects of Social Change in Modern Japan* (Princeton University Press, 1967), 113–150.

this weakening of "moral fiber" was intensely resented among many samurai, especially during the last decades of the Tokugawa regime, and so the puzzle remains. Dore's analysis of education provides an answer to these questions and enables us to pinpoint the "functional equivalents" of Puritanism in Japan.[7]

With private tutors and, from the end of the eighteenth century, in an increasing number of fief schools, the samurai families who could afford it, appear to have educated their sons.[8] In addition, a significant proportion of townsmen and well-to-do farmers sent their sons to temple schools or private tutors, where they learned the rudiments of reading, writing, and arithmetic. The private schools for commoners were in large part responsible for the fact that at the time of the Restoration some 40 per cent of Japanese boys and about 10 per cent of the girls were receiving formal education; the sons and daughters of aristocratic families probably did not constitute more than 6 per cent of the school-age population.[9]

What were the aims of samurai education? In 1786 Hayashi Shihei formulated these aims in a manner that Dore considers representative:

With the eight virtues as your basis [his list is filial piety, respect for elders, loyalty, trust, courage, justice, straightforwardness, and a sense of honor] cultivate a boldness of spirit without losing self-discipline; acquire wisdom and wide learning without despising other people. Do

[7] The following summary does not do justice to the richness of Dore's materials, but it attempts to make a contribution by singling out the issues that appear critical in a comparative perspective.

[8] In 1703 only 9 per cent of all daimyo fiefs had schools, but the unbroken continuity of the samurai ethic makes it probable that a significant proportion had private instruction. By 1814 about one half of all daimyo fiefs and almost all of the large fiefs had schools; by the time of the Restoration only the smallest fiefs remained without them.

[9] This inference is based on a comparison between Dore's estimate of formal schooling and literacy and Abegglen and Mannari's estimate that all ranks of the aristocracy comprised 460,000 out of 7 million households or about 6.1 per cent of the total population in 1872. Cf. James J. Abegglen and Hiroshi Mannari, "Japanese Business Leaders, 1880–1960" (mimeographed paper presented to the Conference on the State of Economic Enterprise in Modern Japan, Estes Park, Colo., June 1963), 9–11. It is, of course, speculative to identify the proportion of children from aristocratic households with the proportion of aristocratic households, since this assumes that the number of children per aristocratic household was identical with the national average. But a sizable proportion of Japanese boys with formal education must have come from households of commoners, since aristocratic households could hardly have made up in excess of children what they lacked in total numbers.

not become weak and feeble; do not lose your dignity; do not sink stagnantly into mere logic-chopping, nor allow yourself to be carried away by prose and poetry. Do not lose your courage; do not become introverted. Do not become an admirer of China who sees no good in Japan. Do not fall in love with novelty or with pleasures of the eye. Practice your military skills with devotion and at the same time learn something of astronomy and geography, of the tea ceremony and of No drama.[10]

Avoidance of book-learning as such, of novelty and pleasure, behavior appropriate to the samurai's rank with proper dignity of bearing and respect for elders, above all self-discipline, wisdom, and an active way of life: these appear to be the principal themes. The literary arts are of secondary significance; their importance lies primarily in providing a medium of instruction through which the pupil can acquire the proper frame of mind, conscious of his duties and earnest in his practice of military skills.

Apparently, the same ideals of conduct were instilled in pupils of commoner origin. To be sure, military skills were the exclusive prerogative of the aristocracy, while the high rank, strutting arrogance, and rentier existence of the samurai were in turn objects of emulation, envy, and ridicule among the commoners. But temple schools and private tutors taught the sons of commoners the art of writing with a single-minded emphasis on proper manners and the right frame of mind. Dore has translated a set of terakoya (temple school) precepts, from which I quote two paragraphs to illustrate the link between literacy, social structure, and the ideology of self-discipline:

To be born human and not be able to write is to be less than human. Illiteracy is a form of blindness. It brings shame on your teacher, shame on your parents, and shame on yourself. The heart of a child of three stays with him till he is a hundred as the proverb says. Determine to succeed, study with all your might, never forgetting the shame of failure. . . . Cooperate with each other to behave yourselves as you should, check in yourselves any tendencies to be attracted to evil ways, and put all your heart into your brush-work.

At your desks let there be no useless idle talk, or yawning or stretching, or dozing or picking your nose, or chewing paper, or biting the end of your brush. To imitate the idle is the road to evil habits. Just concen-

[10] Quoted in Dore, *Education, op. cit.,* 64.

trate whole-heartedly on your writing, giving each character the care it deserves.[11]

There is much more of the same with special enumeration of all the careless or undisciplined ways that the students are admonished to avoid, incidentally giving a pretty graphic picture of the pranks, misdemeanors, and bad habits that Japanese schoolboys seem to have in common with their peers all over the world. Apparently, neither the social aspiration of commoners nor hereditary privilege with its pride of rank were sufficient in themselves to inculcate self-discipline.

In the fief schools as well as in schools for commoners, instruction became a highly formalized affair which was intrinsically dull and meaningless, as Dore points out. Without holding the individual's interest, the teachers apparently insisted on writing and reading as media through which the student should learn proper behavior and the right frame of mind. Tedious repetition, under conditions in which the student's bearing and attitude were subjected to the most detailed scrutiny and control, was the means used to teach self-discipline. It must remain uncertain how far these educational methods succeeded in inculcating the habits of thought and action that proved highly suitable for the rapid modernization of Japan after 1868. All we really know is that the educational system helped to maintain the ideals of the samurai. One might also say that the teachers had a vested interest in these ideals, and that daimyos and bakufu officials encouraged their educational endeavors because they considered these ideals suitable supports of domestic stability. If one goes beyond these statements to the conclusion that in the schools of the Tokugawa period students internalized ideals of conduct and hence actually acquired the drive and discipline that were in evidence later on, one is guilty of the same confusion between cultural prescription and psychological impulse noted earlier.[12]

Certainly, Tokugawa education put a high premium on self-discipline, filial piety, and an activist way of life. But there is evidence that many samurai students did not take to this education

[11] *Ibid.*, 323ff.

[12] This confusion is widespread because all cultural values have such *possible* psychological correlates. In the field of psychological drives or patterns, the *post hoc ergo propter hoc* fallacy is especially hard to avoid, because observation of such drives or patterns invites inquiry into their antecedents, and in most instances it is impossible to document that these antecedents did *not* exist.

with alacrity. Fief edicts frequently deplored the lack of diligence among samurai students and admonished them to greater effort. Moreover, it is difficult to imagine that the personal militancy of the samurai remained unimpaired under a regime that sought to control all manifestations of aggressive or competitive behavior. The fief schools discouraged all forms of rivalry between different schools and strictly prohibited contests or simulated combat among their pupils, even though the ideology and practice of swordsmanship continued unabated. One result of this double-edged policy was that, as Dore comments, "combat was less and less practiced, and swordsmanship and the use of the lance became increasingly a matter of formal gymnastics, and disciplined choreography."[13] Presumably this applied to those pupils who put dignity, respect for elders, self-discipline, and wisdom above the cult of action. There were others, however, whom circumstances and temperament prompted to make the opposite choice. As ronin or masterless samurai, they lived a wayward life by the sword at the expense of most other tenets of the samurai ethic. One can gauge the tensions inherent in Japanese culture before the Restoration when one observes that the Tokugawa regime did not abandon its praise of militancy despite its policy of pacification and the apprehensions aroused by the activities of the ronin.

The famous story of the forty-seven ronin exemplifies many of these themes. At the shogunal court a daimyo has drawn his sword and wounded a high court official, to avenge an insult. As a penalty the daimyo is asked to commit suicide, because by his act he has jeopardized Tokugawa supremacy and the policy of pacification on which it rests. The daimyo's retainers are now without a master; they acknowledge that he had to die, but out of loyalty to him they make every effort to preserve their lord's fief for the members of his family. This effort fails. For two years the forty-seven ronin (the original number is larger, but many withdraw) secretly plan to avenge their lord. After successfully eluding the ubiquitous Tokugawa police, they kill the court official who had provoked their master. As penalty for this violation of the Tokugawa peace, the shogun demands that the forty-seven commit suicide in turn. The conduct of these men exemplifies unconditional loyalty to their master, self-discipline in guarding their secret plans, and complete devotion to the cult of action in the successful consummation of

[13] Dore, *Education, op. cit.,* 151.

their endeavor. The forty-seven ronin epitomize the priorities and contradictions of the ideals of Tokugawa culture. They divorce their wives or have their wives and daughters turn to prostitution so that they can fulfil their pledge of loyalty to their master; and they combine this act of upholding the hierarchy of rank with the unconditional commitment to action that the bakufu simultaneously encouraged and suppressed. The hierarchy of rank is more important than family, while the peace of the Tokugawa is still more important than the hierarchy of rank. Both these priorities are here exemplified by actions that can be turned against others only at the price of turning against oneself in the end.

This true story of the early eighteenth century instantly became the cultural epitome of the samurai ethic, but in restrospect it reads more like an epitaph than an apotheosis. Its heroes serve their master by their deaths, since they can no longer serve him in their lives. Such symbolic consummation of the cult of self-disciplined action points insistently, albeit by implication, to the discrepancy between this cult and the daily round of a retainer's life that characterized the lives of most samurai under the Tokugawa settlement. One would suppose that many of these men, for whom militancy was the mark of rank, were aware at times of the emptiness of that pretense. While the story of the forty-seven ronin certainly upheld the ideal, did it not also underscore the pettiness of militancy without war? At any rate, the ideal heroism of these ronin does not explain whether and how such ideals could be harnessed to meet the contingencies of everyday life, which developed precipitously following the Restoration of 1868.[14] In the Japanese case we certainly have an instance of the discrepancy between cultural ideals and behavior; perhaps we can infer—for the decades preceding the Restoration—a growing ambivalence and even a diminished adherence to these ideals. The question is how such evidence and the more tentative inferences based on it can be related, however provisionally, to the intense and disciplined effort of many samurai immediately following the Restoration.

[14] In 1867 payments in rice to the samurai amounted to 34.6 million yen, while in 1876 the value of yearly interest paid on a commutation basis had fallen to 11.5 million. For a relatively short time the Meiji government cushioned this precipitous decline by allocating a sizable portion of its budgets for stipends to dispossessed samurai, as well as by the more intangible method of ideological support for their high rank. But these short-term methods only delayed for a little the stark necessity of going to work.

Historical instances are numerous in which discrepancies of this kind lead to a decline of an ideal. Under the Tokugawa regime the peaceful existence of most samurai was increasingly at odds with their militant stance, a condition hardly conducive to the vigor and self-discipline that the samurai displayed during the Meiji Restoration. Here some allowance must be made for the accident of timing: we will never know whether the samurai ethic would have become an empty sham in spite of teaching, official propaganda and increased education of commoners, if the Western challenge to Japanese independence had come much later. All we know is that this challenge brought into the open a capacity for self-disciplined action that had been jeopardized (and may well have been diminishing) by the discrepancy between ideal and conduct under the Tokugawa regime.

Before 1868 the samurai ethic was maintained in its entirety by the educational system and by the officials of the bakufu. There is evidence that the militant ideal of self-disciplined and vigorous action could be "domesticated" through the educational system. Dore shows how this ideal was incorporated in the teaching of reading and writing as well as in the "demilitarized" practice of military skills. The spread of Terakoya education and the high level of literacy by the time of Restoration suggests that samurai ideals gradually became ideals for commoners as well.[15] Moreover, the samurai tradition of militancy was kept alive in several ways despite the increasing discrepancies between cultural ideals and behavior. In response to the contrast between high social rank and low economic position the samurai who turned ronin chose to act out the militant aspect of their ethic at the price of neglecting other aspects of its code. For their part, samurai retainers adopted the alternative way of emphasizing rank consciousness and stylized behavior at the price of turning militancy into "disciplined choreography," a pattern also followed by the samurai whose way of life became hardly distinguishable from that of commoners. One im-

[15] The "demilitarized" teaching of the samurai ethic probably facilitated its general applicability, especially among commoners. Dore emphasizes that there is hardly any evidence in Tokugawa Japan of assertions that commoners should be barred from the acquisition of literacy, while such assertions were frequent in Europe on the ground that such a skill would make the lower orders unruly. In this sense the adoption of samurai precepts in the instruction of commoners was a move in the direction of equality despite the rank consciousness instilled by these precepts.

agines that subjectively samurai of every description adhered to
their ideals with that "sensitive pride and the fear of shaming
defeat" (Dore) which most experts consider the exemplary motivational pattern of the Japanese people.[16] In this they were greatly
aided by the bakufu officials, who always upheld the ideal of samurai militancy, even though they suppressed the aggressive conduct
that was an essential part of this ideal. Thus, before 1868, formal
education and official ideology supported ideals some of which it
disavowed in practice.

Since after 1868 the samurai implemented their ideal of disciplined action in economic, political, and intellectual pursuits, one
can infer that the Restoration provided the opportunity to overcome the long-standing, internal contradictions of the Tokugawa
regime. Paraxodically, the same qualities that had sustained a
quiescent and internally contradictory regime for so long now found
a new outlet. As Dore puts it in a telling summary:

Sensitive pride and fear of shaming defeat, the strength of which probably led the majority of samurai to avoid competitive situations and
certainly prompted most educators and teachers of military skills deliberately to refrain from creating them, also meant that—once competition was declared and the race was on—the self-respecting samurai really
did go all out to win.[17]

Thus, the release of pent-up energies was decisive and there is little
doubt that it was occasioned not by internal structural changes but
by an external event, the arrival of Commodore Perry's ships and
the challenge to national preservation that it symbolized. During
the critical period from 1853 to 1868 (the so-called Bakumatsu
period) the national goals of Japanese society were defined unequivocally, perhaps for the first time; the "ethic" of filial piety,
self-discipline, and an activist way of life was greatly reinforced
by the external threat; and the intense social conflicts that ensued
turned primarily on how best to meet the Western challenges.[18]

[16] For a telling description of this pattern, illuminated by evidence from
Japanese history, see Edwin O. Reischauer, *The United States and Japan* (New
York: Viking, 1957), 99–177.

[17] Dore, *Education, op. cit.,* 212.

[18] For a masterly exposition of these conflicts over policy and their compati-
bility with a basic agreement on national goals, see W. G. Beasley, "Introduction," in W. G. Beasley, ed., *Select Documents—Japanese Foreign Policy, 1853–
1868* (London: Oxford, 1955) 1–93.

THE INTERNALIZATION OF BELIEFS

From the perspective of Japanese development one gains a clearer view of the cultural preconditions of development from tradition to modernity. For our purposes the central fact of Tokugawa Japan is the contradiction between official support of the traditional ideal of militancy and official suppression of warlike actions which accord with that ideal. The bakufu officials who upheld the ideal of militancy surely did not wish to encourage the outlawry of the ronin, and they may have had misgivings concerning the increasingly empty pretense of samurai retainers. Yet in effect they encouraged both, and the contrast between official ideology and practice would have undermined the ideological support of the Tokugawa regime in the long run. It is reasonable to suppose that this support was weakening in the decades preceding the Restoration.

Apparently, then, an event external to the society, the sudden jeopardy in which Japan was placed by the Western challenge to her isolation, was responsible in large measure for defining national goals and the redirecting and intensifying actions based on unchanged motivational patterns and unchanged cultural ideals. The Western challenge redefined the situation for large numbers of Japanese, and while it is true that for a time Westernization was "the rage," a wave of Japanization followed in turn, leading to a reaffirmation of cultural ideals and to a reenforcement of filial piety and the sense of hierarchy, which were now compatible with more national unity and economic development than had existed before 1868.

With this interpretation in mind we can turn once again to the problems raised by Max Weber's analysis. That problem consists, as stated earlier, in the hiatus between doctrine and conduct, between the incentives implicit in religious ideas and the internalized impulses that prompt groups of men to act in the manner Weber defined as "inner worldly asceticism." An attempt to elucidate this unresolved question by reference to the Japanese development may appear farfetched. After all, how is it possible to find points of comparison or even analogy between the Western challenge to Japanese isolation and, say, Calvin's or Luther's challenge to Catholic orthodoxy? Yet at an abstract level we deal here with rather similar phenomena. Both cases have to do with the process by which cultural ideals supporting tradition give rise to cultural ideals supporting modernity.

The discrepancy between official ideology and practice in Tokugawa Japan finds its analogue in the pre-Reformation spokesmen of the Catholic Church who upheld the traditional faith but condoned religious practices, like the indiscriminate sale of indulgences, at variance with the ideals of that faith. The same spokesmen also condemned and at times suppressed individuals and movements that appeared to challenge the supremacy of the Church. It is common knowledge that the immediate antecedents of the Reformation were only the last phases of a century-long development in which the Church had had to grapple again and again with the doctrinal, pastoral, and organizational consequences of the hiatus between faith and secular involvement. It is reasonable to suppose that in the course of this development orthodox spokesmen found themselves time and again in a situation similar to that of Tokugawa officialdom. Whatever the differences in culture and social structure, the task of upholding an orthodox doctrinal position while prohibiting and suppressing actions in consonance with orthodox principles is similar in an abstract sense.[19]

For present purposes it is most relevant to note the probable collective effect. Confronted with a patent discrepancy between official doctrine and sanctioned behavior, a large population—whether of Catholic believers or Japanese samurai—becomes divided into hypocrites and true believers. We know too little about this process, but there is ample evidence from both medieval Europe and Tokugawa Japan that the discrepancy between doctrine and practice was welcomed by some and condemned by others. Some used the occasion as an excuse for moral laxity, others became moral rigorists as a reaction against official dishonesty. The proportions of the population responding in one way or the other may never be known. Perhaps no more can be said in the end than that Catholic Europeans had to live with this discrepancy between doctrine and sanctioned behavior for a much longer period than the population of Tokugawa Japan. Prior to the Reformation, the number and intensity of movements for internal reform of the Church probably exceeded the analogous stirring of reform move-

---

[19] This similarity can be analyzed in several ways. See for example, the analysis of this parallelism in the case of Catholic and Communist orthodoxy in Zbigniew Brzezinski, "Deviation Control: A Study in the Dynamics of Doctrinal Conflict," *American Political Science Review,* 56, 1962, 5–22.

ments in Tokugawa Japan prior to the Restoration. It is conceivable that this longer history of spiritual and psychological unrest indicates a greater attenuation of the moral code in Europe than in Japan. Speculative as such reasoning is, it suggests that we must look for some massive cause, affecting large numbers, if we are to explain how a considerable part of a population could turn for a significant period from the hypothesized vacillation between laxity and rigorism to self-disciplined action in this world, to inner-worldly asceticism. The venturesome analogue of the Japanese development suggests that this massive cause may well lie in events external to that self-contained world of religious ideas and moral precepts that Weber analyzed with such insight.

What was the context in which the incentives implicit in religious doctrines became linked with the impulses that prompt men to action?[20] In the case of the Lutheran Reformation it is noteworthy that around 1500 Wittenberg was located in a German frontier region, bordering on areas inhabited by people of Slavic descent. The town had 2,500 residents, of whom 550 were liable to pay taxes. Composed primarily of artisans and local traders, the community provided little opportunity for the development of an urban patriciate. During the cruicial years of Luther's work, Wittenberg had to accommodate between 1,500 and 2,000 students, and Schoeffler shows that under Luther's influence the faculty of the university rapidly became very young indeed. Men in their twenties and thirties predominated, while older professors retired or left the university altogether. Surely, Luther was a very powerful and courageous innovator, who attracted students from far and wide, and who succeeded in transforming the bulk of the faculty into a group of loyal collaborators and followers.[21] Thus Luther created some of the community support he enjoyed. But in the larger context he could do so because Wittenberg provided cultural and political opportunities for his reorientation of established traditions. Located in a linguistic and cultural frontier area, Wittenberg was a natural setting for a cultural and religious appeal based on the vernacular and the original: the translation of the Bible into Ger-

---

[20] The following observations are based on the work of Herbert Schoeffler, *Wirkungen der Reformation* (Frankfurt: V. Klostermann, 1960), containing essays originally published in 1932 and 1936. My brief statement cannot do justice to the subtlety of Schoeffler's analysis.

[21] Both directly and indirectly Luther had special influence with the Elector Friedrich of Saxony, who used his authority to effect these changes of personnel at the university.

man, the use of German in religious ceremonies, and, beyond this, recourse to the texts of classical antiquity in the original rather than dependence on commentaries. This link between religious reform and a revival of humanistic learning also appealed to other regions and universities lacking in tradition, in striking contrast to areas with more established traditions and older universities where these innovations were bitterly opposed for cultural as well as for religious reasons. Schoeffler examines the signatories of the Augsburg Confession (1530) and suggests that they represent "outposts" of German settlement and areas of relatively late Christianization, which either lacked universities altogether or had universities bereft of the scholarly traditions of that period.

On the Continent the Lutheran Reformation became stabilized through the Articles of Schmalkalden (1537) which distinguish between the coercive legal authority of the temporal power and the spiritual authority of the Church, but then place a certain authority over affairs of the Church in the hands of the prince. His duty is to "diligently further God's glory." To this end he must place his authority in the service of the Church, which at the time meant the right and duty to defend correct doctrine and superintend preaching and worship. Thenceforth, acceptance of established, secular authority became an integral part of Lutheran piety—a link which to this day has had repercussions in German society especially. In this instance it is easy to see that to the extent that the incentives implicit in Luther's theological doctrines were internalized, they were internalized in a political context, however difficult it may be to disentangle the religious from the political incentives or to analyze the interweaving of both in a socialization based on Lutheran precepts.

The context of the English Reformation differs greatly from that on the Continent. Schoeffler points to the absence of a religious leadership in any way comparable to that of Luther or Calvin. Initiated under political auspices, the English Reformation lacked a great religious ethos. During several decades of the sixteenth century the government was markedly unstable. Yet each new government gave rise to new, authoritative decisions on Church policy. As a result the English people were exposed to the whole gamut of religious disputes characteristic of the period, an experience which in Schoeffler's judgment created considerable religious anxiety while providing no prospect of a new consensus on religious questions. In this case, religious anxiety is attributed to the uncertainties introduced into Church affairs by a vacillating government which assumed authority over these affairs but proved unable to develop a consistent approach to the organizational and spiritual problems of the Church. Yet each approach to Church policy found its passionate advocates, leading eventually to the formation of sects whose members adhered to their religious convictions all the more stubbornly, the more the authorities continued to vacillate. As Schoeffler puts it:

The English nation is the only great people, which in all its segments was really led into a state of religious need or anxiety (*Not*). Everyone had to make his own decision among several and eventually among many doctrinal systems and principles of church organization, while the state was in no position to take this decision into its own hands.[22]

Having made such decisions under conditions of special uncertainty, the new sectarian communities were anxious to preserve the faith they had had to discover for themselves, and the unity of the congregation which had been forged in the midst of political conflicts and religious disputes. Thus the political context of the English Reformation helps us to interpret the link between the incentives implicit in religious ideas and the internalization of these religious precepts, which Weber has analyzed in part.

There is no need to examine the manifest dissimilarities between the English Reformation and the Japanese response to the Western challenge. In both instances motivation was intensified along established lines, apparently because the context stimulated a heightened concern with the supreme value of personal salvation or national integrity, respectively. The two cases suggests that the cultural-educational preconditions of economic development can be understood more clearly if the internal structure of a society is analyzed in relation to its political structure and international setting.

The Effects of Cultural Patterns

To answer the question of how cultural patterns that support tradition can give rise to cultural patterns that support modernity, I have explored two different settings. The question is especially difficult to answer because such patterns are accessible to the scholar only so far as they are reflected in documents, and documents which do that tend to be "projections" of a cultural minority. Hence the meaning of cultural patterns for large num-

[22] Schoeffler, *op. cit.,* 324.

bers remains inevitably speculative. And yet, without some answer to the question of what these patterns mean, at least to leading strata of a society numbering in the thousands, we cannot expect to understand the cultural preconditions of economic development. This discussion has advanced two suggestions in this respect.

One is that the mass effect of cultural patterns can be understood better if their political context is observed. In the Japanese case the evidence points unequivocally to a massive redirection of effort as a response to the Western challenge. The evidence from the Reformation is much more complex. Yet if it be true as Weber argued that men of that time were very directly concerned with abstract theological doctrines, then it seems just as plausible to suggest that this concern with personal salvation was hard to separate from political controversy at a time when theological and political differences went hand in hand. Political involvement, I suggest, is another side of that devotional piety or innerworldly asceticism that Weber analyzed in Lutheranism and Calvinism, and I believe that the intensification of motives which he emphasized cannot be understood without attention to this aspect.

The other suggestion is more abstract, but perhaps more important. Throughout his work, Weber was concerned with the uniqueness of Western civilization, from Greek philosophy and Roman jurisprudence to the Protestant ethic, capitalist enterprise, and modern science. Since his day a few other countries have accomplished a transition to modernity, aided by the preceding developments of Europe and America but also contributing cultural elements of their own. Japan is an outstanding example. But the number of such countries is quite limited, and the question seems warranted whether across all the differences among them this capacity for development points to some common element. I noted that both Tokugawa Japan and Catholic Europe were characterized by protracted discrepancies between orthodox doctrine and practical accommodations, giving rise to moral tokenism on one hand and moral rigorism on the other. The tensions imparted to both cultures as a result may have prepared the ground for the innovating impact of political challenges and religious ideas.

XI

THE COMPARATIVE ANALYSIS OF HISTORICAL CHANGE

The renewed interest in comparative studies of social change dates from the Second World War. This intellectual repercussion of the war and its aftermath is most apparent in the discontinuities of interest which have marked the work of American social scientists in recent decades. Before the Second World War American scholars devoted their primary attention to the study of American society. Even if one considers the tremendous popularity of theories of social evolution in the United States before the 1920's, one is struck by the fact that these theories were largely applied in Social Darwinist fashion to an interpretation of the competitive economic struggle. The predominant American concern was domestic, in contrast with the trend in Europe, where these theories originated and where they were used to interpret the encounter between the advanced industrial societies of Europe and the peoples and cultures of colonial and dependent areas. With the notable exception of anthropologists, this intellectual insularity of American social scientists may be related to America's anticolonial heritage, just as the renewed interest in comparative studies may be related to America's worldwide political involvements since the Second World War.

As a result, the earlier parochial orientation has declined, as economists, political scientists, and sociologists attempt to assess the relativity as well as the characterists of the American experience. A steadily increasing number of social scientists are concerned with

Reinhard Bendix, from Tom Burns and S. B. Saul, eds., *Social Theory and Economic Change* (London: Tavistock, 1967), 67–86. Revised version of a paper originally presented to the Round Table on Comparative Research, International Social Science Council, Paris, April 22–24, 1965. The essay develops themes presented in more empirical detail in my book *Nation-Building and Citizenship (1964)*.

non-Western areas, especially with regard to problems of "modernization." This concern has benefited markedly from the wartime experience of many scholars, which included extensive training in foreign languages. It has also been affected by the revolution in research methods that modern computers make possible with regard to the storage and evaluation of data. We seem to find ourselves in a period of intellectual transition, and the participants in this reorientation naturally tend to emphasize its novelty.

The shift of emphasis is evident if one compares the preoccupation of scholars with the conventional teaching of history. Typically, the student learns the history of his own country in considerable detail, whereas the histories of other countries are presented to him much more selectively, or not at all. At one time, professional historians defended this conventional method on the ground that the development of each country is unique, so that the obvious concern with education for citizenship coincided with a plausible, intellectual conviction. Yet today historians no longer adhere to this position as firmly as they did some two generations ago. In notable instances they have presented comparative studies of their own. A series of publications has focused on problems of generalization in historical studies. And while preoccupation with national history remain predominant, many scholars so preoccupied are nevertheless concerned with the questions of conceptualization of central interest to social scientists.[1]

Yet the change in intellectual orientation may be more apparent than real. The greater receptivity toward a conceptual and comparative approach to the study of history is not matched by much agreement on what such a program of study implies positively. There is little agreement on what is to be understood by such recurrent terms as "analysis," "change," "social structure," and "comparison." Taking each in turn, I shall try to indicate the issues involved in our use of these terms. My purpose is to propose an

[1] Note the two Bulletins of the Social Science Research Council dealing with the relations between history and the social sciences: *Theory and Practice in Historical Study: A Report of the Committee on Historiography* (New York: Social Science Research Council, 1946), Bulletin 54, and *The Social Sciences in Historical Study: A Report of the Committee on Historiography (ibid.,* 1954), Bulletin 64. See also Louis Gottschalk, ed., *Generalizations in the Writing of History* (Chicago: Chicago University Press, 1963). The statement in the text is especially well illustrated, however, by the many contributions of historians published in the pages of *Comparative Studies in Society and History* (edited by Silvia Thrupp).

approach to the comparative analysis of historical change at an intermediate level of abstraction.[2]

ANALYSIS

At least three divergent approaches to the study of historical change may be distinguished for purposes of orientation. The older, evolutionist approach tended to be classificatory. It assumes that the less developed countries will follow the "steps and sequences of change" through which the more developed have passed already. Analysis becomes a matter of assigning culture traits or even a whole country at a given time to a specific stage of development. Once this is done, it is possible to assess the progressive or regressive significance of ideas and actions, either because the future or next stage is "known" in advance, or because it seems plausible to examine the past of the developed countries for purposes of such retrospective evaluation. To be sure, evolutionist theory is no longer expounded in such simplistic terms. Scholars have become more cautious than their predecessors; concepts of differentiation or increasing complexity are substituted for the idea of progress, and allowance is made for multilinear developments and the reversal or omission of "stages." [3] But while these modifications go

---

[2] Though more directly concerned with the study of historical change, the intention here is similar to that of Merton in his discussion of theories of the middle range. See Robert K. Merton, *Social Theory and Social Structure* (2d rev. ed., Glencoe: Free Press, 1957), 9–10 and *passim*. For certain purposes, higher levels of abstraction may well be useful, and, logically, one cannot speak of intermediate levels of abstraction without acknowledging the existence and possible utility of higher levels as well. However, considerable differences of judgment and emphasis remain with regard to the direct, analytic utility of such higher levels, as the following discussion indicates.

[3] Cf. the recent contributions: Talcott Parsons, "Evolutionary Universals in Society," *American Sociological Review*, 29, 1964, 339–357; R. N. Bellah, "Religious Evolution," *American Sociological Review*, 29, 1964, 358–374; and S. N. Eisenstadt, "Social Change, Differentiation and Evolution," *American Sociological Review*, 29, 1964, 375–386. Regrettably these writers take no note of the important contribution by I. Watt and J. Goody, "The Consequences of Literacy," *Comparative Studies in Social History*, 5, 1963, 304–345. Note also the closely related analysis by Bruno Snell, *Scenes from Greek Drama* (Berkeley and Los Angeles: University of California Press, 1964), *passim*. For scholars interested in evolution, these studies have the great advantage of focusing attention on a more or less documented record of transition from a preliterate to a literate society.

far, it is not clear that the original theory has been abandoned. The proliferation of synonyms for "change," such as "development" or "modernization," with their several adjectives, warns us that this is an area of uncertainty and confusion; the new vocabulary often employs older theories of evolution uncritically.

Related to this older approach, but more modern in its nomenclature, is the view that societies should be analyzed as natural systems. In this perspective a social structure appears as an interrelated, functioning whole with systemic prerequisites, properties, and consequences, which may be identified as a "stage of development." Typically, such analysis runs the danger of reification, which occurs whenever a society is identified as a unit that maintains or changes itself in order to survive as such. I shall comment on this view below, but wish to refer here to one modern tendency related to, but not identical with, this wholistic or systemic approach. I refer to the social-engineering approach, which is oriented toward planned social change. In its view, analysis should aim at the discovery of critical independent variables, since control of these will entail predictable changes in the dependent variables. Indebted to images derived from controlled experiments or from medical practice, this approach is less classificatory than the older evolutionist theory and less organicist than systems theory proper. But, like these theories, its simplifying assumptions and test of truth depend upon a *ceteris paribus* treatment of historical constellations. For example, the record of economic growth in the developed countries is employed as a model, however provisionally, so that historical preconditions reappear as logical prerequisites without which growth cannot occur. In this way the engineering approach comes close to the natural-systems approach in that both operate with the concept of "indispensable prerequisites," though the engineering approach is perhaps more candid in generalizing from the Western experience.[4]

Comparative analysis of historical change attempts a closer ap-

---

[4] In a recent contribution, Lerner suggests that, since rising output per head depends especially upon a people's willingness to change, politicians are well advised to promise economic benefits only after people have changed their ways in the requisite direction. He is silent, however, on how politicians can be induced to act in this manner, or on how people are likely to change in the absence of promises, or why in the movements for independence the value of independence has priority over the value of economic growth. Cf. Daniel Lerner, "Comparative Analysis of Processes of Modernization," paper submitted to International Social Science Council Round Table on Comparative Research, Paris, April 22–24, 1965. Unpublished.

proximation to the historical evidence than is possible on the assumptions of evolutionism, or of systems theory, or of social engineering. As a result, it promises less in the way of prediction and in the way of guiding social actions towards defined goals. Whether this sacrifice is permanent or temporary remains to be seen. Studies of social change in complex societies may hold in abeyance the tasks of casual analysis and prediction while concentrating on the preliminary task of ordering the phenomena of social change to be analyzed further. This task can be characterized by reference to the meaning of change and of social structure.

CHANGE

At the risk of oversimplification, I shall assume that, at a minimum, considerations of change involve two terminal conditions, so that the word "change" refers to the differences observed before and after a given interval of time. Since the future is uncertain, studies of historical change deal in the first place with past changes, the better to understand what the contrasts between before and after are and how they have come about. Naturally, it is hoped that a better understanding of historical changes will contribute to a fuller exploration of developmental possibilities, perhaps even to constructive action, but the relations between knowledge and action are complex and should not be prejudged.

Studies of change, then, depend upon contrasts between social structures before and after change has occurred. Without knowledge of how a later social structure differs from an earlier one, we do not know what changes to look for and explain. This is one reason why studies of this kind use familiar concepts such as feudalism, democracy, totalitarianism, etc., despite the many justified criticisms leveled against these terms. Such concepts express something we want to express, namely, that in some over-all and important, but rather general, sense, an old social structure has passed away and a new one has taken its place. Dissatisfaction with such conventional terms is understandable, but it is no solution to substitute universal terms for these concepts of limited applicability. Almond has suggested, for example, that "interest aggregation" is a term that cuts across all the conventional distinctions between political systems and hence can be applied universally.[5] Such a term has the utility of prompting us to look for "interest aggregation" in unfamiliar social

[5] G. A. Almond and J. S. Coleman, eds., *The Politics of the Developing Areas* (Princeton: Princeton University Press, 1960), 38–45 and *passim*.

structures to which our conventional terms do not apply, but it does not dispense with the utility of terms such as "class" or "estate" which already differentiate—however approximately—more familiar types of "interest aggregation." I suspect that we shall invent new terms to fit the unfamiliar types of "interest aggregation" once we have analyzed them sufficiently, for concepts are the result of inquiry as much as they are its precondition.

What, then, is meant by "social structures" and how do we study them comparatively?

SOCIAL STRUCTURES

Social structures retain certain of their characteristics while individuals come and go. The specification of such enduring characteristics involves abstractions from observations of behavior and from historical evidence. On this basis, studies of social change should be able to state that one type of social structure has ceased to prevail and another has taken its place. Yet to make such an assertion involves the hazards demonstrated by the debates concerning Max Weber's ideal type. Definitions of structures such as feudalism, bureaucracy, etc., usually take the form of enumerating several distinguishing characteristics. Such enumerations necessarily "freeze" the fluidity of social life, as Weber himself emphasized. They say nothing about the strength or the prevalence of a given characteristic, nor do they say anything about structures in which one or another element of the definition is missing. The result has been uncertainty. Abstractions are needed to define the characteristics of a structure and thus they remove the definition from the evidence. Conversely, when we approach the evidence "definition in hand," we often find its analytic utility diminished, because the characteristics to which it refers are in fact neither unequivocal nor general.[6]

Concretely: impersonal definition of rights and duties is one of the distinguishing criteria of bureaucracy. But "impersonal definition" has meant many things: the rights and duties of the classic Chinese bureaucrat and of an English official in the administrative class are worlds apart, even if both are impersonally defined. Nonetheless, the criterion is indispensable if we are to find all instances of bureaucracy or properly identify those instances we do find. Then

---

[6] These and related issues are discussed in Arthur Schweitzer, "Vom Idealtypus zum Prototyp," *Zeitschrift für die gestamten Staatswissenschaften*, 120, 1964, 13–55. The article will be useful even to those who do not follow all of Schweitzer's stimulating suggestions.

we will want to know how general and important the phenomenon of impersonal definition is in a given case. Typically, this involves us in the task of analyzing the methods by which the rights and duties of officials are defined, and the degree to which these definitions correspond to behavior. That analysis will reveal the characteristic discrepancy between formally stipulated methods and actual implementation, and that discrepancy will raise questions about the utility of the criterion ("impersonal definition") with which we started. Thus the criterion employed simplifies the instances to which it applies, and hence its analytic application poses difficulties. The dilemma is genuine, but there are proximate solutions.

Examination of comparative studies suggests, it seems to me, that definitions of social structures are contrast conceptions. Implicitly or explicitly, we define feudalism, capitalism, absolutism, caste system, bureaucracy, and other such terms by contrast with what each of these structures is not. For example, fealty ties are contrasted with contractual ties, absolutist-centralized with feudal-decentralized authority, caste with tribe or estate, impersonal with personalized administration, the unity of household and business with their separation, etc. My suggestion is that contrast conceptions are indispensable as a first orientation (they serve a function as bench marks), which introduces analysis but should not be mistaken for analysis.

Since social structures are defined by several characteristics, more than one contrast conception may be found analytically useful. The choice depends in good measure on the purpose of the inquiry and the historical context. In the emergence of modern bureaucracy, as Weber defined it, the recruitment of officials and their exercise of authority were emancipated from the direct intrusion of kinship relations and property interests. This aspect was prominent as long as hereditary privileges prevailed, but has declined in importance along with the rise of egalitarianism in all spheres of modern life. The exclusion of "every purely personal feeling" remains a valuable desideratum and a proximate characteristic of official conduct, but this condition may not do as much today to insure administrative impartiality as it did when government by a social elite encouraged the intrusion of family loyalties and property interests upon the conduct of public business. That is, recruitment to official positions on the basis of impersonal criteria and the separation of office and incumbent remain characteristics of bureaucracy, but the changed structure of modern politics has altered their significance. For certain purposes it would be useful, therefore, to formulate an early and a later type of bureaucracy, which would take account of this altered environment of government administration.

In this view, the definition of a social structure in terms of a cluster of traits can serve only as a first approximation. On closer inspection, every such trait proves to be an abstraction from the contentions among groups of men. The fealty relation between king and vassal is one of the defining characteristics of feudalism. But the contentions over their reciprocal rights and obligations between these classes of men are resolved in a variety of ways without thereby divesting that relation of the quality of fealty. In this way, social structures are defined by a set of issues which comprise the characteristic areas of contention among the constituent groups of a society. If we then say that one social structure has ceased to exist and another has taken its place, we mean that the terms of reference have changed by which issues are defined, relationships maintained, or contentions resolved. This is the meaning, it seems to me, of Tocqueville's classic specification of the contrast between a feudal and a democratic society.[7]

One corollary of these considerations is that concepts of social structure should be used in two forms. By bureaucracy we mean a depersonalized form of governmental administration, but we know that depersonalization is a matter of degree. Hence we use "bureaucracy" when we wish to contrast one type of administration with another, and "bureaucratization" when we wish to emphasize that the new term of reference ("depersonalized personnel selection") continues to be problematic, an issue whose every resolution creates new problems as well. Similarly, one can distinguish between democracy and democratization, nation and nation-building, centralized authority and the centralization of authority, etc. Such usage will create linguistic problems from time to time. For example, Max Weber's usage of *Vergesellschaftung* instead of *Gesellschaft* had much the same purpose that I suggest here, but there is no proper English equivalent of this word form, and it is not exactly usual in German either. Whatever the linguistic difficulties, we should keep the substantive distinction in mind.

By defining social structures in terms of a set of issues, we not only avoid the reification of concepts but make them "operational." If, in this way, we reformulate Max Weber's definition of bureaucracy, we obtain a specification of the issues over which individuals and

[7] I have used this and other suggestions of the literature in my elaboration of this point in *Nation-Building and Citizenship* (New York: Wiley, 1964).

groups contend in their effort to realize their ideas and maximize their chances, however they define these. The consequence of such contentions is a development in the direction of bureaucratization or debureaucratization, as the case may be. Analysis of such contentions can account for the changing strength of the "traits" which characterize a social structure, but are "never twice the same." [8]

A third corollary is a reformulation of the concept of equilibrium. Having been taken over from feedback mechanisms such as the thermostat or from biological analysis, the term is widely used by social scientists who employ the concept of social system. Such systems are believed to survive as long as they are in condition of equilibrium or return to it. The idea has merit in the very general sense that we combine with the concept of social structure the notion of some stability and identity over time. We must account for such stability as exists. However, I do not consider the concept of equilibrium useful for this purpose, because it is not the social structure or the system that maintains itself in "equilibrium," whatever that means, but men, who, by their actions (however conditioned), achieve a certain degree of stability or fail to do so. Here the definition of social structure in terms of a set of issues helps, because it points to the contentions through which individuals and groups achieve a measure of accommodation or compromise between conflicting imperatives.

By way of illustration, I shall reformulate Max Weber's types of domination in keeping with this perspective. The charismatic quality of a personality proves itself by its supernatural attributes (ultimately by miracles), and thereby gains recognition from the ruled. A leader will claim unconditional acceptance of his authority, but, as Weber says, if the test of this claim remains forever wanting, he will appear forsaken by his God or bereft of his heroic powers. Between the leader's unconditional claims and the followers' secret longing for visible signs of his "gift of grace" this authority relationship will fluctuate one way or another, but it will also endure as long as that tension exists. Similarly, under traditional domination,

[8] I use the example of bureaucracy since, in *Nation-Building and Citizenship*, *op. cit.*, 107–115, I have formulated the implications of the general points made here. Similar points are suggested elsewhere in that volume with regard to the contrast between patrimonialism and feudalism, the plebiscitarian and the representative principle in a democracy, the double hierarchy of government in totalitarian regimes, the relation between central and local authority in Indian history. None of these other concepts is as clearly worked out as the concept of bureaucracy.

authority is exercised by the ruler in conformity with established precedent. Tradition also confers on him a certain latitude, so that the ruler acts arbitrarily in keeping with tradition. But when he regularly infringes upon the limits set by tradition, he runs the risk of jeopardizing the legitimacy of his own position. Guardians of traditional limits and guardians of the king's prerogatives are, therefore, typical groupings under this type of domination. Finally, Weber distinguishes between formal and substantial rationality of law. The legal order exists as long as neither principle is allowed an absolute ascendancy. It is a continuous political and legal task to maintain balance between these antagonistic tendencies, for insistence on some principle of material justice can destroy the legal framework just as exaggerated formalism can undermine confidence in the legal system. In this view, stability of a social structure is not an equilibrium that can be attributed to a system, but the end product of always proximate efforts to maintain stability.

Here may be the place also to comment briefly on a problem raised by a German and by an English historian, both of whom warn us against the dangers of substituting inevitably arbitrary categories for the terms in which the historical participants themselves think about the questions at issue.[9] The point is well taken, I believe, and the definition of social structure suggested here allows us to take account of this subjective dimension. But it is also necessary to go beyond that dimension and define the social structure which eventually results from all these contentions; and that cannot be done in subjective terms alone. Indeed, some abstractions and arbitrariness will be unavoidable in order to freeze the fluidity of

---

[9] See Otto Brunner, *Neue Wege der Sozialgeschichte* (Göttingen: Vandenhoeck und Ruprecht, 1956) and E. P. Thompson, *The Making of the English Working Class* (London: Gollancz, 1963; New York: Pantheon, 1964). In his major work, *Land und Herrschaft* (Vienna: Rudolf M. Rohrer, 1959) and *Adeliges Landleben und europäischer Geist* (Salzburg: Otto Müller, 1949), Otto Brunner reanalyzes feudalism in terms of the legal, economic, and ethical categories employed by those directly involved in feudal relationships, but the volume of essays puts this perspective in the larger context of European social history. Thompson, for his part, wishes to restore the meaning of the term "class" and accordingly he rejects abstract definitions. Class, he says (*op. cit.*, 9), is a historical phenomenon "which *happens* when some men, as a result of common experiences, feel and articulate the identity of their interests as between themselves and as against other men whose interests are different from theirs." Note, incidentally, that the same point is made despite the rather marked difference in political orientation of the two authors.

historical change for purposes of obtaining bench marks, as suggested earlier. It may be that the deliberate employment of static *and* dynamic terms, for example bureaucracy and bureaucratization, democracy and democratization, etc., provides a way of conceptualizing both the group contentions that are an essential part of change and the altered social structures which from time to time result from that change.

COMPARISON

The points discussed may now be considered in relation to the comparative analysis of historical change, and specifically of the "steps and sequences of change in the processes of nation-building and national integration." Ideally, we should be able to consider all such changes in the same terms, and there is a powerful intellectual legacy which invites us to do so. That legacy goes back to the contrast between tradition and modernity which was first formulated in the Romantic period and has been reformulated ever since. Familiar dichotomies such as status and contract, *Gemeinschaft* and *Gesellschaft,* folk and urban society, and others have been given their most systematic formulation in Talcott Parsons's scheme of pattern variables. The utility of these distinctions has been diminished, in my opinion at least, by a tendency toward reification. Nineteenth-century evolutionary theory, for example, imputed to the different aspects of a society "a strain of consistency with each other, because they all answer their several purposes with less friction and antagonism when they co-operate and support each other." [10] Modern reformulations of this idea in terms of systems theory and equilibrium are more sophisticated no doubt, and have an impressive array of analogies to draw on, yet they continue to attribute a "strain of consistency" to social structures such that the "frictions and antagonisms" between the several traits will diminish —in the famous long run.[11]

On these assumptions it is certainly possible to consider all socie-

[10] W. G. Sumner, *Folkways* (Boston: Ginn, 1940), 5–6.

[11] It is a short step from this thought to a metaphoric language which attributes actions of various kinds to society, the famous fallacy of misplaced concreteness against which Whitehead warned. To me, it has always seemed odd that a theory that began by placing *human* action at the center of its attention should end up by referring to the actions of *systems,* though that consequence is probably related to the way in which action was defined in the first place.

ties in comparative terms, irrespective of time and space. This approach has been most fully developed with regard to the social and psychological consequences of industrialization, and in the field of national integration with regard to the study of the central value system.

For the scholar interested in comparative studies, the alternative to this approach is to think in terms of concepts applicable to some, rather than all, societies. This strategy of analysis proceeds in the belief that concepts of universals—even if useful for certain orientating purposes—are so emptied of content that they require specifications in order to be applied to some body of evidence, and these specifications are concepts of more limited applicability. Examples: interest aggregation is a universal concept, whereas class, estate, political party, etc., are more limited; administration (or should I say goal-attainment?) is universal, but administration by disciples or bureaucrats or patrimonial servants is limited, and so on. By "concepts of limited applicability," I mean concepts that are usefully applied to more than one society for a period whose approximate beginning and end are themselves an object of research. Such delimitation is always debatable. But, however difficult in detail, I doubt that it is useful, for example, to speak of class in the absence of a formal legal equality and the freedom of movement and expression that goes with it, or of political parties in the era of politics among cliques of notables, or of the nation-state in the absence of a monopoly of legitimate coercion in the hands of government—although in these and other cases the qualifying criterion is a variable as well as a contrast conception, as discussed earlier. These considerations are equally applicable to "nation-building." The concept "nation" requires delimitation against a period and condition to which it does not apply, and it may be that, with variations in such preconditions, different types of nationhood will have to be formulated. A nation is always in the process of change, for example in the extent to which consensus prevails or different sections of the people have formally equal rights—hence the phrase "nation-building."

With regard to this process, the specification of an early and a late condition is necessary, the "before-and-after" model to which I referred. This is, in fact, a crucial step in the procedure since comparative studies of nation-building depend on the success with which the different dimensions of nation-building can be conceptualized and then compared with one another. In this respect, Stein Rokkan and I have experimented with categories derived from T. H. Marshall, and Karl Deutsch has marshaled a great body of evidence on the physical indexes of nation-building.[12]

In some instances it may even be possible to combine quantitative indexes with more qualitative criteria: for example, in the study of the franchise, which has the unique advantage of involving dichotomous choices such as eligibility *vs.* noneligibility and voting *vs.* nonvoting. The accompanying table is suggestive in this respect:

EXTENSIONS OF THE FRANCHISE AND CHANGES
IN PARTICIPATION IN PRESIDENTIAL ELECTIONS IN
THE UNITED STATES (SELECTED YEARS)

Year	Population (millions)	Percentage of population eligible to vote	Percentage of eligible population that voted
1860	27.6	17	84
1880	50.3	23	78
1900	76.1	25	74
1920	106.5	51	49
1940	132.0	61	62
1952	157.0	62	64
1956	168.9	61	60
1960	180.7	60	64

Source: Murray Gendell and Hans L. Zetterberg, *A Sociological Almanac for the United States* (New York: Scribner, 1964), 54. The table is based on figures originally assembled by R. E. Lane, *Political Life: Why People Get Involved in Politics* (Glencoe: Free Press, 1959), but supplemented for the later years.

With the exception of 1920, the first year adult women had the right to vote throughout the United States, the table gives a graphic picture of the transition from a politics of notables to mass politics under a universal franchise. Voting participation is high as long as voting eligibility exists only for the few, but declines as the franchise is extended. It would be interesting to assemble comparable data for other countries and inquire into the reasons for the differences

[12] T. H. Marshall, *Citizenship and Social Class* (London: Cambridge University Press, 1950) and Karl Deutsch, *Nationalism and Social Communication* (New York: Wiley, 1953). Cf. Bruce M. Russett, Hayward R. Alker, *et al.*, *World Handbook of Political and Social Indicators* (New Haven: Yale University Press, 1964).

that would be revealed—a task that would supplement Almond and Verba's suggestive study by the addition of a historical dimension.[13] But in what way would it enable us to speak of "steps and sequences" in the process of nation-building?

In this respect, comparative studies are obliged to develop a typology of nation-building processes before proceeding further, or so it seems to me. This approach is implied in the work of Max Weber and Otto Hintze, whose comparative studies aim at delineating and distinguishing features of the Western European development.[14] In an effort to account for the initial development of capitalism, Weber is concerned with the larger complex of Occidental rationalism, whereas Hintze restricts himself to the relation between social structure and political institutions and seeks to account for the emergence of modern administration and representation. Comparison for both writers means, in the first place, the use of contrasts with other civilizations in order to define more precisely what they wish to explain. Both rejected the evolutionism of the nineteenth century not only because they criticized its biological analogies, but because they were interested in developments that were true of more than one society but of less than all.[15]

I want to suggest in what ways I think this perspective to be especially useful for the comparative study of recent historical changes, those broadly suggested by the twin terms of industrialization and democratization. In the introduction to *Capital,* Marx pointed out that he had chosen England as his model because it exemplified the "laws of capitalist development," which would govern, by and large, the future development of other capitalist countries. Thus he felt that he could say to his German readers: *de te fabula narratur.* This position is, of course, based on the assumption of necessities emanating from the economic structure of societies, which—in the long run—determine political change including international relations. We can now say, I believe, that the facts do not bear this out. Once industrialization had been initiated, no two countries would go through the same process in similar fashion. Not only were English mechanics used in the early industrialization of Germany, for exam-

---

[13] G. A. Almond and S. Verba, *The Civic Cultures Political Attitudes and Democracy in Five Nations* (Princeton: Princeton University Press, 1963).

[14] Max Weber, *Gesammelte Aufsätze zur Wissenschaftslehre* (Tübingen: Mohr—Siebeck, 1922); Otto Hintze, *Soziologie und Geschichte* (2d ed., Göttingen: Vandenhoeck und Ruprecht, 1964).

[15] Hintze's critique of evolutionism is found in several essays in *Soziologie und Geschichte*; for Weber's critique, see ch. XIII below.

ple, but English institutions were used by German intellectuals as points of reference for the development of German institutions. The point is a general one: industrialization itself has intensified the international communication of techniques and ideas, which are taken out of their original context and adopted or adapted to satisfy desires and achieve ends in one's own country. What is here said with reference to the international repercussions of English industrialization applies, *mutatis mutandis*, to the international repercussions of the ideas of the French Revolution.

English industrialization and the French Revolution altered the terms of reference by which "issues are defined, relationships maintained, and contentions resolved." Looking backward from the vantage point of the eighteenth century, one is justified in emphasizing the continuity of the changes in Western Europe which culminated in these events, and which Weber and Hintze analyzed as distinguishing characteristics of Occidental civilization. That industrialization and democratization emerged from a long and distinctly European development may help to account for the strong tendency of social scientists to consider change a phenomenon that is internal to the societies changing. It is equally legitimate to regard industrialization and democratization as having been initiated at a particular time and place and as constituting a breakthrough to a new historical era. If one considers the great transformations that followed, one is inclined to highlight the contrast between prerevolutionary traditions and postrevolutionary modernity. This contrast has been a dominant theme of social theory from the eighteenth century to the present, and it underlies many generalizations that have been derived from the Western experience.

However, these same perspectives may be used in a different manner. Emphasis may be placed on the persistent distinctiveness of the Western experience, which is as notable in its feudal traditions as in its modern industrialism and democracy. Although long in the making in Western Europe as a whole, the twin revolutions of the eighteenth century came to a head in England and France, and since then this impetus to change has had repercussions in other Western European countries and in European settlements overseas. These repercussions may be considered an extension of the internal continuities of the prerevolutionary development analyzed by Weber and Hintze.

Let me try to characterize these repercussions by restructuring what we know about certain pervasive differences between intellectual and working-class alienation and agitation during the nineteenth century. The alienation of intellectuals is a by-product of industrialization itself, for industrialization creates a mass public and a market for intellectual products and thus accentuates the elitism of some, the populism of others, and the ambivalence of all intellectuals, especially through their awareness of the discrepancies between high culture and popular culture. This general alienation was overshadowed as well as greatly intensified in the countries that witnessed from afar the rapid economic advance of England and the stirring events of the French Revolution, so that their own economic backwardness and autocratic institutions appeared still more backward and autocratic by comparison. Under these conditions a polarization of cultural life has typically occurred between those who would see their own country progress by imitating the "more advanced countries" and those who denounce that advance as alien and evil and emphasize instead the wellsprings of strength that exist among the people and within the native culture. This reaction is typified by the difference between Westernizers and Slavophiles in czarist Russia; recently its convolutions have been analyzed with great subtlety by Levenson.[16] The general pattern has occurred again and again; it has been a mainspring not only of intellectual alienation but also of movements for national independence where these have occurred.

Working-class alienation and agitation during the nineteenth century involved very different processes, as I have argued.[17] Intellectuals could experience industrialization as an emancipation from their previous subservience to the Church and to private patrons. But workers experienced it initially as economic destitution exacerbated by legal and political changes which—under the slogan of individual freedom—made a mockery of their position as members of the community. For workers, alienation meant simply second-class citizenship reinforced by police measures and the ideological indignities heaped upon them through sermons and public debates. As a result, radical agitation among workers represented a protest against this type of discrimination, a point largely obscured by Marx, whose theory of alienation attributes to workers types of dissatisfaction more often found among intellectuals. There is a strong civic component in much working-class agitation that is

---

[16] J. R. Levenson, *Confucian China and its Modern Fate*. Vol. 1, *The Problem of Intellectual Continuity* (Berkeley: University of California Press; London: Routledge & Kegan Paul, 1958).

[17] Bendix, *op. cit.*

missing from the radical agitation of intellectuals, since their citizenship was never in question. And, conversely, the alienation of intellectuals also occurs in countries like the United States in which workers have a strong sense of citizenship and reject radical appeals. However, the two kinds of movement have joined in various blends of socialism and nationalism, where the workers' protest against second-class citizenship and the intellectuals' ambivalence about the comparative backwardness of their country and their own role in it are not sufficiently assuaged.

In Europe these nineteenth-century movements occurred in the context of the emerging nation-state. They were preceded by developments which furthered an absolutist concentration of power, on the one hand, and a more or less individualized citizenry, on the other. At the risk of putting a very complex matter too simply, I would say that the desire of the workers for full citizenship and the search of the intellectuals for a power capable of removing the backwardness of their country had a common precondition in the prior decline of kinship ties, religious belief, linguistic affiliation, and territorial and racial communalism. None of these ties or associations disappeared, but some of them had been weakened by the ascendance of Christianity, others by the Renaissance and the Reformation, and others still in the course of struggles between enlightened absolutism and the estates. It will be recalled that Max Weber's lifework documents the proposition that Christian doctrine and the revival of Roman law militated against familial and communal ties as foci of loyalty that could compete effectively with the universal claims of legal procedure and the Christian faith. By these prior developments men were freed very gradually for such alternative solidarities as those of social class and national citizenship, though the relative decline of "traditional" and the relative ascendance of "modern" solidarities remains an issue to this day and hence a major subject of comparative study in Europe as well.

Here is the place, it seems to me, to refer to that loss of community that has been a recurrent theme of social theory ever since the eighteenth century. The reference can be made without nostalgia or false romanticism, if it is accompanied by an appreciation of these alternative solidarities, and hence by a proper balancing of the assets and liabilities of such a development.

The new nations of today are in a fundamentally different position from the new nations of Western Europe during the nineteenth century. Indeed, the applicability of the term "nation" itself is in question. The long European prehistory, in the course of which familial and communal ties gradually weakened, is notably absent from the societies which have gained their independence since the Second World War.[18] In these societies industrialization has become an almost universal ambition, and the populism of the franchise (if not democracy) an equally universal reality—in good part as a reaction against Western colonialism but still also as a result of influences emanating from Europe. One effect of the right to vote has been that just those familial and communal ties are mobilized politically that militate against the emergence of civic loyalties, and hence against at least one of the preconditions of the nation-state that are familiar to us from the Western experience. The consequence of this new historical pattern may be as great eventually as the consequences of the twin revolutions in eighteenth-century Europe. At any rate, there is no precedent in our experience for the emergence of nations in the context of three competing world systems which can quickly transform every tension of a social structure into an issue of international relations under the threat of nuclear war.

[18] That, it seems to me, is the questionable part of Lipset's analysis in *The First New Nation: The United States in Historical and Comparative Perspective* (New York: Basic Books, 1963), since the achievement of political independence at the end of the eighteenth century is comparable with a similar achievement in the middle of the twentieth century only on the assumption that all achievements of independence by former colonies are comparable—irrespective of time and place. I do not consider the utility of that assumption very great, but whatever it may be it is diminished, it seems to me, by the neglect of the obvious differences between independence movements then and now.

Part C

PREDECESSORS AND PEERS

XII

THE HISTORICAL RELATIONSHIP
TO MARXISM

SOME ALLEGATIONS

Many scholars have felt a sense of affinity for both Karl Marx and Max Weber. Hence they have been interested in what appeared to them compatible or complementary. Even those writers who saw Weber as an alternative to Marx have assumed a close relationship. Moreover, Marxian protagonists tend to exaggerate the impact of Marxist ideas, and detractors of Marxism unwittingly support this view by their emphasis on the pervasive and pernicious influence of the doctrine. At another level, students often read parts of Marx and Weber, but not much else of the German literature, so that the two appear as related progenitors of modern thought. And as the horizon of historical awareness shrinks, it is even hinted sometimes that Weber owed more to Marx than he admitted.

The fact is that Weber and Marx were further apart than these interpretations suggest. One should be aware that the differences between quite heterogeneous thinkers can be minimized if they are compared from a historical distance or on a high level of abstraction. To avoid these distortions, a closer look and a greater sense of discrimination are needed. I am here concerned with the way in which certain ideas were transmitted and transformed in a particular intellectual and institutional setting, rather than with a defense of Weber's originality. I shall deal first with some interpretations that overemphasize the historical proximity or analytical similarity of Marx and Weber. Some clues for a more balanced assessment are provided by Weber's political attitudes toward the Social Demo-

By Guenther Roth. The third section incorporates pp. 433–438 of "Das historische Verhältnis der Weberschen Soziologie zum Marxismus," *Kölner Zeitschrift für Soziologie*, XX: 3, 1968, 432–440.

cratic labor movement and by the fashionable economic determinism in bourgeois circles (section 2). Some intellectual influences that look Marxist from afar were in fact a result of Weber's immediate academic environment (section 3). Lastly, I shall summarize Weber's critique as well as partial adaptation of Marxian notions.

Almost always comparisons between Marx and Weber have been made on the level of the philosophy of history or of the methodology of social science, from Karl Löwith's well-known essay of 1932 up to the recent investigations by Kocka and Bendl-Janoska. The question of the empirical substance of the two men's work has usually remained subordinate.[1] In the United States the prevailing view of Weber's relation to Marx has been shaped, naturally enough, by the men most responsible for the introduction of his writings. As early as 1929 Talcott Parsons declared that *The Protestant Ethic and the Spirit of Capitalism* was "intended to be a refutation of the Marxian thesis in a particular historical case."[2] In a 1945 sketch of German sociology Albert Salomon alleged that Weber "became a sociologist in a long and intense dialogue with the ghost of Karl Marx" and that the main purpose of *Economy and Society* was the re-examination of the "Marxian sociological thesis." At the same time Gerth and Mills suggested not only that "throughout his life, Max Weber was engaged in a fruitful battle with historical materialism," but added: "Yet there is a definitive drift of emphasis in his intellectual biography toward Marx."[3]

This view of a close affinity between Weber and Marx has also

---

[1] Cf. Karl Löwith, "Max Weber and Karl Marx," in Dennis Wrong, ed., *Max Weber* (Englewood Cliffs: Prentice-Hall, 1970); Judith Janoska-Bendl, *Methodologische Aspekte des Idealtypus. Max Weber und die Soziologie der Geschichte* (Berlin: Duncker und Humblot, 1965), 89–114; Jürgen Kocka, "Karl Marx und Max Weber. Ein methodologischer Vergleich," *Zeitschrift für die gesamten Staatswissenschaften*, 122, April 1966, 328–357.

[2] Talcott Parsons, "Capitalism in Recent German Literature," *Journal of Political Economy*, 37, 1929, 40.

[3] Albert Salomon, "German Sociology," in Georges Gurvitch and Wilbert Moore, eds., *Twentieth Century Sociology* (New York: Philosophical Library, 1945), 596; H. Gerth and C. W. Mills, eds. and trans., *From Max Weber* (New York: Oxford, 1946), 63. Salomon's view was taken over by S. M. Miller in his introduction to *Max Weber: Selections* (New York: Crowell, 1963), 7; Salomon is also the starting point for Irving Zeitlin's extreme reduction of Weber to the level of a Marxian elaborator; see his *Ideology and the Development of Sociological Theory* (Englewood Cliffs: Prentice-Hall, 1968), ch. XI. Gerth and Mills' view is reflected in N. J. Demerath III and Phillip Hammond, *Religion in Social Context: Tradition and Transition* (New York: Random House, 1969), 54n.

been aided by a loose interpretation of Marx's historical materialism. Recently several English writers have interpreted Marxism in
such a fashion as to make it all-inclusive and even quasi-Weberian
insofar as multiple causation is admitted. To Eric Hobsbawm it
appears "entirely wrong . . . to think of historical materialism as an
economic (or for that matter a *sociological*) interpretation of history." [4] Sidney Pollard has agreed with J. Witt-Hansen that contrary to the various social sciences "historical materialism deals
with the human society and history *as a whole*." [5] Once Marxism is
conceived in this universalist manner, it becomes possible, for instance, to support the view that "the whole of Weber's sociology of
religion fits *without difficulty* into the Marxian scheme." [6] But in
becoming all-embracing, Marxism loses its distinctive character.

In the 1890's, during Weber's early career, there was already a
certain theoretical rapprochement between Marxists and academic
men in spite of mutual political recriminations. The aging Engels
explicitly acknowledged the importance of reciprocal influences
between substructure and superstructure, insisting only that the
economic factor was the "ultimate" one. At the same time economic
determinism became fashionable in Weber's generation. Otto
Baumgarten, his cousin, later reminisced: "Before the [First World]
War all of us—but most of all the youngest and the labor leaders
with their powerful aspirations—tended toward a strict determinism, which derided the freedom of will with a certain sense of exaltation and asserted the complete dependence of our actions on the
circumstances as well as the entrapment of our alleged freedom of
will within the causal nexus." [7] Ernst Troeltsch, too, asserted a
profound influence of Marxism on his academic colleagues, including Tönnies and Weber. However, the two claims refer to two diverse, if not contradictory, kinds of influence. Otto Baumgarten had
in mind economic determinism; its politically most important variant was the Marxism of the labor movement. By contrast, Troeltsch
thought of the Marxian dialectic, which was largely ignored by the
socialist theoreticians.

[4] Eric Hobsbawm in his introduction to Karl Marx, *Pre-Capitalist Economic
Formations* (New York: International Publishers, 1965), 17. My emphasis.
[5] J. Witt-Hansen, *Historical Materialism: The Method, the Theories* (Copen-
hagen, 1960), Book i, 36, quoted by Sidney Pollard, "Economic History—A
Science of Society?," *Past and Present*, 30, April 1965, 14. My emphasis.
[6] Georg Lichtheim, *Marxism. An Historical and Critical Study* (New York:
Praeger, 1961), 385. My emphasis.
[7] Otto Baumgarten, *Meine Lebensgeschichte* (Tübingen: Mohr, 1929), 298.

Troeltsch's view is presented here at some length because he appears to have been the first to assert a pervasive Marxian influence on Weber at the same time that he gave Marxism an all-inclusive, and hence highly indistinct, meaning. Troeltsch contrasted the dialectic as a holistic, dynamic approach with the static, piecemeal, causal approach of positivism. Once idealist, the dialectic had become socially concrete in the works of Marx and Engels. Troeltsch conceded that most academic scholars rejected the dialectic in either Hegelian or Marxian form, but added that "one must not be deceived by a scholar's methodological declarations about his actual methodology." [8] Therefore, he argued that the works of Plenge, Tönnies, Bücher, Sombart, and Weber

retained a dynamic view of the individual totalities . . . and an orientation toward the socioeconomic basis of all these historical movements and connections—features which separate this kind of research from the historical monographs that are completely alienated from any philosophical context and also from the kind of historiography that flirts with the merely causal laws of intellectual life. All of this [dynamic orientation] derives from Marxism. However, in the course of this reception Marxism loses importance as universal history. General development is replaced by individual developments. Their comparison leads, not to universal history, but to sociology, into which the scientific elements of Marxism are dissolving today. . . . Max Weber declared his methodological affinity to Rickert. This implies a renunciation of every kind of dialectic or organicist notion of development. For him such a notion is pure romanticism and fallacious emanationist logic. For the same reason he consciously abandoned universal history and replaced it by comparative sociology, which . . . eradicates the last remnants of historical teleology. . . . However, in his research Weber too adopted the broad perspective of the big sociological complexes and the great lines of development. In this regard Marx, in particular, seems to have made a deep and lasting impression on him. The concomitant causal checks and the attention to individual motivation merely add that enormous empirical richness distinctive of all of Weber's works. Everywhere he addressed the Marxist question about the relation between sub- and superstructure to the images (Bilder) of these great configurations and in this way achieved the most interesting and important results of his research. Thus, in his Roman Agrarian History he elucidated the history of landed property or, as Marx said, the secret history of the Romans, and clarified on this basis the decline of antiquity. . . . In his "Agrarian Conditions of Antiquity" the same per-

[8] Ernst Troeltsch, Der Historismus und seine Probleme (Tübingen: Mohr, 1922), 366. The following quotation is from 361 and 367ff.

spective was extended to ancient Egypt and Asia, contrasting the irrigation empires and their compulsory labor with the Western inland economies and their free labor, and showing as well the difference between the ancient polis and the medieval commercial city. Weber brilliantly illuminated the rise of modern capitalism in his inquiries into Calvinist Puritanism as the source of the economic mentality required by it, without failing to notice that Puritanism in turn came under the wheels of economic class formation and without overlooking the many causal components involved. Finally, in his studies on the "economic ethic of the world religions" he applied the [Marxist] viewpoint to all the great religions and demonstrated that the problem of sub- and superstructure does not permit any general solution, but always and everywhere must be resolved in terms of the specific context and the individual configuration. All of these inquiries are fragments of an inclusive evolutionary and sociological view, which rethinks Hegelian and Marxian thought in a completely new, if essentially sociological, manner and provides historiography with new insights of the greatest significance.

Troeltsch's interpretation, then, goes in two directions. On the one hand, Weber's work appears strongly influenced by Marx and to have a Marxian quality; on the other, it seems to transcend the Marxian dialectic. Troeltsch wanted to prove some bourgeois scholars better Marxians than the Social Democratic theoreticians, whose economic determinism and monism he scathingly criticized. This seems to have tempted him to go beyond the evidence and to blur the lines separating actual historical influence, structural similarity, and qualitative difference. Perhaps more importantly, Troeltsch pictured a grand sweep of epochal ideas, minimizing crucial intellectual differences, because he wanted to accomplish a historically grounded synthesis of ideas that might give a new value basis to Western civilization after the trauma of the First World War.[9]

[9] Troeltsch wrote his interpretation after his friendship with Weber had fallen apart during the First World War. Increasingly he claimed intellectual independence from Weber, who had always gone out of his way to emphasize it before a doubting public. In exaggerating the Marxian influence on Weber, Troeltsch may have had an ulterior motive, but this cannot be proven; instead, his assertion needs to be examined on the basis of the available evidence. Troeltsch's ambivalence is reflected in his obituary and perhaps in his refusal of Marianne Weber's request to speak at Weber's funeral. The obituary is reprinted in René König and Johannes Winckelmann, eds., *Max Weber zum Gedächtnis* (Cologne: Westdeutscher Verlag, 1963), 43–46; cf. Eduard Baumgarten, ed., *Max Weber: Werk und Person* (Tübingen: Mohr, 1964), 489, 624.

Troeltsch's *Historism and Its Problems* appeared in 1922, two years after Weber's death. A reply was left to Tönnies. Like Sombart, Tönnies was closer to Marx than Weber was; unlike Weber, both wrote biographical accounts of Marx and histories of socialism. In their own way, they professed to be followers of Marx. This makes it all the more striking that Tönnies protested Troeltsch's sweeping attributions: "I leave it to other critics to judge the impact of Marxist thought beyond its partisans, but I would like to mention that my own basic ideas developed independently and were linked to it only afterwards." [10] Tönnies resolutely sided with Weber: "I don't go along with Troeltsch's view that the transition from theoretical analysis to 'cultural synthesis' is inescapable. . . . I strictly separate cognition and volition. Weber's remarks in 'Science as a Vocation' fully correspond to my own attitude, as I have always maintained it. It is not surprising that Weber's speech caused anguish to Troeltsch's mind." [11]

In contrast to Tönnies, Weber did not give a detailed account of the intellectual influences that shaped his work. These must, therefore, be reconstructed from occasional remarks and from the substance of his writings. Since Tönnies objected to Troeltsch's interpretation, it appears advisable to take a closer look at Weber's actual relationship to Marxism.

POLITICAL ATTITUDES OF THE YOUNG WEBER

Weber grew up during the most dramatic years of German industrialization, when the great agrarian and industrial interest groups organized themselves and became politically influential. His political awareness was awakened in the period of the antisocialist laws (1878–90), which coincided with his student years. His early political thinking was greatly affected by the existence of the Social Democratic labor movement and the class cleavage pervading Imperial Germany. At the end of the period, in 1891, Marxism became the official creed of the Social Democratic Party after a rather slow

[10] Ferdinand Tönnies, "Troeltsch und die Philosophie der Geschichte," in *Soziologische Studien und Kritiken* (Jena: Fischer, 1926), II, 396. As early as in the first edition of *Gemeinschaft und Gesellschaft* (1887) Tönnies acknowledged five influences on his thinking: (1) Comte and Spencer; (2) Schaeffle, Adolph Wagner, and Rodbertus; (3) Sir Henry Maine; (4) Otto Gierke; (5) Marx. Cf. *op. cit.*, I, 34ff.

[11] *Op. cit.*, II, 420.

advance.[12] It is certain that by that time Weber knew at least the Marxism of the party agitators. Marianne Weber reports in her biography that by the late eighties Weber had developed a strong interest in the conditions of the working classes: "This new orientation was determined, not by the heartbeat of charity, as in the mother's case, but at first by a political motive—making the masses affirm the state and freeing them from the socialist embrace. However, mother and son shared the same goal: the mitigation of class differences and a more equitable distribution of burdens and goods. Soon after Weber also developed sympathies for the fate of those fettered to joyless mechanical work." [13] Weber's first concrete information about the attitudes of Social Democratic workers dated from the early nineties, when he befriended Paul Göhre, a theology student who had worked incognito in a factory and written a widely acclaimed account of his experiences.[14]

About 1890 Weber met Pastor Friedrich Naumann. He collaborated with him in the Evangelical-Social Congress and helped him found the abortive National-Social Association in 1896. Naumann and Göhre wanted to establish an anti-Marxist working-class party guided by the Christian idealism of educated men. Weber had his doubts about this combination and discussed it together with the Marxist indoctrination of the workers in Naumann's *Die Hilfe* (Dec. 6, 1896):

It would be a step forward to win over the upwardly mobile classes of the workers for a patriotic workers' party. This would mean the workers' intellectual emancipation. Freedom of thought is not tolerated by the Social Democratic party, since it hammers Marx's fragmented system as a dogma into the heads of the masses. As every city missionary in Berlin can report, among the Social Democrats freedom of conscience exists only in rhetoric, not in fact. However, in a class party there would be no room for us, especially if you [Naumann] want to exert a new pressure on conscience by demanding that the Christian faith be professed in political meetings. . . . You should realize that a party that knows no other principle than "Down with the haves" is the caricature of a party. All upwardly mobile strata of the population, including

[12] On the gradual adoption of Marxism by the Social Democratic leadership, see my *Social Democrats in Imperial Germany* (Totowa: Bedminster, 1963), ch. VII.

[13] Marianne Weber, *Max Weber: Ein Lebensbild* (Tübingen: Mohr, 1925; repr. Heidelberg: Schneider, 1950), 172.

[14] Paul Göhre, *Drei Monate Fabrikarbeiter* (Leipzig: Grunow, 1891).

those of the working class, would for this reason become the natural
opponents of the National-Social movement. You would retain only
the bottom of society. A party which counts only on the have-nots will
never seize power. If you choose the criteria of the "bleeding hearts"
(*miserabilistische Gesichtspunkte*), reminiscent of the Ethical Culture
movement, you will become jumping jacks, people who, whenever their
nerves are affected by the sight of economic misery, react by moving at
one time to the right, at another to the left, sometimes against the
agrarians, then against the stock exchange or big business. Such reactions do not amount to a political position.[15]

Politically, then, Weber considered himself an opponent of
Marxism as well as of politically naïve humanitarianism. He also
opposed the fashionable concern with the "economic viewpoint"
in many political and intellectual areas. In his inaugural address of
1895 he remarked that "a perspective advancing in such a self-
possessed manner is in danger of succumbing to certain illusions
and to overestimate the explanatory power of its own notions. . . .
It is one of the delusions rooted in the modern overestimation of
the 'economic factor,' in the common sense of the term, to believe
that national solidarity cannot survive the tensions of antagonistic
economic interests, or even to assume that political solidarity is
merely a reflection of the economic substructure composed of those
changeable interest constellations. That approximates the truth
only in periods of fundamental social change." [16]

QUASI-MARXIST INFLUENCES

The moot question is whether, despite his political opposition to
economic determinism and Marxism, Weber's early scholarly work
was significantly influenced by the writings of Marx and Engels.[17]

---

[15] Reprinted in Eduard Baumgarten, ed., *op. cit.,* 331f.

[16] Weber, "Der Nationalstaat und die Volkswirtschaftspolitik," *Gesammelte
politische Schriften,* Johannes Winckelmann, ed. (Tübingen: Mohr, 1958),
15, 18.

[17] In her biography Marianne Weber mentions nothing about an early Marxist influence. Her edition of the young Weber's letters appeared in the Nazi
period (1936). If there were any references to Marx and Engels, they may have
been omitted. A volume of later letters, already set into type, was destroyed for
political reasons. Most of the letters seem to be lost.

In the second half of the 1880's the following Marxist literature had some
currency in Germany: Marx and Engels, *The Communist Manifesto* (1848, but
widely read only since the seventies); Marx, *A Contribution to the Critique of
Political Economy* (1859); Capital, I, 1867; II, 1885; *The Misery of Philosophy*

Two recent publications have asserted a formative Marxist influence. Vernon K. Dibble compared Weber's contribution to the agrarian surveys of the *Verein für Sozialpolitik* in the early nineties with that of the five other authors and found it striking that Weber had a much better grasp of economic group relations than the others, who took an individualist position or looked at the workers only from the employers' viewpoint. Dibble inferred from this difference that "Weber took Marx seriously, and learned from Marx." Also without evidence, Eduard Baumgarten has seen in Weber's dissertation of 1889 *(On the History of the Medieval Trading Companies)* a "viewpoint unmistakably oriented toward Marx." [18]

The passages cited by Baumgarten deal with the household as the original unit of production and consumption. True enough, Engels too viewed the household, not the individual family, as the primeval economic unit in his *Origin of the Family, Private Property and the State* (1884), but he cited as a source for German history Andreas Heusler's *Institutions of German Private Law*,[19] which Weber mentioned many years later in his Sociology of Law. In the section on family and sib (paragraph 130, pp. 271–76) Heusler explained that according to ancient German law the family was an organization of household members, not just of blood relatives. Since Weber studied Roman and German private law intensively in the 1880's, it is reasonable to assume that as a law student he was familiar with Heusler's work. At the least, Weber's early views on the household do not prove a Marxist influence.

Marxist students even allege that Weber's second dissertation, *Roman Agrarian History in Its Bearing on Public and Private Law* (1891), is merely an explication of Marx's dictum that the "secret

---

(French 1847, but German only 1885); Engels, *Anti-Dühring* (1877–78); *Origin of the Family, Private Property and the State* (1884, fourth ed., 1892); August Bebel, *Woman and Socialism* (1879, revised in 1891 on the basis of Engels' *Origin*); *Die Neue Zeit* (a Marxist journal edited by Karl Kautsky). Werner Sombart reports that Marx was rarely read in the seventies, except by Adolph Wagner, Albert Schäffle, Adolf Held, and "a few overly ambitious tailors' journeymen." According to Sombart, before 1883 there were only 20 publications on Marx; between 1884 and 1894, when the third volume of *Capital* was published, there were 58; between 1895 and 1904, the number jumped to 214. See W. Sombart, *Das Lebenswerk von Karl Marx* (Jena: Fischer, 1909), 4ff.

[18] Vernon K. Dibble, "Social Science and Political Commitments in the Young Max Weber," *European Archives of Sociology*, IX: 1, 1968, 99; Eduard Baumgarten, ed., *op. cit.*, 410.

[19] Andreas Heusler, *Institutionen des deutschen Privatrechts* (Leipzig, 1886), 2 vols.

history [of the Roman Republic] is the history of its landed property," although the same sentence states that such knowledge "requires but a slight acquaintance." [20] However, it is unlikely that Weber's strong opinions about the ruthlessness of ancient capitalism were greatly affected by the few scattered remarks in *Capital*, since his teachers Theodor Mommsen and Levin Goldschmidt held similar views. Anticapitalist sentiments, incidentally, were widespread among the German professoriate, the guardian of humanist tradition, and in his 1895 inaugural address Weber pointed out that the workers "would find few traces of a community of interest with the capitalists if they searched the study of a German scholar." [21]

In his *Universal History of Commercial Law*, dedicated to Mommsen, Goldschmidt wrote of the "epoch of the greatest moral degeneration of the Roman state, when the ruling strata, profiting from the most barefaced exploitation of the provinces, indulged in the wildest speculation and most ruthless capitalism; when the owners of the latifundia had become big industrialists, and the demand for luxuries by the old and new aristocracy, which had amassed fantastic wealth through war, plunder and extortion, could be satisfied only by the most extended world trade." [22]

This view is echoed in Weber's *Roman Agrarian History* where he writes of "capitalist exploitation" in the wake of the Roman conquests: "It is likely that the political domination of a large polity has never been so lucrative." [23] It is not clear whether by 1891 Weber had read the two volumes of *Capital* available at the time. Among many references Goldschmidt also listed the first volume in connection with the transformation of money into capital. Hence Weber knew at least something about *Capital* through him. By contrast, it can be demonstrated that he dealt early and intensively with the writings of Karl Rodbertus (1805–75), the conservative socialist squire who studied the ancient economy more thoroughly than Marx. Weber cited Rodbertus in the *Roman Agrarian History* and later used his notion of the *oikos*—the large patrimonial household —in "Agrarian Conditions of Antiquity" (1908–9) and in *Economy*

[20] Karl Marx, *Capital* (New York: Modern Library, 1936), 94. The phrase about "the secret history" of the Romans was cited by Troeltsch (above) and Gerth and Mills, *op. cit.*, 10.

[21] Weber, "Der Nationalstaat und die Volkswirtschaftspolitik," *op. cit.*, 23.

[22] Levin Goldschmidt, *Universalgeschichte des Handelsrechts* (3d, completely revised ed., Stuttgart: Enke, 1891), 60. (1st ed. 1864; 2d ed., 1875.)

[23] Weber, *Die römische Agrargeschichte in ihrer Bedeutung für das Staats- und Privatrecht* (Stuttgart: Enke, 1891), 6.

and Society. He early rendered a balanced judgment, which is similar to his later evaluation of Marx and Engels in that it combines frank recognition with sharp disagreement. In 1893 he wrote to Lujo Brentano: "If I may permit myself to say so, I was somewhat surprised about the great harshness of your evaluation of Rodbertus —or perhaps you do not refer to his historical studies, especially on Rome. Although most of his reconstructions appear to me completely erroneous, I do believe that he has mightily furthered the study of the subject matter. Most of the time he misses, but not blindly. Almost always he touches on a central point, and frequently even his most obviously one-sided statements and hypotheses have appeared to me extraordinarily fruitful and suggestive." [24]

Rodbertus contrasted the more or less self-contained *oikos* with the capitalist enterprise, a central dichotomy for Weber. This distinction was also important for Goldschmidt, like the organization of capital and labor. Goldschmidt was particularly concerned with capitalist forms of organization, but he also gave some attention to the rise of associations of small producers, another development studied by Weber.

Weber wrote his second dissertation, which secured him the *venia legendi*—the right to academic teaching—under August Meitzen, whom he once pointedly called his teacher, thus denying that he had been Schmoller's pupil. In the late eighties Meitzen was at work on his monumental comparative study *The Settlement and Agrarian Structure of the Western and Eastern Germanic Tribes, Celts, Romans, Finns and Slavs* (3 vols., 1895). Meitzen too was interested in the historical antagonism between property and labor. In the Germanic settlement with its equal parceling *(Flurgemeinschaft)* he perceived an "emancipation of labor from property," that means, from the large cattle-owners. To him this proved that equalitarianism was an inherent quality of the Germanic folk spirit. As against such a spiritualist interpretation Weber advanced a "materialist" one; he considered the narrowing of economic opportunities a major cause of equal land distribution. This kind of realism led to Weber's epithet, "the bourgeois Marx," in the 1920's. However, most of the time he attributed more weight to political and military, rather than economic, "real factors" *(Realfaktoren)*.

Under Meitzen's influence Weber for a while employed the analogical method, which belonged to the arsenal of evolutionary

[24] Marianne Weber, ed., *Max Weber: Jugendbriefe* (Tübingen: Mohr, 1936), 364.

constructs.[25] Marxism too appeared to Weber as an evolutionary theory, corresponding to the contemporary self-image of the Marxist theoreticians. The analogical method presupposed that all peoples, or at least certain groups of peoples, would pass through the same stages. Communal property in Indian villages or low esteem for agriculture among Bedouins were cited as valid explanations for undocumented stages of Germanic antiquity. Marx fully endorsed this kind of analogical reasoning:

A ridiculous presumption has latterly got abroad that common property in its primitive form is specifically a Slavonian, or even exclusively Russian form. It is the primitive form that we can prove to have existed amongst Romans, Teutons, and Celts, and even to this day we find numerous examples, ruins though they may be, in India. A more exhaustive study of Asiatic, and especially Indian forms of common property, would show how from the different forms of primitive common property, different forms of its dissolution have been developed. Thus, for instance, the various original types of Roman and Teutonic private property are deducible from different forms of Indian common property." [26]

In contrast to Meitzen, Marx did not devote much time to a systematic exploration of early agrarian structures. Weber, however, followed Meitzen's substantive interests and methodology in the *Roman Agrarian History*. Meitzen also taught him the general strategy of studying ideas and institutions in terms of material group interests—a "method whose value I learned to know and to esteem nowhere as well as under him." [27] As early as 1890, then, Weber asked the general question: "Which social strata and interest groups constituted the dominant political force" in a given situation? Were policy shifts on the part of a political community the "deliberate result of pressures by certain interest groups"? This may be called a quasi-Marxist approach, but it was adopted from Meitzen, not Marx.[28] However, Weber soon became acquainted with Sombart's interpretation of Marx.

[25] See below, first section of ch. XIII.

[26] Marx, *Capital, op. cit.,* I, 89. Marx considered this point important enough to retain it from *A Contribution to the Critique of Political Economy.*

[27] Weber, *Römische Agrargeschichte, op. cit.,* 5, 6.

[28] Gerth and Mills mention only Marx and Nietzsche as Weber's predecessors in "interpreting ideas in terms of their intended or actual service rather than in terms of their face value," *op. cit.,* 61. On the relationship between Marx and German historical scholarship see Georg von Below, *Die deutsche Geschichtsschreibung* (Leipzig: Meyer, 1916). Below tried to show that the influence of

Critique and Adaptation of Marxism

In the nineties Werner Sombart was the most energetic, if ambiguous, academic champion of Marxism. Weber felt an affinity to his fighting spirit. He befriended Schmoller's *enfant terrible* and even proposed him in 1897 as his successor to the economics chair in Freiburg. In his personal relationship with Sombart, Weber again demonstrated his ability to combine recognition with sharp differences of opinion and to maintain collaboration over many years. From 1904 they worked together as editors of the *Archiv für Sozialwissenschaft*, continuing many interests of its socialist founder, Heinrich Braun. In their joint statement of editorial policy, Weber wrote: "Like the science of *Sozialökonomik* since Marx and Roscher, our journal is concerned not only with economic phenomena but also with those which are 'economically relevant' and 'economically conditioned'. . . . The scientific investigation of the general cultural significance of the social-economic structure of the human community and its historical forms of organization is the central aim of our journal." [29]

The two men regarded the conventional antisocialism of the time as intellectual inertia, if not outright political stupidity. Mixing declamatory affirmation with sweeping critique, Sombart claimed that his own work was the fulfillment of Marx's. Typical of his stance is the obituary on Frederick Engels in *Die Zukunft*. He criticized the Hegelian formalism of Marx and Engels, the insufficiently clarified concept of law in the "Marxist theory of evolution," and the fuzziness of the terminology.[30] But he also charged that his colleagues had neglected both the reception and the sys-

Marxism on German economic historians was minimal and that instead a good deal of Marx's work can be viewed as a variant of German Historism. According to Below, Meitzen received the main impulse for his comparative agrarian studies from local and regional history and from his practical experiences as commissioner for land assessment in Silesia.

[29] Weber, "Objectivity in Social Science and Social Policy," in Edward Shils and Henry Finch, eds. and trans., *The Methodology of the Social Sciences* (New York: Free Press, 1949), 65, 67.

[30] Sombart, "Friedrich Engels," separate reprint from *Die Zukunft*, Berlin, 1895: "The frequently cited passage in which Marx sketches the materialist interpretation of history (the 1859 preface to the *Critique of Political Economy*) even speaks metaphorically of an 'ideological' superstructure" (15). Weber adapted the terminology of sub- and superstructure in his popular lecture on "The Social Causes of the Decay of Ancient Civilization" (1896), trans. by Christian Mackauer, *Journal of General Education*, V, 1950–1, 75–88.

tematic critique of Marxism. Most of all, his championship of Marx served to emphasize his difference from his erstwhile teacher Schmoller: "What separates me from Schmoller and his school is the constructive element in the ordering of the material, the radical postulate of a uniform explanation from last causes, the reconstruction of all historical phenomena as a social system, in short, what I call the specifically theoretical. I also might say: Karl Marx." [31]

After 1895 Sombart moved progressively away from his own brand of Marxism. By contrast, Weber never had a Marxist phase. He accepted the heuristic utility of historical materialism but advanced the following critique:

(1) Historical materialism is unscientific, insofar as it is mono-causal; there are no ultimate causes;
(2) The same economic substructures can have different kinds of political and cultural superstructures;
(3) Historical materialism and socialism are not necessarily linked;
(4) The socialist theory of marriage and property is historically untenable;
(5) The deterministic component of Marxism is undermining its ethical motives.

Weber's earliest critique involved the theories of marriage and property in early history and the vaunted "future society" (Zukunftsgesellschaft). These theories were not specifically socialist, but they enjoyed great popularity in the socialist literature. The most popular socialist book from the 1880's to the First World War was August Bebel's *Woman and Socialism* (1879), which for a long time was also unrivaled as the most vigorous feminist statement in German literature. The 1891 edition popularized Engels' *Origin of the Family, Private Property and the State*. In the conclusions of his *Roman Agrarian History* (1891) Weber suddenly referred to Bebel in an ironic aside, defending the moral import of marriage for all strata. The context was the transition, in the later stages of the Roman Empire, from the condition of the barracks slaves to that of hereditarily attached peasants, who were permitted families of their own and conditional land use, in Weber's view a decisive change for the better:

[31] Sombart, *Der moderne Kapitalismus* (Leipzig: Duncker und Humblot, 1902), I, xxix.

The moral significance of this development need scarcely be emphasized. One must remember that at the beginning of the Empire Bebel's ideal of legal marriage [i.e., freely contracted and dissoluble marriage] was realized *de facto* among the upper strata, *de jure* for citizens in general. The consequences are known. In this study it has not been possible to show the connection between the influence of the Christian ideal of marriage and this economic development, but it should be obvious that the separation of the slaves from the manorial household was an element of profound internal recovery (*Gesundung*), which was by no means bought too dearly with the relapse of the "upper ten thousand" into centuries of barbarism.[32]

Four years later, in his inaugural address, Weber spoke of the "villain of matriarchy," and during the years of his illness and public silence he appended a note to his wife's monograph on *Fichte's Socialism and Its Relation to the Marxian Doctrine,* in which he denied the absence of exclusive property claims in early history:

It is scarcely worth mentioning even vis-à-vis a reader who is not an economist that the absence of property in the primeval society is a fiction. Only the owners of property, its uses, hence its practical importance, have changed. The consumer communism of the contemporary nuclear family is the last remnant of the communism of larger associations in matters of property, production and consumption. Historically, there never was a time when some group did not advance exclusive property claims.[33]

In Weber's stead, his wife wrote a positive statement of the historical development of marriage and property arrangements over the ages, *Wife and Mother in Legal History*.[34] In part, it elaborated a theme anticipated in the *Roman Agrarian History*: the Roman family and the economic impact of Christianity. Weber himself, however, treated matriarchy and "the socialist theory based on it" only briefly in *Economy and Society* (about 1910) and cursorily in his last lectures (1919–20), where he remarked that "an ingenious error is more fruitful for science than stupid accuracy." [35]

[32] Weber, *Römische Agrargeschichte, op. cit.,* 274f.

[33] Marianne Weber, *Fichte's Sozialismus und sein Verhältnis zur Marx'schen Doktrin* (Tübingen: Mohr, 1900), 102. The quotation is identified as Max Weber's opinion. Marianne Weber's Marxist sources were *The Communist Manifesto, Capital,* and *Socialism: Utopian and Scientific.*

[34] Marianne Weber, *Ehefrau und Mutter in der Rechtsentwicklung* (Tübingen: Mohr, 1907).

[35] For the last two quotes cf. Weber, *General Economic History* (New York: Collier, 1961), 40.

Similarly, Weber believed that the Marxian theory of capitalism could be adopted without any anticipation of the historical likelihood of socialism:

Marxism is subsumed under the idea of socialism only in the sense that it endeavors to prepare the development of the socialist society of the future. However, somebody can adhere to the so-called materialist interpretation of history, he can adopt Marx's theses about the developmental tendencies of capitalism as much as the epigoni still do, and yet believe that, if a stationary condition of human want satisfaction should recur, the future social order might well be an organism suffused with monopolies and hence authoritarian controls, an organism that might incorporate very complex antagonistic interests; indeed, he may believe that this is a developmental necessity.[36]

If this statement reflects Weber's grave doubts about the future and his disbelief in the socialist utopia, he also rejected the basic claim of historical materialism. At the first meeting of the German Sociological Association in 1910 he said:

I would like to protest the statement by one of the speakers that some one factor, be it technology or economy, can be the "ultimate" or "true" cause of another. If we look at the causal lines, we see them run, at one time, from technical to economic and political matters, at another from political to religious and economic ones, etc. There is no resting point. In my opinion, the view of historical materialism, frequently espoused, that the economic is in some sense the ultimate point in the chain of causes is completely finished as a scientific proposition.[37]

Weber also criticized Marxism for blurring the difference between technological and economic phenomena. He argued that different superstructures could rest on the same kind of technology. Instead of emphasizing technology, he directed his attention to modes of appropriation and expropriation. This is another "quasi-Marxist" position, but in fact denotes a difference from Marxism. Weber told the Sociological Association:

To my knowledge, Marx has not defined technology. There are many things in Marx that not only appear contradictory but actually are found contrary to fact if we undertake a thorough and pedantic analysis,

[36] Marianne Weber, *Fichte's Sozialismus, op. cit.,* 1. Quote identified as Weber's position.
[37] *Verhandlungen des Ersten Deutschen Soziologentages* (Tübingen: Mohr, 1911), 101.

as indeed we must. Among other things, there is an oft-quoted passage: The hand-mill results in feudalism, the steam-mill in capitalism. That is a technological, not an economic construction, and as an assertion it is simply false, as we can clearly prove. For the age of the hand-mill, which extended up to modern times, had cultural "super-structures" of all conceivable kinds in all fields.[38]

Although Weber referred to Marxism most frequently as an economic interpretation of history, he did not overlook its ethical and prophetic qualities. The *Communist Manifesto* was for him not only "a scientific achievement of the first order," but also a "prophetic document." [39] If the workers were motivated by a vague sense of the basic injustice of the economic order, Marx and intellectuals of his kind were driven by their sense of moral outrage. Marianne Weber, investigating the natural-law components of Marxism, concluded that "the contradiction that condemns the existing social order to extinction is not an organic defect of its structure, but the contrast between the natural—and that means for Marx, the ethical —purposes of the social order and the actual state of affairs. The organic defect had to be construed if the ethical postulate was to be satisfied." [40] The trouble with Marxism, as the Webers saw it, was this fusion of natural-law beliefs with a deterministic social theory. Socialist thinkers first advanced substantive natural law against the formalistic natural law of the bourgeoisie, but then undermined their own position by positivistic relativism and "Marxist-evolutionist considerations." [41]

As a secular creed, Marxism opposed revealed religion, prominently in the rationalist polemics of Engels, August Bebel, and Karl Kautsky—polemics that appeared shallow to Weber. He did not overlook the compensatory functions of religion or its uses for legitimation and pacification, but he had a much more profound and sympathetic interest in religiously inspired ethical conduct. At the same time, he did not put a one-sided spiritualist interpretation in place of the one-sided materialist one that Engels, for one, had presented when he wrote: "Calvin's creed was one fit for the boldest of his time. His predestination doctrine was the expression of the

[38] *Op. cit.*, 95f.
[39] Weber, "Der Sozialismus," *Gesammelte Aufsätze zur Soziologie und Sozialpolitik* (Tübingen: Mohr, 1924), H. F. Dickie-Clark, trans., *Socialism* (Durban: Institute for Social Research, University of Natal, 1967), Occasional Papers No. 11, 25.
[40] Marianne Weber, *Fichte's Sozialismus, op. cit.*, 112.
[41] Weber, *Economy and Society* (New York: Bedminster, 1968), 872.

fact that in the commercial world of competition success or failure does not depend upon a man's activity or cleverness, but upon circumstances uncontrollable by him." [42]

If it must remain questionable whether Weber knew this passage, it can be shown that by the nineties the relationship between Calvinism and capitalism had become an internal academic issue and that he wrote *The Protestant Ethic and the Spirit of Capitalism* in response to other studies, not just as a discourse against historical materialism. He acknowledged particularly the earlier work of three colleagues, Eberhard Gothein, Werner Wittich, and Georg Jellinek. [43] To Sombart the impact of Calvinism and Quakerism on capitalist development even appeared as "too well-known a fact to require detailed explanation." [44] Weber, who had presented his thesis as early as in his Heidelberg lectures (1897–98), was not deterred by Sombart's dismissal of the issue in 1902 and stated his case more fully in the following year. He declared openly that the formulation of his case was influenced by Sombart's work. In writing his essay at the time he did, Weber perhaps also responded to Schmoller, who observed in a review of Sombart: "Whatever Marx and the Social Democrats have against the capitalist—the 'hunger for profit' and the untrammeled ruthlessness toward the worker's welfare— concerns primarily the manner in which the individualist drive for acquisition developed between 1500 and 1900 and cut itself loose from most earlier moral and social restraints. These phenomena must be investigated if one wants to understand today's economy." [45]

Such investigations, then, can be considered at least indirect responses to Marxism, but for the scholarly research of the time the primary challenge was the given historical issue, behind which the polemical interest in a "critique of ideology" remained secondary. This appears to me especially true of Weber's writings in the so-

[42] Engels, English introduction to *Socialism: Utopian and Scientific* (London, 1892), in *Marx and Engels on Religion* (New York: Schocken, 1964), 300f. German version in Marx-Engels, *Werke* (Berlin: Dietz, 1963), vol. 22, 300.

[43] This paragraph paraphrases pages lxx–lxxi of my introduction to *Economy and Society*, *op. cit.* For Jellinek's influence on Weber, see below chapter XVI, second part; on the general familiarity in the literature of the eighteenth and nineteenth century with the relation between religious dissent and economic motivation, see Bendix, "The Protestant Ethic—Revisited," chapter XVI, first part.

[44] Sombart, *op. cit.*, 381.

[45] Gustav Schmoller in *Jahrbuch für Gesetzgebung, Verwaltung und Volkswirtschaft*, 27, 1903, 298.

ciology of religion and of *Economy and Society,* where he pushed popular, ideologically saturated theories aside insofar as they obstructed his exposition. In brief, almost incidental remarks, he turned in *Economy and Society* against evolutionism, Social Darwinism, the romantic glorification of the rural neighborhood, and racist and nationalist creeds, as well as against dogmatic historical materialism, but without singling out the latter.

The most specific adaptation of a Marxist concept on Weber's part may well be the use of "class" in *Economy and Society.* Here too Sombart may have been a catalyst. However, in contrast to Sombart's elaboration of the Marxist class concept in his *Socialism and Social Movement in the 19th Century* (1896), Weber included the dimension of international stratification, power prestige, and imperialism. Moreover, he integrated the class concept into a typology of status groups and parties, the other two phenomena of power distribution in the political community. One of his polemical targets was "that kind of pseudo-scientific operation with the concepts of class and class interests which is so frequent these days and which has found its most classic expression in the assertion of a talented author that the individual may be in error about his interests, but that the class is infallible"—a reference, it seems, to none other than the young Georg Lukács.[46] As against this class reification by a new breed of Marxian metaphysicians, Weber insisted on his own empirical dialectic of class and status.

In conclusion, Marxism was for Weber primarily the materialist interpretation of history as understood at the time by friend and foe. As a critic of conventional wisdom, he sometimes went out of his way to stress Marxism's scholarly contributions and to acknowledge its impact. However, historical materialism appeared also as part and parcel of evolutionism. After Weber had convinced himself of the inherent inadequacies of the evolutionary theories, he began to grope his way toward a typological approach, which became his answer to the dilemmas of the evolutionary schemes, Marxism included. His critique of historical materialism, then, must be seen as part of his broader critique of evolutionism. Therefore, the next chapter will deal with this critique and the genesis of the typological approach.

[46] Weber, *Economy and Society, op. cit.,* 930. Weber knew Lukács well when he wrote this passage. Lukács first wrote down his theory in a Hungarian essay of 1919, "Tactics and Ethics"; see his *Schriften zur Ideologie und Politik,* Peter Ludz, ed. (Neuwied: Luchterhand, 1967), esp. 9, 18f., 31. Lukács later adapted Weber's class terminology in *History and Class Consciousness* (1923).

However, before turning to this theoretical issue, I shall address myself briefly to a concrete organizational phenomenon, the German Social Democratic Party, as it was perceived by Weber and Robert Michels. Just as the influence of Marxism on Weber has been overemphasized, so it has sometimes been assumed that his views of the Social Democratic labor movement were shaped by Michels. Since an alternative interpretation of the movement and an alternative theory of bureaucratization and democratization is involved, the matter has more than purely biographical interest.

POSTSCRIPT: WEBER AND ROBERT MICHELS ON THE SOCIALIST LABOR MOVEMENT

Weber and Michels were close political allies in spite of substantial disagreements. We have seen in chapter I that Weber tried hard, if unsuccessfully, to save Michels' academic career in Germany when it was blocked because of his activities on behalf of the Social Democratic Party. In turn, Michels expressed his closeness to Weber in the dedication to the first German edition of his *Political Parties:* "To my dear friend Max Weber, that upright man who does not shy away from vivisection if it is in the interest of science, with greetings from a kindred soul." [47]

In his work Michels postulated that all large-scale organizations inevitably develop oligarchic controls, the famed "iron law of oligarchy." [48] This appeared to him as a special dilemma for democratic and socialist organizations: they strive for the emancipation of the masses, but their leaders tend to perpetuate themselves

[47] Michels, *Zur Soziologie des Parteiwesens in der modernen Demokratie* (1911). In the second edition (1925) Michels again acknowledged Weber's influence and mentioned that for its revision he took into consideration a lengthy critique by Weber. However, he added that he did not learn much that was new from Weber's posthumously published treatment of parties in *Economy and Society*—understandably so, since Weber had communicated his views to Michels many years earlier.

[48] For an account of Michels' academic influence and of political reactions to his work, see S. M. Lipset's introduction to Michels' *Political Parties* (New York: Collier, 1962); for a qualification of Lipset's earlier assessment, see his introduction to M. Ostrogorski, *Democracy and the Organization of Political Parties* (New York: Anchor, 1964), xiii.

Revised version of an excursus in Guenther Roth, *The Social Democrats in Imperial Germany* (Totowa: Bedminster, 1963), 249–256.

through monopoly of skills, control of communication channels, and the very gratitude of the masses. Even worse, professional leaders of a democratic party or a labor union ultimately tend to fail the masses by developing an overriding concern with organizational survival. Michels wrote from the perspective of Rousseau's ideal democracy, which rejected the principle of popular representation because it involved a diminution, if not a destruction, of popular sovereignty and freedom.

Michels asserted his "iron law" in an apodictic fashion which may have hidden an underlying ambivalence. His intellectual ambiguities were paralleled by a vacillating career. To begin with, his family background was remarkably heterogeneous. The descendant of a wealthy Catholic family in the Rhineland, he became an active officer in the predominantly Protestant Prussian army. Soon, however, he rejected his upper-class background and the military career and became instead a socialist with syndicalist and anarchist predilections.[49] But his upper-class origins, syndicalist inclinations, and "objective" scholarly work impaired his relations with the German Social Democrats, for whom he campaigned in Marburg in 1906–7. Unable to find a footing either in the Social Democratic Party or in the German university, he chose Italy as his elective country, becoming a lecturer at the University of Turin in 1907. He joined the syndicalist wing of the Italian labor movement, but soon frustration made him withdraw again. In 1914 he accepted a chair at the University of Basle in Switzerland, from which he observed the seeming triumph of the "iron law of oligarchy" in the First World War. A disappointed idealist, who despaired about his own "iron law" and about the permanent political crisis in Italy, France, and Germany, he came to consider authoritarian regimes historically inevitable and finally accepted a professorship from Mussolini in 1928.[50]

When Michels' book appeared, the radical socialist Left benefited

---

[49] Compare Michels' own pertinent description of the young bourgeois enthusiast turning to socialism in *Political Parties, op. cit.,* 241.

[50] These biographical details rely on Werner Conze's thoughtful postscript to the 1957 German edition (Stuttgart: Kröner); on Michels' Italian period, see also Juan Linz, "Michels e il suo contributo alla sociologia politicia," introduction to Michels, *La Sociologia del Partito politico nella Democrazia moderna* (Bologna: Il Mulino, 1966), 7–119; Linz, biographical article on Michels in the *International Encyclopedia of the Social Sciences* (New York: Macmillan and Free Press, 1968).

from its arguments, often built on its own testimony. Yet it was also part of the academic critique of the Marxist belief that administrative and political problems of large-scale organization would be easily manageable under socialism. A major representative of this critique was Max Weber. The two men agreed that the German labor movement as it was could not offer a radically different form of social organization; it constituted no revolutionary threat; the movement tended to become an end in itself and its leaders "conservative." However, their basic premises and final evaluations differed. For Weber the basic premise was the national welfare; for Michels, an internationalist syndicalism which Weber called an "apolitical ethos of brotherhood."

Since the nineties, Weber had been strongly under the influence of M. Ostrogorski's monumental volumes on *Democracy and the Organization of Political Parties,* which analyzed the rise of modern party organization in England and the United States.[51] Ostrogorski showed in detail how mass suffrage and industrialization resulted in the creation of party machines mobilizing the masses in quasi-military fashion. Oligarchic controls and mass manipulation were the inevitable outcome. Ideological differences between parties tended to become blurred under the identical pressures of organizational requirements. Weber pointed out to Michels that the German Social Democratic Party was, "outside the Anglo-Saxon realm, the only one which is technically fully developed," although it has "by contrast . . . something like a *Weltanschauung*" and thus is "not just a technical machine," as are the parties in the United States.[52] In a similar vein he explained to a distinguished audience at the 1905 convention of the Verein für Sozialpolitik what would happen to the Social Democratic party

under the pressure of compelling conditions, particularly under the pressure of the feeling of powerlessness which predominates in the ruling circles . . . , as everybody knows who looks behind the scenes. Of course, its representatives would deny this, but this does not change matters. The party cannot become anything else but a party of the American *genre*, committed . . . to a few slogans . . . , a party which exists for its own sake and that of its office-holders. Just as the workers in the factories are supposed to knuckle under according to the theory

[51] Ostrogorski's work was first published in French in 1893 and in English in 1902.

[52] Letter of March 26, 1906, quoted in Wolfgang Mommsen, *Max Weber und die deutsche Politik* (Tübingen: Mohr, 1959), 124.

of the lords of the big business syndicates, and just as these gentlemen and all of us are supposed to bow before the State, everybody in the party is supposed to do so before the ruling bosses. The workers have acquired this lack of character in our State . . . and in our quasi-military factories.[53]

Weber urged the empirical study of basic problems of leadership, organizational structure, social composition, and ideology. Michels was understandably interested at first in the role of the intellectuals and especially of the reformists, but eventually he took up these broader problems, at least in part under Weber's influence. Weber, who published Michels' studies in his *Archiv* from 1906 on, outlined some research topics in 1905, in the same issue, incidentally, in which he presented the first part of *The Protestant Ethic and the Spirit of Capitalism*. Weber's catalogue of research topics included:

(1) The relationship between the organized elite of the labor movement and the masses of followers; (2) The impact of non-proletarian groups within the party versus the necessity to appeal to non-proletarian groups outside the party during election campaigns; (3) The character and the background of the elements controlling the local organizations and the party newspapers; (4) The professional politicians who live "off" or for the party—explicit comparisons to be made with American parties despite the ideological differences; (5) Difference between academically trained members and those who, due to the class barriers, could not acquire higher education; (6) Universal tendencies of parties to become an end in themselves for their followers; (7) Resulting tendency of Social Democratic office-holders (*Parteipfründner*) to oppose a radical course no less than a clearly reformist one—comparisons to be made with the conflicts of liberal and orthodox theologians on Apostolic writings; (8) Interest of the trade unions in "conservative" party tactics; trade union dependence on the party, due to the need for having the voice of a large party in parliament to fight the chicaneries of the officials and the police—the real cause of the proletarian class consciousness; drawback of this dependence; other parties not interested in wooing labor; relatively small material gains for labor are the result; (9) Extent to which the trade unions are likely to take over the party; possible irrelevance of trade union domination in view of strategic position of the

---

[53] *Verhandlungen, Schriften des Vereins für Sozialpolitik*, 116, 1906, 389f. Weber purposively exaggerated such statements. He replied to Michels' protests against his similar address at the 1907 convention that he had addressed "the cowards of his own class as a 'class-conscious bourgeois.' " He wanted to diminish their fears of the Social Democrats. Cf. letter of Nov. 6, 1907, quoted in Mommsen, *op. cit.*, 123.

party, especially the need to appeal to unorganized masses; (10) Importance of everyday operations and tactical questions, such as the mass strike, over program demands and theoretical issues.[54]

If Michels took up some of Weber's suggestions, he did not link his analyses directly to Ostrogorski's work, to which he referred only occasionally. Yet his *Sociology of Parties in Modern Democracy* appears as a supplement to Ostrogorski's study.[55] However, instead of dealing with liberal and conservative parties, as Ostrogorski had done for the Anglo-Saxon democracies, Michels turned to the labor movements in semiauthoritarian Germany; in Italy, which did not have a genuine parliamentary monarchy; and in the French Third Republic, which suffered from a persistent crisis of legitimacy. But in contrast to Ostrogorski and Weber, Michels did not pay much attention to the political systems under which these movements operated; given his premises of the "iron law," such differences appeared fairly immaterial—a perspective which influenced for a long time the French, German, and American literature on the sociology of parties.

Similarly to Michels wavering between the affirmation of syndicalist ideals and the skeptical recognition of organizational realities, Weber—to use his own distinctions—vacillated in his evaluation of the Social Democrats between an "ethic of absolute values" *(Gesinnungsethik)* and an "ethic of responsibility" *(Verantwortungsethik)*—that is, a pragmatic ethic. Weber well understood the organizational dilemma of the Social Democrats, but he had little sympathy for the Social Democratic dualism of radical rhetoric and moderate practice. He criticized the party's lack of revolutionary enthusiasm no less than its refusal to declare itself openly a reform party;[56] for him this dualism was "petty-bourgeois" timidity. Weber attended the important 1906 party convention in Mannheim and reported to Michels in disgust:

Mannheim was a miserable affair. . . . Ten times at least I heard Bebel and Legien emphasize "our weakness" [that is, the movement's weakness]. On top of it, there were all the extremely petty-bourgeois attitudes, the self-satisfied physiognomies of innkeepers, the lack of *élan,*

[54] Weber, postscript to R. Blank's "Die soziale Zusammensetzung der sozialdemokratischen Wählerschaft Deutschlands," *Archiv für Sozialwissenschaft und Sozialpolitik,* 20, 1905, 550ff.
[55] The misnomer of Michels' book was perhaps due to its being a parallel to Ostrogorski's broad title.
[56] Cf. letter to Michels of Feb. 1, 1907, quoted in Mommsen, *op. cit.,* 122, 149.

and the inability to move to the right if the road to the left is blocked or appears to be so—these gentlemen no longer scare anyone.[57]

While Michels still believed in 1907 that the political emancipation of the working class could be derived from its economic indispensability, Weber argued:

Indispensability in the economic process means nothing, absolutely nothing for the power position and power chances of a class. At a time when no "citizen" worked, the slaves were ten times, nay a thousand times as necessary as is the proletariat today. What does that matter? The medieval peasant, the Negro of the American South, they were all absolutely "indispensable." . . . The phrase contains a dangerous illusion. . . . Political democratization is the only thing which can perhaps be achieved in the foreseeable future, and that would be no mean achievement. . . . I cannot prevent you from believing in more, but I cannot force myself to do so.[58]

Michels did not deny that the German labor movement was a vehicle of democratization, but this was not enough for him. For Weber, democratization held out the promise that the coalition between big business and the Junkers might be destroyed, enhancing Germany's prestige and power in the world. The basic difference between Michels and Weber eventually came to be the interpretation of the very organizational phenomena on whose existence they agreed. For Michels the "iron law of oligarchy" left no way out. Weber overcame his original exasperation with the bureaucratization of political parties and recognized its positive consequences. Party machines with a system of patronage and co-optation could devote themselves more realistically to problems of national leadership than purely ideological groups or parties of notables. In his discussion of charismatic domination, he compared English and German party developments and concluded that "in certain respects the chances of charisma are greatest in the first case. A patronage party makes it much easier, *ceteris paribus,* for impressive personalities to win the necessary following than do the petty-bourgeois organizations of notables of the German parties, particularly of the liberal ones, with their programs and *Weltanschauungen* which are forever the same." [59]

[57] Letter of Oct. 8, 1906, quoted *ibid.,* 122.
[58] Letter of Nov. 6–7, quoted *ibid.,* 97, 121.
[59] In contrast to Michels' tendency to absolutize generalizations, Weber added cautiously: "But it is probably impossible to generalize successfully. The in-

Although Weber did not foresee the Fascist and Communist combination of bureaucracy and extremist ideology and was by no
means detached about the Social Democrats, his general approach
to party organization appears to me superior to Michels' because it
was more concerned with alternatives then with "iron laws." In
later decades, however, Michels' book became more influential than
Ostrogorski's stout volumes and Weber's massive fragments; paradoxically, Ostrogorski was eclipsed in the United States despite the
fact that Michels did not focus on the Anglo-Saxon realm. American
social scientists were stimulated as well as handicapped by the
pessimistic orientation of Michels' thesis, which produced much
repetitive confirmation and some incisive qualification; the latter
contributed fruitfully to the development of theories of institutionalization.

---

ternal dynamics of party organization and the social and economic conditions
of each concrete case are all too intimately interwoven in any given situation":
Economy and Society (New York, Bedminster, 1968), 1133.

XIII

THE GENESIS OF THE
TYPOLOGICAL APPROACH

In Weber's student days unilinear evolutionism and mono-casual theories were widely held; Herbert Spencer exerted considerable influence on the generation of Weber's teachers. Although the unilinear conception was gradually abandoned, schemes of developmental stages or theories of cycles remained popular throughout Weber's lifetime; Oswald Spengler fascinated many young students in the last years of Weber's life. As against general theories of social change, Weber became increasingly concerned with the actual changes and vicissitudes of Occidental history. He did not think that the ranking of economic, political, legal, and religious factors in a general scheme of development was possible. Therefore, historical inquiry had to decide their relative impact in a given instance.

HISTORICAL LAWS AND THE USES OF ANALOGY

As a young scholar, Weber too had been under the sway of evolutionary thought. In his *Roman Agrarian History,* he employed August Meitzen's categories of Indo-Germanic development. At the time he still considered it "scientifically correct to say that if a trend dominant in the metropolitan center is not yet prevalent in the outlying areas it is because for the time being other tendencies oppose it. It is possible to construe the general developmental law in terms of mere tendencies that can be hindered by stronger local ones. Hence I considered it methodologically correct to proceed for the time being from an agrarian development inside the most advanced provinces of the Empire without further detailed investigation [of

By Guenther Roth: written for this volume.

the outlying areas]." [1] When Weber wrote his second major study of antiquity in 1908, he declared that he had erred in his attempt to apply Meitzen's evolutionary categories to heterogeneous conditions.[2] By that time he had presented his critique of evolutionary assumptions, historical laws, and analogical reasoning, but he was only just beginning to work out his own typologies as an alternative.

His first critique of historical laws of development appeared in 1903, when he returned to writing after his prolonged illness. This was a critical examination of Wilhelm Roscher, whose works he had first read in his Heidelberg student days.[3] Roscher had formulated his views in the 1840's and taught until the nineties. Searching for historical laws *(Entwicklungsgesetze)* of state and economy, he believed in their divine origin and, therefore, in their ultimate inscrutability. In perceiving universal laws he differed from the Historical School in jurisprudence, but he shared its belief in peoples as historical "individuals" and embodiments of the folk spirit. He advocated especially the study of antiquity, because its peoples had passed through their natural stages. He urged that ancient literature be compared with Romanic and Germanic literature for the sake of discovering the developmental patterns of all literature.

In Weber's view, such a search for historical constants and repetitions missed the vocation of history, which is to find the reasons for, and the meaning of, historical changes. Roscher's approach appeared unable to achieve any "causal transparency," because parallels and regularities are not self-explanatory but constitute merely the beginning of research.

If we strive for intellectual understanding of the reality about us, of the way in which it was by needs individually determined in a necessarily individual context, then the analyses of those *parallels* must be undertaken solely from the viewpoint of elucidating the specific meaning of concrete culture elements with regard to concrete, intelligible causes and consequences. In this case the parallels would merely be a means of comparing several historical phenomena in their full individuality for the sake of identifying their specific character.[4]

---

[1] Weber, *Die römische Agrargeschichte in ihrer Bedeutung für das Staats- und Privatrecht* (Stuttgart: Enke, 1891), 4.

[2] Weber, "Agrarverhältnisse im Altertum," *Gesammelte Aufsätze zur Sozial- und Wirtschaftsgeschichte* (Tübingen: Mohr, 1924), 287; abbr. *GAzSW*.

[3] Weber, "Roscher und Knies und die logischen Probleme der historischen Nationalökonomie" (1903–6), *Gesammelte Aufsätze zur Wissenschaftslehre* (Tübingen: Mohr, 1951).

[4] *Op. cit.*, 14.

Instead of using parallels for the ultimate purpose of arriving at laws, subsuming lower under higher regularities, Weber stressed their utility for the formation of historical concepts. Of course, this utility depended on the given case; parallels could be illuminating as well as misleading. At any rate, they were meant to serve causal analysis, not to represent explanations in their own right. In his "Critical Studies in the Logic of the Cultural Sciences" (1906) Weber pointed to the widespread confusion in the literature, from Roscher to Karl Bücher and Eduard Meyer, between explanation in terms of cause and of law, a confusion made worse by the linguistic habit of speaking of the "causal law" *(Kausalgesetz)*. He advocated "mere" causal analysis: "The historian's problem of causality . . . is oriented toward the attribution of concrete causes, and not toward the establishment of abstract 'uniformities' *(Gesetzlichkeiten)*." [5]

After his critique of Eduard Meyer (in the first part of the "Critical Studies") Weber clarified the categories of objective possibility and adequate causation, which involve an inherently comparative mental experiment. He wanted to demonstrate that every historian, whether he knows it or not, undertakes some kind of mental experiment in assessing a given case, in fact that he is forced to be explicit about it when his interpretation is challenged. [6] The historian's mental experiment is, however, not yet a systematic undertaking using parallels and analogies for the construction of ideal types and generalizations. Weber emphasized that "the comparison of 'analogous' events is to be considered as *one* means of this imputation of causal agency, and indeed, in my view, one of the most important means and one which is not used to anywhere near the proper extent." [7]

Weber's essay on the controversies about ancient Germanic social structure—still untranslated, although it was intended for presentation at the St. Louis Congress of 1904—shows clearer than the critique of Eduard Meyer how he took a step closer to historical typology. [8] At issue was the historical significance of manorial dom-

[5] Weber, "Critical Studies in the Logic of the Cultural Sciences," in Edward Shils and Henry Finch, eds. and trans., *The Methodology of the Social Sciences* (New York: Free Press, 1949), 168. Shils and Finch translate *Zurechnung* as "correlation," but the term is easily confused with the statistical notion; hence, I prefer to speak of "attribution." Weber did not have in mind the correlation approach which today is often used as an alternative to a causal approach.

[6] Cf. *ibid.*, 177, 183.

[7] *Ibid.*, 130.

[8] Weber, "Der Streit um den Charakter der altgermanischen Sozialverfassung in der deutschen Literatur des letzten Jahrzehnts" (1904), *GAzSW*, 508–556.

ination, of large-scale land ownership, broadly speaking. For a time, many historians believed that most of the political and economic history of Germany could be explained monocausally from this institution. In view of the dearth and ambiguity of historical sources, some scholars attempted to buttress their view of the historical primacy of manorial domination in Europe by drawing on analogies with contemporary primitive peoples or tribes. This implied universal stages of development, an assumption for which Weber saw no empirical justification. He insisted that it was the business of cultural history to explain change from the viewpoint of current concerns—how the major institutions and values of the present had come about; this was a problem-oriented, subjectivist rather than a law-oriented, objectivist endeavor. The search for analogies and the comparison of developmental stages were just heuristic devices.

Weber's own use of analogy was twofold: illustrative, helping the reader visualize a phenomenon by reference to something with which he was familiar, and typological, drawing on similar phenomena for the sake of formulating typologies. Weber considered unfeasible the kind of analogy that relied too much on a single trait without taking into account other internal or environmental features. As an example he cited an analogy used by Richard Hildebrand and Werner Wittich: If contemporary nomads such as Bedouins and Kirghiz look down upon agricultural labor, the Germanic tribes of Caesar's time, presumably also nomads or seminomads, must have done likewise. As against this kind of analogy, Weber offered, albeit illustratively, a more adequate one:

If one wants to search at all for such distant analogies as the Kirghiz and Bedouins, the traits of an "autarkous state" [an allusion to Fichte's collectivist utopia] found among the Suevi will remind one much more of the robber communism that existed in antiquity on the Liparian islands or—if the expression be permitted—the "officers' mess communism" of the ancient Spartans—or the grand booty communism of the Caliph Omar. In one phrase, these traits are the outcome of "warrior communism." They can easily be explained as of purely military interest . . . They would scarcely be in tune with the living conditions of a tribe stagnant at the nomadic stage and ruled by large-scale cattle owners in a patriarchal manner.[9]

The reference to "officers' mess communism" was an illustrative

[9] *Op. cit.,* 523.

analogy drawn from the clubhouse life of the officer corps in Imperial Germany and was meant to be familiar as well as ironically alienative; like Thorstein Veblen, Weber enjoyed pointing out historical residuals. The three other cases more closely resembled one another than the more "distant" analogies criticized, albeit in each case there was likely to be some ground for scholarly disagreement. Important for Weber's comparative approach was that the examples made up a type (warrior communism).

CLEAR TYPES AND RULES OF EXPERIENCE

If there are no "whole societies," unilinear developments, universal stages, or causal master keys, the varieties of historical structure must be conceptualized in a different way. Weber's alternative was the ideal-typical approach, which appeared more static only in comparison with the long-range evolutionary schemes or the monocausal theories. Instead of searching for a basic causal agent throughout the ages, he tried to rank factors in a given historical case. He believed that this could be accomplished only with the help of clear concepts and rules of experience. Causal explanation "requires as an indispensable preparation the isolation (that means, abstraction) of the individual components of the course of events, and for each component the orientation toward *rules of experience* and the formulation of *clear concepts*. This should be taken into account especially in the economic field in which inadequate conceptual precision can produce the most distorted evaluations." [10] By "clear concepts" Weber meant not just carefully defined general concepts but historically derived ideal types. Problematical for historical investigation was not the abstractness and selectiveness of the types; in this regard the evolutionary stages and Marxist concepts, too, were ideal-typical. Rather, the challenge lay in the empirical adequacy of the concepts. Weber granted that "all qualitative contrasts in reality, in the last resort, can somehow be comprehended as purely quantitative differences in the combination of individual factors." [11] However, after formulating an analytical problem, the researcher's task consists in discerning significant historical differences, although "historical reality always

---

[10] Weber, "Agrarverhältnisse," *op. cit.,* 288.

[11] From the introduction to the essays in the sociology of religion, in H. Gerth and C. W. Mills, eds. and trans., *From Max Weber* (New York: Oxford, 1946), 292.

appears in mixed forms." [12] As Weber put it in a methodological aside on the construction of religious types: "Those features *peculiar* to the individual religions . . . but which at the same time are important for *our interest,* must be brought out strongly." [13] Thus, even though Weber agreed with the epistemological view of the world as an infinite manifold—"the continuous stream of actual phenomena" [14]—his approach was based on the assumption that it was fruitful to reduce social reality to intelligible typological proportions. This was a nominalist position, distinguishing Weber from men like Hegel and Marx, who believed that concepts and objects were intrinsically related.

The construction of typologies presupposed certain historical judgments. Weber gave so much attention to political typology because of his conviction that the form of rulership affected both social stratification and the economy. In *The Protestant Ethic and the Spirit of Capitalism* Weber made it plain that he did not propose to pit an idealist interpretation against a materialist one, but in the essay on Germanic social structure he stated his judgment about the historical primacy of the political factor unambiguously:

The oldest social differentiation of Germanic and Mediterranean prehistory is, as far as we can see, determined *primarily politically, in part religiously,* not, however, primarily economically. Economic differentiation must be considered more as a consequence and epiphenomenon or, if you want it in the most fashionable terms, as a "function" of the former, rather than vice versa. . . . It means a reversal of the usual causal relationship to view the later manorial constitution not as a consequence but as the original basis of the privileged position of the high-ranking families. The historical primacy of manorial domination appears highly unlikely, first of all, because in an age of land surplus mere land ownership could not very well be the basis of economic power.[15]

In addition to such a specific historical judgment, Weber took into account certain "rules of experience" for the formulation of clear historical types. Before setting up his types of authority, he drew upon the following historical rules: (1) Legitimation is important because "simple observation shows that . . . he who is more favored feels the never-ceasing need to look upon his position as in

[12] Weber, *Economy and Society* (New York: Bedminster, 1968), 1002.
[13] *From Max Weber, loc. cit.*
[14] Weber, *Economy and Society,* 945.
[15] Weber, "Der Streit," *GAzSW,* 554f.

some way 'legitimate,' upon his advantage as 'deserved,' and the
other's disadvantage as being brought about by the latter's 'fault' ";
(2) "The sociological character of domination will differ according
to the basic differences in the major modes of legitimation"; (3)
Rulers use coercion in addition to legitimation; hence, the typology
must deal with domination "insofar as it is combined with administration"; (4) "It is a fact, after all, that only a limited variety of
different administrative techniques is available" to rulers and their
staffs.[16]

These rules were complemented by another rule that Weber considered empirically undeniable: the state was "the most important
constitutive element of every civilization *(Kulturleben),*" just as
law was for a civilization "the most important form of normative
regulation." [17] This statement had nothing to do with Hegelian
state metaphysics. It was meant as a plain observation about the
major civilizations, and indeed did not necessarily conflict with the
Marxian view of the state as the executive committee of the ruling
class. Weber pointed merely to the structural importance of the
state among other organizations; he distinguished this rule from
the prevailing legal definition of the state, which postulated its
sovereign powers, by stressing empirical variation: in society as an
arena of contending associations, the state was not necessarily more
powerful than religious groups or economic interest groups.

Weber first elaborated his political typology, still without the
label "sociology," in "Agrarian Conditions of Antiquity" (1908–9).
This book-length study for the *Handwörterbuch der Staatswissenschaft* (where it first appeared under this narrow rubric) presented
a substantive theory of ancient capitalism and related it to what
Weber considered the crucial variable, the political structures. For
this reason he constructed a politico-military typology of the ancient
polities with a limited and open developmental scheme.[18] His next
step, in *Economy and Society* (1909–13) was a typology broad
enough to encompass the last two and a half millennia. This time
he also included law and religion, the latter partly because of its

---

[16] Weber, *Economy and Society,* 953, 947, 948, 1309.

[17] Shils and Finch, *The Methodology, op. cit.,* 67. In the English text the
sentence: "The most important constitutive element of every civilization *(Kulturleben)* is the state, and the most important form of its [the civilization's]
normative regulation is law" was telescoped and reads erroneously: "The state
is the most important form of the normative regulation of cultural life."

[18] For a summary of the typology, see my introduction to Weber, *Economy
and Society, op. cit.,* xlviii–li.

inherent importance, partly because of the controversies about *The Protestant Ethic*. *Economy and Society*, the real title of which, significantly, is *The Economy and the Arena of Normative and De Facto Powers*, was intended to bring into one analytical orbit political and administrative organization, religious, ethical, and legal prescription, and the economic resources of the historical actors.

The theoretical point of departure for the political typologies of *Economy and Society* was comparative constitutional theory. Weber openly acknowledged his indebtedness to Georg Jellinek's "coinage of the concept of the 'social theory of the state,' clarifying the blurred tasks of sociology." [19] Since little attention has been given to this literary relationship, the next section will show the development from constitutional theory to sociological typology by a comparison of Jellinek and Weber.

FROM CONSTITUTIONAL THEORY TO SOCIOLOGICAL TYPOLOGY

Georg Jellinek (1851–1911) played a major role in redefining the theory of the state as an empirical discipline rather than a normative science. His *Allgemeine Staatslehre* was a systematic argument for institutional analysis, which he had advocated for many years as a necessary supplement to the history of ideas.[20] Jellinek belonged to those scholars who insisted on the logical difference between a normative and a causal approach and on the methodological difference between the social and the natural sciences. Jellinek's work, comprising, in modern terms, the fields of "comparative constitutional law" and "comparative government," was the dominant achievement in its field for a whole generation. It was conceived at a time when the theory of the state had fallen into neglect. Public opinion was preoccupied with social instead of constitutional issues, and new publications, Jellinek noted in his Preface with chagrin, were likely to arouse public interest only if dressed "in the fashionable garb of welfare politics or sociology." Sharing Weber's disdain for sociology in the conventional sense, Jellinek firmly opposed the integration of the theory of the state into all-inclusive sociological schemes:

[19] From Weber's memorial address on Jellinek, in René König and Johannes Winckelmann, eds., *Max Weber zum Gedächtnis* (Cologne: Westdeutscher Verlag, 1963), 15.

[20] Georg Jellinek, *Allgemeine Staatslehre* (1st ed. 1900; 2d rev. ed., Berlin: Häring, 1905).

In view of the immaturity of the new science [of sociology] and the lack of a recognized method, extremely broad leeway is given to individual arbitrariness; hence, no confirmed results providing new knowledge have been gained. Just as was true previously of the openly metaphysical philosophy of history, so nowadays the irreconcilable opposition of contrasting views emerges sharply in those empirically adorned speculations. Hence, it is not surprising that, serious researchers apart, an obtrusive scientific demi-monde endeavors to prosper in the guise of this discipline, which belongs to the fashion of the day.[21]

In order to keep straight the difference between philosophical speculation and empirical observation, Jellinek distinguished between ideal types and empirical types. Thus, ideal types were not "objects of knowledge but of faith, hence the striking similarity of doctrinaire attitudes in politics to religious fanaticism." By contrast, empirical types were "derived inductively," through careful comparison of the individual states, their organization and functions."[22] Weber, while fully agreeing with the distinction, preferred to call the latter "ideal types," since he wanted to emphasize the abstracting and selective quality of all concepts—and perhaps also to indulge his penchant for nominalist irony.

Jellinek saw no viable alternative to the typological approach in the theory of the state. He stated bluntly that the scholar can create only "types or isolated portraits—a third approach is methodologically impossible." The typological approach had greater practical value:

From the viewpoint of the practitioner, the type proves to be a heuristic instrument, since it is feasible, with a high degree of probability, to draw certain inferences from the type for the life of the individual state. The applicability of the same type points to an analogous course (*Gestaltung*) of similar polities in the future. When we speak of the lessons of history, we have in mind—whether we know it or not—the typical element in human affairs. Only because similar events repeat themselves under similar conditions can history become our schoolmistress. Only because the functioning (*Leben*) of the state has constants in its flux is scientific politics possible, that means, a theory of the intelligible (*vernünftige*) structure of the state.[23]

Great care, however, had to be observed in constructing types; overly inclusive types were too abstract and devoid of heuristic

[21] *Op. cit.*, 67.
[22] *Op. cit.*, 34f.
[23] *Op. cit.*, 40.

value. Jellinek suggested that types should be construed from phenomena with some historical relationship, some common historical ground, although he conceded that comparisons going even further might have some value. Weber agreed with Jellinek's caveat in general, but went beyond him in building types from historically unrelated phenomena. He stated his rationale in the essay on Eduard Meyer:

The cultural development of the Incas and Aztecs has left, relatively speaking, very few historically relevant traces; thus, a cultural history, in Eduard Meyer's sense, of the genesis of contemporary culture can perhaps be silent about it. If this be true—as we shall presume here—our knowledge of the Incas and Aztecs constitutes, in the first instance, neither a "historical object" nor a "historical cause," but rather a "heuristic means" for the formation of concepts in cultural theory (*kulturtheoretische Begriffe*); *positively,* we may use our knowledge of the Incas and Aztecs, as a rather peculiar specimen, to construct the concept of feudalism, for example; *negatively,* to set off certain concepts employed in the study of European cultural history from those quite different cultural traits, thus enabling us, with the help of this comparison, to undertake a more precise genetic study of the historical distinctiveness of European cultural development.[24]

Weber's decision to go beyond Jellinek in the construction of his typology and to draw together historically unrelated phenomena was an effort to help solve one major issue of his time, namely, the applicability of concepts to differing contexts and periods. Men like Eduard Meyer argued that terms of modern economics could be applied to antiquity; others asserted that concepts like feudalism should be limited to the European Middle Ages. Weber considered it grossly misleading to apply modern categories to older conditions, and outright impossible to form adequate individual ideal types without prior comparison with similar phenomena. Hence he supplemented them with a series of concepts linking similar phenomena in various areas and epochs.

The most important feature of Jellinek's *Allgemeine Staatslehre* was his so-called "two-sided theory of the state," still an issue in German constitutional theory. As against the older literature, Jellinek claimed that the theory of the state should have two components: the state could be viewed as a "legal institution" (as was customary), but also as a "social phenomenon," a "total social con-

[24] Weber, *Gesammelte Aufsätze zur Wissenschaftslehre, op. cit.,* 258; for a different translation, cf. Shils and Finch, *The Methodology, op. cit.,* 155f.

figuration"; hence, the *Staatslehre* should be divided into the "social theory of the state" *(soziale Staatslehre)* with its causally explanatory approach, and the "constitutional theory" *(Staatsrechtslehre)* with its normative-dogmatic character.[25] With this separation Jellinek took a major step beyond the Aristotelian tradition embodied in Roscher's *Politik* (1892), which dealt with the "nature" of the state and its "natural" forms. Weber moved further by devising a purely institutional typology of rulership in terms of basic modes of legitimation and differentiated modes of administration. He took some of the major building blocks of his typology from Jellinek's edifice, in which the theories of legitimation appeared partly in the "social theory of the state," as did the historical types of the state (ancient-oriental, Hellenic, Roman, medieval, modern). However, the features of public authority and sovereignty, the administrative and representative arrangements, and the "forms" of the state—the varieties of monarchic and republican government—appeared in the "constitutional theory of the state." This division had primarily pragmatic rather than logical grounds. Although Jellinek insisted on a social theory of the state, he was, after all, bound to some extent by the conventional dimensions of constitutional theory, and this led him at times to a somewhat arbitrary separation of topics. Weber, however, was free to ignore the difficulties arising from Jellinek's dual approach and to combine the separately treated components into unified sociological types.

Jellinek distinguished five basic theories of legitimation on these grounds: (1) Religious and theological, for example, the state as Divine creation; (2) Power, the pendant of (1), since in both cases plain subordination is demanded; (3) Legal, the state as a product of law; (4) Ethical, the state as an ethical necessity; (5) Psychological,

[25] Jellinek presupposed a separation of politics as a practical art *(Kunstlehre)* from the theoretical discipline of the *Staatslehre*. Their confusion in the older literature had contributed to the indiscriminate mixture of practical, normative, and causally-explicatory elements. In the subsequent controversies, especially during the Weimar Republic, two solutions to Jellinek's methodological syncretism were sought: The first was best represented by Hans Kelsen's resolute separation of sociology and jurisprudence in favor of a "pure theory of the state"—a peculiar form of legal positivism; the second was championed in Rudolph Smend's "integrated theory of the state" and Hermann Heller's *Staatslehre*, which endeavored to provide a normative as well as empirical foundation for the democratic and socialist welfare state. On these constitutional and normative debates, see Wolfgang Schluchter's excellent exposition in his *Entscheidung für den sozialen Rechtsstaat: Hermann Heller und die staatstheoretische Diskussion in der Weimarer Republik* (Cologne: Kiepenheuer und Witsch, 1968), ch. I.

the state being a natural propensity of man as a "political animal."

Weber abandoned Jellinek's five kinds of legitimation in favor of a threefold scheme of "ultimate" grounds of justification: traditionalist, charismatic, and legal-rational. For Jellinek, patrimonialism, feudalism, and patriarchalism were legal justifications: patrimonialism postulated the state as the private property of the ruler; feudalism viewed it as a contractual relationship, and patriarchalism as a matter of family, rather than property, law. Weber subsumed these three legal theories under traditionalist authority.

Whereas the category of "legal-rational" legitimation was a central component of liberal constitutional theory, "charismatic" legitimation was Weber's own innovation. It is well known that he adapted the term from the work of the legal historian Rudolf Sohm. According to Sohm, the Christian church was not based on manmade law; it was sustained by the faith of its believers in its supernatural legitimation. Weber broadened the notion of "grace" (charisma) so that it would encompass the phenomenon of warrior communism. His decision to contrast traditionalist and charismatic legitimation appears to be closely linked to his critique of the manorial thesis, according to which political rulership had originated in land ownership. Throughout history, Weber observed, power had been seized by leaders with a voluntary following; from the military chieftains of early history to the Bonapartist demagogues and parliamentary leaders of his own time, legitimacy had been claimed on purely personal (charismatic) grounds.

In line with his sociological emphasis on the empirical validity of norms—an emphasis linked to his critique of Rudolf Stammler —Weber proceeded from the three basic modes of legitimation to a historically inclusive typology of political organizations—the first part of the Sociology of Domination in *Economy and Society*. Historically, the power of legitimation rested mainly in the hands of religious agents; throughout history this created the tension between the secular and the priestly authorities—the second part of the Sociology of Domination. Finally, the typology had to give equal attention to the problem of revolution, the usurpation of legitimate powers. This became the third (unfinished) part, with its focus on the Occidental city as a historically crucial form of nonlegitimate rulership.[26]

Thus did Weber elaborate Jellinek's social theory of the state

[26] For details on the Stammler critique, see my introduction to Weber, *Economy and Society, op. cit.*, lxi; on the structure of the Sociology of Domination, see *ibid.*, lxxxii–xciv.

into a sociology of domination. For the construction of his types he used the latest historical literature, but he passed over some older works. Among his predecessors in the study of legitimacy and usurpation as well as the conflict between secular and sacred authority was Jacob Burckhardt, who investigated the rise of the state as "a work of art" in his famed *Civilization of the Renaissance in Italy* (1860). Yet there is no reference to it in *Economy and Society*, perhaps because Burckhardt was not concerned with "clear concepts" and systematic typology. The omission does not mean that Weber had a low opinion of Burckhardt. To the contrary, he repeated a remark by Georg Jellinek, who had known Burckhardt personally: "You felt that you stood before one of the great men on this earth." [27] There are some notable affinities as well as differences between Burckhardt and Weber—the subject of the next chapter.

[27] *Max Weber zum Gedächtnis, op. cit.,* 214.

XIV

JACOB BURCKHARDT

Max Weber's scholarly work encompasses the most divergent themes of nineteenth-century intellectual history. The extraordinary tensions in his life may stem from this as well as from his precarious psychological condition. For Weber's work reflects a debate with Marx, with utilitarianism, the German historical school, the philosophies of Dilthey and the Neo-Kantian school at Marburg, the evolutionists, the antirationalist doctrines of Schopenhauer and Nietzsche, and the dominant Social Darwinism of his own day. These many-sided confrontations are one reason for Weber's pervasive influence on modern thought.

Aspects of this synthesis have been discussed by Alexander von Schelting, Talcott Parsons, Dieter Henrich, H. Stuart Hughes, Wolfgang Mommsen, myself, and others, although a comprehensive account remains to be written. I wish to contribute to this discussion by drawing attention to the themes of Weber's work that provide comparisons and contrasts with the work of Jacob Burckhardt, a scholar of comparable breadth and acumen. The two men were alike in important respects, despite equally notable differences to which I shall refer in the concluding section. Critics of the German historical school, they continued its tradition in their own ways. Opponents of the Hegelian philosophy of history, they developed views of social change indebted to it. Deeply influenced by the antirationalist tradition of their day, they sought to combine its insights with an affirmation of the values of Western civilization. Weber and Burckhardt both believed that in human affairs reason plays only a

Reinhard Bendix, "Jacob Burckhardt and Max Weber," *American Sociological Review*, 30:2, April 1965, 176–184. First read at the annual meeting of the American Sociological Association, Montreal, 1964.

small part, while man's struggle for power greatly affects the course of events. Their writings may be compared with regard to these themes.

REASON AND THE WILL

The idea that the will and the affections are ascendant over man's capacity to reason pervades much of nineteenth-century social thought. With its emphasis on power, Social Darwinism at the end of the century is part of a reaction to the Enlightenment, of which Arthur Schopenhauer is an early and prominent representative. Schopenhauer consciously reverses the broad tradition of Western rationalism by making man's intellect a function of his will and divesting his reason of all competence in the fields of religious belief and moral judgment. Reason is a necessary instrument, to be used for good or evil, but it has no inherent moral qualities. Will, however, is of the essence of man, who "wants everything for himself, wants to possess all, dominate at the very least, and wants to destroy whatever resists his will." [1] Accordingly, the intellect is above all a weapon in the struggle for existence. As such, intellect aims at the pursuit of truth, but the will constantly interferes with this natural tendency, so that the prejudices of estates, classes, nations, and religions determine and faltify our judgment.[2] For Schopenhauer all that is genuine in man arises from the unconscious, like other forces of nature. He concedes that eventually the intellect can free itself from its subservience to the will and develop a capacity for objective knowledge. But for him such knowledge largely consists in unmasking the lies and prejudices with which men disguise the lust and brutality of their nature.

Nietzsche develops this idea of the supremacy of the will over the intellect, though he differs in other respects from Schopenhauer's pessimistic, antievolutionist philosophy. By unmasking lies and prejudices Nietzsche offers not only an iconoclastic critique of European culture but a biological reductionism and a dual ethic for masters and slaves which fit in only too well with the climate of opinion in the years following the Franco-Prussian War of 1870–71.

In his essays on the sociology of religion Weber utilizes the in-

[1] Quoted in Hans Barth, *Ideologie und Wahrheit* (Erlenbach-Zürich: Eugen Rentsch, 1961), 194. I have relied partly on Barth for this brief synopsis of Schopenhauer's position.
[2] *Ibid.*, 197.

sights of this antirationalist tradition. "Not *ideas,* but material and ideal *interests* directly govern men's conduct." [3] Each type of interest has its own dynamic, yet each depends on the other to maintain its direction or momentum. In analogy to Kant's famous dictum concerning facts and concepts, one can say that, according to Weber, material without ideal interests are empty, but ideal without material interests are impotent. Thus the Protestant Ethic concludes with the familiar statement that the materialistic and the spiritualistic interpretation of culture and history are equally legitimate, heuristic principles. Weber uses this dual orientation as the starting point of his analyses; he regards any tendency to generalize one *or* the other perspective as something "best left to the dilettantes, who believe in the 'unity' of the 'group-psyche' and its reducibility to one formula." [4]

This emphasis on interest exemplifies Weber's indebtedness to the antirationalist tradition that Hans Barth has traced from Bacon's theory of idols through Helvetius' analysis of prejudices to Marx's theory of ideology, on the one hand, and on the other to Schopenhauer's and Nietzsche's efforts to uncover man's will and affect behind every manifestation of thought and reason. Weber clearly accepts this searching critique of the Enlightenment. But for him the ideal interests of estates, classes, nations, and religions are not so much prejudices to be unmasked as they are beliefs to be understood in their own right, however true it might be that men use such beliefs to disguise their grasping and deceitful nature. Since human selfishness and passion tend to use ideas for their own ends, his studies in the sociology of religion fully explore the passionate interests involved even in the most esoteric beliefs. But Weber is not concerned with the need to uncover man's lust and brutality. Rather, he is concerned with the significance of man's conventionality for an understanding of his behavior. The routine of conduct borders on a mechanical conformity that involves little or no subjective awareness. He therefore devotes the very first part of *Wirtschaft und Gesellschaft* to a discussion of the "meaning of meaning" at the level of usage and tradition. And in his sociology of religion he examines the question repeatedly: how and to what extent do beliefs that are consciously shared only by a tiny, intellectually ar-

[3] H. Gerth and C. W. Mills, eds. and trans., *From Max Weber* (New York: Oxford, 1946), 280.
[4] Weber, *Gesammelte Aufsätze zur Religionssoziologie* (Tübingen: Mohr, 1926), I, 205f.; cf. *The Protestant Ethic and the Spirit of Capitalism,* trans. by Talcott Parsons (New York: Scribner, 1958), 284.

ticulate minority affect the behavior and beliefs of the people at large? Thus for Weber passion, material striving, *and* ideation are basic features of the human condition.

Comparable themes appear in the works of Schopenhauer and Burckhardt. For Schopenhauer, philosophy deals with the enduring nature of things, while history deals with singular occurrences that are never twice the same. Hence the true philosophy of history consists in the identification of this same, unchanging nature beneath the diversity of appearances and events. What endures in the midst of universal change, according to Schopenhauer, are "the basic qualities of man's heart and head—many bad, a few good." [5] Burckhardt appears to echo these statements. He opposes Hegel's philosophy of history, as Schopenhauer did, stating that "our point of departure is the only central point that endures and is accessible for us—man suffering, striving, and doing, as he always was and is and shall be." [6] Yet Burckhardt's meaning is not the same as Schopenhauer's. He is interested in man's culture-creating capacities rather than in uncovering the lust and brutality beneath the apparent change of events. I have no evidence that Weber was influenced by Burckhardt in this respect, but Burckhardt's *Griechische Kulturgeschichte* (first published in 1898) contains a formulation that resembles Weber's basic approach. According to Burckhardt, cultural history

goes to the heart of past mankind; it declares what mankind *was, wanted, thought, perceived and was able to do.* In this way cultural history deals with what is constant, and in the end this "constant" appears greater and more important than the momentary; a quality appears to be greater and more instructive than an action. For actions are only the individual expressions of a certain inner capacity, which is always able to re-create these same actions. Goals and presuppositions are, therefore, as important as events.[7]

---

[5] Arthur Schopenhauer, *Die Welt als Wille und Vorstellung* (Munich: Piper, 1911), II, 501f., 506. In rejecting Hegel's concept of world history as the manifestation of a rational design Schopenhauer asserts that only the individual's life career has coherence. Events have meaning only as they are related to the will of the individual. See *ibid.*, 504.

[6] Burckhardt, *Weltgeschichtliche Betrachtungen* (Stuttgart: Kröner, 1963), 5f. Subsequent references are to this edition.

[7] Burckhardt, *Griechische Kulturgeschichte* (Stuttgart: Kröner, 1952), I, 6. The similarity of this position to that of Weber is not affected by the latter's critical appraisal of the work, which was reconstructed posthumously from lecture notes (1898) and appeared several years after Weber's *Roman Agrarian History* (1891). In his "Agrarian Conditions of Antiquity" (1908) Weber

This emphasis on man's "inner capacity," his goals and presuppositions, is quite similar to Weber's explication of the logical and behavioral corollaries of religious doctrines; it is also similar to Weber's emphasis on subjective meaning in his definition of sociology. Both scholars affirm the enduring importance of man's consciousness.

But the similarity goes well beyond this starting point. Burckhardt posits state, religion, and culture as the three great spheres of thought and action *(Potenzen)*, the first two stable and hierarchical and the third representing the element of change. The emphasis on state and religion was the major theme of Ranke's world history, with its tendency to spiritualize force and power. Burckhardt's preoccupation with culture as the element of freedom and spontaneity is, therefore, an expression of his humanistic values. But his purpose is neither naïve nor idealistic; his effort is to interpret the conflicts of culture with the power concentrations of state and religion, and his reflections culminate in a discussion of historical crises, not in romantic theories of organic growth and spiritual principles. It may be said of Burckhardt as well as Weber that his view of the historical world accentuates the tragic conflicts of man's political, religious, and cultural impulses, combining the pessimistic realism of the antirationalist tradition with an affirmation of man's cultural potential.

In their opposition to the evolutionist optimism of their contemporaries, both scholars use the same argument. Burckhardt begins his lectures on the study of history with ironic comments on the idea of progress. In his final chapter he unmasks the conventional judgments about "happiness and unhappiness in world history" as so many optical illusions—the results of impatience, cheap self-satisfaction, or a matter of taste, political sympathy, or the desire for security. He reminds his readers that they would have felt desperately unhappy in the great age of Pericles, just as in his book on the Italian Renaissance he punctuates his description of cultural efflorescence with reminders of political instability and dissolution. We know from Burckhardt's letters of his profound pessimism concerning modern culture. The last chapter in the *Welgeschichtliche Betrachtungen* (1868) ends with the observation that a series of new

---

judged that Burckhardt's work "ignored all of modern research and the monumental sources. Hence his perspectives can be utilized only with reservations, albeit they are often highly illuminating. The economic factor, incidentally, is scarcely taken into account": Weber, *Gesammelte Aufsätze zur Sozial- und Wirtschaftsgeschichte* (Tübingen: Mohr, 1924), 283.

wars are in the making, that the political structures of the great nations (Burckhardt says *"Kulturvölker"*) are marked by instability and transition, that the spread of education and communication is accompanied by a rising consciousness of suffering and impatience. Yet Burckhardt concludes by evoking the human spirit that is also at work in all these phenomena. Contemporaries may be unable to perceive that this spirit is building a new mansion, but the quest for such knowledge is for Burckhardt the supreme goal. This is the classical belief in the mutability of fortune, noting the seeds of destruction at the pinnacle of power and prosperity, but also the emergence of new life in the midst of anarchy and despair.

Weber comes quite close to this attitude, though he did not achieve the personal serenity that Burckhardt did.[8] The principal theme of his scholarly work is the "disenchantment of the world" in which he sees the distinguishing feature of Western civilization. Weber explores many aspects of this process: the decline of charismatic inspiration and the growth of formalism in law, the displacement of adventure-capitalism by types of enterprise based on rational bookkeeping methods, and others. His emphasis on the growth of rationalism might appear consistent with nineteenth-century evolutionary theories, but this is misleading. For Weber all types of rationalism are ambivalent. The great theme of his *Ancient Judaism,* for example, is the ascendancy of Old Testament prophecy with its monotheistic creed over the magical beliefs and practices of the Baal cult. Yet the study ends with an analysis of the legalism of Rabbinical Judaism following the Babylonian Captivity and thus emphasizes the irrational ritualism emerging from the decline of magic. Again, in his *Protestant Ethic* Weber shows that methodical conduct was a response to the religious anxiety induced by the doctrine of predestination. But Puritanism anathematizes *all* activities that turn men away from God. Art is suspect because it appeals to man's sensuality; sleep is condemned if it exceeds the necessary minimum. Since Puritanism militates against the sentiments of love and friendship that encroach upon the service the believer owes to God above all purely mundane obligations, inner-worldly asceticism may have a rationalizing effect on economic activities. But it also exacts a high price in demanding an atrophy of natural feeling in man's cultural and personal life. Hence Weber emphasizes not only the peculiar rationalism of Occidental civiliza-

---

[8] For documentation on the latter point, especially with regard to Weber's attitude toward death, cf. Eduard Baumgarten, ed., *Max Weber: Werk und Person* (Tübingen: Mohr, 1964), 658–678.

tion, but the anguishing deprivations it entails—a perspective that informs all of his substantive work and is kindred in spirit to that of Burckhardt.

POWER AND CULTURE

For Weber, man's striving to impose his will, even against the resistance of others, is a universal attribute of all human actions, though not an ultimate determinant of any.

The idea is not original with him. Versions of it were as widely accepted in his generation as Freud's theory of libidinal impulses was later, and it was vulgarized just as readily. Two forms of that vulgarization should be noted. The American variant of Social Darwinism, for example in the work of William Graham Sumner, joined the doctrine of economic laissez-faire with the theory of social evolution. The result was a defense of the Gilded Age, sanctioning the success of the few and the deprivations of the many as inevitable outgrowths of the struggle for survival.[9] In the Imperial Germany of Weber's generation the same kind of thinking prevailed, but there Social Darwinism merged with national power politics. The difference is easy to understand. The strength and relative isolation of American society made it possible for the concern with power to remain an internal affair,[10] but Germans of the same generation had just experienced the emergence of their country as an industrial society and a world power. In celebrating the "survival of the fittest" the vulgarizations of the day linked the economic with the political struggle, the internal with the external affairs of the country. By adding the special accents of racism and the pseudo-political dreams of empire, marginal figures like Langbehn or Moeller van den Bruck helped to stir up that unholy mixture of cynical *Realpolitik* and pretentious romanticism that has been a German liability since the early nineteenth century.[11] Weber be-

[9] For documentation, see Richard Hofstadter, *Social Darwinism in American Thought* (Boston: Beacon, 1955), esp. chs. 3 and 5.

[10] Note how readily American social theory even today emphasizes the structural aspects of a society to the exclusion of concern with its international setting. This particular abstraction has strong affinities with the Marxist tradition before Lenin, as well as with the basic assumptions of social anthropology, but its utility is doubtful except under properly specified, limiting conditions.

[11] This "mixture" antedates the Franco-Prussian War of 1870–71, as Ernst Troeltsch notes in his emphasis on the hiatus in political thought between Germany and England. See Ernst Troeltsch, "The Idea of Natural Law and Humanity in World Politics," in Otto Gierke, *Natural Law and the Theory of*

longs in this context, as is evident from his inaugural lecture at Frei-burg. But current German efforts to construe his scholarly work from this vantage point alone seem just as mistaken as the tendency of some interpreters to underrate his preoccupation with the power phenomenon. Weber shares this preoccupation not only with the Social Darwinists of his time, but with Schopenhauer, Nietzsche, and Burckhardt. For this reason it is worth-while to observe the way he reconciles an emphasis on power and a related distrust of reason with humanistic values and transforms them into instru-ments of analysis. Two examples from his work will illustrate this point.

During the First World War, in 1916, Weber referred twice to Burckhardt and the burden of power:

We are a great power, and that is the ultimate reason for the war. . . . Are the "little" nations—the Swiss, the Dutch, the Danes, Norwegians, and Swedes—any less valuable? No German would assert that. In history both the power states and the outwardly small nations have an enduring mission. . . . Only in small states . . . is genuine democracy possible as well as an aristocracy based on achievement. In the mass state both are transformed beyond recognition. Inevitably the popularly elected administration or one staffed by notables is replaced by bureaucracy, and the popular militia by the disciplined army. That is the inescapable fate of a people organized in a mass state. For that reason Jacob Burck-hardt adjudged power an element of evil in history. All of us appreciate that fate has permitted one part of our people, the Swiss Germans, to cultivate the virtues of the small state. . . . But why did we voluntarily accept the fateful burden of power? Not out of vanity, but because of our responsibility before history.[12]

This grave sense of responsibility is a persistent theme in Weber's political writings. But if some moral values are more easily fulfilled in the small state, others can at least be approximated in the power state, even for the masses. Unlike Nietzsche, Weber wishes to see

---

Society (Boston: Beacon, 1957), 214 and passim. For documentation and analysis of the ideologies of the Gründerjahre see Harry Pross, Vor und nach Hitler (Olten: Walter, 1962), 81–103 and passim; Fritz Stern, The Politics of Cultural Despair (Berkeley: University of California Press, 1961), and Fritz Bolle, "Dar-winismus and Zeitgeist," Zeitschrift für Religions- und Geistesgeschichte, 14, 1962, 143–178.

[12] Weber, "Deutschland unter den europäischen Weltmachten," Gesammelte politische Schriften, J. Winckelmann, ed. (Tübingen: Mohr, 1958), 170f. In the same year (1916) Weber restated this point with reference to Burckhardt in "Between Two Ethics" ("Zwischen zwei Gesetzen"), 139.

these values embodied in the people's way of life as well. Writing
about the farm laborers of the provinces east of the Elbe River, he
says:

We want to cultivate and support what appears to us as valuable in
man: his personal responsibility, his basic drive toward higher things,
toward the spiritual and moral values of mankind, even where this
drive confronts us in its most primitive forms. Insofar as it is in our
power we want to create the external conditions which will help to preserve—in the face of the inevitable struggle for existence with its suffering—the best that is in man, those physical and emotional qualities
which we would like to maintain for the nation.[13]

Here Weber sees the nation's struggle for power as a means to promote personal and cultural values for the masses, but this is the
statement of a political goal. Elsewhere he makes clear that the
prestige of nations, but not necessarily the development of their
culture, depends on their power position. Germany after 1870
showed no unequivocal cultural gains that were commensurate with
her increasing power. "Pure art and literature that is typically
German did *not* develop in the political center of Germany." [14]
Thus, much as he is concerned with the "meaning" of the struggle
for power Weber remains acutely aware of the ambiguous relations
between power and culture. He is convinced that man's striving to
impose his will on others pervades all human relationships. But
the analysis of multiple interrelations makes it impossible for him
to turn the power phenomenon into a general theory of society. In
his view power is an aspect of all human relationships and hence
can explain none of them. He distinguishes himself from his contemporaries in that for him power is the starting-point of analysis,
not a main explanatory factor as for the antirationalist tradition.[15]

   In his analysis of the manifold relations between man's ideal and
material interests Weber seeks to vindicate the relative autonomy
of ideas in man's assertions of his will, even in the midst of the "inevitable struggle for existence." One could dismiss this approach

[13] Quoted from Weber's speech in 1894 before the *Evangelisch-Soziale Kon-
gress,* in Marianne Weber, *Max Weber* (Heidelberg: Schneider, 1950), 159.
   [14] Weber, *Economy and Society,* ed. and trans. by C. Roth and C. Wittich
(New York: Bedminster, 1968), 926.
   [15] See *ibid.,* 942, for Weber's statement on the pervasiveness of power. For a
description and analysis of the mentality of Weber's German contemporaries,
cf. Herman Lübbe, *Politische Philosophie in Deutschland* (Basel: Schwabe,
1963), 173–238.

as ponderous philosophizing about mundane affairs, reflecting that mixture of *Realpolitik* and romanticism mentioned earlier. But this does scant justice to the enduring contribution of Weber's sociology of religion. In commentary on this work too much attention has been given to Weber's debate with Marx, not enough to his debate with Nietzsche. Although he is stimulated by both authors, Weber takes issue with their "reductionist" arguments.

Marx treats ideas as epiphenomena of the organization of production, and in his "positive critique" of "historical materialism" Weber accepts this perspective. Thus each of the great world religions is to him the expression of a religious elite: Confucianism, for example, is the ethic of government officials in the Chinese dynasties; Hinduism, the product of cultured literati who functioned as house priests and experts on ritual propriety. But

the specific nature of a religion is [not] a simple "function" of the social situation of the stratum which appears as its characteristic bearer . . . [nor] is it a "reflection" of a stratum's material or ideal interest situation . . . However incisive the social influences . . . a religious ethic receives its stamp primarily from religious sources.[16]

Nietzsche treats ideas as epiphenomena of organic life. Where Marx argues that the beliefs of the masses are a result of exploitation and will be completely altered when the ruling class is overthrown, Nietzsche contends that such beliefs reflect the true nature of the people. The masses are born to be slaves, and their slave morality finds consummate expression in the Christian idealization of suffering. Hence, for Nietzsche,

the moral glorification of mercy and brotherliness is a "slave revolt in morals" among those who are disadvantaged. . . . The ethic of "duty" is thus considered a product of repressed sentiments for vengeance on the part of banausic men, who "displace" their sentiments because they are powerless. . . . They resent the way of life of the lordly stratum who live free of duties.[17]

Weber accepts this perspective also as a fruitful starting point and he underscores especially an element of rationalization that Marx *and* Nietzsche emphasize.

[16] *From Max Weber, op. cit.*, 269f.
[17] *Ibid.*, 270.

In treating suffering as a symptom of odiousness in the eyes of the gods and a sign of secret guilt, religion has psychologically met a very general need. The fortunate is seldom satisfied with the fact of being fortunate. Beyond this he needs to know that he has a *right* to his good fortune.[18]

Thus Weber certainly recognizes the element of rationalization in religious ideas. Yet for him such ideas possess a momentum and direction of their own. With specific reference to Nietzsche's theory of resentment, Weber emphasizes that it cannot explain the several ways in which the "negative evaluation of suffering has led to its religious glorification." Hence the reductionism common to both Nietzsche and Marx provides Weber with hypotheses to be tested rather than general explanations.

Weber's concern with power may be compared and contrasted with Burckhardt's. Burckhardt states that power is always the prior element, because it is the natural consequence of human inequality. Like Weber he is sensitive to the human cost: states originate in terrible crises and exact a tremendous price in human suffering.[19] Accordingly, he scoffs at the fashion of his day to evaluate history in terms of "great states" and treats the suffering of the people with equanimity—the same point Weber makes in his critique of Nietzsche.

These questions involve the objectivity of scholarly judgments and Burckhardt is as concerned with this problem as Weber, although unlike Weber he rejects the idea of a scientific approach. Awareness of human suffering leads Burckhardt to assert that one should retain the expression "unhappiness" in historical studies. But, at the same time, all judgments about "happiness" are relative and should be excluded altogether.[20] These considerations are linked to his discussion of "historical greatness," a category he regards as indispensable in historical studies, however provisional and relative our use of it remains.[21] In his view the great man is not a model to be followed, but rather an exception who expresses something transcending the individual: "It appears that there is a mysterious coincidence between egoism of the individual and what one calls the general benefit or greatness, the glory of the whole." [22]

[18] *Ibid.*, 271.
[19] Burckhardt, *Weltgeschichtliche Betrachtungen, op. cit.*, 32.
[20] *Ibid.*, 260.
[21] *Ibid.*, 209ff.
[22] *Ibid.*, 242. See also *ibid.*, 232ff., for passages briefly summarized here.

In these reflections Burckhardt is at one with writers from Goethe to Nietzsche, from Carlyle to Sumner, in their fascination with the great men of power. But Burckhardt makes clear, as many others did not, that greatness must be distinguished from power, and that neither has much to do with happiness. He tries to depict "great men" as they really are, peculiarly exempt from ordinary moral rules, judged leniently even for monstrous crimes if their actions are successful, passionate in their ambition for glory, and endowed with a sense of brute power which looks on men in terms of their subordination and utility. Not every period finds its great men, nor does every great ability find its appropriate occasion. But Burckhardt satirizes the tendency of his time to assume that it could conduct its affairs without great men and that virtue would prevail in their absence, as if small men would not also become evil when they encounter resistance.[23] Thus a dispassionate judgment demands that we recognize great men for the extraordinary evil that is in them as well as for their critical importance. "Great men are necessary for our life, so that the world historical movement frees itself periodically and abruptly from forms of life that are dead and from ruminating idle talk."[24]

This synopsis of Burckhardt's view suggests striking similarities to Weber's concept of charisma as a source of historical change. Weber, like Burckhardt, emphasizes the inherent cultural significance of this phenomenon, its absolute transcendence of routine, and its independence from ordinary moral standards, as well as the basic distinction between greatness and mere power.[25]

SCHOLARSHIP AND ACTION

Parallels of the kind discussed may be due to one writer's direct influence on another, or to the indebtedness of both to the same intellectual tradition. In the present case this distinction cannot be made for lack of evidence, though much direct influence of Burckhardt on Weber is unlikely in view of the differences between the two.[26] In conclusion I wish to emphasize these differences.

[23] *Ibid.*, 247.
[24] *Ibid.*, 248.
[25] Note here that Weber distinguishes between Nietzsche's "ethic of nobility" and the biological (Darwinian) embellishments with which Nietzsche almost buries the basically moral core of his doctrine, which Weber considers enduring. See Baumgarten, *op. cit.*, 648.
[26] Weber acknowledged Burckhardt's "greatness," but with ambiguous praise.

Burckhardt was forty-six years older than Weber. In personal terms the two men could hardly have been more different. Serene and contemplative, Burckhardt was a humanist who pursued his cultural studies as a work of art, remote from the modern world and in conscious opposition to its cultural and political tendencies. Weber was scholarly and passionate, a man of science and action as well as a humanist, consciously standing in the midst of affairs both large and small. Cultural studies were for him second best to political action and decision-making, though events and personal disability barred him from active participation. Weber affirmed the world in which he found himself despite his foreboding perception of its threatening tendencies.

Like Schopenhauer, Burckhardt thinks of history as the most unscientific of all the disciplines, although history provides us with much that is worth knowing. He speaks of the "systematic harmlessness" of his exposition, which is in keeping with the "continual transitions and mixtures" that characterize history, and which allows him to move rapidly among different periods and cultures. In this way he can bring out parallels and affinities—a chronological philosophy of history would emphasize contrasts instead. Clear concepts, he feels, belong to logic and philosophy, not to history.[27] Accordingly, Burckhardt's aim is to acquire wisdom for all time rather than knowledge that may be useful at the next occasion. In this connection he emphasizes the theme of impotence or alienation that appears so often in modern commentary:

Over against the great historical powers the contemporary individual feels completely impotent; as a rule he comes to serve either the attacking or the defending party. Few contemporaries have discovered for themselves a vantage point outside events, few are able to come to terms with things intellectually, and [even for them] there is not much satisfaction in it and they cannot fend off an elegiac feeling, because they must abandon all others to their bondage.[28]

In one of the few references to him, Weber pointed out that "if a historian has a distinctive personality, that means, if he advances sharply accentuated evaluations, casual analysis may be greatly facilitated, but by their very impact these evaluations can also impair the empirical validity of the individual results. For both aspects Jacob Burckhardt is an eminent example." Weber, "Knies und das Irrationalitätsproblem" (1906), Gesammelte Aufsätze zur Wissenschaftslehre (Tübingen: Mohr, 1951), 125.

[27] Burckhardt, Weltgeschichtliche Betrachtungen, op. cit., 83.

[28] Ibid., 8f.

For Burckhardt this vantage point of freedom in the midst of general bondage is provided by his personal identification with Basel and Switzerland, though even he occasionally expresses frustration and discontent despite his affirmation of the small state and of civic virtue.[29]

Like Burckhardt, Weber emphasizes the "seamless web" of history; in his writings he moves even more freely among different periods and cultures than Burckhardt does. But Weber wants to advance science where Burckhardt offers reflections; Weber formulates concepts that Burckhardt leaves to the logicians; Weber accentuates differences where Burckhardt searches for the similar and repetitive; Weber is committed to the search for truth, which Burckhardt considers a lesser good than the search for beauty. Ultimately, Weber puts scholarship in the service of a *vita activa* and thus binds himself to that "stream of necessities" from which Burckhardt sought to free himself through contemplation. In his scholarly work Weber persists in seeking to make intellectual allowance for the role of ideas and innovation in human affairs, to find an answer to the question "how anything new can ever arise in the world, oriented as it is towards the regular and the empirically valid." [30] But Weber lived in Wilhelmian Germany, amidst events he was powerless to alter, and in a society whose dominant values did not leave him unaffected. His career was marked by violent outbursts of temperament as well as by stoic resignation; both reactions may be seen as efforts to fend off the bondage that Burckhardt witnessed from afar. Toward the end of his life Weber said to his wife: "It could be even that I *am* a mystic. Just as I have 'dreamed' more in my life than one should really permit oneself to do, so I am nowhere really, *entirely* at home. It is as if I could (and would) withdraw myself as well and entirely from everything." [31] In view of the emotional and intellectual tensions in his life, it is not remarkable that at times Weber felt sympathetic to the mood that dominated Burckhardt's life. But for Weber, withdrawal from involvement and contemplative freedom were probably temptations or weaknesses to which he never permitted himself to yield.

Perhaps the most moving contrast between Burckhardt and Weber concerns the pursuit of knowledge itself. For Burckhardt

[29] For a searching analysis of Burckhardt's position in this respect, cf. Karl Schmid, *Unbehagen im Kleinstaat* (Zürich: Artemis, 1963), 201–229.

[30] Weber, *Economy and Society, op. cit.*, 321.

[31] According to a conversation reported by Baumgarten, *op. cit.*, 677.

knowledge of the future is neither desirable nor probable, and the general craving for such knowledge appears to him an "astrological impatience" that is "truly foolish." [32] Volition and striving occur for their own sake, an expression of man's inner capacities which would become confused or disoriented were we to know in advance the day of our death (or, collectively, the decline of our civilization). "A future known in advance is a contradiction *(Widersinn)*." [33] But such knowledge is also improbable. Wishes, hopes, and fears stand in the way; we do not know the latent forces and unpredictable psychological contagions that can suddenly transform the world; and four centuries of argument (now made ubiquitous by the press) have created a din that thoroughly obscures impending changes. Yet for Burckhardt knowledge of the past has great value, especially when it is entirely free of concern for our welfare and indeed of all mundane interests. Properly pursued, such knowledge bears witness both to the conditions of an epoch seen from its own perspective and to the enduring quality and the continuity of the human spirit. [34]

For Weber such contemplative knowledge with its emphasis on the art of appreciation is one of the ends men seek. It is an end that led Burckhardt to reject modern civilization and its belief in progress. Similarly, for Tolstoy modern man always looks forward and is never at peace, not even in death, which is a pointless instant in the progress of a world devoid of God. Weber respected this position but did not share it. From him intellectual clarity was as valid an end of knowledge as contemplation. In his view honesty demanded that men recognize the void of a world without God as well as the ambivalence of all gains made in the name of progress. He acknowledges that today scientists are dedicated to the advancement of knowledge but do not ask what ends this knowledge will serve, because increased technical mastery is to them a self-evident good. In the modern world, increasingly a world of such technical specialists, contemplation and intellectual clarity for their own sake are at a discount. Describing these conditions in his essay, "Science as a Vocation," Weber seeks to preserve the integrity of contemplation, intellectual clarity, and the pragmatic approach to the pursuit of knowledge; and yet he acknowledges that each of these ends is in jeopardy. Like Burckhardt Weber probes into the irrational

[32] Burckhardt, *op. cit.*, 14.
[33] *Ibid.*
[34] *Ibid.*, 18f.

foundations and consequences of knowledge, but unlike Burckhardt and with a skeptical fortitude reminiscent of the classics he endeavors to advance social science.[35]

[35] A fuller exposition of Weber's views on knowledge in relation to those of Marx, Tocqueville, and Durkheim is in Reinhard Bendix, *Embattled Reason. Essays on Social Knowledge* (New York: Oxford, 1970), *passim*. See also Karl Löwith, "Die Entzauberung der Welt durch Wissenschaft," *Merkur*, 18, June 1964, 501–19.

XV

TWO SOCIOLOGICAL
TRADITIONS

DURKHEIM AND WEBER

Academic disciplines are wedded to the idea of progress through knowledge. As a result nearly all have a disturbed relationship with the past. For some the history of the discipline is an antiquarian pursuit, typically the preoccupation of those who are not in the forefront of research. Yet the new knowledge which supersedes past accomplishments quickly becomes obsolescent. The ideal scientist is thus chained to the wheel of progress and believes in the supreme importance of his task, however small. At the same time he must be reconciled to the rapid obsolescence of his own contribution, however large.

For others the history of their discipline is not cast off so easily. Past accomplishments loom large where the pursuit of knowledge consists in the specification and elaboration of previous work. In the social sciences and humanities scholars are also chained to the wheel of progress. But where the obsolescence of knowledge is ambiguous, it is uncertain how the idea of progress applies. Faced with that uncertainty adherents of the disciplines often split in their attitude toward the past. Some treat it as the history of past errors, which has little to teach us; others, as the history of past insights and failings, from which we have much to learn. Both groups may be surprised by the renascence of old ideas, and present pursuits are often dogged by unresolved issues of the past.

These reflections apply to a field like sociology in which, during the past generation, we have moved from a complete rejection of evolutionist ideas to their rediscovery. Indeed, the field abounds

---

By Reinhard Bendix. Written for this volume.

with uncertainty toward its past, including the classic contributions of nineteenth-century social thought. Some thirty years ago Talcott Parsons synthesized the writings of Weber and Durkheim in order to provide a theoretical foundation for the discipline.[1] Yet Weber and Durkheim were at opposite poles as social theorists and their divergence is still characteristic of the field. In 1966 Edward Tiryakian showed that nowhere in the writings of the two men is there a citation or other manifest evidence that they were aware of each other's work, although the productive careers of both were contemporaneous.[2]

However, several factors worked against a direct confrontation of the two men. Durkheim's major writings extended from *The Division of Labor* (first published in 1893) to *The Elementary Forms of the Religious Life* (first published in 1912). Since their author was also editor-in-chief of *L'Année sociologique,* to which Weber subscribed, it is improbable that Weber was not aware of his contribution. On internal evidence it seems likely that Weber actually discussed Durkheim's *Rules of Sociological Method* (first published in 1895), as I indicate below, but otherwise circumstances militated against an intellectual interchange. Until his debilitating illness in 1897 Weber's work had been that of an economist and legal historian. When he resumed his scholarly work in 1903–4 he proceeded to define his theoretical position in direct confrontation with German historicism and the welfare ideology of German civil servants, as manifested in the Verein für Sozialpolitik. When in that context Weber defined his work as sociological, he thought of it as a discipline auxiliary to historical studies. And when he wrote his chapter on the sociology of religion for *Economy and Society,* Durkheim's *Elementary Forms* (1912) had not been published. During the war communications were disrupted. Finally, since Weber's purpose was diametrically opposed to that of Durkheim, he might have considered it pointless to pursue the matter.

From the standpoint of Durkheim's career the situation is much simpler. His major work was published before Weber became prominent as editor of the *Archiv für Sozialwissenschaft* in 1904. Weber's essays in the sociology of religion appeared in that journal with an introductory note saying that ethnographic materials had

---

[1] Talcott Parsons, *The Structure of Social Action* (Glencoe: Free Press, 1949), see esp. 661–677.

[2] Edward Tiryakian, "A Problem for the Sociology of Knowledge," *European Journal of Sociology,* VII, 1966, 330–336.

been excluded. Moreover, several of the essays appeared during World War I and Weber's most systematic statement was published in 1920–21, after both men had died. During the war years Durkheim was preoccupied with France's national struggle against Germany. Under the circumstances he may not have found time to read Weber's complex essays, which appeared to deal with aspects of religion altogether different from those in which he was interested.

These are conjectures. In the absence of direct evidence we must rely on the substantive work of both scholars in order to interpret the relationship between them. For us the works of both are classics of modern sociology. But they had good reason to feel that their respective contributions—to the extent that they became aware of the other's work—were in different fields of study.

THE NATURE OF THE DISCIPLINE

Durkheim's and Weber's uses of the term "sociology" support this interpretation. Durkheim conceived of his work as a direct continuation of Comte and Mill. Where they had been content with general inquiries into method, he would "construct a method . . . more precise and more exactly adapted to the distinctive characteristics of social phenomena." [3] His aim was to treat social phenomena scientifically, "to extend scientific rationalism to human behavior." Once behavior is reduced to relationships of cause and effect, "these relationships can then be transformed by an equally logical operation, into rules of action for the future." [4] To advance this program one must completely accept the fundamental principle of sociology, namely the objective reality of social facts.

This science . . . could be brought into existence only with the realization that social phenomena, although immaterial, are nevertheless real things, the proper objects of scientific study. To be convinced that their investigation was legitimate, it was necessary to assume that they had a definite and permanent existence, that they do not depend on individual caprice, and that they give rise to uniform and orderly relations.

This view of the matter runs counter to the widespread bias that attributes to man unlimited power over the social order, and fears

[3] Emile Durkheim, *The Rules of Sociological Method* (Chicago: University of Chicago Press, 1938), lx (from the author's introduction).
[4] *Ibid.*, xxxix-xl (from the author's preface to the first edition).

TWO SOCIOLOGICAL TRADITIONS

that man would have to submit in complete impotence if the existence of collective forces were admitted. Durkheim's principal purpose is to liberate sociology from the illusion of omnipotence or the fear of impotence. In society as in nature man must learn "that his power over things really begins only when he recognizes that they have a nature of their own." [5]

At one point in his discussion Durkheim seems to conceive his task in the same terms as Weber. He wants his sociology to occupy a middle ground between the nominalism of the historians and the realism of the philosophers, between the view that collective life is infinitely heterogeneous and the view that it obeys general laws deriving from human nature.[6] But for Durkheim this intermediate position consists in the concept of social species or type of society, with reference to which analysis distinguishes between normal functions and pathological conditions. On this basis Durkheim's sociology aims at a scientific knowledge of cause and effect on which rules of action for the future can be based.

Weber's sociology also aims at an intermediate position between the nominalism of the historians and the realism of universal generalizations, though for him the latter referred less to philosophy than to the stage constructions of social evolution. But when Weber came to write his own conceptual exposition after 1913, he made no reference to Durkheim's book on method of 1895. The reason appears to be that his proposed terminology was formulated with a view to his own distinctive approach to sociology.[7] He emphasized the limited role of sociology. Its object is

to formulate type concepts and generalized uniformities of empirical process. This distinguishes it from history, which is oriented to the causal analysis and explanation of individual actions, structures, and personalities possessing cultural significance.[8]

Concepts and generalizations begin with a wide knowledge of the world, but cannot reflect this fullness of experience. In a given case

[5] Ibid., lvii-lviii (from the author's preface to the second edition).
[6] Ibid., 76–78.
[7] Weber emphasized the ambiguity of the term "sociology," and the limited meaning he gave to it, but apparently believed that his formulations of basic concepts made explicit what "all empirical sociology really means when it deals with the same problems." See Max Weber, Economy and Society, G. Roth and C. Wittich eds. and trans. (New York: Bedminster, 1968), I, 3–4. See also xciv-xcviii of the introduction by Guenther Roth.
[8] Ibid., I, 19.

authority-relations may be feudal, patrimonial, bureaucratic, and charismatic at the same time. Analysis must abstract from this experience to arrive at clear concepts, each of these aspects having been defined precisely. This precision rests on logical integration, which necessarily isolates what is connected and simplifies what is complex. "It is probably seldom if ever that a real phenomenon can be found which corresponds exactly to one of these ideally constructed pure types." [9] Thus Weber's sociology aims at a formulation of types and generalizations which must abstract from reality to be precise, and which by virtue of that precision can serve as an aid to the analysis of concrete cases or situations.

Looked at this way Durkheim's and Weber's approaches appear diametrically opposed, though both wanted to extend "scientific rationalism to human behavior." Durkheim modeled his sociology after the natural sciences, Weber did not. Durkheim was confident that this new discipline would greatly extend man's control over society. Weber did not share this optimistic view of progress through science. Durkheim was a social evolutionist who conceived of change as a sequence of social species or types. Weber considered such theories heuristic devices only, which should not be confused with a historical development. For Durkheim types of society or social organization are objective social facts with reference to which we can and must distinguish between health and morbidity. For Weber types of society are mental constructs which are indispensable aids in the analysis of selected empirical data. He would have considered Durkheim's distinction between normal and pathological aspects of a social type unscientific, because it claimed scientific status for ethical judgments based on uncertain biological analogies.

What Is a Social Fact?

The difference between the two writers is one of purpose and approach. Durkheim wanted to extend the domain of science to the study of social facts, whereas Weber wanted to provide existing social studies with a better foundation than they possessed. Accordingly Durkheim insisted repeatedly that social facts had distinctive properties which must be recognized if the study of society were to become scientific. By contrast, Weber did not pioneer a new field. His substantive studies as well as his theoretical work treated

[9] *Ibid.*, I, 20.

old themes and known materials with a new precision and from the standpoint of new questions. These differences are apparent in Durkheim's and Weber's divergent definitions of "the social fact," and in their sociological studies of religion.

Durkheim deliberately pioneered the field of sociology as an academic discipline.[10] "Social facts are a subject matter *sui generis.* This separate category of facts "consists of ways of acting, thinking and feeling, external to the individual, and endowed with a power of coercion, by reason of which they control him." [11] Among these facts are legal and moral regulations, religious faiths, and economic or political systems, as well as less institutional "social currents" like the language one speaks or the fashions one follows. They retain an identity over time regardless of who abides by the rules, speaks the language, etc.—in Durkheim's opinion an indication that they are external to any individual. They also have in common a power of constraint, so that individuals who violate rules or deviate otherwise find themselves restrained or punished.

In his comments on this definition Durkheim stressed three points. First, social facts cannot be defined by their universality. All Frenchmen speak French, but the manifestations of the language in each individual are distinct from the collective aspects of the language, such as its idioms, vocabulary, syntax, dialects, etc. Second, "because beliefs and social practices come to us from without, it does not follow that we receive them passively or without modification." [12] Instead, we individualize them, as in the habitual turns of phrase which one adopts unwittingly. Against his critics Durkheim stressed the "range of individual shades" which goes together with social convention, although he also stressed the limits beyond which deviation cannot go without adverse repercussions. Third, very often we do not feel the constraint or coercion of the collectivity any more than we feel oppressed by the air we breathe. We may cling to and love the institutions that compel us; we may find our welfare in adhering to them and in the constraint they impose.[13]

These specifications refer to "social facts" as collective causes which become manifest through the individual but are not reducible to his consciousness and actions. Neither motives nor utility

[10] See Terry Clark, "Emile Durkheim and the Institutionalization of Sociology in the French University System," *European Journal of Sociology,* IX, 1968, 37–71.

[11] Durkheim, *op. cit.,* 3.

[12] *Ibid.,* lvi, n.7.

[13] *Ibid.,* liv, n.5.

(and hence neither psychology nor teleology) can account for the social forces which transcend the individual's consciousness and therefore can exert pressure upon him.[14] Nor can they account for the effects of human action, since these depend upon society rather than subjective intentions. Durkheim states:

When the explanation of a social phenomenon is undertaken we must seek separately the efficient cause [or collective force] which produces it and the function it fulfils. We use the word "function," in preference to "end" or "purpose," precisely because social phenomena do not generally exist for the useful results they produce. We must determine whether there is a correspondence between the fact under consideration and the general needs of the social organism. . . .

And this can be done, because society is a system formed by the association of individuals and as such "represents a specific reality which has its own characteristics."[15] It is a question of determining "how the phenomena comprising [social life] combine in such a way as to put society in harmony with itself and with the environment external to it." Thus the effort to show the causes of social facts must be supplemented by showing their "function in the establishment of social order."[16]

In turning now to Weber's approach, note should be taken of his more limited conception of the field. Sociology is to concern itself "with the interpretive understanding of social action and thereby with a causal explanation of its course and consequences." The emphasis is on "interpretive understanding" because "the acting individual attaches a subjective meaning to his behavior," whether he does so explicitly or tacitly. This understanding is to be distinguished from all those favoring or hindering circumstances which condition the individual but which "are devoid of meaning insofar as they cannot be related to an intended purpose." On the other hand, action is both meaningful and specifically social insofar as the individual "takes account of the behavior of others and is thereby oriented in its course."[17]

Emphasis on the subjective meaning of action as the proper focus of sociology may be compared with Durkheim's approach to this subjective dimension. We saw that Durkheim acknowledged a

[14] *Ibid.,* 101.
[15] *Ibid.,* 95, 103.
[16] *Ibid.,* 97.
[17] Weber, *Economy and Society,* I, 3–4, 7.

range of individual modifications within the prevailing conformity. He chose not to study them, either because individual attitudes are too varied to allow scientific treatment or because the psychological analysis of such attitudes (where possible) must miss the external constraint of collective forces, which is the proper object of sociology.[18]

Weber's approach to "favoring or hindering circumstances" which are devoid of meaning is more complex. Fortunately, his discussion of the problem is so explicit that one might see it as an answer to the Durkheimian position.[19] Weber begins by saying that sociology in his sense is "restricted to subjectively understandable phenomena," which exist only in individual human beings. In this restricted view there are many "processes and uniformities" which are not sociological because they are not "understandable" in the sense defined. These "conditions and stimuli . . . of action" must be treated by methods other than those of interpretive sociology.

> For [these] other cognitive purposes it may be useful or necessary to consider the individual, for instance, as a collection of cells, as a complex of biochemical reactions, or to conceive his psychic life as made up of a variety of different elements, however these may be defined. Undoubtedly such procedures yield valuable knowledge of causal relationships. But the behavior of these elements, as expressed in such uniformities, is not subjectively understandable. This is true even of psychic elements because the more precisely they are formulated from a point of view of natural science, the less they are accessible to subjective understanding.[20]

With these other purposes in mind it is certainly possible to derive uniformities from the observation of various elements, and to explain individual phenomena by subsuming them under these uniformities. Sociology in Weber's sense takes account of these uniformities as of any other facts "not capable of subjective interpretation." But the ascertaining of such uniformities "is never the road to interpretation in terms of subjective meaning." [21]

[18] See Durkheim, *Rules*, 95, 100–102.
[19] The following analysis is based on Weber, *Economy and Society*, I, 12–18. Sentences in quotation marks which are not otherwise identified are taken from these pages.
[20] *Ibid.*, I, 13.
[21] Incidentally, Weber makes clear that the distinction between understandable uniformities and uniformities devoid of meaning is not the same as that between qualitative analysis and quantitative method. See *ibid.*, I, 12.

Still, there are contexts in which it is convenient or indispensable to treat such uniformities as social collectivities and hence as if they were individual persons. Weber mentions states, associations, business corporations, and foundations as examples, but his reference is more broadly to "collective concepts derived from disciplines" other than sociology in his meaning of the term. Since Durkheim states explicitly that the external constraint of society is a social fact independent of the individual, Weber would have to consider this "collective concept" as derived from another discipline. In turn, Durkheim would have rejected Weber's specification that "for the subjective interpretation of action in sociological work these collectives must be treated as *solely* the resultants and modes of organization of the particular acts of individual persons, since these alone can be treated as agents in a course of subjectively understandable action." [22] But then Durkheim considers such "acts of individual persons" as too varied to be suitable for scientific study.[23]

For his part Weber believes that a subjective interpretation of action can make legitimate use of collective concepts, provided certain cautions are observed. First, concepts of collectivities like nation, family, an army corps, etc., are often indispensable if an intelligible terminology is to be obtained. But the sociological use of these terms always refers to the "actual or possible social actions of individual persons." For example, the jurist treats a corporation as the performer of legally significant actions. By contrast, the sociologist would treat the same phenomenon in terms of the covert or overt beliefs which the major executives of the corporation associate with a given transaction.

Second, concepts of collectivities have a meaning in the minds not only of functionaries like executives or judges, but in those of ordinary individuals. Terms like "nation" or "state" may be used sociologically in this sense. Individuals take account of the behavior of others in their belief that these collectivities (reference groups) exist and/or that they have normative authority.

Third, functional concepts of collectivities are for Weber the most problematic. He readily accepts an analysis of the "relation of 'parts' to 'whole'" for purposes of illustration and as a "provisional orientation," but rejects concepts of collectivities when they are endowed with a misplaced concreteness, to use Whitehead's

[22] *Ibid.*, I, 13.
[23] Durkheim, *Rules,* 95.

phrase. Such reification occurs when actions and thoughts or feelings are attributed to the collectivity. In Weber's view this seductive short cut to interpretation should be avoided, because it confuses distinct levels of analysis.

In the case of social collectivities, precisely as distinguished from organisms, we are in a position to go beyond merely demonstrating functional relationships and uniformities. We can accomplish something which is never attainable in the natural sciences, namely the subjective understanding of the actions of the component individuals . . . This additional achievement of explanation by interpretive understanding, as distinguished from external observation, is of course attained only at a price—the more hypothetical and fragmentary character of its results. Nevertheless, subjective understanding is the specific characteristic of sociological knowledge.[24]

Here is perhaps the most crucial distinction between Weber and Durkheim. For Weber functional analysis is a preliminary orientation; for Durkheim it is a major objective. For Weber's sociological purposes "there is no such thing as a collective personality which 'acts'." [25] Contrast this with Durkheim's statement: "When the individual has been eliminated, society alone remains. We must, then, seek the explanation of social life in the nature of society itself." [26] Thus Weber always hesitates to ascribe actions or ideas to collectivities, while Durkheim does so freely. One could say that Weber accepts the fragmentary character of sociology as he understands it and thus relinquishes the goal of establishing sociology as a science. On the other hand, Durkheim emphasizes functional relationships in the interest of science and attributes actions and feelings to society. The import of this difference in orientation is best seen in their respective studies of religion.

SOCIOLOGY OF RELIGION

Both scholars devoted a major part of their work to religion. Durkheim chose to examine religion in a primitive nonliterate tribe in the belief that from this he could deduce the essence of religion in all societies. Weber, in *The Protestant Ethic,* but still more in his comparative studies, chose to investigate the early age of religious creativity. His analysis of Confucius, Lao-tse, Buddha,

[24] Weber, *Economy and Society,* I, 15.
[25] *Ibid.,* I, 14.
[26] Durkheim, *Rules,* 102.

the Old Testament prophets, and others examined the divergent world views of the great civilizations.

Certain differences between the two authors derive from these starting points. In searching for the essential characteristics of all religion—its "elementary forms"—Durkheim devotes much attention to problems of definition, to the supposed origins of religious phenomena, and correspondingly little or no attention to religious functionaries or theological doctrines. With Weber it is the other way around. Though greatly concerned with the clarification of concepts, his discussion of religion begins with an explicit refusal to define it; it is concerned, not with "religion," but with religious behavior as a particular type of social action. Furthermore, Weber eschews questions of origins and explicitly acknowledges the omission of ethnographic materials. His analysis comes into its own with an analysis of "the prophet" as the first of several types of religious leaders and functionaries. Beyond that he develops a typology of theological doctrines and then returns to the problem of the Protestant Ethic: the relation between doctrine and conduct.[27]

The two scholars differ not only in subject matter and emphasis but in their fundamental orientation. By studying primitive religion Durkheim wants to characterize "an essential and permanent aspect of humanity."

One must know how to go underneath the symbol to the reality which it represents and which gives it its meaning. The most barbarous and the most fantastic rites and the strangest myths translate some human need, some aspect of life, either individual or social. The reasons with which the faithful justify them may be, and generally are, erroneous; but the true reasons do not cease to exist, and it is the duty of science to discover them.[28]

Durkheim defines "all known religious beliefs" as presupposing a division of the world into the sacred and the profane. And he attempts to show that this division is similar to that between society and the world of empirical objects.

[27] See *Economy and Society*, II, 399–400, 420 and *passim*. The first section of the sociology of religion is given the title "The Origin of Religion." This perpetuates an erroneous impression which the editors studiously avoid otherwise, namely that Weber stood in the tradition of social evolutionism. True to his behavioristic emphasis, Weber is discussing the social psychology of religious beliefs.

[28] Emile Durkheim, *The Elementary Forms of the Religious Life* (London: Allen & Unwin, 1957), 2–3.

Like all the powers of gods and spirits, society "gives us the sensation of a perpetual dependence." [29] The norms and taboos of the community exercise an imperious moral authority over our thoughts and actions. Unwittingly we comply with the usages and conventions of those surrounding us, and in this way society controls our daily lives.

We speak a language that we did not make; we use instruments that we did not invent; we invoke rights that we did not found; a treasury of knowledge is transmitted to each generation that it did not gather itself, etc. It is to society that we owe these varied benefits of civilization, and if we do not ordinarily see the source from which we get them, we at least know that they are not our own work. . . .

Thus the environment in which we live seems to us to be peopled with forces that are at once imperious and helpful, august and gracious, and with which we have relations. Since they exercise over us a pressure of which we are conscious, we are forced to localize them outside ourselves, just as we do for the objective causes of our sensations.[30]

Yet these outside forces inspire different sentiments in us. The world of objects in its empirical characteristics arouses in us no sense of respect; we treat it matter-of-factly, though elsewhere Durkheim declares that our ways of thinking about this world are also conditioned by society. But where these outside powers compel a sense of complete dependence and awe, they belong to the realm of the sacred as distinguished from the profane.

This sketchy résumé makes clear that for Durkheim religious beliefs are automatically the beliefs of everyman. The choice of primitive religion makes it plausible to assume a universal religious consensus. Religious functionaries merely express the beliefs of the whole group, and nonliterate societies do not involve the complication of systematic theological doctrines.[31]

Weber too goes "underneath the [religious] symbol to the reality." But he sees that "reality" in the mundane or innerworldly meaning of religious behavior, not like Durkheim in the outside powers of society which impinge upon us. Men certainly experience

[29] *Ibid.*, 206.

[30] *Ibid.*, 212.

[31] Durkheim, of course, generalized his findings. Thus, in *Suicide* (London: Routledge & Kegan Paul, 1952), 170, he specifically mentions the different views of suicide in Catholic, Protestant, and Jewish theology only to dismiss them as irrelevant for an understanding of behavior.

such transcendent powers. But for Weber this religious experience involves "the notion of 'super-sensual' forces that may intervene in the destiny of people in the same way that a man may influence the course of the world about him." [32] The reference is thus not only to the intervention of higher powers, but also to its mundane analogue and meaning. Hence Weber does not dismiss the reasons with which the faithful justify the rites and myths of their religion, though he puts special emphasis on the ideas and interests of religious functionaries or of classes and status groups. Not the essence of religion as in Durkheim, but the condition and effects of religious behavior are of interest to him.

The most elementary forms of behavior motivated by religious or magical factors are oriented to *this* world. "That it may go well with thee . . . and that thou mayest prolong thy days upon the earth" (Deut. 4:40) expresses the reason for the performance of actions enjoined by religion or magic. . . . Furthermore, religiously or magically motivated behavior is relatively rational behavior, especially in its earliest manifestations. It follows rules of experience, though it is not necessarily action in accordance with a means-end schema. Rubbing will elicit sparks from pieces of wood, and in like fashion the mimetical actions of a magician will evoke rain from the heavens. The sparks resulting from twirling the wooden sticks are as much a "magical" effect as the rain evoked by the manipulations of the rain-maker. Thus, religious or magical behavior or thinking must not be set apart from the range of everyday purposive conduct, particularly since even the ends of the religious and magical actions are predominantly economic.[33]

The tendency to consider religious or magical behavior a thing apart originates with us. Certain interpretations appear "irrational" and certain acts based upon them are dubbed "magical" only from our modern standpoint. But for Weber the question is how the believer himself looks upon such beliefs and practices.

The person performing a magical act will distinguish "between the greater or lesser ordinariness of the phenomena in question." Not every object can serve as a source of special powers, nor does every person have the capacity to achieve the ecstatic states which in primitive experience are the condition for achieving certain effects. Those objects and persons that do, possess charisma. The distinction between extraordinary and ordinary phenomena parallels Durkheim's distinction between the sacred and the profane. But for

[32] Weber, *Economy and Society*, II, 402.
[33] *Ibid.*, 399–400.

Weber the accent is on the innerworldly effect which the believer hopes for, and expects from, the charismatic object or person. There is, indeed, the believer's special sense of awe and reverence. But whereas Durkheim attributes this sentiment to our sense of dependence upon society, Weber attributes it to the hopes and fears with which the believer regards the extraordinary powers attributed to a fetish or magician. The difference is basic. For "the sensation of a perpetual dependence" is shared by all alike, whereas the believer's search for extraordinary powers singles out the objects and persons that are believed to possess these powers.

This is the reason why Weber's study of religion focuses attention on religious elites and Durkheim's study does not. Charisma may inhere in an object or person; it is seen as a natural endowment that cannot be acquired. It therefore becomes a question of developing the criteria by which its presence may be recognized, a procedure which lends itself to monopolization. Knowledge of the criteria and the act of recognition are made an arcane art. However, charisma may also be produced artificially. In that case it is usually assumed that the objects or persons already possess a dormant propensity that can be awakened by special rites or ascetic practices. It becomes a question of performing these rites or practices in an authentic manner. Again this puts a premium upon knowledge of what is authentic. Moreover, the belief in the charismatic endowment of objects or persons is associated—by a process of abstraction—with "the notion that certain beings are concealed 'behind' and responsible for the activity of the charismatically endowed natural objects, artifacts, animals or persons." [34] This belief in spirits gives special significance to those who are thought to possess magical powers with which to command the spirits.

The professional necromancer—Weber calls this the oldest of all "vocations"—turns ecstasy into an enterprise. For ecstasy "represents or mediates charisma" and thereby establishes special powers over the spirits in the eyes of the layman. Ordinary men search for, and seek to control, those extraordinary phenomena, which can assist them in affliction and in the success of everyday affairs. They need help from those extraordinary men whose charismatic gifts enable them to communicate with the spirits and demons. In this way, the formation of elites lies at the very root of religious experience.

It is surprising to look back from this perspective to Durkheim's

[34] *Ibid.*, 401.

Elementary Forms, which might be expected to deal with similar phenomena. Fully half of this book is devoted to a study of elementary religious beliefs, yet there is hardly a mention of the magicians, sorcerers, shamans, and other functionaries who propound these beliefs. In fact, Durkheim distinguishes between the "popular representation as it is spontaneously formed from common experience," which he finds among the Australian tribes, and the "late and philosophic elaborations" which obscure rather than illuminate that experience.[35]

Weber's position is very different. His most systematic account may use Durkheim's phrase "elementary forms" but it uses it to refer not to religion itself, but to the innerworldly orientation of religiously motivated behavior, to religious hopes for a good life in this world. And in a footnote explaining the omission of ethnographic materials, on which Durkheim's study was based entirely, Weber states that his study "was necessarily dealing with the religious ethics of the classes which were the culture-bearers of their respective countries. We are concerned with the influence which *their* conduct has had." [36]

Thus Durkheim and Weber approached the study of religion from diverse standpoints and with different purposes in mind. Durkheim wanted to analyze the universal essence of religion and for this purpose had recourse to its most "elementary forms" in primitive society. Every religious phenomenon is reduced ultimately to that same "external coercion" which constitutes for Durkheim the evidence of a collectivity as an autonomous force. There is a certain monotony in this explanation which Durkheim regarded with evident enthusiasm, since in his eyes it held out the promise of "rules of action for the future," though he nowhere says what these might be.

For his part Weber made it quite clear that he considered such an approach useful only as a prolegomenon to sociological studies in his sense. Even a complete knowledge of psychological and sociological uniformities or regularities could do no more than provide the background for the interpretation of culturally significant phenomena.

[35] See Durkheim, *Elementary Forms,* 264 and *passim.* One can see in this view a reflection of Durkheim's anticlericalism just as one may see in Weber's detached, but sympathetic, study of religious doctrines an echo of attitudes evoked by his mother's religiosity.

[36] Weber, *Economy and Society,* II, 420, n.1. Note that Weber wrote this chapter before 1913 and hence before the publication of Durkheim's *Elementary Forms* in 1915.

Let us assume that we have succeeded by means of psychology or otherwise in analyzing all the observed and imaginable relationships of social
phenomena into some ultimate elementary "factors," that we have
made an exhaustive analysis and classification of them and then formulated rigorously exact laws covering their behavior. What would be the
significance of these results for our knowledge of the historically given
culture or any individual phase thereof, such as capitalism, in its development and cultural significance? As an analytical tool, it would be as
useful as a textbook of organic chemical combinations would be for our
knowledge of the biogenetic aspect of the animal and plant world. In
each case, certainly an important and useful preliminary step would
have been taken. In neither case can concrete reality be deduced from
"laws" and "factors." . . . The real reason is that the analysis of reality
is concerned with the configuration in which those (hypothetical) "factors" are arranged to form a cultural phenomenon which is historically
significant to us. Furthermore, if we wish to "explain" this individual
configuration "causally" we must invoke other equally individual configurations on the basis of which we will explain it with the aid of those
(hypothetical) "laws."[37]

With this emphasis there could be no meeting of minds between
the two scholars, even if they had confronted each other directly.

Two Foundations of Modern Sociology

Accordingly, sociology counts among its classics two scholars
whose work manifests an almost complete divergence of method
and substance. The differences between Durkheim and Weber may
be attributed to temperament and circumstance. A later observer
can ignore these and extract certain common themes from the work
of both. This is best done from the standpoint of belief in sociology
as a natural science, which automatically moves this work of synthesis closer to Durkheim than to Weber.[38] However, one can also

---

[37] Weber, " 'Objectivity' in Social Science," *The Methodology of the Social
Sciences,* Edward Shils and Henry Finch, eds. and trans. (New York: Free Press,
1949), 75.

[38] This was a major contribution in Parsons' *Structure of Social Action,* 661–
677. The difference of my intepretation from that of Parsons is best seen in relation to the parallel between Weber's concept of "charisma" and Durkheim's
concept of the "the sacred." Parsons sees a simple parallel. I note that belief in
charisma is the prime basis for the divergence between an elite of religious functionaries and the religiosity of the masses. Durkheim's concept of the sacred cannot accommodate this distinction, because this awe-inspiring representation of
the entire collectivity encompasses all its members regardless of the distinctions
among them.

emphasize the differences between the two scholars as I have done, to make clear that modern sociology is beholden to two traditions.

One of these is Baconian or Saint-Simonian in inspiration. It takes its cues from the natural sciences as nonscientists tend to interpret them: disciplines whose major goal is the discovery of general laws and whose principal utility consists in the power of control which the application of these laws is expected to put at man's disposal. This is the legacy upon which Durkheim based the major orientation of his work. The other tradition has a developmental orientation; its inspiration goes back to Burckhardt and Tocqueville. It takes its cues from disciplines whose major goal is to discover the genesis of historical configurations and whose principal utility, if that is the word, consists in the cultivation of human judgment. This is the legacy upon which Weber based the major orientation of his work. To me the tension-ridden but creative interplay between these two traditions, rather than the absorption of one by the other, appears as the foundation of modern sociology.

XVI

THE PROTESTANT ETHIC—REVISITED

EARLIER LITERATURE

In his article on "Respect for Work and Cleanliness," Nikolai A. Mel'gunov touches on themes which are largely associated in our minds with the work of Max Weber. The aristocratic contempt for manual work and more broadly for any kind of specialization, the association of industriousness with religious dissent and with Protestant dissent particularly, the general view that labor is a burden which in Russian culture as in Catholicism is related to the frequency of holidays, the observable differences between Protestants and Catholics in the Rhineland—these and other themes can be found in Weber's work. Yet Weber himself considered these notions a commonplace in the literature. He believed that his own study offered a more probing analysis of the relation between the Protestant Ethic and that complex of attitudes toward economic activities which he designated as "innerworldly asceticism." "It is thus not new that the existence of this relationship is maintained here. Laveleye, Matthew Arnold, and others already perceived it. What is new, on the contrary, is the quite unfounded denial of it. Our task here is to explain the relation.[1] Here Weber hints at, rather than refers to, an earlier literature in which writers had commented on the innerworldly significance of Protestantism. No doubt he was unaware of Mel'gunov, but a brief survey of this other

---

[1] Max Weber, *The Protestant Ethic and the Spirit of Capitalism* (New York: Scribner, 1958), 191, n.23. See also 280, n.96.

Reinhard Bendix, "The Protestant Ethic—Revisited," *Comparative Studies in Society and History*, IX:3, April 1967, 266–73; comment on Philip Shashko, "Nikolai Alexandrovich Mel'gunov on the Reformation and the Work Ethic," *ibid.*, 256–65. I should like to acknowledge the valuable assistance of Jean Guy Vaillancourt.

literature will suggest that many nineteenth-century writers wrote commentaries similar to Mel'gunov's.

The Belgian writer Emile de Laveleye was the author of a textbook on economics that was widely used in the eighties and nineties of the last century. In a chapter entitled "Influence of Philosophic and Religious Doctrines on the Productiveness of Labor" he specifically linked evangelical Christianity with the economic prosperity of countries, noting that the equalitarianism and the simple life-style of Protestants favored economic progress while intolerance was harmful to it. Laveleye also mentioned Voltaire's observation that there were no poor to be found among the Quakers in England and the Mennonites in Holland.[2] In addition, he published a pamphlet comparing Protestantism and Catholicism in their relation to freedom and prosperity obviously intended as a partisan argument in the religious conflicts of his country. Laveleye makes an invidious contrast of Protestant virtues and Catholic vices, among which the effects of both on economic affairs are mentioned incidentally. But in introducing the German edition of this work the political theorist J. C. Bluntschli was more specific. Writing in 1875, Bluntschli pointed out, as Mel'gunov had, that in the Catholic Rhineland the most important factories were in the hands of Protestants. He also noted that much of German literature and science has been the work of Protestants rather than Catholics, although he also mentioned that Catholics were relatively more prominent in music and the arts—a point of some importance in Weber's own study.[3]

Weber refers to Matthew Arnold as another writer who had noted the close relation between Protestant dissent and economic enterprise. Yet Arnold comments on this relationship only incidentally; he largely takes it for granted. His concern is with the cultural implications of Puritanism, and it is probable that he stimulated Weber as well as Bluntschli in this respect. At one point Arnold speaks of the English middle class as having "entered the prison of Puritanism" at the beginning of the seventeenth century and having "had the key turned upon its spirit here for two hundred years." Driven by their sense of the power of conduct, the middle class gained by what it became, "and the whole nation with

[2] Emile de Laveleye, *Elements of Political Economy* (New York: Putnam, 1889), 44. The book was published originally in 1882.

[3] See Emile von Laveleye, *Protestantismus and Katholizismus in ihren Beziehungen zur Freiheit und Wohlfahrt der Völker* (Nördlingen: Beck'sche Buchhandlung, 1875), *passim* and iv-v of Bluntschli's preface.

them; they deepened and fixed for this nation the sense of conduct. But they created a type of life and manners, of which they themselves are slow indeed to recognize the faults, but which is fatally condemned by its hideousness, its immense ennui, and against which the instinct of self-preservation in humanity rebels.[4] In this and many similar passages Arnold refers to the Puritan pattern of conduct—less in terms of its accomplishments than of its great emotional and cultural liabilities, though he recognizes both sides. That recognition is found in Weber's analysis as well. But while Arnold approaches this phenomenon as a critic of culture, Weber deals with it in functional terms. In his view, the Puritan devaluation of emotional attachments, of sensual enjoyment, and of the world of art is the price that must be paid if the daily conduct of affairs is subjected to so exacting and fear-inspired a discipline of the spirit.

John Keats and H. T. Buckle are two other writers to whom Weber referred. Both commented on the role of religion in Scotland, with particular emphasis on the soul-destroying dread induced by the church. Keats noted that there was much linguistic similarity on the neighboring shores of Scotland and Ireland, but yet a great cultural difference. Though both countries were poor, Scotch cottages were neat, clean, and comfortable; they were palaces by contrast with the hovels of Ireland. But the boys and girls of Scotland stood in terrible awe of the Elders: ". . . they are formed into regular Phalanges of savers and gainers. Such a thrifty army cannot fail to enrich their country, and give it a greater appearance of comfort, than that of their poor rash neighborhood—these Kirk-men have done Scotland harm; they have banished puns, and laughing, and kissing . . . "[5] Here is a clear, if incidental, statement concerning the particular phenomenon on which Weber was to focus his attention: poverty, a carefree enjoyment of life, and Catholicism on one hand; comfort and cleanliness, saving and gaining, and a fear induced by a life-repressing Presbyterianism on the other.

What Keats spoke of in an incidental comment was the subject of lengthy analysis in Buckle's *Civilization in England*. Again there is a contrast between adjacent countries, but Buckle compares the effects of Protestantism in Scotland and in England rather than of Irish Catholicism and Scotch Presbyterianism. For Buckle Protes-

---

[4] From the essay on "Equality" (1878) in Lionel Trilling, ed., *The Portable Matthew Arnold* (New York: Viking, 1949), 595.

[5] John Keats, *Complete Poetical Works and Letters* (Cambridge: Houghton, Mifflin, 1899), 310. The quotation is from a letter, written in July 1818, to Keats' brother Thomas.

tantism is the mark of progress and civilization in contrast with Catholicism, yet in practice even the same religion may have divergent effects depending upon the cultural level of the population. "While in England Protestantism has diminished superstition, has weakened the clergy, has increased toleration, and, in a word, has secured the triumph of secular interests over ecclesiastical ones, its results in Scotland have been entirely different; and that, in that country, the Church, changing its forms without altering its spirit, not only cherished its ancient pretensions, but unhappily retained its ancient power." [6] In Scotland, the Protestant movement "never produced the effects which might have been expected from it, and which it did produce in England." [7]

From the standpoint of Weber's later analysis the most interesting part of Buckle's discussion is contained in a chapter on "The Scotch Intellect during the Seventeenth Century." According to Buckle, Scotland presented the paradox of a people "liberal in politics" but at the same time "illiberal in religion." For a hundred and twenty years after the establishment of Protestantism, the rulers of Scotland, by their neglect or persecution of the church, had driven the clergy into the arms of the people with the result of strengthening the democratic spirit, since the clergy *and* the people were thwarted by the upper classes.

But these very circumstances, which guarded the people against political despotism, exposed them all the more to ecclesiastical despotism. For, having no one to trust except their preachers, they trusted them entirely, and upon all subjects. The clergy gradually became supreme, not only in spiritual matters, but also in temporal ones. . . . In fairness to them, we ought to acknowledge that the religious servitude into which the Scotch fell during the seventeenth century, was, on the whole, a willing one, and that, mischievous as it was, it had at least a noble origin, inasmuch as the influence of the Protestant clergy is mainly to be ascribed to the fearlessness with which they came forward as leaders of the people, at a period when that post was full of danger, and when the upper classes were ready to unite with the crown in destroying the last vestiges of national liberty.[8]

Buckle did not neglect to mention that toward the end of the seventeenth century the energy of the Scottish people turned away from

---

[6] Henry Thomas Buckle, *Civilization in England* (New York: Appleton, 1861), II, 153.

[7] *Idem.*

[8] *Ibid*, II, 260f.

religious controversy to the new channel of commercial enterprise, but this reference occurs in the context of discussing the general pacification of Scotch society and the decline of feudal institutions and loyalties.[9] The greater part of Buckle's attention was devoted rather to a detailed examination of "ecclesiastical despotism." For all its obvious partisanship, this discussion presents an impressive survey of seventeenth-century literature, which contains many of the themes mentioned by Mel'gunov, on which Weber commented later. Quoting at length from the sermons of the period Buckle characterized the spiritual mutilation of the people. Here is part of his own summary of that presentation:

To be poor, dirty, and hungry, to pass through life in misery, and to leave it with fear, to be plagued by boils, and sores, and diseases of every kind, to be always sighing and groaning, to have the face streaming with tears and the chest heaving with sobs, in a word, to suffer constant affliction, and to be tormented in all possible ways; to undergo these things was deemed a proof of goodness, just as the contrary was a proof of evil. It mattered not what a man liked; the mere fact of his liking it, made it sinful. Whatever was natural, was wrong. The clergy deprived the people of their holidays, their amusements, their shows, their games, and their sports; they repressed every appearance of joy, they forbad all merriment, they stopped all festivities, they choked up every avenue by which pleasure could enter, and they spread over the country a universal gloom.[10]

There is in this picture a degree of spiritual blight that left no room even for those habits of "foresight and of provision for the future" that played so important a role in Weber's subsequent study.[11] At the same time Buckle gives a very vivid impression of what Weber calls at one point the "power and torment of those metaphysical conceptions." It is possible that Weber's emphasis on the religious dread induced by the doctrine of predestination was partly influenced by Buckle's colorful account.[12]

Reference to this consideration brings us closer to Weber's specific concern with the behavioral correlates of particular religious

[9] *Ibid.*, II, 236ff.

[10] *Ibid.*, II, 314.

[11] Cf. *ibid.*, II, 313, where Buckle specifically identifies thoughts about the future as incompatible with complete resignation to the divine will.

[12] Cf. Weber's own stress on the importance of this consideration in his "Kritische Bemerkungen zu den vorstehenden 'kritischen Beiträgen,' " *Archiv für Sozialwissenschaft und Sozialpolitik*, XXV, 1907, 248 and *passim*.

doctrines. In this respect several other historical references are revealing. After mentioning Keats, Buckle, Laveleye, and Arnold, Weber cites the case of the Mennonites in East Prussia whom Frederick William I tolerated as "indispensable to industry, in spite of their absolute refusal to perform military service." Weber calls this an especially striking instance of the fact that "a religious way of life and the most intense development of business acumen" went together.[13] Frederick William is well known for his ruthlessness in promoting the military capacities of his country. The abuses practiced by his military recruiters are documented with specific reference to the Mennonites. All but one of the Mennonites forced into service and subjected to various tortures resisted steadfastly on religious grounds, and Frederick William decided to banish the entire Mennonite community, preferring other Christians who did not reject military service. But then the Königliche Kriegs- und Domänenkammer of Königsberg petitioned the king in March 1732, on the ground that execution of this edict would damage the royal revenue and His Majesty's other interests to a considerable extent, because as industrialists and as peasants the Mennonites were of the greatest benefit to the land and their presence guaranteed the royal coffers a considerable income. The king responded by granting the Mennonites the desired exemption and assuring them of royal protection on condition that they would found and develop textile factories. Thereupon most Mennonites returned to Königsberg.[14] The contemporary evidence concerning the economic efficiency of the Mennonites must have been impressive if officials of this particular king were willing to risk his displeasure, and the king permitted himself to be dissuaded from his previous course of action.

A number of other references to the then existing literature may be passed in briefer review. Weber noted William Petty's observations on the economic prosperity of Holland, which Petty attributed to the presence of religious dissent, an explanation which he formulated as a general principle.[15] Weber also cites Eberhard Gothein, who specifically emphasized the importance of the Calvinist dias-

[13] Weber, *Protestant Ethic, op. cit.,* 42.

[14] See W. Mannhardt, *Die Wehrfreiheit der Altpreussischen Mennoniten* (Marienburg: Hermann Hempels Wwe., 1863), 118–120. I have no evidence that Weber used this particular publication, but it is the one dealing most specifically with the incident to which he referred.

[15] See Charles H. Hull, ed., *The Economic Writings of Sir William Petty* (Cambridge: The University Press, 1899), I, 261–264 and *passim*.

pora as a seed bed of capitalistic economy,[16] and the similar theme
which recurs in the writings of J. E. T. Rogers.[17] In referring to
these observations Weber pointed out that the evidence was rather
equivocal, even though it suggested a general affinity between Protestantism and the promotion of trade. French, Spanish, Dutch,
Austrian, and Prussian statesmen had at times protected dissident
Protestant minorities in an effort to promote trade and industry.
But it was not clear whether the economic drive of these sectarian
communities was to be attributed to the economic superiority of
the culture from which they had come or "perhaps to the immense
influence of exile in the breakdown of traditional relationships." [18]
At any rate, the fact that in a good many cases Catholics in a minority position had *not* become prominent in trade and industry argued against attributing too much importance to minority status
as an explanatory variable.[19]

There were still other writers to whom Weber referred in support of his view that there was some kind of relationship between
Protestantism and the development of trade and industry. Manley,
Temple, Montesquieu, Heine, Macaulay, Carlyle, Wiskemann,
and others are among the older writers mentioned; Ashley, Doyle,
Bernstein, Cunningham, and Hermann Levy among the younger.
These references to the literature are quite incidental and the omission of still other writers has no significance.[20] What emerges from
this survey is simply that Mel'gunov's brief essay is part of a consid-

---

[16] See Eberhard Gotheim, *Wirtschaftsgeschichte des Schwarzwaldes* (Strassburg: Trübner, 1892), 673–714.

[17] See J. E. T. Rogers, *Holland* (New York: Putnam, 1900), 51 (originally
published in 1888); the same author's *The Economic Interpretation of History*
(New York: Putnam, 1889), 74–84 and *The Industrial and Commercial History
of England* (New York: Putnam, 1892), 35ff.

[18] Weber, *Protestant Ethic, op. cit.,* 43. In a footnote Weber adds: "The migration of exiles of all the religions of the earth, Indian, Arabian, Chinese, Syrian,
Phoenecian, Greek, Lombard, to other countries as bearers of the commercial
lore of highly developed areas, has been of universal occurrence and has nothing
to do with our problem." *Ibid.,* 189, n.13.

[19] *Ibid.,* 39–40.

[20] There is a relevant passage, for example, in Alfred Marshall which is among
the more perceptive of these earlier commentaries. It links the "isolation of each
person's religious responsibility" among Puritans with the "sturdy thorough-
ness of work in the manufacturing arts." See Alfred Marshall, *Principles of
Economics* (New York: Macmillan, 1895), I, 36–39. The book was originally
published in 1890. My colleague Neil Smelser informs me that similar comments
occur rather frequently among English writers of the early nineteenth century
who discussed the development of trade and industry.

erable earlier literature commenting more or less fully on the relation between religious belief and economic behavior and in that context on the particular significance of Protestantism. Accordingly, Weber's seemingly casual comment should be taken seriously, that the burden of proof was on those who denied this relationship. He took it as probably true but still in need of a more specific formulation and causal explanation. This particular focus is worth recalling in view of the large critical literature dealing with specific instances exemplifying, or "refuting," the relationship Weber had posited. The point is that in embryonic form such a literature already existed at his time. He was aware of it and apparently believed that for purposes of understanding this posited relationship not much more could be gained by a further accumulation of instances. Even today students might read Weber's essay differently if they were made aware that Weber assumed rather than tried to prove the existence of a positive relation between Protestant piety and economic growth. His effort was to understand the relation on the assumption that it existed. In more modern terminology: once a correlation has been demonstrated, even if it is a weak one, it still needs to be interpreted.[21]

Weber's interpretation took the form of an ideal typical construction; his reasoning may be restated in the following form. Assume the existence of a positive relation of undetermined magnitude between Protestant piety and the "capitalist spirit." Isolated instances of a relation between certain religious doctrines and capitalist enterprise, and also isolated instances of the capitalist mentality unrelated to religious belief, have occurred throughout history, but the first development of a capitalist system occurred in Western Europe and specifically in England. Since the material preconditions of that system have existed elsewhere, but did not give rise to an economic development comparable with that of England, some part of this "breakthrough" must be attributed to favorable cultural factors. And since the previous literature had shown many divergent relations between Protestantism and capitalist enterprise, the task as

---

[21] That it might be weak on occasion was clear not only from Buckle's discussion, among others, but was explicitly stated by Weber himself. After emphasizing the combination of "capitalistic business sense" and the "most intensive forms of piety" especially in the case of Calvinism, Weber adds the footnote: "This, of course, was true [of Calvinism] only when some possibility of capitalistic development in the area in question was present." See *Protestant Ethic, op. cit.*, 190, n.16.

Weber saw it was to isolate conceptually how certain religious beliefs and a particular mentality of economic behavior could be related to one another. All this is evident in Weber's original text, which emphasizes that the moral awakening which seriously affected practical life can only be understood in the light of the dogmatic beliefs which influenced the men of that day to an extent that is difficult to appreciate today. Weber states that he would present these religious ideas "in the artificial simplicity of ideal types. For just because of the impossibility of drawing sharp boundaries in historical reality we can only hope to understand their specific importance from an investigation of them in their most consistent and logical forms.[22] As long as one does not deny the influence of the "great traditions" (Redfield) on behavior, analysis of their patterns is likely to proceed along such lines as Weber suggested. Yet ideal typical constructions of this kind pose special problems. They deliberately simplify and exaggerate the evidence in order to "draw sharp boundaries in historical reality." Thereby analysis is removed from the ambiguities and complexities of the behavioral context, and special steps are needed in the subsequent analysis of the latter.[23] This distance between concept and evidence is a general problem, of course. But it may be suggested that with regard to the issues posed by Weber's analysis, historical developments since his day have substantially increased our opportunities of utilizing his insights in a wider framework.

Other cultural patterns than those of sectarian Protestantism have produced that work ethic and systematization of economic behavior which Weber called "innerworldly asceticism." Accordingly, it is possible to broaden the scope of Weber's analysis in keeping with his own approach to comparative analysis. Once attention shifts away from the focus on the peculiarities of Western civilization, one can reverse the Weberian approach by starting with evidence of "innerworldly asceticism" and then search for the factors (many of them secular rather than religious) which have contributed toward such patterns of economic behavior. Such analyses, say of Russian or Japanese developments, can only gain from a precise understanding of Weber's original contribution.

[22] *Ibid.*, 97–98. Note also Weber's statements on 90–92 where the purpose of his study is carefully delimited. Not many of Weber's critics have been nearly as careful in this respect.

[23] For this aspect of Weber's methodology in a comparative context, see ch. X above.

JELLINEK AND WEBER

A major source of inspiration for Weber's *Protestant Ethic and the Spirit of Capitalism* was Georg Jellinek's essay *The Declaration of the Rights of Man and of Citizens* (1895; English trans., 1901).[24] Weber acknowledged Jellinek's influence, speaking of his friend's "proof of religious traces in the genesis of the Rights of Man . . . which gave me a crucial stimulus . . . to investigate the impact of religion in areas where one might not otherwise look."[25] Weber paralleled Jellinek's study by linking the spirit of capitalism, rather than the declaration of rights, to religious beliefs. He went to work on this problem soon after coming to Heidelberg in 1896, where Jellinek taught. Weber presented his thesis in the classroom before the onset of his illness forced him to postpone its literary elaboration until the second half of 1903.[26] If Jellinek's particular stimulus made him turn to the varieties of Protestantism in the Anglo-Saxon countries, his scholarly concern with the social impact of Christian beliefs was in fact older, as we have seen in ch. XII.

In his essay Jellinek dealt with the practical importance of natural-law doctrines for constitution-building. He criticized the Historical School for dismissing such doctrines as empty dreams instead of studying how they became embedded in political realities. Jellinek opened his case by rejecting an older view, embraced

[24] George Jellinek, *Die Erklärung der Menschen- und Bürgerrechte* (Leipzig: Duncker & Humblot, 1895; 2nd. ed., 1904); Jellinek, *The Declaration of the Rights of Man and of Citizens. A Contribution to Modern Constitutional History* (New York: Holt, 1901), Max Farrand, trans. One of the few writers who mentioned Jellinek in connection with Weber's *Protestant Ethic* was Paul Honigsheim; see his "Max Weber als Soziologe" (1921), reprinted in *On Max Weber,* Joan Rytina, trans. (New York: Free Press, 1968), 126. For affirmative and critical opinions on Jellinek's thesis in the later literature, see Roman Schnur, ed., *Zur Geschichte der Erklärung der Menschenrechte* (Darmstadt: Wissenschaftliche Buchgesellschaft, 1964).

[25] From the memorial address on Jellinek, reprinted in René König and Johannes Winckelmann, eds., *Max Weber zum Gedächtnis* (Cologne: Westdeutscher Verlag, 1963), 15.

[26] Cf. Weber, "Antikritisches zum 'Geist' des Kapitalismus," *Archiv für Sozialwissenschaft,* XXX, 1910, 177, reprinted in Johannes Winckelmann, ed., *Max Weber: Die protestantische Ethik.* Band II: *Kritiken und Antikritiken* (Munich: Siebenstern, 1968), 150.

This section was written by Guenther Roth.

especially in France, according to which Rousseau had been a formative influence upon the French Declarations of 1789 and 1791; he pointed out that the *contrat social* denied any natural rights. Comparing the French and American Declarations, Jellinek found that the French formulations were an incomplete imitation, not so much of the American Declaration of Independence, but of the constitutions of Virginia, Pennsylvania, and other states. Whereas in France the Declarations were accused of having undermined the political community, in the United States they seemed to have furthered the building of the state. Thus the causes of the French troubles should be found elsewhere.

Next, Jellinek turned to the questions of the historical roots of the American Bill of Rights, comparing England and America. He noticed that English constitutional history did not know inalienable rights of the individual; the Bill of Rights was primarily a catalogue of governmental duties. At any rate, whatever rights were construed as a reflection of these duties had a traditionalist legitimation. In the colonies, however, these rights were posited as being grounded in nature, not tradition. Whereas natural law had remained a mere set of unenforceable ideas in earlier centuries, it became constitutional law in America. Jellinek saw the explanation in the victory of Congregationalism in New England, where, in contrast to the homeland, it succeeded in institutionalizing the principle of inherent, natural rights both in religion and politics. Freedom of conscience was the starting point for the other political rights, which lawmakers had to accept as given, not granted. Jellinek concluded that "the idea of legally establishing inalienable, inherent and sacred rights of the individual is not of political but religious origin. What had been held to be a work of the Revolution was in reality a product of the Reformation and its struggles. Its first apostle was not Lafayette but Roger Williams." [27] Of course, beyond the Reformation, the causal chain could be traced back even further into the past. Jellinek pointed to some antecedents, such as the relative weakness of Roman law in England and the persistence of Germanic notions about the rights of the people vis-à-vis the ruler—themes repeated in *Economy and Society*. However, Jellinek's main purpose was to identify a causal connection between two phenomena insufficiently studied in the past.

Establishing a historical connection between two phenomena was also Weber's research strategy, which he had adopted as early

[27] Jellinek, *The Declaration, op. cit.,* 77.

as 1891, when he defended his *Roman Agrarian History* against anticipated objections:

I have my doubts about the degree to which I managed to prove in detail the nature of these relationships [between surveying methods and public and private law], but I consider it a gain if their mere existence has been proven—as I would like to believe. . . . After all, the existence of a *connection between two historical phenomena* can be visualized not *in abstracto* but only by presenting a logically consistent view of the manner in which it came about concretely.[28]

In *The Protestant Ethic* Weber followed this guideline by asking himself: How can the causal connection between a set of religious beliefs and the economic activities of the believers be made likely with a tolerable degree of historical certainty? He took it for granted that "these two cultural components were at the time not related to one another in terms of a 'lawful' dependency, such that where x (ascetic Protestantism) is, there must be y (capitalist spirit) without exception—in view of the causal intricacies of historically complex phenomena, this must be accepted *a priori*." [29]

Weber was fully aware of the precarious nature of historical reconstructions. He accepted as one of the facts of the scholar's life that "the concept of historical certainty is simply relative, and [that] historical research must make do with the sources at its disposal." [30]

[28] Weber, *Die römische Agrargeschichte in ihrer Bedeutung für das Staats- und Privatrecht* (Stuttgart: Enke, 1891), 2.
[29] Weber, "Kritische Bemerkungen," in Winckelmann, ed., *Die protestantische Ethik, op. cit.*, II, 29f.
[30] *Römische Agrargeschichte, op. cit.*, 3.

INDEX